John Denvir

The Irish in Britain

From the Earliest Times to the Fall and Death of Parnell. Second Edition

John Denvir

The Irish in Britain
From the Earliest Times to the Fall and Death of Parnell. Second Edition

ISBN/EAN: 9783744730532

Printed in Europe, USA, Canada, Australia, Japan

Cover: Foto ©ninafisch / pixelio.de

More available books at **www.hansebooks.com**

THE
IRISH IN BRITAIN

FROM

THE EARLIEST TIMES

TO THE

FALL AND DEATH OF PARNELL

BY

JOHN DENVIR

SECOND EDITION

LONDON
KEGAN PAUL, TRENCH, TRÜBNER & CO., Ltd.
PATERNOSTER HOUSE, CHARING CROSS ROAD
1894

PREFACE TO THE SECOND EDITION.

THE two years that have passed since the appearance of the first edition of "The Irish in Britain" have been among the most eventful in Irish history. But, though our cause has, during that period, made giant strides, the time has scarcely yet come when a satisfactory history can be presented of the struggle still going on, which we believe to be the final rally for Ireland's freedom.

It is still true to say that no portion of our race has borne a more distinguished part in this struggle than the Irish in Britain.

When the General Election of 1892 found the Irish Parliamentary Party with an empty treasury, their prompt and generous contribution gave heart and hope to Ireland. It proved to her that an appeal to her children at home and abroad would not be made in vain. In answer to Ireland's call the sinews of war were poured in, and the Irish Party were sent back to Parliament, somewhat less in number, it is true, than before the Parnell crisis, but still overwhelmingly representative of the people of Ireland. The best proof of returning unity, and that the forces of faction were diminishing, was that the Parnellite party in Parliament entered upon the General Election with thirty-two members and came out of it with but nine.

The General Election placed Mr Gladstone in power by

a comparatively small majority. Even that majority the great Liberal leader would not have had but for the splendid organisation of our people on this side of the Channel.

The carrying of the Home Rule Bill of 1892 through the House of Commons by Mr Gladstone brought us almost within sight of that promised land, which, at one time—when we were the Ishmaelites of the British Empire—few of us had ever hoped to see.

The rejection of the Bill by the House of Lords was only what was expected. The breaking down of that barrier is but a question of time. Meanwhile we must not lose heart if we find the struggle longer than we expected. With perseverance we must win. Let us judge the future by what has already been accomplished.

Often has her emancipation seemed within Ireland's grasp, but never since the invader set foot on her shores did she appear to be so near freedom and happiness as now.

In point of material progress the terrible struggle of so many years waged by our people in this country still continues to bear fruit. In intelligence, education, and influence, their march is still onward and upward, and there seems no reason to doubt that they are reaching the end of one of the saddest and yet most remarkable stories in history. It is the fervent belief of those who know them best that our mother Ireland will have no less cause to be proud of them in a prosperous future than she has had in an arduous past.

CONTENTS.

BOOK I.

EARLY IRISH COLONISTS AND MISSIONARIES.

CHAPTER I.
PAGE
Early Irish Settlements in Britain—The Scots and Picts . . 1

CHAPTER II.
Ireland and Scotland—St Columbkille and Iona . . . 3

CHAPTER III.
Ireland and England—The Missionaries from Iona—Irish Art in Britain 10

BOOK II.

THE AGE OF FEUDALISM.

CHAPTER IV.
The Normans in England—"Base Diarmid M'Murrough"—The Irish in the Scottish and French Wars, and in the Wars of the Roses—In the Tower—At Tyburn 15

BOOK III.
"THE REFORMATION."
CHAPTER V.

The Irish Chiefs become English Nobles and Land-grabbers—
"The Reformation"—Shakespeare's Sketches of Irishmen
—Irish Music in Britain 29

CHAPTER VI.

The Stuarts—The Infamous "Court of Wards"—Persecution—
Duplicity of Charles I.—The Rising of 1641—Valour of
Irish Soldiers in Britain—Colkitto and his Antrim men—
Early Irish Colony in London—Martyrdom of Oliver
Plunkett—James II. loses his crown 40

CHAPTER VII.

Irish Genius during the Stuart Reigns 59

BOOK IV.
THE PENAL DAYS.
CHAPTER VIII.

Persecution again—The Jacobite Rising of 1745—Thurot's
Expedition 64

CHAPTER IX.

The Irish in London in the Eighteenth Century—Burke and
Sheridan—Relaxation of the Penal Code—Scottish "No-
Popery" Riots—The Gordon Riots in London—Irish
Victims—The United Irishmen in England—Father O'Leary 76

CHAPTER X.

Distinguished Irishmen of the Eighteenth Century . 95

BOOK V.

FROM THE UNION TO EMANCIPATION.

CHAPTER XI.

Martial Law—Catholicity at the Opening of the Nineteenth Century—The Fight for Emancipation 97

BOOK VI.

O'CONNELL AND THE REPEAL AGITATION.

CHAPTER XII.

Catholic Progress—Orangeism—Accession of Victoria—The Chartists 107

CHAPTER XIII.

The Census of 1841—Where the Irish were then to be found throughout Great Britain 113

CHAPTER XIV.

Opening of the Repeal Agitation—Father Mathew—Thomas Davis 117

BOOK VII.

THE FAMINE.

CHAPTER XV.

"Gone with a Vengeance" 120

BOOK VIII.

YOUNG IRELAND.

CHAPTER XVI.

PAGE

The *Nation* Newspaper—The Young Irelanders—Ribbonism—The Irish Confederation—The Young Irelanders in Great Britain—Terence Bellew M'Manus 125

CHAPTER XVII.

The Confederates in Great Britain organise and arm themselves 138

CHAPTER XVIII.

Thomas D'Arcy M'Gee and the Young Irelanders in Scotland . 142

CHAPTER XIX.

The Rising—M'Manus at Ballingarry—Arrests in England and Scotland—Arrest, Trial, and Transportation of M'Manus—His Death 146

BOOK IX.

IRISH PROGRESS IN BRITAIN.

CHAPTER XX.

The Great Immigration—Location and Condition of our People 153

CHAPTER XXI.

"Spreading the Faith"—The War of Creeds and Races . . 157

CHAPTER XXII.

Catholic Development—Restoration of the Hierarchy in England—The "Papal Aggression" Mania—Tenant Right—"The Pope's Brass Band"—Riots again—Treason of the Sadlier-Keogh gang—Catholic disabilities in the Army, Navy, and Public Institutions—Fate of Sadlier and Keogh 160

BOOK X.

FENIANISM.

CHAPTER XXIII.

PAGE

James Stephens and the Phœnix Conspiracy—Jeremiah O'Donovan (Rossa)—The Brotherhood of St Patrick—The M'Manus Funeral—The Irish Revolutionary Brotherhood in England and Scotland—Informers at Work—Seizure of the *Irish People*—Arrests in England—The Liverpool Irish Volunteers 176

CHAPTER XXIV.

Arrest of Stephens—True Story of his Escape, told by John Devoy, one of his Rescuers—Devoy and Stephens on the chances of a Rising in 1865—More Arrests in England—Arms for Ireland 189

CHAPTER XXV.

Suspension of the Habeas Corpus Act—Stephens reaches France—Gladstone and Cardinal Manning on Fenianism—Fenian recruits from the Army—The Informer Corydon—More Arms for Ireland—Rickard Burke 204

CHAPTER XXVI.

New Year's Day, 1867—The Hour has come, but not the Man—How the Fenian Chiefs "squandered the Money of the Irish Servant Girls"—Preparations for the Rising—The Plot to seize Chester Castle—M'Cafferty—Flood—Davitt 215

CHAPTER XXVII.

The Rising in Ireland 224

CHAPTER XXVIII.

Fenian Alarms in England—Arrest and Rescue of Kelly and Deasy—"God save Ireland"—The Manchester Martyrs—The Clerkenwell Explosion 228

CHAPTER XXIX.

Michael Davitt 244

CHAPTER XXX.

Retrospective—Church Progress—The Irish in Liverpool—The Irish in Birmingham—"No-Popery" Riots again . . 248

BOOK XI.

HOME RULE—THE LAND LEAGUE—THE IRISH NATIONAL LEAGUE.

CHAPTER XXXI.

The Home Rule Confederation of Great Britain—Isaac Butt—An Active Policy demanded—The Convention of 1877—Parnell succeeds Butt as President of the Home Rule Confederation 263

CHAPTER XXXII.

Release of Fenian Prisoners—The Land League—The General Election of 1880—Overthrow of the Tory Government—Liberal Coercion—Gladstone's Land Bill—Imprisonment of the Irish Leaders—Attempted suppression of *United Ireland* 281

CHAPTER XXXIII.

Abandonment of Coercion and a Relapse into it—The Tredegar Riots—The Irish in South Wales—A. M. Sullivan . . 294

CHAPTER XXXIV.

The Irish National League of Great Britain—The 1885 Election —The Balance of Power—Supporting the Tories . . 314

CHAPTER XXXV.

Mr Gladstone a Convert to Home Rule—His Defeat in Parliament and at the Polls 321

CHAPTER XXXVI.

The Bye-Elections—"The Flowing Tide"—The League prepares for the next Election—Our Muster Roll . . . 323

CHAPTER XXXVII.

The *Times* Forgeries—The "Flowing Tide" still sweeps on— William O'Brien 329

CHAPTER XXXVIII.

The Forgeries Commission again—The British Spy "Le Caron" —Pigott the Forger—Explosion of the Conspiracy—Flight and Suicide of Pigott 344

BOOK XII.

THE FALL AND DEATH OF PARNELL.

CHAPTER XXXIX.

Parnell's Sin—His Deposition—The Irish in Britain reject him —Ireland condemns him at the Polls—Kilkenny—Sligo— Carlow—Death of Parnell—Freedom still in sight . . 362

BOOK XIII.

THE IRISH IN BRITAIN TO-DAY.

CHAPTER XL.

	PAGE
The Census of 1881 and of 1891	383

CHAPTER XLI.

The Irish in the various Districts of Great Britain . . . 389

CHAPTER XLII.

Distinguished Irishmen of the Nineteenth Century . . 458

CHAPTER XLIII.

A Few Parting Words 460

THE IRISH IN BRITAIN.

BOOK I.

EARLY IRISH COLONISTS AND MISSIONARIES.

CHAPTER I.

EARLY IRISH SETTLEMENTS IN BRITAIN—THE SCOTS AND PICTS.

BORNE on the foremost waves of colonisation that proceeded from the early home of mankind in the East, and peopled the continent of Europe, came that great branch of the human family—the Celts.

They, too, in that far-away age, unlit by the lamp of history, and barely appreciable in the vague and mysterious light of tradition, were the first to trust their lives and fortunes to the mercies of the great western sea; and, after enduring perils and privations far greater than fall to the lot of colonists of to-day, they were the first to settle down and make a permanent resting-place in these islands.

How many years elapsed before the wandering tribes who took possession of the country we now call Ireland, had learned to associate themselves inseparably with the land they dwelt in, we know not; but it is certain that, long before the invasion of Britain by the Romans, the change had taken place: the records of their earlier wanderings had faded into a mere theme for bards and romancers, and the Irish race as a distinct nationality had entered into existence.

We are told that, during the period in which the Romans

were gradually withdrawing from Britain, and after they had entirely abandoned it, the inhabitants of that country suffered severely from the incursions of the "Picts and Scots,"—warlike tribes, who ravaged and devastated all before them in the periodical forays which they made from the north of the island. There is considerable difference of opinion as to the origin and final lot of the people to whom the name " Picts " was applied by the Romans (apparently in consequence of their supposed custom of painting their bodies when going into battle). It seems evident, however, that they were the original settlers in the northern part of the island, Celtic in blood, with perhaps a strong admixture of the Scandinavian element among them. The name became prominent in the fourth, and finally disappeared in the ninth century, and some writers have chosen to assume that at this later epoch the *people* also disappeared. How we are to suppose this disappearance occurred—whether by emigration, or extermination, or otherwise, no one has attempted to tell us ; and the theory seems to have originated in the minds of men unwilling to do credit to the glorious work of the Irish missionaries, who Christianised and civilised the tribes of Alba—the ancient native name of Scotland. As to the real reason for the disappearance of the name of the Picts, there appears no ground for doubting that this race ultimately became assimilated with the Scots, who came, as will be seen, from Ireland, just as—still later —the savage Norsemen became Christianised and transformed into the more cultured, though not less warlike, Normans, after contact with the Celtic civilisation of Gaul.

The "Scots" who figure in the incursions referred to, were undoubtedly warriors who had crossed over from Ireland (one of the many names of which was Scotia) and made common cause with the unconquered kindred tribes of Alba in warring against the Roman invaders and the Romanised Britons. The earliest of these immigrations mentioned by authentic records took place about the year 258, from Antrim into Argyle,* where the strait is less than twenty-five miles wide. Other adventurers followed at

* Argyle=*Airer Gaedhal*, the territory of the Gael.

intervals, but this is the earliest record we have of the Irish in Britain.

They were a warlike and adventurous race, those old Irish pagans. They did not confine their incursions to the neighbouring island, but carried their banners and left their footprints in many parts of the Continent itself. During one of these expeditions it was, and while the Romans still lingered in Britain, that our national apostle, St Patrick, was carried off—whether from Gaul, Britain, or Alba, is still a subject of controversy—and borne into captivity in Ireland.

CHAPTER II.

IRELAND AND SCOTLAND—ST COLUMBKILLE AND IONA.

"This monastic nation, therefore, became the missionary nation *par excellence*; while some came to Ireland to procure religious instruction, the Irish missionaries launched forth from their island. They covered the land and seas of the West."—MONTALEMBERT'S "Monks of the West."

As the years rolled on, from the time of the immigration into Scotland in 258, successive settlements were made, and the hold of the Scots upon the soil became firmer, until, after a couple of centuries had elapsed, a very large extent of territory was occupied by them. The leader of one expedition was an Ulster chief, Carbre Reada, and, from him, his companions and their descendants were named Dalreathians, and their territory Dalriada. The connection with the mother country was closely kept up, the language, habits, dress, and customs remained the same,* and the life of the colony was in every respect a counterpart of that of Ireland itself. There seems to have been, in fact, a kind of federal alliance by which the Scots of Ireland and those of Alba were pledged mutually to assist one another in time of need. In due course, when Ireland had received Christianity, the colonists coming thence began to bring with them the teachings and practice of the

* Lament of Deirdre.

true faith. The first missionary of whom tradition speaks was the great St Kiaran, and to this day there are parishes bearing his name in Cantire, Islay, and Carrick, in everlasting tribute to his memory. The year 503 marks an important historical epoch. Fergus, the son of Eric, a prince of the house of Niall, came over with a large contingent to the help of the Scots of Alba, who were in sore straits under the attacks of the Picts, and he established the colony on a firm basis as a kingdom. It would be impossible to say what the boundaries of his kingdom were, as they varied and extended as time went on; but, in addition to Argyle, they soon embraced the present Ross-shire and the western part of Perth.

A few years after the settlement of Fergus, St Columba, or Columbkil—whose name is indissolubly connected with the early history of the Irish in Britain—was born. His baptismal name was Crimthain. The name by which he is better known was given to him later in life. His character was such that it makes him one of the most fascinating studies in history, and his whole life is a striking illustration of St Augustine's celebrated apophthegm that of our weaknesses we can make a ladder by which to attain heaven. The old monks who wrote of him in their chronicles almost lose command of themselves in the fulness of their admiration, and matter-of-fact biographers of the present day who deal with the period in which the saint lived, show that they too have been unable to resist the spell. Of all the lives of St Columbkil (Columba of the churches,—he is said to have founded 100 monasteries and 365 churches, and ordained 3000 priests) the most interesting is that of his relative and successor, St Adamnan (or Eunan). From him we learn that his great patron was born in Gartan, in the County of Donegal, about 520. His father, Feidlimid, was the son of Fergus, grandson of Conal Gulban, and great-grandson of Niall of the Nine Hostages. Feidlimid's wife, the saint's mother, was Aethonia, daughter of Mac Nave, a Leinster chieftain nearly related to Cathair, the supreme monarch of Ireland. St Columba in his boyhood drank in learning from the lips of St Finnian, called the wise, and, after much study, he was ordained priest in his thirty-sixth year. For six years he worked with an energy and zeal that made his name famous throughout the land, and during that time he founded monasteries at Durrow, Kells, Swords, Arran, Boyle, Raphoe, Tory Island, Drumcliff, Derry, and many other places.

At the end of that time, he received the inspiration which led him to the great work of his life, and, accompanied by twelve companions, he left Ireland—or Scotia, as Adamnan terms it—and set out for the shores of Alba. Conall, son of Congal, the King of Scots, and Columba's own relative, received him cordially, and granted to him the island of Hy, better known now as Iona or I-Columbkil, whereon to build a monastery. Favoured by the special grace of God, this small spot of earth became, before many years, the centre of Christianity and learning for the west of Europe, and from its shores countless saints and holy men went forth to gather into the true fold the pagan tribes of Alba and Britain.

Here for thirty-five years did Columba labour. His love of Ireland was wondrously deep. "My sad heart ever bleeds," he says; "there is a grey eye which is ever turned towards Erin, but never in this life shall it see Erin, nor her sons nor her daughters. I look over the sea, and great tears are in my eye;" and again—"Death in faultless Erin is better than life without end in Alba." "Young traveller," he says to one of his monks returning home, "take my heart with thee and my blessing. Carry my blessing across the sea. If death should come upon me suddenly, it will be because of my great love for the Gael." But, deep as his love was, Adamnan only mentions two visits made by him to Ireland, and these appear to have been necessitated by events of national importance, and to have been brief in duration.

After he had built the church and monastery at Iona, he set out for his apostolic journey to the Picts. Near Loch Ness was the royal residence of Brude, their king, and, as in the case of St Patrick, Columba's conversion of the monarch was his first step to gaining the conversion of the people. After winning over whole tribes to Christianity on the mainland, he traversed the whole of the islands on the western coast, everywhere meeting with the most extraordinary success, performing miracles, and founding churches. Nor did he fail to study with heart and soul the welfare of his kinsmen in Alba. The immediate successor of Conall, the king who befriended the saint on his first arrival, was Aidan, or Aedh. This king was solemnly consecrated by Columba—the first authentic record of such an event in the country—upon the *Lia Fail*,* or Stone of Destiny, which Aidan's ancestor, Fergus, the first King of Scots, had brought from Ireland. Between priest and ruler thenceforth a bond of union remained and grew stronger as time went by, many benefits resulting from it, both to Aidan's people and to Iona. In the reign of Aedh, King of Ireland, it became necessary to hold a great convention on Irish soil in order, amongst other things, to settle a point of difference which had arisen between the Scots of Alba and the mother country. This gathering took place at Drum-ceath, and hither Columba came, attended by a suite of one hundred persons, which included thirty abbots or bishops and Aidan himself. The question at issue was the desire to impose a tax upon the colony, and the claim of the Irish king received the support of many learned and influential men—among them St Colman of Dromore. Hitherto the King of Scots had been compelled to furnish a contingent of land and sea forces whenever his royal kinsman at home went to war, and, in addition, he had paid an annual "eric." Against the new tribute Aidan and Columba urged every reasonable argument. As the discussion went on and waxed hotter, the Irish king declared that he would go in person to Alba and collect the tribute by force. At this threat, Columba rose and solemnly declared that thenceforth the Scots of Alba should be free for ever from the yoke. This declaration of the saint was in truth the establishment of the Scottish nation, and the fact that no attempt to controvert it was made by the Irish kings or people shows that the love of liberty was strong and consistent.

After seeing the seed which he had planted in Iona grown into a mighty tree, whose far-reaching branches swept as far north as Iceland, and whose fame had spread to the

* This stone is now under the Coronation Chair in Westminster Abbey.

bounds of the known world, Columba's noble life was ended in 597. The scholar, hero, and saint died as he had lived—in the midst of his toil, and, as the pen dropped from his weakening fingers, he expressed a desire that his friend and successor Boethin should finish the task upon which he was engaged. Just after matins on the Sunday morning, while the clear, peaceful air was still echoing the chant of his beloved monks, his soul passed to Heaven.

Scotland was occupied at the time of Columba's death by — roughly speaking — four nations. These were the Scots, the Picts—occupying the largest part of the country—the Britons of Strathclyde, and the Saxons of Northumbria, who had extended their kingdom to the Frith of Forth. Conflicts between all these races were unceasing, and it was in the face of such difficulties that the brave Irish monks carried out their noble work and Columba's successors sent forth their apostolic messengers. About 678 a severe check was given to the Saxons at the battle of Drumnechtan, at which the Saxon king of Northumbria, Egfrid, was slain. With manly generosity the Scottish conquerors brought his body to Iona, where it was buried with due honour by St Adamnan, the sixth successor and biographer of St Columba.

A word of notice is due to this wise and holy man. He was born about 624 in Donegal, being descended on his mother's side from the same Conal Gulban who was an ancestor of St Columba. After many years of monastic work, he was elected in 679 Abbot of Iona, which at this period was at the very height of its fame, and covered with ecclesiastical buildings. Kings of no less than four nations lay buried there, and its Abbot's jurisdiction was acknowledged by an immense number of monasteries throughout Alba.

Dean Munroe, who wrote from actual survey in 1569, describes the royal tombs of Iona. He tells us that on one was written—" *Tumulus regum Scotiæ,*" which the chronicles declared covered forty-eight crowned Scots Kings. On the south was another tomb inscribed—" *Tumulus regum Hiberniæ,*" in which lay four kings of that country; and on the north side was another inscribed—" *Tumulus regum*

Norwegiæ." Besides these, most of the Lords of the Isles and many other chiefs were buried there.

In the "Annals of the Four Masters" we frequently find such interesting records as the following—" Age of Christ, 979. The first year of Maelseachlainn Mor . . . in sovereignty of Ireland. Amhlaeibh, son of Sitric, chief lord of the foreigners of Ath-cliath, went to Hy on his pilgrimage, and he died there after penance and a good life"

Shakespeare, in his tragedy of "Macbeth," speaks of this sainted island as the burial place of the Scottish monarchs. Here is part of the dialogue between Macduff and Rosse after the murder of the king—

" *Rosse.* Where is Duncan's body?
Macduff. Carried to Colme-kill;
The sacred storehouse of his predecessors,
And guardian of their bones."

It was the Iona of this day which called forth the eulogium of Dr Johnson, who termed it—" that illustrious island, luminary of the Caledonian regions, whence savage clans and roving barbarians derived the knowledge and the blessings of religion. That man is little to be envied whose patriotism would not gain force upon the plains of Marathon, or whose piety would not grow warmer among the ruins of Iona."

During his period of office at Iona, St Adamnan carried on his labours in the true spirit of a disciple of Columba. In 701 we find him making a journey to York to intercede with Alfrid, king of the northern Saxons, for the release of some Irish prisoners who had been carried off in a foray into Meath. Alfrid was an old friend of the saint. They had met years before in Ireland, and doubtless it was the monarch's experiences of his sojourn there that prompted him to write his celebrated "Itinerary of Ireland." As might have been expected, Adamnan's plea was not refused, and he had the satisfaction of restoring some sixty captives to their homes.

We may now turn to an event which can be looked upon as the turning point in the history of Alba. For years struggles had been going on between the Scottish and Pictish kingdoms, alternating with intervals of peace, or periods in which both peoples joined to repel their common enemies. During one of the periods of friendly intercourse an intermarriage took place between the royal houses. The offspring of this marriage, Alpin, was succeeded by his son Kenneth as king of Scots. On a vacancy occurring in the Pictish succession, during the reign of Kenneth, he claimed the Pictish crown, and, in 842, succeeded in uniting both peoples under his sway. Before long the races had so far amalgamated that any distinction between them was impossible, and the name of the Picts may be said from this period to have disappeared.

The Scots of Alba had now become so firmly welded together that we may cease to regard them as any longer an Irish colony, but rather a distinct people. In fact, we find that, in describing Kenneth's reign, the country begins to be called by historians by the name of Scotland. The close and friendly relations between Scotland and Ireland, however, were still kept up, nor did the origin of their ancestors fade from the memory of the Scottish people.

The hierarchy of the northern part of Ireland kept up an ecclesiastical protectorate over Iona for several centuries. As late as 1203 we read of them exercising this authority. The "Four Masters" regularly record the deaths of the Abbots of Hy. True to their traditions of liberty, when many of the Scottish people under Somerled, Lord of the Isles, and ancestor of the Macdonalds, revolted against the introduction of the feudal system, the Irish lent their arms, as on many another occasion, to fight the battle of the people against despotism.

Reverence for the memory of Columb-kil was long cherished in Scotland, and more than one of its monarchs was proud to bestow on his heir at the baptismal font the name of Malcolm—"servant of Columba."

CHAPTER III.

IRELAND AND ENGLAND—THE MISSIONARIES FROM IONA—
IRISH ART IN BRITAIN.

"It is not generally known, or, if known, it is overlooked, that Ireland, after the six centuries which follow the introduction of Christianity, was the seat of the industrial arts and the school of the West. Residence there was considered essential to establish a literary reputation; and to her seminaries and universities students flocked from every part of Christendom. They were Irish missionaries who first presented to the illiterate Saxon the rudiments of literature, science, architecture, music, and even the means of shaping the letters used in writing the English language. Irish monks were the workmen who built most of the early Christian edifices. Old St Paul's Cathedral in London, and the magnificent roof that spans Westminster Hall, were of Irish design. At that time Ireland was the Christian Greece—the centre of scholastic enlightenment and enterprise."—JOSEPH COWEN.

DURING the course of the events narrated in the last chapter great changes had taken place in the southern part of the island of Britain, now known as England. The faith had originally been introduced by Christians among the Roman conquerors, and, after lingering for several centuries, it received vitality and impetus by communication with Ireland. We see the best proofs of this connection in the oldest ecclesiastical remains now to be found in England. These are the ancient stone crosses which are to be found in various parts of the country. The fury of the "Reformation" period destroyed many of them, but some still remain—generally in out-of-the-way villages or churchyards—mute, yet eloquent witnesses of the days when they were erected to commemorate the victory of the Cross over paganism and ignorance. They are to be found principally in the west of England—this in itself is strong evidence of their origin—and their shape and ornamentation leave no doubt in the mind of the antiquary that they were copied from the great Celtic crosses which are among the chief glories of Ireland.* The history of the early British Church

* Among the crosses that might be instanced are those of St Columb in Cornwall, Sandbach, and West Kirby, Cheshire.

For authorities, see Rimmer's "Ancient Stone Crosses," Mr Blight's "Cornish Antiquities," &c.

may be briefly summarised thus :—In 156, Lucius, the king of Britain, sent to Rome asking for the establishment of Christianity in his country. In 314 progress had so far been made that the British Church was represented by three bishops (those of London, York, and Caerleon-on-Usk probably) at the Council of Arles. Laws for regulating the Church were laid down at the Council of Brevi in 519. At the latter date, however, its lot was not a peaceful one. The first landing of the Saxons had taken place, and each successive year saw the invaders growing in strength, and the British being driven more and more into the remote parts of the country. In 586 the last of the British bishops took refuge in the fastnesses of Wales, and paganism was once more rampant from north to south.

But if the forces of evil were at work in the south, the servants of God were no less active in the north. From the shores of Iona the little fleets of boats were continually speeding away wherever the voice of duty called, whether far away to the bleak Faroes, among the scattered isles of the Hebrides, or southward to the uttermost extremities of Britain. The annals of Britain at this period are the annals of Iona and Lindisfarne. Wherever the trace of Christianity as then existing has remained to modern times, it is in connection with an Irish monk, or church or monastery founded by one. It was at this period that holy men like Aidan, Cuthbert, Colman, and Finian spent their lives in the great work of winning souls for Christ. St Aidan came to Northumbria in 635. By divine blessing, the king, Oswald, was a convert who had himself been instructed at Iona, and he assisted the missionaries in the work of converting his people, even acting as interpreter—translating the sermons of the monks from Celtic into Saxon.* St Aidan founded the famous monastery of Lindisfarne, or Holy Island, which repeated the work of Iona. Aidan was succeeded by Finian, who brought with him from Iona twelve disciples. They converted the Middle Angles, Mercians, and East Saxons, whose chief city was London, which, however, existed from the days when the Britons held sway, the name itself being Celtic—signifying the "fort of

* Ven. Bede.

ships." Another Irish missionary among the East Saxons was St Fursey.* The foundation of the Abbey of Melrose (Maol-rois) was laid under Aidan's directions by Eata, who was its first abbot. He was succeeded, first, by the pious Boisil, and next by the celebrated St Cuthbert. This great saint was an Irishman. This has been controverted, but we have it on undoubted authority that up to the time of the "Reformation," an inscription on the rood-screen of Durham Cathedral stated specifically that he was of Irish birth. The researches of the Most Rev. Dr Healy, coadjutor Bishop of Clonfert, prove still more conclusively that St Cuthbert was an Irishman. He shows the errors into which Archbishop Eyre and Canon Consitt have fallen. "In the library of the Dean and Canons of York," says Dr Healy, "is the oldest manuscript copy of that very 'Irish Life' of Cuthbert, which cannot be rejected or ignored, without at the same time throwing doubt on several of the most authentic memorials of the ancient church of Durham." From this "Irish Life" we learn that this great saint was undoubtedly an Irishman. The monastery of Malmesbury was founded at the same period as Melrose by another learned Scot, Macduff. One of the most renowned saints of this age was Kentigern, also called St Mungo, bishop of Glasgow, whose unceasing labours made him famous between that city and Wales itself. The cathedral of St Asaph marks the spot in the peaceful vale of Clwyd where he erected a monastic building, which he entrusted to his disciple, St Asaph.

Nor is it merely by tradition or history that we can judge of the work of these holy men. They have stamped their individuality and the lessons of their lives indestructibly on the face of the country, in the churches they built, and the monasteries they founded. Many of these have passed away, but we know that the great ecclesiastical edifices, which are among the crowning glories of Britain to-day, were often built on the time-worn foundations of the early buildings of the Irish monks, thus binding us to those noble souls in precious and enduring links. Amongst the most valued treasures of our museums and libraries we count the wonderful illuminated manuscripts which Columba and his

* Ven. Bede.

disciples produced, and which cannot be paralleled in the art-work of any people. Westwood, in his "Anglo-Saxon and Irish Manuscripts," where he gives beautiful fac-similes of these, says: "The study of these works has incontestibly proved that, at a period when the pictorial art may be said to have been almost extinct in Italy and Greece, and, indeed, scarcely to have existed in other parts of Europe—namely, from the fifth to the end of the eighth century—a style of art had been originated, cultivated, and brought to a most marvellous state of perfection in these islands, absolutely distinct from that of any other part of the civilised world, and which, having been carried abroad by numerous Anglo-Saxon and Irish missionaries, was adopted and imitated in the schools founded by Charlemagne, and in the monasteries established or visited by the former, many of which, in after ages, became the most famous seats of learning." On this subject Mr Digby Wyatt observes that, "In delicacy of handling and minute but faultless execution, the whole range of palæography offers nothing comparable to these early Irish MSS., and those produced in the same style in England." The chief existing manuscripts of this school in this country are the "Gospels of Lindisfarne," in the British Museum; the "Book of St Chad," at Lichfield; and the "Hereford Gospels," in the Cathedral Library of the city of Hereford.

As time went on, and the Church in Britain waxed strong and vigorous, as we might naturally expect, we hear less and less of the Celtic missionaries, and we find their places taken by great Englishmen like Bede. Still, from time to time, in the ancient records, we hear of holy men coming from Ireland, either of their own choice or at the invitation of friends in England. Among these were the good Irish monks of Glastonbury, who educated St Dunstan, and the three monks who left home in 891, and were graciously received by the Saxon King Alfred.

It must not be supposed, however, that the pious missionaries of whom we have spoken were the only Irishmen whose feet were led into Britain. From the days of the first invasion of the "Picts and Scots" to the era of the Norman Conquest, we are frequently confronted with accounts of invasions from the north, in which the Scots

of Erin and Alba made common cause in forays into
Britain. For a considerable period the attacks of the
Danes gave the people of the three countries enough to
do to hold their own at home. The wild Norsemen
made sad havoc wherever they carried their banners, and
in many places swept away all trace of the work of the
early missionaries. We read of the abbots of Lindisfarne
over and over again flying before them, and carrying
wherever they went their greatest treasure — the body of
St Cuthbert. In 937, Athelstan, King of England, gained
the decisive victory of Brunanburgh over the combined
forces of the Danes, Scots, and Britons. The "Four
Masters" tell us that, in 985, Iona was plundered by the
Danes on Christmas night, and that they killed the abbot
and fifteen servitors of the church along with him. Next
year, however, a great slaughter was made of the Danes
who had plundered Hi, three hundred of them being slain.
It would seem as if contact with the Danes corrupted some
of the Irish, for we read of a band of Irish pirates who
arrived in 1049, in six-and-thirty ships, in the mouth of
the Severn, and, after landing, devastated the surrounding
country, and killed many of the natives in battle. Probably
these pirates were really Danes, who had settled on the east
coast of Ireland. We hear of these on other occasions
assisting their kinsmen to gain the supremacy they afterwards obtained in England. They were also the principal
merchant-traders of the period, carrying between Ireland
and Britain and the Continent. A considerable slave-trade
was carried on with Bristol, where they obtained Saxon and
British children, and carried them to Ireland and the Continent. It has been surmised that the Irish oak used in the
roof of Westminster Hall was brought over by them.

In 1051, Harold, son of Earl Godwin, quarrelled with his
monarch—King Edward the Confessor—and fled to Ireland,
where he remained in security for two years. When he
returned, the seeds of great events had been sown, for,
earlier in the same year, William, Duke of Normandy, had
made a visit to the court of King Edward, which, no doubt,
helped to fix him in the determination he afterwards carried
out of securing for himself the crown of England.

BOOK II.
THE AGE OF FEUDALISM.

CHAPTER IV.

THE NORMANS IN ENGLAND—" BASE DIARMID M'MURROUGH "
—THE IRISH IN THE SCOTTISH AND FRENCH WARS,
AND IN THE WARS OF THE ROSES—IN THE TOWER—
AT TYBURN.

THE sun that set on the blood-stained field of Hastings saw the triumph of a new order of things, which created a revolution in the social and political condition—first of England, and afterwards of Ireland and Scotland.

It was not to be expected that a people with Celtic quickness of apprehension like the Irish could look on unmoved at the triumph of William, Duke of Normandy, at Hastings. Their sympathies were on the side of the Saxons, and when, a little later, Godwin, Edmund, and Magnus, the sons of the unfortunate monarch Harold, appeared amongst them, they readily offered their aid to begin anew the struggle against the Normans. The Earls Edwin and Morcar were still keeping up a desperate and stubborn resistance to the invaders, and it seemed possible, by co-operating with them, to rally the broken and scattered Saxons to another effort. An Irish expedition, in sixty-six vessels, accompanied the three Saxon princes, entered the mouth of the Avon, and besieged Bristol. The odds were, however, against them. The men against whom they were striving were the foremost masters of military science in Europe, and, secure in their fortified city, with an unlimited food supply behind them, they held out until Edwin and Morcar had been driven back into Northumberland. Abandoning their first project, the sons of Harold sailed down the channel and made a second and more successful descent upon the south coast. They defeated the first hostile force they encountered, and the people flocked from every side to their aid. In the Vale of Tamar a second battle took place, and the Irish and Saxons were defeated with great loss. Retreating as best they could, the survivors betook themselves to their ships, and returned to Ireland. The next hostile meeting between the Irish and Normans was destined to take place on the soil of Ireland itself.

The opening incident of the lamentable tragedy which ended in the enslavement of our country—the crime of one wretched Irish prince—took place in Ireland itself; but from time to time the scene changed to this side of the Irish Sea. In this way, about the middle of the twelfth century, there landed on the shores of England an Irishman, whose name has never since been breathed by his countrymen but with execrations, a name accursed—to be mentioned only with such as Judas Iscariot. This was the infamous Diarmid M'Murrough, king of Leinster, who, flying from the wrath of his countrymen on account of his adultery with the wife of the Prince of Brefni, sought the aid of England to restore him to his kingdom, and to work the downfall of Ireland. He followed King Henry to Aquitaine, and there swore allegiance to him. The letters-patent which Henry gave him set forth that—"Whoever within the bounds of our territories shall be willing to give him aid, as our vassal and liegeman, in recovering his territories, let him be assured of our favour and license on his behalf." With this document in his possession, M'Murrough reached England, and pursued his way to Bristol, in the neighbourhood of which city, and along the southern coast of Wales, he hoped to find a number of the semi-robber Norman barons willing to enlist under his standard. Contiguity to Ireland also determined him in making Bristol his centre while hatching his treason against his country. Giraldus Cambrensis says: "Here he sojourned for some time, making a liberal expenditure, as on account of the ships which made frequent voyages from Ireland to that port (Bristol), he had opportunities of hearing the state of affairs in his own country and among his people." It is not our province here to trace the history of the Normans in Ireland. We know that M'Murrough's treachery was only too successful, and how the work of subjugation was begun.

From time to time the history of our people at home and here become so interwoven that the state of the Irish in Britain cannot well be shown without introducing some part of the history of Ireland itself. Otherwise it is intended here to describe only the fate and fortunes of those of our countrymen who have been for many centuries making this country their temporary or permanent home, also referring to those passing through Britain, such as the Irish bishops on their way to the Council of Lateran in the twelfth century.

One part of the policy of successive English kings and ministers for the gradual conquest of Ireland, and to keep it securely in their grasp, was to obtain wherever possible the sons and heirs of noble Irish families as hostages. This did not imply any harsh treatment. On the contrary, these youths were educated and brought up in all the learning and refinements of the age. The first incident of the kind took place in 1180, when the son of Roderic O'Connor, the ill-fated Ard-Righ of Ireland, was conveyed to the English Court by St Laurence O'Toole, Archbishop of Dublin.

In 1243 the Norman barons in Ireland—many of whom, like the Geraldines, were becoming "more Irish than the Irish themselves"—were summoned by the English king to assist him in the war with France. It is recorded that Richard MacWilliam Burke accompanied the English forces, and died on the expedition. Two years later a similar appeal was issued for the war in Wales to the Lord Justice of Ireland and the Anglo-Irish generally—also to one of the native chiefs, Felim O'Connor. It is the cruel fate of subject nations that, having lost their own freedom, they are sometimes found in the train of their conquerors, making war on the liberties of others. Such now was the position of O'Connor. King Henry was besieging the castle of Gannoc (Diganwy) in Carnarvon. He was sorely pressed for aid, as will be seen by the following note of Dr O'Donovan to his translation of the "Annals of the Four Masters":— "Mathew Paris gives in his 'Chronicles' at this year a letter said to have been written at the time by a nobleman in Henry's camp, which conveys a vivid idea of the distressed condition of the English army before the Irish had joined them. In substance, it is as follows: 'The king with his army lyeth at Gannocke, fortifying that strong castle, and we live in our tents thereby, watching, fasting, praying, and freezing with cold. We watch for fear of the Welshmen, who are wont to invade and come upon us in the night time; we fast for want of meat, for the halfpenny loaf is worth fivepence; we pray to God to send us home speedily; we starve with cold, wanting our winter garments, having no more than a thin linen cloth between us and the wind. There is an arm of the sea under the castle where we lye, whereto the tyde cometh, and many ships come up to the haven, which bring victuals to the camp from Ireland and Chester.' All this time, says Mathew Paris, the king was looking impatiently for the Irish forces, mused with himself, fretted with himself, the wind serving, and yet said nothing. At length their sails were descried, and Maurice Fitzgerald and the Prince of Connaught presented themselves in battle array before the king. Hanmer adds, 'When all the forces joined together, the Welshmen were overthrowne, the king manned and victualled his castles, returned into England, gave the Irishmen leave to return, winking awhile in policie at the tarriance and slow coming of Maurice Fitzgerald.' Hanmer also remarks that, on the return of Maurice Fitzgerald, the Lord Justice, to Ireland, he performed a successful expedition against the Irish of Ulster, but that this was of no avail, for the king, whose displeasure was inexorable, dismissed him from his office, and appointed Sir John, the son of Geoffrey de Marisco, in his place. Maurice Fitzgerald, after some contests with the Irish and the new Lord Justice, took upon him the habit of St Francis, in the monastery of Youghal, where he died in 1256."

In 1247, Conor O'Murray, Bishop of Kilmacduagh, died at Bristol, and nine years later, Flann MacFlynn died at the same place. The mention of these two deaths by the "Four

Masters" shows that the connection and trade between Ireland and Bristol remained constant all this time.

Although Felim O'Connor, like Maurice Fitzgerald, had incurred the displeasure of the English king for his tardiness in coming to his aid in Wales, this was overlooked on account of his being an independent or semi-independent prince in Ireland. It was not thought politic to show the same resentment against the Irish chieftain as against the Norman-Irish baron. On the contrary, he received marks of favour, for, when on his behalf the Archbishop of Tuam, with ambassadors, came to England in 1255 to complain of the inroads made on his territory by the Normans, a royal charter was in the following year given to him granting to him and his heirs dominion over five baronies.

The following shows the close connection between Ireland and Scotland in the thirteenth century. In 1258, at a council of the Kinel-Conell, Donell Oge, the son of Donnell More O'Donnell, was elected to the chieftainship. He had just returned from Scotland, and the "Four Masters" state that he spoke the Albanian Gaelic, so that he had probably been educated in that country.

The usage in the old monastic schools, when students from many lands flocked to them, attracted by the fame of the great teachers who resided within their walls, was to divide the little colony of scholars according to their nations. Thus, when in 1092, the churches and schools of Armagh were burned, we read that among the parts which suffered most was a street of Trian-Saxon—that is, the third of the Saxons—the division of Armagh in which the Saxons resided. There had now been growing up in England for many years the great University of Oxford, and we might, not unreasonably, expect that among its scholars and teachers would be found some of Irish birth. This expectation is confirmed by the account given in the chronicles of the intestine troubles which took place in 1274, when it is mentioned that Irishmen were in residence at that time. Dr Newman says: "In Oxford there was from the earliest time even a street called 'Irishman's Street,' and the Irish were included there under the 'nation' of the southern English." Later on, indeed, we hear of individual ecclesiastics that they had graduated in Oxford, and of one, Faltach, Bishop of Meath, who died there. One of the most notable, perhaps, in his way, was Richard Fitz Ralph, a native of Dundalk, who became chancellor of the university in 1333. Fourteen years later he was made Archbishop of Armagh, and was the great champion of the secular clergy in a lengthened controversy with the religious orders in Ireland. He died at Avignon in 1361.

We have now to turn from the scanty narration of occasional visits into England to an important epoch which was opening in Scotland, in which the name of Ireland and of Irishmen occur with considerable frequency. In 1286, Alexander III., King of Scotland, died, leaving as his heiress his only child Margaret, the "Maid of Norway." On her death, which took place shortly after, a host of competitors for the throne arose, the chief being Robert Bruce and John Baliol. In 1292, King Edward I. of England, who had been referred to as arbitrator, decided in favour of Baliol, giving his decision as Baliol's feudal lord. The Scottish nobles by no means concurred in this theory, and when, a little later, Edward invaded France, they caused Baliol to enter into an alliance with the French King against his English suzerain. Edward promptly turned his offensive operations against Scotland, and marched thither with an army of 40,000 men, which he had raised for his French war. He summoned to his assistance from Ireland, the Earl of Ulster, the Lord Justice Wogan, the Geraldines, Butlers, Vernons, de Genvilles, Birminghams, Poers, Purcells, de Cogans, de Barrys, de Lacys, d'Exeters and others, early in 1296. The Earl of Ulster sailed with a fleet of his own, and the other nobles obeyed the call with alacrity. They fought through most of the campaign, and after being thanked and feasted by Edward at Roxburgh, they returned home, the object of the English king having been gained by the capture of Baliol. Edward's followers, as may be seen from their names, were mostly drawn from the Norman-Irish of the Pale. On the other hand, there can be no doubt that the Scotch on this, as on later occasions, had the assistance of many of their native Irish friends. Edward's hope of securing such a speedy triumph soon proved unfounded.

Wallace rose and kindled the flames of disaffection, so that in 1299, and again in 1303, the Norman-Irish barons, and with them some of the Irish chiefs, were summoned anew to join the English forces and march into Scotland. In 1307, Edward the First died, and by this time, Bruce had established himself securely in the affections of his people. Magee remarks, "There is ample evidence that the claims of kindred were at this period keenly felt by the Gaels of Ireland for the people of Scotland, and men of our race are mentioned among the companions of Wallace and the allies of Bruce." He says later, "Irish adherents followed the fortunes of Wallace to the close; and when Robert Bruce, after being crowned and seated in the chair of the MacAlpine line, on the summit of the hill of Scone, had to flee into exile, he naturally sought refuge where he knew he would find friends." When, indeed, he left his exile, he was accompanied by a large body of Irish troops. "In 1314, the second Edward prepared," says Magee, "an overwhelming force for the expedition (the campaign into Scotland, which he intended should be decisive), summoning, as usual, the Norman-Irish Earls, and writing in different language to his 'beloved cousins,' the native Irish chiefs, not only such as had entered into English alliances at any time, but also notorious allies of Bruce, like O'Neil, O'Donnel, and O'Kane. These writs were generally unheeded; we have no record of either Norman-Irish or native Irish chiefs having responded to Edward's summons, nor could nobles so summoned have been present without some record remaining of the fact. On the contrary, all the wishes of the Irish went with the Scots, and the Norman-Irish were more than suspected of leaning the same way. Twenty-one clans, Highlanders and Islemen, and many Ulstermen fought on the side of Bruce at the field of Bannockburn; the grant of 'Kincardine O'Neil' made by the victor king to his Irish followers remaining a striking evidence of their fidelity to his person and their sacrifices in his cause. The result of that glorious day was, by the testimony of all historians, English, as well as Scottish, received with enthusiasm on the Irish side of the Channel."

It may be here noticed that, with the accession of King

Robert Bruce to the throne, the old Scoto-Irish line of kings may be said to have ceased. Edward the First, during the period in which his forces held Scotland, did his best to eradicate all evidence of national independence. With this view he carried off or mutilated many of the old records, and brought to England the crown and sceptre of Baliol, and the sacred stone on which the Kings of Scotland had been crowned from the days of Fergus, the first King of Scots, who had brought it from Ireland. Sir Walter Scott, speaking of this stone says: "Its virtues are recorded in the celebrated leonine verse — '*Ni fallat fatum, Scoti, quocunque locatum Invenient lapidem, regnare tenentur ibidem*,' which may be rendered thus—

> Unless the fates be faithless found,
> And prophets' voice be vain,
> Where'er this monument is found,
> The Scottish race shall reign.

The stone is still preserved, and forms the support of King Edward the Confessor's chair, in Westminster Abbey, which the sovereign occupies at his coronation, and is in itself a very curious remnant of extreme antiquity."

At the battle of Halidon Hill in 1333, we find Sir John D'Arcy, who commanded the Anglo-Irish troops, much commended for the bravery of himself and his men; and in 1347, they again distinguished themselves at the Siege of Calais under the Earls of Kildare and Desmond. "From this time forward," says Magee, "it became a settled maxim of English policy to draft native troops out of Ireland for foreign service, and to send English soldiers into it in times of emergency. For fully four hundred years we have records of Irishmen fighting the battles of Britain on the continent of Europe. In 1418, King Henry V. was carrying on a war against France, and we are told that, among his followers were a number of Irishmen. Thomas Bottiler (Butler), the prior of the Knights Hospitallers at Kilmainham, with a large contingent attended Henry at the Seige of Rouen. Hall says: 'they did do their devoir as that none were more praised, nor did more damage to their enemies.'" For the following year there is a record in the "Four Masters" that—"Thomas Bocagh, the son of the Earl of Ormond, went to assist the King of England in the war with France, and died while on the expedition. The greater number of those who went with him from Ireland died likewise, either in England or France."

This French war is doubly interesting from the fact that Shakespeare, in his play of "Henry V.," has introduced an Irishman as taking part with the English army in the seige of Harfleur. It is a proof of the universality of Shakespeare's genius that such a minute detail as the presence of Irishmen in this campaign did not escape him. Froude, who has notoriously done more to misrepresent Ireland and Irishmen than almost any writer, living or dead, has seized on this incident to indulge in a little congenial criticism. As if he could not even interpret Shakespeare's words except in a distorted way, he writes in his "English in Ireland" thus: "Careless of antiquarian pedantry, Shakespeare drew his men and women as he saw them around him, and Fluellen, Captain Jamie, and Captain Macmorris, are the typical Welshmen, Scot, and Irishmen, as they were to be met with in Elizabeth's train bands. Fluellen, hot-blooded, voluble, argumentative, is yet most brave, most loyal, and most honourable. Among his thousand characters there is not one which Shakespeare has sketched more tenderly, or with a more loving and affectionate irony. Captain Jamie is a 'marvellous falerous gentleman,' well read in the ancient wars, learned 'in the discipline of the Romans,' and able to hold discourse on them with any man; but shrewd and silent, more prone to listen than to speak, more given to blows than to words, and determined only to 'do good service or ligge in the ground for it.' Macmorris, though no less brave than his companions, ready to stand in the breach while 'there are throats to be cut or work to be done,' yet roars, rants, boasts, swears by his father's soul, and threatens to cut off any man's head who dares to say that he is as good as himself. Captain Jamie never mentions Scotland; we learn his country from his dialect, and from what others say of him. Fluellen, a Welshman to the last fibre, yet traces his Welsh leek to the good service which Welshmen did 'in a garden where leeks did grow' at Crecy, under the English Edward. He delights in thinking that all the waters of the Wye cannot wash His Majesty's Welsh blood out of his body. Macmorris, at the mention of his nation, as if on the watch for insults from Saxon or Briton, blazes into purposeless fury—'My nation? What ish my nation? Ish a villain, and a bastard, and a knave, and a rascal! What ish my nation? Who talks of my nation?'"

Of course, it is manifestly absurd to be building up elaborate theories on the mere creatures of the dramatist's inspiration; the striking thing is that Froude appears to go out of his way to look at the character of Macmorris in the most unfavourable light. To any ordinary person reading the play, a somewhat different impression would be given. He is first mentioned by Gower, an officer in King Henry's army, in the following words:—

"*Gower.*—The Duke of Gloster, to whom the order of the siege is given, is altogether directed by an Irishman; a very valiant gentleman, i' faith."

It is true that Shakespeare credits Macmorris with extravagancies of speech, but he also makes Gower describe him as an officer of engineers and a man of military science, considerable enough to have gained for him the most important position in connection with the whole of the operations then going on—that is, adviser to the commander-in-chief. If Macmorris is to be taken as a type of his fellow-countrymen, surely such an important feature as this is worthy of mention. Although Shakespeare depicted the Irish soldier of fortune more fairly than Froude would have us believe, he would not be likely to have had any very friendly feeling towards our nation. Doubtless, he had heard of the pageant of Shane the Proud, with his body-guard, through the streets of London, and of the havoc they had made among the choicest troops of Elizabeth; and he would like the "Irishry" none the more for the waste of English blood and treasures in the efforts to subdue the northern chieftains who carried on the struggle after the treacherous murder of Shane. It might be asked, Where did Shakespeare get the name which he has given to his Irish Captain? Probably it is a version of the name M'Murrough, which, by the time of Queen Elizabeth, must have been tolerably familiar to English ears. At the very date of the siege of Harfleur there was an Irish prince of that name, Donough M'Murrough, son of Art Kavanagh, imprisoned in the Tower of London. He was ransomed after nine years' captivity by his clansmen, who gave him such a welcome home as he would not have received in any other country of the world.

In the great struggle which marks the period into which we have now advanced—the "Wars of the Roses"—as might have been expected, the Norman-Irish barons bore a prominent part. Indeed, if we may credit Shakespeare's authority, without their assistance the struggle could not have been well begun. In the second part of the play of "Henry VI." (Act iii., Scene 1), he makes the Duke of York accept the command of the expedition into Ireland as a step towards securing the crown. Later on (Act iv., Scene 9), on his return, this announcement is made to the king—

> "*Messenger.*—Please it, your grace, to be advertised,
> The Duke of York is newly come from Ireland;
> And, with a puissant and mighty power
> Of gallowglasses and stout kernes,
> Is marching hitherward in proud array."

If the gallowglasses and stout kernes remained with him, as presumably they did, they, no doubt, rendered a good account of themselves at the first battle of St Albans, which terminated decisively in favour of the Yorkists. What seems to vouch for the accuracy of Shakespeare is the undoubted fact that the Norman-Irish barons, with the exception only of the Earl of Ormond, were staunch adherents of the Duke of York. The Earl would almost naturally take the opposite side in the quarrel to the Geraldines, on account of the standing feud between his family—the Butlers and the Fitzgeralds. James, the fifth Earl of Ormond, fought, with a body of his retainers, in every battle from St Albans to Towton, where he was taken prisoner. His estates were confiscated, an act of attainder was passed against his family, and he himself was executed by Edward IV. The attainder was afterwards reversed, and the estates restored.

There can be no doubt that during the long years of bloodshed and unrest caused by these wars, when the English "Pale" in Ireland was growing more limited in area every year, and when almost all the Norman-Irish barons and their feudal vassals were being drained from the country to recruit the Yorkist ranks, had only a capable leader appeared among the native Irish, they could with ease have rid themselves for ever of the English connection. The most probable explanation is, that during this period the country was practically in the hands of the native Irish, so that they felt no pressure of any kind from without, and did not realise the necessity for taking measures against any future danger to their liberty. When the great contending English houses were united in the person of Henry VII., the ministers of England were left perfectly free to strengthen anew the connection with Ireland. The accession of Henry did not by any means, however, quell the partisan feeling in favour of the house of York, as witness the encouragement given to Lambert Simnel and Perkin Warbeck, who made in succession claim to the crown. Simnel pretended to be the Earl of Warwick, and the Earl of Kildare presented him as such to the people of Dublin. He was proclaimed king at Christ Church Cathedral, in May 1487, under the style of "Edward VI." The army he raised in Ireland, largely composed, however, of foreign soldiers, was defeated, after landing in England, at Stoke Acton. This was the last invasion of England that took place from the side of Ireland. The second pretender to the English crown, Warbeck, also tried to gain adherents in Ireland, but with little success. One Irishman, however, seems to have stood by him, and to have followed his fortunes to the last. This was John Waters, who had been Mayor of Cork, who was executed along with him. King Henry VII. never forgave the Norman-Irish lords the part they took in the recent troubles, and towards the Earl of Kildare he showed especial enmity. He removed him from the position of Lord Deputy, putting the Archbishop of Dublin in his place. This prelate was succeeded, after a brief interval, by Sir

Edward Poynings—famous, or infamous, by reason of the Act which is named after him, and which he was instrumental in compassing. Poynings arrested the Earl of Kildare on a charge of treason, and sent him as a prisoner to London, where he was placed in the Tower. The idea, no doubt, was to remove the head of the semi-independent Anglo-Irish barons, and thus leave the ground clear for a scheme which might bring Ireland under complete and direct control of the English crown. With this view, also, the statute alluded to, known as Poynings' Act, was adopted. It provided that, thereafter, no legislation whatever should be proceeded with in Ireland, unless the bill to be proposed were first submitted to the king in council in England, and returned certified under the great seal of the realm.

Henry's policy, however, was not so short-sighted as to keep in the position of an enemy, if it could be avoided, a man so capable of being a powerful friend. Another circumstance also had weight in moving the king to conciliate the head of the Geraldines. In 1495, a visit was paid by Hugh Roe O'Donnell to James IV. of Scotland, and reports were brought to the English Court of the cordial welcome which the Irish chief received from the young Scottish king. The "Four Masters" tell us that a solemn covenant was entered into by both parties mutually to assist each other in all their exigencies. Probably these disquieting circumstances prompted King Henry, after a time, to adopt a new attitude towards the Earl of Kildare, for, after being liberated and married to a cousin of the king, the Geraldine was sent back in triumph to Ireland as deputy in 1503.

The enemies of the Kildare family, however, had been strengthened and increased during the absence of the Earl, and were determined not to yield the supremacy to him without a struggle. For thirty years there was continued strife between the house of Kildare and its enemies, chief of these being, as usual, the Ormonds. This enmity pursued Garrett Oge when he became Earl of Kildare, and though, for a time, he was able to baffle his opponents, they at length prevailed. He felt compelled to go over once more to the Court of Henry VIII. to vindicate his conduct. His appeal, however, was of no avail, and he was seized and thrown into the Tower of London. The reported execution of the Earl drove his son—known in Irish history as "Silken Thomas"—into rebellion. After a desperate resistance, he too found himself a captive in the Tower, and with five of his uncles was executed at Tyburn on the 3rd of February, 1537, the Earl himself having in the meantime died in captivity on the 12th of December 1534.

We have now arrived at a distinct epoch, with which may be opened another period in the history of the Irish in Britain. Looking back at the ground already traversed, we see that—with the exception of the early Irish colonisation of Scotland—no settlement, of any extent, of the Irish people had as yet been made in Great Britain. Probably the first to settle here were Irish traders in London, Bristol, and Liverpool. In Leland's time, this must have gradually been becoming more apparent in Liverpool, for in his "Itinerary" he says, "Lyrpole, *alias* Lyverpoole, a pavid toune, hath but a chapel. Walton, a four miles off, not far from the se, is paroche church. The King hath a castalet there, and the Erle of Derby hath a stone house there. Irish marchantes come much thither as to a good haven. At Lyrpole is small custume payed that causith marchantes to resorte thither. Good marchandis at Lyrpole and moch Yrish yarn that Manchester men do buy there."

BOOK III.

"THE REFORMATION."

CHAPTER V.

THE IRISH CHIEFS BECOME ENGLISH NOBLES AND LAND-GRABBERS — "THE REFORMATION" — SHAKESPEARE'S SKETCHES OF IRISHMEN—IRISH MUSIC IN BRITAIN.

No doubt it will be considered by many people a proof of the perversity which they declare to be characteristic of the Irish race, that, given in Ireland certain circumstances which appear to have worked a uniform result in other European nations, the Irish people have taken a course entirely distinct from their neighbours, and, indeed, held it as their greatest glory that they have done so. It is laid down as an axiom that "the blood of the martyrs is the seed of the Church," and that Christianity has been introduced into the various countries of the world with the hallowed bodies of its martyred saints as its basis; but Ireland gave the exception to the rule by accepting the faith from the hands of St Patrick without a drop of blood being shed. At the period into which we have now arrived, the spectacle was seen of half Europe—with England in the van—rejecting the spiritual supremacy of the Pope, and pronouncing in favour of new and startling doctrines. In some countries, doubtless, the majority of the people proved true to Rome, but in these cases their fidelity was always made easier from the fact that the ruling powers remained true also. Indeed, it would almost appear as if the prevalence of the condition of things arising from the feudal system in the continental nations and in England accounted for the fidelity or non-fidelity of the people to Catholicity, for the rule was that, where the rulers became Protestant, the people also became Protestant.

Although there had been a considerable fusion between the two races in Ireland, there were at this time, broadly speaking, two classes of rulers—the great barons of Norman blood and the native Irish chiefs. The former were always as independent as they dared be; the latter were practically free from any outside control. The problem for English ministers was how to curb the power of the one, and bring the other under control. To subjugate the whole country by force of arms was an impossible task; to attempt a conquest of the free clans by means of the barons was to increase the power of the latter. The solution of the difficulty was found in a novel and ingenious, if unscrupulous, way. One by one the great Irish chiefs were courted and cajoled. Honours were heaped on them, and, finally, when it was thought that the ground was ready, it was suggested to them that they should receive titles of nobility from the crown. How was this to be done? In the simplest manner possible. They were to make their submission to the crown, transfer their tribe lands to the king—to be sure, merely as a matter of form—then to receive their new titles, and to have the lands handed over to them as feudal tenants of the crown. Probably it appeared to them a mere pleasing ceremony whereby they were mightily advantaged without any cost to themselves. Flattered by the incense wafted towards them, overcome by the compliments showered on them by crafty statesmen and a covetous monarch, impelled also, it must be said, by their own cupidity and personal ambition, they shut their ears to the voice of conscience, and yielded to the tempters.

From that hour the real conquest of Ireland began. The old law of Tanistry, which had regulated the succession to the chieftainships, was set aside, the Brehon laws, which had been looked to as the basis of social and national life, the relationships between chief and clan, the very right to live in the land which bore them, all these were involved in a common destruction by the act of these Irish chiefs. That their act was utterly illegal and unjustifiable was evident even to themselves. The chief of the O'Briens, when overtures were first made to him, indignantly replied that, though he was captain of his nation, yet he was still but one man. The land which they were handing over to the king was never theirs to give; they but held it in trust for their people, the meanest of whom had as much possession in it as the chief. The very office which they were bartering away was one to which they had been elected by the people, and the people could depose them from it. And yet, with the knowledge of all this, a few years saw the wholesale transformation of free Irish chiefs into feudal lords and vassals of a foreign king. Murrogh O'Brien, the same who expressed the sentiments stated above, became Earl of Thomond; his nephew, Donagh, Baron of Ibrackan; Ulic MacWilliam Burke, Earl of Clanrickarde and Baron of Dunkellin; Hugh O'Donnell, Earl of Tyrconnell; FitzPatrick, Baron of Ossory; Kavanagh, Baron of Ballyan; and Con O'Neil, Earl of Tyrone. It is an unpleasant truth that the majority of the Irish visitors to Great Britain at this time came either as prisoners to the Tower of London, or upon such disgraceful business as the bartering away of the rights of their people.

"The imposing ceremony," says Magee, "of the transformation of these Celtic chiefs into English Earls has been described by an eye-witness. One batch was made at Greenwich Palace, after High Mass, on Sunday the 1st of July 1543. The Queen's closet was richly hanged with cloth of arras and well strewed with rushes for their robing room. The King (Henry VIII.), received them under a canopy of state, surrounded by his Privy Council, the Peers spiritual and temporal, the Earl of Glencairn, Sir George Douglas, and the other Scottish commissioners. The Earls of Derby and Ormond led in the new Earl of Thomond, Viscount Lisle carrying before them the sword. The Chamberlain handed his letters-patent to the Secretary, who read them down to the words *cincturam gladii*, when the King girt the kneeling Earl baldrick-wise with the sword, all the company standing. A similar ceremony was gone through with the others, the King throwing a gold chain having a cross hanging to it round each of their necks. Then, preceded by the trumpeters blowing, and the officers-at-arms, they entered the dining-hall, where, after the second course, their titles were proclaimed aloud in Norman French by 'Garter-king-at-Arms.' Nor did Henry, who prided himself on his munificence, omit even more substantial tokens of his favour to the new Peers."

This was the first batch. Other Irish chiefs went through the same process later on. Their brand new English titles were accompanied in some cases by gifts of abbey lands and plunder from the dispossessed monasteries, which brought a weakening of their respect for the religion of their forefathers. This, together with the policy of keeping as hostages in England the sons of the principal Irish chiefs, is an explanation of the fact that we find, after the change of religion began in England, that a number of the heads of the old Irish families had lost their faith, while the great bulk of their countrymen clung to it with desperate tenacity. The accession of Queen Mary to the English throne caused a slight break in the proselytising policy commenced in the previous reign. Mary's reign also brought a ray of sunshine to several Irish exiles. One of these, O'Connor of Offaly, was languishing a prisoner in the Tower, but his heroic daughter, Margaret, "relying on the number of her friends and relatives in England, and on her knowledge of the English language," according to the "Four Masters," braved the dangers of the journey, and threw herself at the queen's feet. Mary's heart was touched, and she released the chief. One of these relatives referred to would probably be Donagh O'Conor, who had gone to England in 1548 to help in the war against the French and the Scots. Others of the banished Irish had amnesty extended to them during the reign of Mary Tudor. Among these were the sons of the Earl of Kildare—Garrett and Edward. For sixteen weary years they had been banished from Ireland, and had been sojourning in Italy and France; longing for some chance to return to their native land. With them also came back the heir of the house of Ossory.

But Mary reigned only for a brief five years, and her successor, Queen Elizabeth, brought with her all the fury of "Reformation" zeal, increased tenfold by the brief check it had received. Not that it was exercised always, for occasionally, for State reasons, it was deemed politic to conciliate the native Irish. Thus, in 1561, we find Shane O'Neill paying a visit to London, and being received by the queen with all honour. John Mitchell, in his "Life of Hugh O'Neill," describes, in graphic language, how "He proceeded to London with a gallant train of guards, bareheaded, with curled hair (as if the Statute of Kilkenny had never been passed) hanging down their shoulders, armed with battle-axes, and arrayed in their saffron doublets—an astonishment to the worthy burghers of London and Westminster."

Shane's visit was due to the revolution, effected by the change of Irish chief into English earl, made in the reign of Henry VIII. Upon the O'Neills the late king had conferred the rank of Earls of Tyrone and Barons of Dungannon, but setting aside what were termed the "Queen's O'Neills," the clansmen of Tyr-owen had conferred upon Shane what was to them and him a far more honoured title, THE O'NEILL, and in him England found one of the most determined opponents she had ever encountered on Irish soil. The result of Shane's interview with Elizabeth was that for the present he was left undisturbed as Prince of Ulster, his destruction being meanwhile planned by treachery.

But one who proved an even more famous O'Neill than this, Hugh, who had been recognised by Elizabeth as Baron of Dungannon, "in his father's right," was being carefully trained at the English court in every accomplishment of the age, ready to be brought forward at the proper moment, in accord with the oft-repeated policy of England, to be a thorn in the side of his country. For once this fiendish policy failed, for this Irish youth, Hugh O'Neill, trained carefully as he had been in the Reformed religion, with the Earldom of Tyrone and every honour conferred upon him, throwing aside these in after years, proved himself one of the most skilful and courageous champions of creed and country that Ireland ever produced. Before he himself was finally overthrown, Hugh O'Neill defeated in succession England's ablest soldiers. Anticipating a triumphant conclusion to the campaign of one of Elizabeth's generals who fought against O'Neill—the ill-fated Essex—Shakespeare thus compares the reception which he believes awaits him in London on his return from the Irish Wars, to the greeting the citizens gave to the fifth Henry on his return from the French Wars—

> "*Chorus.*—As by a lower but by loving likelihood,
> Were now the general of our gracious empress
> (As in good time he may) from Ireland coming,
> Bringing rebellion broached on his sword,
> How many would the peaceful city quit
> To welcome him?"

This was shown to be but the vain imaginings of the poet's brain, for Essex proved no match for O'Neill in either diplomacy or war, and, instead of meeting the triumphant reception pictured by Shakespeare, he returned to the foot of Elizabeth's throne to be spurned by her as a defeated and disgraced man.

By this time Irishmen were no strangers in the metropolis. Its streets had seen many an Irish chief and noble brought in chains to perish miserably in the gloomy dungeons of the Tower; many a young Irish heir, obtained by force or cunning, had been educated in the London court, until he had forgotten the faith and language of his childhood, and had learned to lisp and languish in the gardens of Greenwich as well as the most accomplished of English-born courtiers; many an Irish soldier who had enrolled himself under the flag of England to fight in France, or Scotland, or the Low Countries; and many an Irish chief, too, who had come over on some errand of appeal, little witting that justice was of no consideration when English interests were to be advanced.

Something of this, no doubt, Shakespeare, the great English dramatist, saw, or had read or heard of, though his knowledge of Irish affairs seems limited enough, and bears a very close resemblance to the ignorance and prejudice which characterise many English writers to-day in dealing with the same subject. It is evident that most of what he knew he got from the soldiers who had been in the Irish Wars, for it is generally only Irish military terms he uses. Thus, in "Macbeth," (Act i., scene 1):—

> "—— The merciless Macdonwald
> (Worthy to be a rebel ; for, to that
> The multiplying villainies of nature
> Do swarm upon him) from the western isles
> Of kernes and gallowglasses is supplied."

In "Richard II.," the king speaks of the—

> "rough rug-headed kernes"

against whom he is organising his forces ; an expedition of such a formidable character that, to embark in it, he was compelled to put "the realm in farm." In "Henry VI." (Part Second, Act iii., Scene 1), one of his characters announces that—

> "The uncivil kernes of Ireland are in arms,
> And temper clay with blood of Englishmen."

Again, in the same play, the Duke of York thus describes Jack Cade—

> "In Ireland have I seen this stubborn Cade
> Oppose himself against a troop of kernes ;
> And fought so long, till that his thighs with darts
> Were almost like a sharp-quilled porcupine.
>
> . . . . . .
>
> Full often, like a shag-haired crafty kerne,
> Hath he conversed with the enemy ;
> And, undiscover'd, come to me again."

In another passage Shakespeare affords an interesting trace of the Irish sojourners in England during his day. The various annotators of his plays were for many years floored by an apparently unmeaning passage in "Henry V." (Act iv. scene 4)—

> "*Pistol.*—Yield, cur.
> *French Soldier.*—*Je pense, que vous estes le gentilhomme de bonne qualite.*
> *Pistol.*—Quality ? *Callino custore me!* Art thou a gentleman ?" &c.

It is amusing to note the various readings gravely laid down in the attempts to decipher Pistol's strange expression. Malone (going so far, indeed, that he ought to have known enough to read the whole riddle) suggested that it was only the burden of an old song which he had discovered in a book, entitled " A Handful of Pleasant Delites, containing sundrie new Sonets, newly devised to the newest Tunes," &c., by Clement Robertson and others, 16mo, 1584. In this is a sonnet of a lover in praise of his lady with *Calen o custure me* sung at every line's end, thus—

> " When, as I view your comely grace,
> *Calen o custure me.*"

It remained for Samuel Lover, in our day, to entirely clear up the mystery. The following extract from the " Talbot Papers" (vol. ii. fol. 18), which he quotes, gives the first step :—

" We are in frolic here in Court ; much dancing in the Privy Chamber of country dances before the Queen's majesty, who is exceedingly pleased therewith. Irish tunes are at this time most pleasing."—*Letter from the Earl of Worcester to the Earl of Shrewsbury, dated September 19th, 1602.*

Here is evidence that the glorious melodies of Ireland had already been brought over to England, and were familiar in the very presence of royalty, a fairly good guarantee that they would spread pretty widely through the whole country. How these were brought here first it is hard to say. Perhaps some English soldier, with more refinement than was usual at that period, had heard and learned some of the airs sung by the native allies of the English during the campaign against Hugh O'Neill. Perhaps some Irish harper had been brought back in the train of some English nobleman ; or, more likely still, perhaps these songs, that pleased the ear of the haughty queen, were the sad reminiscences of the music of their early youth, sung by Irish captive chiefs fettered in the Tower of London, or as hostages degraded to the position of Elizabeth's courtiers—

> " The stranger shall hear thy lament on his plains ;
> The sigh of thy harp shall be sent o'er the deep,
> Till thy masters themselves as they rivet thy chains,
> Shall pause at the song of their captive, and weep."—*Moore.*

"Mr Boswell," writes Lover, in tracing the origin of the expression put into the mouth of "Pistol," "in his edition of Shakespeare, says, in noticing Mr Malone's emendation, that Mr Finnegan, master of the school established in London for the education of the Irish poor, says the words mean, 'Little girl of my heart for ever and ever.' Now, this is not the meaning, and I cannot but wonder that, with so much literary discussion as has taken place on the subject, the true spelling, and, consequently, the meaning of the burden, have remained until now undiscovered. The burden, as given in the 'Handful of Pleasant Delites,' and copied by Malone, is, '*Calen o custure me*,' which is an attempt to spell, and pretty nearly represents, the sound of '*Colleen oge astore*' (*me* being expletive or, possibly, a corrupt introduction), and these words mean, 'Young girl, my treasure.'"

Boswell gives the air of the song "*Callino castore me*" as he found it in Playford's "Musical Companion," 673. Shakespeare's idea appears to be this : Pistol, addressed in French, replies with the first foreign words that came into his head, suggested, no doubt, by the similarity of sound between "*qualite*" and "*callino.*" The air is given in Bunting's collection, and is stated to be the very oldest we possess.

Probably as early as Shakespeare's own days, and certainly soon after, during the Stuarts' reigns, Irish dramatists and composers enriched the music and literature of England. Thus, in O'Keeffe's "Poor Soldier," the music of "The rose tree in full bearing" is the same old Irish air to which our national poet, Moore, wrote "I'd mourn the hopes that leave me." Hardiman, speaking of the song known in Scotland as "Maggy Lauder," says : "The air as well as the words of *Maggy Laidir*, though long naturalised in North Britain, is Irish. When our Scottish kinsmen were detected appropriating the ancient saints of Ireland (would that they would rid us of some modern ones) they took a fancy to its music. Not satisfied with borrowing the art, they despoiled us of our sweetest airs." Hardiman had in his mind, no doubt, such airs as our "Aileen Aroon," known in Scotland as "Robin Adair," and the "Cruiskeen lawn," to which the air of "John

Anderson, my jo," bears a strong resemblance. These, and many other airs were, no doubt, brought over to Scotland by wandering Irish harpers or pipers, who were frequently, like Carolan, O'Connellan, and O'Kane, composers also.

The fact has been mentioned that, while in the face of the apostacy of many of the nobility and heads of the old Irish families, the people of Ireland strenuously resisted all attempts to enforce the new creed and customs upon them. A singular instance of this is given in the case of the Desmond family. At the end of the sixteenth century the young Earl of Desmond was in custody in London. He had been kept as a hostage for his father's loyalty, and had been trained in such learning and ideas as were considered most fitting for him. Hugh O'Neill had lent his counsel and assistance to another claimant to the headship of the Desmond family, and it was felt by Queen Elizabeth's advisers that it would be a bold stroke to restore the young man, whom they believed the people would recognise as the rightful earl in opposition to O'Neill's ally. Accordingly, the youth was sent by Cecil, the chief secretary, to Sir George Carew, the governor of Munster, with permission for the latter to use his charge according as it might seem expedient. Carew sent him as an experiment into Limerick, with what result will be seen. Carew's own account of the matter is most interesting ("Pacata Hibernia," book i., ch. xiv.). "And to Master Boyle his lordship gave secret charge, as well to observe the Earle's waies and cariage, as what men of quality or others made their addresses unto him, and with what respects and behaviour they carried themselves towards the Earle, who came to Kilmallock upon a Saturday, in the evening, and by the way, and at their entry into the towne, there was a mighty concourse of people, insomuch as all the streetes, doares, and windowes, yea, the very gutters and tops of the houses, were as filled with them, as if they came to see him whom God had sent to be that comfort and delight their soules and hearts most desired; and they welcomed him with all the expressions and signs of joy, everyone throwing upon him wheat and salt (an ancient ceremony used in that province, upon the election of their new mayors or officers, as a prediction of future peace and plenty). That night the Earle was invited to supper to Sir George Thornton's, who then kept his house in the towne of Kilmallock, and although the Earle had a guard of souldiers, which made a lane from his lodgings to Sir George Thornton's house, yet the confluence of people that flockt thither to see him was so great, as in halfe-an-houre he could not make his passage through the crowde, and after supper he had the like encounters at his returne to his lodgings. The next day, being Sunday, the Earle went to church to hear divine service, and all the way his country people used loud and rude dehortations to keep him from church, unto which he lent a deaf ear, but, after service and the sermon was ended, the Earle comming forth of the church, was railed at and spat upon by those that, before his going to church, were so desirous to see and salute him, insomuch as, after that publike expression of his religion, the towne was cleared of that multitude of strangers, and the Earle from thenceforward, might walk as quietly and freely in the towne, as little in effect followed or regarded as any other private gentleman. This true relation I the rather make, that all men may observe how hateful our religion, and the professors thereof, are to the rude and ignorant sort of people in this kingdome. For, from thenceforward, none of his father's followers (except some few of the meaner sort of freeholders) resorted unto him, and the other great lords in Munster, who had evermore been overshadowed by the greatnesse of Desmond, did rather feare than wish the advancement of the young lord. But the truth is, his religion, being a Protestant, was the only cause that had bred this coyness in them all; for if he had been a Romish Catholike, the hearts and knees of all degrees in the province would have bowed unto him." It was evident that the unfortunate young man was of no use in the direction where it was hoped he might have been a valuable tool, and so he was sent back to London, where he died shortly after.

It is worthy of note, that among the Catholic missionaries and laymen who suffered for the faith in England during Elizabeth's reign, several were of Irish birth.

Half the people of England were still Catholics three

hundred years ago. A rapid falling off would, no doubt, follow the extinction of the English hierarchy, which took place in 1585, and the martyrdom and banishment of so many of the clergy. But in the darkest hour the lamp of faith was never wholly withdrawn, for, in 1598, the Catholics of England were placed under an Archpriest, his jurisdiction extending also to Scotland—the last of whose bishops was then in exile, and died abroad in 1603.

CHAPTER VI.

THE STUARTS—THE INFAMOUS "COURT OF WARDS"—PERSECUTION — DUPLICITY OF CHARLES I.— THE RISING OF 1641—VALOUR OF IRISH SOLDIERS IN BRITAIN—COLKITTO AND HIS ANTRIM MEN—EARLY IRISH COLONY IN LONDON—MARTYRDOM OF OLIVER PLUNKETT—JAMES II. LOSES HIS CROWN.

IT is only right to begin a new chapter with the accession of James I. to the English throne. From the Saxon period to the end of the sixteenth century, Ireland was practically a sealed book to the English people; they knew nothing of the manners and customs of its natives, and historians and writers of all kinds, from Giraldus Cambrensis to Fynes Morison, had been able to repeat the most ridiculous fables as genuine facts, and gain credence for them. Now, however, there was a closer touch if not a more friendly connection between the two countries. Elizabeth's troops had penetrated into districts which had never known the foot of a hostile foreigner before. On the other hand, many Irishmen had taken service in the English army, and had found other opportunities of visiting England in the way of commerce. Before many years they had gained a footing in various ways in the metropolis. Knight surmises that the costermongers of the Stuart period must have been largely Irish, basing his theory on the dialect which the early dramatists make these persons use in their plays. There was a reason, too, why a closer connection should now take place between Ireland and this country, in the fact that James I., as King of Scots, was a lineal descendant of the old Irish kings, and it may be easily understood that this idea—absurd enough though it might seem at the present time—had a certain influence among the Irish of that day. The reception which he gave the chiefs of Tyr-owen and Tyr-connell, whom Mountjoy the deputy brought to England, encouraged still further the belief that the new monarch was one who could sympathise with the aspirations of a people whose blood he had inherited. For the moment they forgot the treacherous manner in which he had treated one of their own chiefs, Brian na Murtha O'Rourke, while he was yet only King of Scots. This incident is worthy of a passing notice. O'Rourke, who had made a gallant stand at home against the invaders, had fled to Scotland for safety, but James handed him over to the English government. A manuscript history of Ireland (dated 1636), preserved in the Royal Irish Academy, describes his trial:—"Brian O'Rourke, the Irish potentate, being thus by the King of Scots sent into England, was arraigned in Westminster Hall; his indictments were that he had stirred up Alexander M'Connell and others to rebell. This being told him was interpreted (for he understood no English), he said he would not submit himself to tryel of twelve men, nor make answer except the queen satt in person to judge him. The Lord Chief Justice made answer that whether he would submit himself or not to a tryal by a jury of twelve, he should be judged by law according to the particulars alledged against him. Whereto he replied nothing but—'If it must be soe, let it be soe.' Being condemned to dye he was shortly after carried into Tyburne to be executed as a traitor, whereat he seemed to be nothing moved, scorning the Archbishop of Caishill (Miler M'Grath) who was there to counsill him for his soule's sake, because he had broken his word, from a Franciscan turning Protestant." Hardiman says:—"The Londoners exulted at his death. Even 'the brightest, meanest of mankind,' forgot his philosophy to be witty on the occasion." "He, O'Rourke, gravely petitioned the queen that he might be hanged with a *gad* or *withe*, after his own country fashion which doubtless was readily granted him" (Bacon's Essays). But the world has now to decide which of the two men, the brave but betrayed Irishman, or the corrupt judge, most deserved the *gad*. This petition, however, if any such was sent, shows that O'Rourke relied on the queen, and that his real object was to apprise her of his condemnation. Sir Richard Cox, in his virulent "History," inserts another anecdote from Philip O'Sullivan, worth relating:—"Being asked why he did not bow his knee to the queen, he answered that he was not used to bow. 'How, not to images?' sayd an English lord. 'Aye,' says O'Rourke, 'but there is a great deal of difference between your queen and the images of the saints.'" This Irish chief was executed and his head placed on a spike on London Bridge.

Whatever hopes were entertained by the Irish people in James I., on the strength of ties of kindred, were speedily dissolved. He set himself to the task of stamping out the religion of his mother with determination and severity. A deputation from Ireland, which waited on him in 1603, for the redress of some grievances, he reprimanded harshly, and four of its members he committed to the Tower. He enlarged the "Court of Wards" established by Queen Elizabeth. In former reigns, we have seen how it was a settled policy of England to get possession of the scions of the chief Irish families, as hostages or otherwise, so as to train them up to be a scourge to their country. Since the commencement of the "Reformation," the same atrocious system had been carried out, with the addition that as the children grew up, they were taught to hate the faith of their fathers. Some thus trained in England returned to the national and religious faith of their ancestors—like the great Hugh and Phelim O'Neill. Others brought up in the infamous "School of Wards," but too well served the fiendish purpose for which they had been educated. Such were the Duke of Ormond and Murrough O'Brien, Lord Inchiquin —"Murrough of the burnings." At the commencement of King James's reign there were not less than 300 of these Irish children in the Tower of London, or at the Lambeth schools. These proselytising schools at Lambeth were the prototypes of similar institutions existing up to our own times, the influence of which, in successive generations, is, no doubt, one of the causes why, considering the constant immigration from Ireland, the number of Catholics in Britain is not greater than it is. We have seen how one appeal to James's sense of justice was treated by him. A second appeal, in the shape of a dutiful remonstrance, was drawn up by the principal Anglo-Norman Catholics of Ireland, but their spokesman, Sir Patrick Barnwall, was seized and conveyed to the Tower, and other delegates were imprisoned in Dublin Castle. A third deputation, which came later on, was treated in a similar fashion. The latter was a gross instance of the perversion of forms of law and order so familiar to English rule in Ireland. The Irish Parliament was summoned by writs in 1613, and, in order to swamp the Catholic representatives, who were certain to be in a majority, a royal charter established forty additional boroughs, where the constituencies were mere shams. Each of these returned two members. The indignation at this was naturally great, and manifested itself on the day Parliament assembled, and the election of a speaker became necessary. The Catholics refused to take part in the election of a speaker until the question of these "rotten boroughs" had been dealt with, and seeing the difficulty the Lord Deputy prorogued Parliament. The Catholic members sent Lutrell and Talbot to represent their grievance to King James, who answered them by sending Lutrell to the Fleet prison and Talbot to the Tower. Some sort of a compromise was, however, patched up, and Parliament met, to dissolve shortly afterwards.

In 1623 a vicar apostolic was appointed for England, Scotland still remaining under the same jurisdiction, but in the same year Pope Gregory XV. directed the vicar apostolic to cease from exercising jurisdiction in Scotland, where the Catholics were afterwards placed under a "Prefect of the Missions."

Another of the worthless Stuarts, Charles I., came to the throne in 1625. He was married in the same year to Henrietta Maria of France, and the Catholics began to hope for better times, now that there was a queen professing the same faith as themselves. But however well disposed Charles, himself, may have been, he did not resist the pressure from the House of Commons to put the law in force against "recusants," thus flagrantly breaking one of the articles of his marriage treaty with the King of France. His compliance did not satisfy the Puritan party in the House of Commons, for already the contest had commenced between king and parliament, which only ended, after a struggle of twenty-three years, by the death of Charles on the scaffold.

In 1628, the king was anxious to increase the army in Ireland by 5000 men, but the difficulty was how to provide for their support. At the suggestion of the Deputy, Lord Falkland, the General Assembly of the leading Catholics of Ireland, with "several Protestants of rank," offered to the king, in return for certain "graces," the sum of £120,000. Some of these graces provided for greater security in the titles to their estates, whether of Catholics or Protestants, while the Catholics stipulated that they should be allowed to practise in the courts of law, and to sue the livery of their lands out of the Court of Wards, on taking an oath of civil allegiance instead of the oath of supremacy. It can well be understood that the Catholics would gladly make almost any sacrifice for this latter concession, since the Court of Wards could take the Catholic heir, if he were a minor, and educate him in the Protestant faith, while, if of age, he was refused the livery of his lands till he abjured his religion by taking the oath of supremacy.

There was a protest from the ultra-Protestant bigots in Ireland and England against a price being thus put upon the practice of "Popery and Idolatry." The king wanted the money, yet could not afford to offend the Puritans. Following the advice of Thomas, Lord Wentworth (afterwards Earl of Strafford), he had recourse to the basest deceit, whereby he took the money of the Irish Catholics, yet so arranged that while apparently conceding to them the "graces," they never got them. He signed the agreement for the concession of fifty-one "graces," and Parliament was to be immediately called in Ireland to confirm his act. He received from the Irish agents in London bonds for £120,000 (equal to ten times that amount now), to be paid in three annual instalments of £40,000. The delegates from the Irish General Assembly, having paid the first instalment, returned to their country with instructions to the Lord-Deputy to call Parliament together immediately to confirm the act of the king. Charles, however, counselled by Wentworth, secretly instructed Falkland to see that the writs summoning Parliament were so prepared as to be informal. The Deputy carried out his instructions so that no Parliament was held to confirm the treaty made by the king. Lingard says:—"The writs undoubtedly were illegal, but the error, whether it were intentional or not, might have been remedied by the issue of other writs in a more legal form. Nothing, however, was done. The Irish, though surprised, waited with patient reliance on the honour of the sovereign, nor did it yet enter into their minds to suspect that he would receive their money and refuse to redeem his pledge." It is needless to say that that the Irish Catholics never got the "graces."

In 1629, four years after the accession of Charles to the throne, Pope Urban VIII. granted faculties to Father William Ogilvie, as Prefect of the Missions for Scotland, where the Catholics were numerous, particularly in the Highlands and islands. Father Ogilvie died in 1631. His successor was an Irishman. After the Confiscation of Ulster the Irish clergy of the northern province were bitterly persecuted, yet not only did they keep the faith alive among the remnant of the Ulster clans, and their glorious hierarchy intact, but were able to assist their brethren in Scotland. So we find that, on the death of Father Ogilvie, Bishop Magennis of Down and Connor, was placed over the Scottish Mission. In 1635, Father Cornelius Ward, a Franciscan, became the Scottish Prefect.

In 1638 Charles added to his difficulties with the English Parliament, by attempting to force the English Liturgy upon the Scots. The Puritans there were furious, and formed what was known as the "Solemn League and Covenant." The subscribers pledged themselves (1) to renounce "Popery;" (2) to resist religious innovations, and to defend one another against opposition. The Covenanters, as they were called, invaded England and overcame the king's troops.

In 1640, during the time that these fanatics held sway in Scotland, Father Patrick Hogarty, another Irish Franciscan, became Prefect of the mission, on the retirement of Father Ward, and held the office for eight years.

Meanwhile Strafford, who had succeeded Falkland as Lord-Deputy in Ireland, was determined to make his master, Charles, as "absolute as any sovereign in Christendom," and on the first rumour of the Covenanters' invasion of England was able to remit to the king a large sum from the Irish treasury and to offer the services of the army of 10,000 foot and 1000 horse he had raised in Ireland. He was recalled to take command of the royal forces engaged against the Covenanters, with whom, however, the king was compelled to conclude a treaty.

Strafford's career in Ireland had been one series of acts of robbery and tyranny. Not for these, but that the fruits of his plunder were, they well knew, to be used against themselves, did the Parliamentarians resolve upon his destruction. When Parliament met he was impeached for high crimes and misdemeanours—the chief of which were in connection with his Irish administration. The condemnation and execution of Strafford followed.

We have now reached the memorable year 1641, when the Irish, seeing the success which had attended the rising of the Scottish Covenanters, under like circumstances, and the bitter feud between Charles and the English Parliament, conceived the time opportune to strike a blow for their political and religious freedom. A general rising took place on the 23rd of October. The plan included the seizure of Dublin Castle, and, with it, the Lords Justices Borlase and Parsons, who, though acting for the absent Lord Lieutenant, were, all along, so far as they dared, in the interest of the English Parliament. The rising succeeded all over Ireland except at the chief point—Dublin Castle. Here the plan of the confederates was betrayed, and Colonel MacMahon and Lord Maguire, who were to have carried out this part of the enterprise, were seized and sent to England, where they were afterwards condemned and executed.

For several years, after this, with the exception of Dublin and the small tract of country surrounding it, and a few other places—sometimes lost, sometimes won, according to the varying fortunes of war, Ireland was, in everything but name, an independent nation. But the Catholic Confederates professed all along to be fighting for King Charles, even while he repudiated them. Indeed, this was one of Ireland's lost chances. The native Irish might have won their freedom had they cast off the alliance with the Anglo-Irish Catholics of the Pale, with whom the war was not for nationality, but for liberty of conscience and a faithless king. As this is one of the most complex chapters in our history, a few words of explanation may be necessary.

For two years the Irish Confederates had found themselves opposed by both English factions—Parliamentarian and Royalist—in Ireland. Charles's Lieutenant-General, the Marquis of Ormond, did all he could to subdue them, but, in the end, found himself cooped up in Dublin, while the Parliamentary army under Monroe, sent from Scotland to put down the rising in Ireland, met with no success, being confronted in the north by that unrivalled soldier—Owen Roe O'Neill.

Civil war had now broken out in England between the King and Parliament, and the false Charles found it expedient to ask, through Ormond, for a truce with the Irish Confederates. In return, certain concessions were to be made to the Catholics of Ireland. Unfortunately, at this time the Anglo-Irish formed the majority in the Supreme Council —the governing body of the Irish Catholics of both races, and the truce asked for was concluded on the 15th of September 1643. The folly of the truce was shown, when it was seen that the king and Ormond, now Lord Lieutenant, had not the power, if they had the will, to carry out its provisions on their side.

While the Irish were, as usual, betrayed by Charles, he got the full benefit of the cessation of hostilities, for Ormond was able to send troops over to England to his assistance. "In November 1643," says Lingard, "four Irish regiments landed at Mostyn, in Flintshire. Their reputation more than their numbers unnerved the prowess of their enemies. No force ventured to oppose them in the field, and, as they advanced, every post was abandoned or surrendered." At

Nantwich they met with their first check. While besieging this quaint old Cheshire town, Lord Fairfax, with a much superior force, advanced upon them. After a desperate struggle 1600 of them surrendered. Among these was Colonel Monk, who was afterwards the most prominent figure in the restoration of the Stuarts to the throne. He and many of the officers and soldiers joined the Parliamentarians, so that it is probable that these levies sent by Ormond to the assistance of Charles, were chiefly drafted from his own troops and largely made up of soldiers of fortune. The remainder would appear to have made their way to Prince Rupert in Lancashire, for we read of Irish fighting under him about this time.

On the 18th of August 1643 Colonel Hugh MacMahon and Lord Maguire, who had been captured and sent to England in connection with the projected seizure of Dublin Castle in 1641, escaped from the Tower of London, and took refuge in a house, probably belonging to a fellow-countryman, in Drury Lane. Here they lay concealed until the 20th of October, when one of them happening to call to somebody in the street, the voice was recognised, and both were recaptured and afterwards executed. The following are the incidents connected with the last days of Lord Maguire. He was brought to the bar on the 10th of November 1643, at the Court of King's Bench, London, for conspiracy to take the castle of Dublin. He was convicted, and, on Thursday, February 20th, 1644, was drawn on a sledge through London from the Tower to Tyburn. He was cruelly tormented by the Sheriff with questions as to his "crimes." He repeatedly asked to be allowed to die in peace, but without avail. Addressing the people who came to see his execution, he said, "I do beseech all the Catholics that are here to pray for me. I beseech God to have mercy on my soul." And so he met his end with a courage worthy of his ancient race and with the fortitude and devotion of a martyr for his persecuted faith.

"Two Irish deputations," says M'Gee, "one Catholic, and the other Protestant—proceeded this year (1644) to the king, at Oxford, with the approval of Ormond, who took care to be represented by confidential agents of his own.

The Catholics found a zealous auxiliary in the Queen, Henrietta Maria, who, as a co-religionist, felt with them, and, as a French woman, was free from insular prejudices against them. The Irish Protestants found a scarcely less influential advocate in the venerable Archbishop Usher, whose presence and countenance, as the most Puritanical of his prelates, was most essential to the policy of Charles. The king heard both parties graciously—censured some of the demands of both as extravagant and beyond his power to concede—admitted others to be reasonable and worthy of consideration—refused to confirm the churches they had seized to the Catholics; but was willing to allow them their 'seminaries of education,'—would not consent to enforce the Penal law on the demand of the Protestants—but declared that neither should the undertakers be disturbed in their possessions or offices. In short, he pathetically exhorted both parties to consider his case as well as their own, promised to call together the Irish Parliament at the earliest possible period; and so got rid of both deputations, leaving Ormond master of the position for some time longer."

Although the troops that crossed from Ireland, whether native Irish or the Anglo-Irish levies of Strafford or Ormond, had often, in addition to the perils of war, much bigotry and prejudice to encounter, they invariably sustained the military reputation of Ireland. Of none of these is this more true than of the stout Ulstermen, led by Alaster MacDonnell—known as Colkitto (the left-handed), who formed the backbone of the army which, under the gallant Montrose, did such splendid service for King Charles. At the battle of Marston Moor, fought on July 2nd, 1644, the Royalists under Prince Rupert, found themselves opposed and defeated by the army of the English Parliamentarians, aided by a force sent by the Scottish Covenanters—these having formed a "Solemn League" in the previous year. They were to defend each other, the Scots were to supply 21,000 men to aid in the war, and Popery, Prelacy, Heresy, and Schism were to be put down. It was necessary for the royal cause to detach, if possible, this Scottish contingent, or, at all events, to create a diversion in their rear. For this purpose the king, a week after the battle of Marston Moor, gave to the Earl of Antrim a commission to raise troops in Ulster, to cross over to reinforce Montrose, who was about to raise the royal standard in Scotland.

The Earl raised a body of men among the glens of Antrim, and placed them under the command of his kinsman, Colkitto. Better troops and better leader could not have been found for such an expedition. These were not men of the stock of the Lowland Scotch of King James's Ulster Plantation, many of whom, having had to disgorge their ill-gotten gains, would about this time be found in the army of Monroe, which afterwards met such a decisive defeat at Benburb, by Owen Roe O'Neill. Colkitto's followers were of a purely Celtic strain, having nothing in common with the bulk of King James's planters, and though quite as Irish in feeling, and of a kindred race to the other native Ulster clans, were, perhaps, still nearer akin to the men of the Highlands and Islands of Scotland, with whom there had been for centuries a constant communication, and who were about to be their companions in arms.

MacDonnell and his followers succeeded in crossing into Scotland, and having taken and fortified the castle of Mingary, they marched to meet Montrose at the appointed rendezvous in Athol, which he had reached in disguise, and with but two attendants. Having now the Irish troops as the nucleus of an army, he, says Lingard, "unfurled the royal standard, published his commission from the king, and summoned the Highland clans to his aid. To the astonishment of the Covenanters, an army appeared to arise out of the earth in a quarter the most remote from danger; but it was an army better adapted to the purpose of predatory invasions than of permanent warfare. Occasionally it swelled to the amount of several thousands; as often it dwindled to the original band of Irishmen under MacDonnell. These, having no other resource than their courage, faithfully clung to their gallant commander in all the vicissitudes of his fortune; the Highlanders, that they might secure their plunder, frequently left him to flee before the superior number of his foes."

Sir Walter Scott, in his "Legend of Montrose," makes

some interesting references to the Irish troops of Colkitto. He makes one of his characters say that they spoke—"neither Saxon nor pure Gaelic." But the difference between the language spoken in their native Antrim glens and that of their Highland companions in arms was no greater than that between the present dialects of two English counties. Indeed, to this day, an Irish scholar can read quite easily a book printed in Gaelic, or understand a sermon such as that, at the Iona pilgrimage of 1888, preached by the Catholic Bishop of Argyle and the Isles.

There was yet another tie between many of these "sea-divided children of the Gael"—the tie of a common creed, for great numbers of the Highlanders, like their brethren from Ireland, still clung to the Catholic faith, which has been preserved among many of them even to our own times. There was a community of suffering, too, between them, for the good Irish-Franciscan, Father Hogarty, who came from Ireland to be Prefect of the Scottish Mission, had been thrown into prison in the previous year, and still remained there.

The dress and weapons of the Irish and Highlanders were somewhat similar. One of the personages in the "Legend of Montrose," speaks of how insufficiently armed Colkitto's Irishmen are, whereupon Dugald Dalgetty, that quaint creature of Scott's prolific brain, whose name has become synonymous with that of a soldier of fortune, declared that, providing—"one-third have muskets, he prefers the pike for the rest." Speaking of the Irish in the Continental Wars, Sir Walter makes Dalgetty say when he hears of their Irish allies—"The Irish are pretty fellows. I desire to see none better in the field. I once saw a brigade of Irish, at the taking of Frankfort on the Oder, stand to it with sword and pike until they beat off the blue and yellow Swedish brigades, esteemed as stout as any that fought under the immortal Gustavus."

The first engagement fought by Montrose was at Tippermuir, where he completely routed the Covenanters, and opened for himself the way to the ancient town of Perth, where, on the 1st of September, a plentiful supply of military stores and provisions became the spoil of the victors. The good burghers of Perth no doubt looked with as much astonishment on the sinewy forms and martial bearing of the Irish soldiers of Montrose as did the London citizens in the days of Queen Bess on the followers of Shane the Proud. They left but little trace of their presence in the picturesque old town that looked down upon the Tay. They were not the last Irish invaders, though, who appeared in Perth, for there has been a more peaceful invasion here as elsewhere in our own time, and you will at this moment find them there, making their way in the world fairly well,—natives of the "old sod," not as a rule from Ulster, like most of the Irish settled in Scotland, but chiefly from the western province.

"From Perth," continues Lingard, "Montrose's army marched to Aberdeen; the Lord Burleigh with his army fled at the first charge; and the pursuers entered the gates with the fugitives. The citizens had experienced the severity of Montrose when he fought for the Covenant; they found that he was not less vindictive now that he commanded for the crown. The pillage continued four days; the Highlanders disappearing with the spoil; and Argyle approached with a superior force. Montrose, followed by the enemy, led his Irishmen into Banff, proceeded along the right bank of the Spey, crossed the Mountains of Badenoch, marched through Athol into Angus, faced the Scots at Fairy Castle, and suddenly retraced his steps into the north. Argyle, fatigued with his obstinate and fruitless pursuit, returned to the Castle of Inverrera, where he reposed in security, amidst mountains deemed impassable to an army. But neither the obstacles of Nature nor the inclemency of the season could arrest the impetuosity of Montrose. He penetrated through defiles choked up with snow, compelled his enemy to save himself in an open boat on the sea, and spent seven weeks in wreaking his vengeance on the domains and the clansmen of the fugitive." Thus passed the December of 1644 and the January of 1645. Lingard then proceeded to describe how—"Shame and passion brought Argyle again into the field. He overtook the plunderers at Inverlochy, in Lochaber, but, afraid of the prowess of Montrose, refused to mingle in the fight, and from a boat in the midst of the lake viewed the advance of the enemy, the shock of the combatants, and the discomfiture of his men. The conquerors now bent their steps to the south, and Dundee must have yielded to their repeated assaults, had not a more numerous enemy approached, formed of new levies, intermixed with veterans from the Scottish forces in England and Scotland. Dundee was saved, and the Royalists regained by rapid marches their fastnesses in the north. Such was the short and eventful campaign of Montrose."

There cannot be a doubt but that the victories of Montrose and his Irish and Highlanders created a powerful diversion in favour of King Charles, causing, as we have seen, a considerable portion of the troops sent against him by the Covenanters to be withdrawn into Scotland. History might have had another story to tell had the troops of Montrose been all like his Irish soldiers. The rest were no less courageous, but, as Sir Walter Scott says,—"When a battle was over, the Highlanders wanted to return home. This is the reason why Montrose, with all his splendid successes, never gained a permanent footing in the Lowlands." Thus it came about that his hitherto uninterrupted career of success was broken on the field of Philiphaugh, where, on the 13th of September 1645, most of his Irish followers were cut to pieces. Colkitto, after a heroic resistance, escaped from the slaughter with a handful of his Antrim men, and ultimately reached Ireland, where he joined the army of the Confederates. He fought in the battle of Knocknos, on the 12th of November 1647, against the infamous "Murrough the Burner," and was treacherously slain, not in the fight, but after he had been made prisoner. Scott speaks of him as having been "brave to intrepidity and almost to insensibility, complete master of his weapons, and always ready to show the example in the extremity of danger." Sir Walter says also, that "Numerous traditions are still preserved in the Highland glens concerning Alister MacDonnell, though the name of Montrose is rarely mentioned among them."

And no wonder MacDonnell and his followers were remembered, for, during their brilliant campaign, there must have been many hours of relaxation, when the light-hearted, high-spirited Irishmen found a hearty welcome at many a

Highland fireside, and many a Highland gathering. Who can doubt but the old airs, so many of which are now claimed by both nationalities, were sung, or played on harp or pipe—who can doubt but the old heroic stories of Finn Mac Coul, and Ossian, and Cuchullin, were told by men and women sprung from a common stock and now for a brief period drawn together by a common cause? During that eventful time they must have often feasted and revelled together, or mourned over a common sorrow—a friend who had died in the course of Nature, or a clansman slain in battle, over whose bodies the wild, plaintive Celtic keen would be raised. And, closest tie of all, can we doubt, though the "Solemn League and Covenant" had sworn to extirpate "Popery," and though the Irish-Franciscan Prefect of the Mission was still in prison, but that some Hiberno-Scotic priest would seek out the clansmen who still clung to the old faith despite fire and sword and gibbet, to minister to the sick and the dying, and to say for them the "mass on the mountain" so familiar in Ireland in the dark days of the Penal Laws?

Macpherson gave his Ossianic poems to the world as translatious from the Gaelic. Many of his critics say he invented them. There may be some truth in each theory; as in Ireland, the Ossianic stories, such as those, no doubt, told by Colkitto's followers, would be found floating about in the Highland glens, and these probably formed the basis at least of Macpherson's work.

In the records of the trials and struggles of the Catholic Church in Scotland in those days, we find that Father Hogarty, the Prefect of the Scottish Mission, was released from prison at the end of five years, and returned to Ireland in 1648.

During the seven years which had just passed, the Irish Catholics had been able to win religious freedom with their swords, so that over the greatest portion of Ireland the clergy had found protection. In England they had been hunted like wolves, so that the priest's hiding-place became a necessary adjunct to the house of many Catholic gentlemen. There were then a few places only where the Catholic faith could be practised without molestation. These were the chapels of the ambassadors from Catholic countries. Preaching in 1882, on behalf of the Church of St Anselm and St Cecilia, in Lincoln's Inn Fields, London, which dates from 1648, when Charles I. was being hard pressed for his life and crown, Cardinal Manning said—"This is the oldest Catholic church now in London, since the great wreck called the Reformation robbed the Church of all its old sanctuaries and altars. The ambassadors of Foreign Powers to this country were alone permitted in those days to have a chapel of their own, and this chapel of the Sardinian Embassy now remains as the Church of St Anselm (a Sardinian saint) and St Cecilia." Round it, just as we see now wherever a Catholic church is erected, gathered the first considerable Irish colony in London, which, afterwards, appears to have spread westward towards St Giles's, where the Irish are still numerous.

On the 30th of January 1649, King Charles, having fallen into the hands of the Parliamentarians, was executed at Whitehall. To do him justice, it must be said that he was not a persecutor by nature. It was only when pushed on by the canting hypocritical faction who profaned the name of liberty that he became so. Whatever toleration they could extort or buy from the king—though he often cheated them in the bargain, there was nothing but bitter and merciless persecution for Irishmen and Catholics to be expected at the hands of the faction now in power. So it continued for the next ten years under the Commonwealth, as the English republic, established after the execution of Charles was called, and during the protectorate of Oliver Cromwell.

But during even these dark days of persecution, the Catholics of England and Scotland were ministered to, at the risk of their lives, by heroic missionary priests, educated mostly on the Continent. The line of English Vicars Apostolic was kept up, and, in 1653, five years after the return of his predecessor to Ireland, another Prefect Apostolic was appointed for Scotland.

Another, and perhaps the most worthless of all the Stuarts, Charles II., was, after numerous vicissitudes, brought back from exile and placed on the English throne in 1660. The Irish parliament, owing to the confiscation carried out by Cromwell, had at this time a large majority of Protestants in both houses. The heads of a "Bill of Settlement" of landed property, which dealt unjustly with the Irish Catholics, having been forwarded to England, Sir Nicholas Plunkett and Colonel Talbot were sent over to advocate the rights of their co-religionists. They met with the usual reception of such delegates. Colonel Talbot was sent to the Tower, and an order of council was issued, that "no petition or further address be made from the Roman Catholics of Ireland as to the Bill of Settlement."

The following is an illustration of the bitter feeling existing in this country against everything Irish at this time—1666. A trade had been growing up for some time—the importation of cattle—between Ireland and England, and it occurred to some one that here was a point at which a blow could be struck at Ireland. The time chosen was a very curious one, while hundreds of unfortunate people were deprived of shelter and food by the great fire of London, so that destitution almost unheard of prevailed in the great city. A gift of fifteen thousand bullocks had been raised and sent over from Ireland to alleviate the distress. The English parliament affected to consider that this was only a sop to enable the Irish dealers to extend their trade in cattle, and, accordingly, an enactment was passed by both Houses of Parliament (meeting most opposition in the House of Lords) that the importation of Irish beef into England was "a nuisance to be abated."

The hatred of Catholics and Irishmen was fomented by a number of sham "Popish Plots," got up by a number of impostors, chief of whom was Titus Oates, of infamous memory. It has been reserved for our own days to furnish anything like a parallel for the villainy of these plots. The only difference is that while, undoubtedly, Oates was the greatest scoundrel of those concerned in the "Popish Plots," the wretched Pigott was by no means the worst of the conspirators against the Irish leaders. Among other things, Oates pretended to have discovered a plot on the part of the Catholics to murder the king, and place the Duke of York, his brother (afterwards James II.), on the throne. Many innocent people were, in consequence, condemned and executed.

The most illustrious victim of the Popish Plot mania was Oliver Plunkett, Archbishop of Armagh, whose martyrdom is thus described by Lingard—
"He had been thrown into prison on the usual charge of having received orders in the Church of Rome; when the promises of reward to informers induced some of the king's witnesses, as they were called, to select him for a principal conspirator in the pretended Irish plot. But they dared not face the man whom they had accused in their own country. At the trial it was said that they were gone to England, and Plunkett, instead of obtaining his discharge (May 3rd, 1681), was compelled to follow them. At his arraignment the chief justice granted him a respite of five weeks to produce evidence from Ireland; but his messenger was driven back by contrary winds; his witnesses were delayed by the difficulty of obtaining passports; the officers in Dublin refused copies of any document without an order from the Council in London; and, in consequence of these delays, his means of defence did not reach the English coast until three days after his condemnation. The informers deposed against him that he had been raised to the dignity of primate for the purpose of preparing a way for the invasion from France; that he had made a survey of the coast, and fixed on the harbour of Carlingford for the debarkation of the French army; that he had collected large sums of money, had ordered musters of all Catholics able to bear arms, and had organised a force of 70,000 men to join the invaders, massacre the Protestants, and establish the Catholic worship. Plunkett replied that his was a most extraordinary case, for, had he confessed himself guilty of these offences in his own country, yet an Irish jury must have acquitted him from their personal knowledge that the charge could not by any possibility be true. But he had been brought away from a place where his own character, the conduct of his accusers, and the state of the country were known, to be tried before men whose ignorance of all these things rendered them incapable of forming a correct judgment of his guilt or innocence. Had his evidence arrived he should have shown that the witnesses against him were men undeserving of credit, apostate friars whom he had

punished for their immorality, and convicted felons who had forfeited their reputation. But of such aid it was not in his power to avail himself because it was still on the road. The only thing which he could now oppose to the oaths of the accusers was the solemn asseveration of his innocence, and the utter improbability that he had been able to collect sufficient money for the support of an army, when it was well known that he could never raise an income of £70 a year for his own subsistence. The jury, however, found him guilty, and when the Earl of Essex, who had been Lord Lieutenant of Ireland, solicited his pardon, declaring from his own knowledge that the charges against him could not be true, the king indignantly replied—'Then, my Lord, be his blood on your conscience. You might have saved him if you would. I cannot pardon him, because I dare not.' Plunkett suffered, and was the last of the victims sacrificed to the imposture of the Popish Plot."

Early in 1685, King Charles II., being on his deathbed, received the rites of the Catholic Church from Father Huddleston, who, it was said, had saved his life at the battle of Worcester. He died on the 16th of February, and his brother was immediately proclaimed king. The accession of James II. to the throne was an evil alike for England and Ireland. He was, though nominally a Catholic, a man of immoral life, and with scarcely a redeeming feature in his character. He did more harm to Catholic interests than the efforts made during the two centuries since his reign have been able to repair, and how he could have succeeded in attracting so much support and sympathy must always remain an inexplicable puzzle. When he reached the throne the English people were still under the spell of terror caused by the villainous stories of Oates and Bedloe. To these imaginary terrors James succeeded in giving a fresh impetus by importing bodies of troops from Ireland. The English regarded this as an insult and a menace, and their terror and hatred of everything Irish increased a hundredfold. The fires of sedition, carefully kindled and fed, grew greater and greater, so that when the invaders, under William of Orange, invited over by the conspirators, appeared on English soil, the anti-Irish feeling was at its height. The first engagement, after William landed at Torbay, was at Wiscanton. Here he encountered a body of Irish troops under the gallant Sarsfield, to whose bravery and splendid qualities even Macaulay pays a high tribute. The fact that it was a body of Irishmen who were the first to stand in the gap against the invaders, added to the terror and detestation with which they and all their fellow-countrymen were regarded. The handful of brave Irish soldiers brought over by James—"not enough," as Macaulay said, "to hold down the single city of London or the single county of York, but more than enough to excite the alarm and rage of the whole kingdom,"—became the objects of popular vengeance, wherever detached bodies of them were met with. "All London," says M'Gee, "lighted with torches, and marshalled under arms, awaited during the memorable 'Irish night' the advent of the terrible and detested regiments brought over by Tyrconnell: some companies of these troops quartered in the country were fallen upon by ten times their number, and cut to pieces. Others, fighting and inquiring their way, reached Chester or Bristol, and obtained a passage home. They passed at sea, or encountered on the landing-places, multitudes of the Protestant Irish, men, women, and children, flying in exactly the opposite directions."

When Viscount Dundee raised the royal standard in Scotland, Irish troops were sent to his aid, and these behaved with the same gallantry as did their fellow-countrymen fifty years before, under Montrose. How King James fared in Ireland and how he lost his crown are matters of history.

CHAPTER VII.

IRISH GENIUS DURING THE STUART REIGNS.

THE inflow of learned and holy men to England from Ireland which was so remarkable before the Norman conquest, after that era proceeded in a gradually lessening measure. They were to be found, as has been mentioned, at the universities of Oxford and Cambridge, and their acquirements obtained for them not infrequently high ecclesiastical promotion. It is to be doubted if they came in any numbers as late as the "Reformation," but if they did, that event entirely checked the practice. But it opened at the same time new careers; and during the persecutions of Elizabeth and James I. more than one Irish priest enrolled himself in the ranks of those fearless missionaries who lived the lives of hunted outlaws in the effort to keep up the faith in England. Late in Elizabeth's reign the University of Trinity College, Dublin, was founded on the site and from the plunder of the old Monastery of All Hallows. Of course its *alumni* were Irishmen of the new religion, for the most part born of English settlers of comparatively recent date; nevertheless, they were born on Irish soil, breathed the pure Irish air, and did not scruple to avow themselves Irishmen, as who shall question their right, provided only they loved and honestly desired the advantage of the country of their birth. From the walls of the young university came forth an array of ecclesiastics—men like Usher and Jeremy Taylor—whose names were the brightest gems of the Protestant establishment in Ireland; and before long many of the keen intellects and ambitious minds began to feel that the sphere at home was too limited, and that there was more room for them, and more fame and wealth besides, to be found in the metropolis of England. It must always be so when one country is under the heel of another; the conquered province can furnish no worthy field for the genius of her sons, and she sees them perforce gradually drifting away from her to spend their brains and energies in the service of others. Those Irishmen who began gradually to find their way over to London in the reign of James I., and, in an increasing stream, in the reigns of Charles II., James II., and William III., were the forerunners of the many hundreds of brilliant Irishmen who to-day are to be found in the great city, competing in the learned professions, in the ranks of art and science, on the stage, in the press, or in any walk of life which calls in a higher degree for the exercise of the mental powers. How many of them from that day to this have made the weary journey, have entered the metropolis with no other capital than their mother-wit, their native courage and sanguine temperament — some to be engulfed in the waves, to perish after a short and unequal struggle, others to attain marvellous success, the majority to toil on against heavy odds, doing great work for which the world will never give recognition, building up monuments for other men and leaving no record after them but the ever-increasing legacy of devotion to motherland which burns so brightly in the breasts of the Irish exiles of to-day. The pioneers of Irish genius, to whom allusion has been made, would find themselves in a very different atmosphere from that of the London of to-day. No doubt their Irish tongue would have received the criticism and raillery of the would-be wits of the period, as it has often done since, and their provincial habits and tricks of attire would have met with considerable adverse comment. Still in religion and blood most of these were nearer akin to their English neighbours and fellow-students than Irish exiles of later times, and even their accent was nearer, if we may believe some philologists, to the English pronunciation of the period than what is called the Irish brogue of to-day is—the latter having remained constant while the English pronunciation has varied. Again, to have got to London at all pointed to the probability of influential patrons or private wealth, either of which advantages would have been no slight recommendation. Some of our young Irish adventurers would have been brought thither, like Richard Stanihurst, the historian, to pursue their legal studies. Others, even at that early date, would seem to have been inspired by the dramatic fire, a not infrequent development of Celtic genius. Such a man was Ludovic Barry, the first Irish dramatist who wrote in the English tongue, and whose comedy of "Ram Alley," or "Merry Tricks," was a favourite with Londoners in the first decade of the seventeenth century. Others again, the greater part of whose lives is more intimately connected with their own country, were led to London to find a suitable field for the publication of their writings, or, it might be, for the purpose of consulting the various libraries which existed there, in the interest of historical and scientific knowledge. Under this head would come the celebrated Protestant Archbishop Usher and also Sir James Ware, who first came to London in 1626, to obtain material for his work on "The Antiquities of Ireland." Accompanying him on this visit was one of the most painstaking and almost the last of the native Irish annalists, Duald Mac Ferbis, who gave him great assistance in his researches. In 1639, Ware was made a privy councillor, and in the same year he published "The Writers of Ireland." In 1644 he waited on the king at Oxford, as one of the delegates from the Earl of Ormond. On his way back to Ireland, he was captured by the Parliamentarians and sent to the Tower. Here he lay for ten months, but was then exchanged. He returned to Dublin where he remained for two years more, but in 1647 his bad fortune returned, and he was, on the surrender of the city, sent as a hostage to London. Here he was detained until 1649, when he was ordered to quit the country, and he betook himself to France. A few years later he published his "Works ascribed to St Patrick," "Annals of Ireland," and "Lives of the Irish Bishops." He died in 1666, and was buried in St Werburghs, Dublin.

Sir John Denham, born in Dublin in 1615, was one of the chief ornaments of the literary world during his century. His best known poem, "Cooper's Hill," was written at Oxford in 1643. Dryden speaks of it as "a poem, which for majesty of style is, and ever will be, the standard of good writing." Speaking of Dryden reminds one of the unfortunate poet Flecknoe, whom he pilloried as "MacFlecknoe." This writer was born in Ireland in 1600, and was in his early years a Jesuit. He died nine years later than Denham, whose death is recorded in 1678. Sir John Denham was a staunch Royalist, but these had not a monopoly of Irish genius. Roger Boyle, Earl of Orrery (the "Merciless Broghill" of Duffy's stirring poem) was just as determined a Parliamentarian. He wrote numerous plays and poems. One of the well-known poets of the Stuart reigns was the Earl of Roscommon. He was a friend of Dryden, and wrote verses of great force and elegance.

Many other Irishmen attained eminence in the world of letters at this period, including Thomas Duffet, a poet; George Farquhar, a dramatist and actor; Nahum Tate, who became Poet Laureate; and Dr Nicholas Brady, who was joint author with Tate of a metrical version of the Psalms of David.

It will be seen that most of these literary Irishmen of the Stuart reigns came from the ascendancy caste, which has more or less dominated Ireland ever since. The irrepressible Irish Celt was, however, gradually coming to the front, as he always does when he gets anything like a fair chance, and made a prominent figure among the distinguished men of the following century.

BOOK IV.

THE PENAL DAYS.

CHAPTER VIII.

PERSECUTION AGAIN — THE JACOBITE RISING OF 1745—
THUROT'S EXPEDITION.

THE Revolution of 1688-90 has been celebrated as a triumph of civil and religious liberty. It was but the triumph of a faction—a faction composed of men who did not understand liberty as equal rights for all. It could not, however, be said of them that they did not value freedom. They valued it so highly, indeed, that they wanted it all for themselves, and would give none to others—least of all to Catholics or Irishmen. For these the "Glorious Revolution" meant a renewal of the persecutions and plunderings arising out of the "Reformation" in these islands.

The history of the Irish settlers in Britain since the expulsion of King James II. is interwoven with the struggles, trials, and triumphs of the Catholic religion during the same period. Here and there throughout the land there were noble English and Scottish families that still held on to the ancient creed. Their tenantry in some cases remained Catholic too, as may be still seen in some parts of Lancashire, where there are villages in which the whole of the people have always retained the faith of their fathers. But the stream of English Catholicity seemed like a river becoming gradually lost in the sands of a desert, until it became strengthened, deepened, and revivified by the immigration from the land of St Patrick and St Columba, which first began to gather force about the middle of the last century.

The reign of James II. had been a breathing time for the Catholics of England and Scotland. It was hoped that better days had dawned for the Church. In 1687, two Vicars Apostolic were appointed for England, and a number of churches and religious houses were opened. On January 30th, 1688, Pope Innocent XI. created four districts or vicariates—the *London, Midland, Northern,* and *Western.* Of existing Catholic missions there are less than a score dating from this period. This, however, is no indication of the number of churches and chapels then in existence, many of which ceased to be used for Catholic worship or were wrecked or destroyed in the penal days that followed. Thus we find that a church and convent were, in 1687, built by the Franciscans in Birmingham. Masshouse Lane still marks their site. But the hopes of the Catholics seemed to crumble away at the very whisper of the intended invasion of William of Orange. The buildings erected by the Franciscans did not remain long unmolested, for they were burnt and pulled down by the rabble of Birmingham on the 2nd of November 1688, two days before the landing of William.

During the eighteenth century the number of men of Irish birth famous in British science, art, and literature was marvellous. A mere catalogue of their names would almost fill a chapter. But as the systematic policy of successive British governments, with but short intervals, had been the extermination of the Irish who held on to the old faith, or the driving of them into a state of savagery, it is not surprising that, of those who came to seek their fortunes and attained eminence in England, the greater portion were from the ascendancy caste in Ireland. The great bulk of the Irish people at this time had really no legal existence. They were considered to be no higher in the social scale than were the negro slaves in America previous to the great civil war.

But the race which had survived such oppressions, and had even increased and multiplied under them, must have possessed extraordinary vitality. For them learning had been made a crime by Act of Parliament. They could only obtain it by stealth and at the risk of severe penalties. But England found that wherever the hardest toil had to be

E

done the strong arms of these Irish slaves—for what else were they?—were invaluable. Accordingly we find them, early in the eighteenth century, crossing the channel, as they have been doing ever since, to reap the harvests of England and Scotland, or to labour on the quays of London, Bristol, or Liverpool. Crushed and starved as they had been, they still had powerful frames and courageous hearts. With proper food and training, they made the finest soldiers in Europe. Some of the Irish regiments raised for King James were afterwards incorporated into the British army. Since then hundreds of thousands of men of our race have borne the flag of England to victory in every part of the world. But their prowess brought no throb of exultation to the national heart. On the contrary, the more firmly they cemented British supremacy with their blood, the more securely were they fastening the chains on the limbs of their own race at home. Ireland knew that many a son of hers had been driven by misfortune to wear the uniform of the British soldier, and never forgot that even these were her children. But she watched with more loving eyes the flight of her darling "wild geese"—as the Irish recruits for European armies were then called; and when at length they stood victors over their olden oppressors at Fontenoy, she hoped soon to welcome them home to strike the shackles from her limbs. So, indeed, the exiled Irish did in some degree loosen their country's chains, for it was only when the army or navy of Britain at any time met with a check that, bit by bit, any part of the fiendish penal code was relaxed.

Our countrymen who crossed the channel in such large numbers to reap the harvest, generally returned home each season. Those who made their homes in England and Scotland mostly settled in the larger towns. From time to time we shall follow their fortunes and glance at their mode of life in these places.

As Liverpool contains the most compact, and, after London, the most numerous body of Irish of any town in Great Britain, some reminiscences of it will be interesting. It would appear from old Leland that long before Manchester men commenced to get their American cotton through Liverpool, or to construct their great canal to bring it to their own doors, they came to Liverpool for "Yrish yarn," to use in what was then, probably, the staple trade of the place. No doubt too, as at present, our countrymen were to be found on the quays of Liverpool, landing the yarn and other goods, and very likely there were Irish hands in Manchester working at the yarn, just as now we have multitudes of them engaged in the cotton manufactures of that great city. An old tradition in Liverpool carries back the connection between the town and Ireland to a more remote time than is spoken of by Leland. There has been much controversy as to the birthplace of St Patrick, and whence he started on his mission to our forefathers. France and Britain contend for the honour. Among other places in this country Liverpool claims a certain connection with our national saint, for in the "Annals" of that town, published in the local Directory, mention is made of a tradition that St Patrick sailed from the Mersey for the conversion of Ireland. Less apocryphal than this is another legend. It is said that, at the junction of Great Crosshall Street and Marybone, there formerly stood what was known as "St Patrick's Cross." It is a remarkable fact that, in the erection of religious edifices, the ministers of the Catholic Church have shewn a wonderful aptitude in seizing upon local circumstances in the choice of a site, as well as in the naming of the shrine. Thus, close to the spot where formerly stood St Patrick's Cross, and in Great Crosshall Street, not far from the street called after Our Lady, there is now erected one of the finest churches in England, designed by the younger Pugin, and dedicated to the Holy Cross. The Irish exiles of our own day have, in addition to this, erected, in another part of Liverpool, a church called after the name of their patron saint. What more natural, then, that some such men as the Irish "marchantes," spoken of by Leland, should have erected here a memorial cross in honour of St Patrick?

The old church of St Nicholas having been seized by the "reformers," there appears to have been no attempt at Catholic worship in Liverpool for a long interval. The following entry from the burial register shews the disabilities under which Catholics laboured at the time, and is also a further indication of the trade between Ireland and Liverpool spoken of by Leland, John Synett, being an Irish sea captain, settled in Liverpool :—" 1618, Aug. 12th.—John Synett, an Irishman, born in Wexforde, master of a barke, was excommunicated by the B. of Chester for being a Catholic recusant, and so dying at his house in Liverpoole, was denied to be buried at Liverpoole churche or chappell, and therefore was brought and buried in the said burial place of Harkirke, in ye afternoon of ye third day of August, 1612." The Harkirke was a piece of land at Crosby, in which Catholics were interred who had been refused burial at their [parish church. In 1701, Nicholas Blundell, of Crosby, sent his chaplain to minister stealthily to those in Liverpool, who still remained true to the old faith. Mass had then to be said in a private house, a proportion of those who attended, judging from some of the names that have been handed down to us, being Irish. Some idea of the extent of the little congregation in 1727 may be formed from the number of palms, 256, given out on Palm Sunday that year. It was nine years later, the population of Liverpool being then about 18,000, before there was a regular Catholic chapel. It was in Lumber Street, an obscure thoroughfare. The entrance was by a passage from Edmund Street, Oldhall Street, and the building was designedly made as unpretentious looking as possible, having the external appearance of a warehouse. This was a Jesuit mission, but later in the century (1783) it was transferred to the Benedictines, who still retain it.

In 1731 there were two Vicars Apostolic—for the Highland and Lowland districts respectively—appointed for Scotland. There had been one Vicar Apostolic for the whole of Scotland since 1694. There are districts in the Highlands and Islands of Scotland that have always, even up to our own time, remained Catholic, but the additional Vicar Apostolic appointed in 1731 would probably be in consequence of the considerable influx into Glasgow, Edinburgh, and the Lowlands of Scotland, chiefly Ayrshire and Wigtonshire, from the North of Ireland. Indeed, just as regularly as the swallows return in summer, as the Connaught peasant has crossed over to work in the fens of Lincolnshire and other

English counties, so has his brother from Donegal come, from time immemorial, to work for the Scottish farmers. Though, as a rule, they returned home each year, many remained and settled permanently. There are a number of the surnames in Ayrshire and Wigtonshire, like that of the Scottish national poet, Burns, which are apparently of Irish origin. The forefathers of many bearing such names were Catholics from the North of Ireland, from whence the Irish of Scotland still come in large numbers. But from the want of priests and the means of practising their religion, the Catholic faith had almost died out in these parts, until the influx of Irish during the present century, and particularly the last fifty years, gave it renewed vitality.

In 1745, so strong had the Jacobites, as the supporters of the Stuart dynasty were called, become, that a determined and almost successful effort was made to replace the ancient line upon the throne of Britain. The Jacobite rising of 1715 had been readily put down: not so the rising of 1745, an account of which enters legitimately into a history of the Irish in Britain; for the sinews of war were found by Irish exiles, and the military operations were mainly directed by skilled officers of the Irish Brigade in the service of France. Prince Charles Edward, grandson of James II., led the expedition on behalf of his father, who had assumed the title of James III. The Waterses, father and son, Irish bankers at Paris, advanced 180,000 livres between them, and Walsh, an Irish merchant at Nantes, put a privateer of eighteen guns into the venture. Sir Thomas Geraldine was the agent of Charles Edward at Paris, and among others who accompanied the expedition, which started from France for Scotland, were Sir Thomas Sheridan, the prince's preceptor, who, with Colonels O'Sullivan and Lynch, Captain O'Neil, and other officers of the Brigade, formed a portion of the staff. Fathers O'Kelly and O'Brien also accompanied the expedition.

"On the 22nd of July 1745," says Thomas D'Arcy M'Gee, from whose history of Ireland most of these details are taken, "with seven friends, the prince embarked in Walsh's vessel, the *Doutelle*, at St Nazaire, on the Loire, and on the 19th of July landed on the northern coast of Scotland near Moidart." The royal standard was unfurled at Glenfinan, on the 19th of August, and among those who rallied round it were Clanronald, Cameron of Lochiel, the Laird of M'Leod, and others. The entire force consisted of but 1200 men. They were formed into camp by O'Sullivan, who, from then until the fatal day of Culloden, took the chief command. By the time Prince Charles Edward's troops had reached Edinburgh, a French ship, containing arms, supplies, and Irish officers, arrived in Scotland, and arrangements were made in France that certain Irish regiments with French troops were to be sent to reinforce the Jacobites. After this 1000 men, under Lord John Drummond, were shipped from Dunkirk and arrived at Montrose. By this time the prince and his heroic little army had reached Manchester, where they were well received. Thence they penetrated to Derby, where the officers refused to advance further towards London with so small a force, and retreat was reluctantly decided upon. A gallant stand was made at Carlisle, and a victory gained at Falkirk. But the army led by the Duke of Cumberland so completely outnumbered the prince's forces, that, during the months of February, March, and part of April, 1746, Edinburgh, Perth, and Glasgow had to be evacuated. The final stand was made at Culloden on the 16th of April 1746. The ground was selected by O'Sullivan as being best fitted for Highland warfare. He formed the army, which mustered less than 5000 men, into two lines; the great clans—the Ogilvies, Gordons, and Murrays being in the first, and the Irish and French in the second. "Four pieces of cannon flanked each wing, and four occupied the centre. Lord George Murray commanded the right wing, Lord Drummond the left, and Brigadier Stapleton the reserve. The British formed in three lines 10,000 strong, with two guns between every second regiment of the first and second line. The action commenced about noon, and before evening half the troops of Prince Charles lay dead on the field and the rest were hopelessly broken. The retreat was pell-mell, except where a troop of Irish pickets, by a spirited fire, checked the pursuit, which a body of dragoons commenced after the Macdonalds, and Lord Gordon's regiment did similar service. Stapleton conducted the Irish and French remnant to Inverness, and obtained for them, by capitulation, 'fair terms and honourable treatment.'" Charles remained on the field until the last, and then had to be dragged away by O'Sullivan. "From that time forth O'Sullivan, O'Neil, and a poor sedan-carrier of Edinburgh, called Burke, accompanied the prince in all his wanderings and adventures among the Scottish Islands. At Long Island they were obliged to part company, the prince proceeding alone with Miss Flora Macdonald. He had not long left when a French cutter hove in sight and took off O'Sullivan, intending to touch at another point and take in the prince and O'Neil. The same night she was blown off the coast, and the prince, after many other adventures, was finally taken off at Badenoch, on the 15th of September 1746, by the *L'Heureux*, a French armed vessel, in which Captain Sheridan (son of Sir Thomas), Mr O'Beirne, a lieutenant in the French army, and two other gentlemen had adventured in search of him."

While there was any chance of the success of Charles Edward Stuart, the Catholics and Irish remained unmolested, but, when it was evident that his fortunes were waning, popular vengeance was wreaked on those supposed to be his sympathisers. As an example of this: after the Jacobite army had retreated from Derby, and had arrived north of Liverpool, the mob attacked and destroyed the little Catholic chapel of that town. The old chapel was rebuilt, and in our own time (1845) was replaced by a stately church, designed by Pugin. Within recent years (1885) this building was removed, stone by stone, to another site in Highfield Street. The ground where it stood, and great tracts of the neighbouring streets, inhabited largely by an Irish population, were taken for the new station of the Lancashire and Yorkshire Railway. But, though all traces of it have been long swept away, there are still Catholic Irishmen in Liverpool who heard mass in St Mary's old chapel in Lumber Street. During the last century, among the clergy ministering to the Catholics of Liverpool, was a Jesuit priest, Father Anthony Carroll. The *Xaverian*, for May 1887, a monthly magazine, published by the Jesuit Fathers of St Francis

Xavier's, Liverpool, gives the following account of him :—
" He was born in Ireland, September 16th, 1722, and
entered the Society at Watten, on September 7th, 1744.
He was professed of the four vows eighteen years later.
Immediately after his ordination, at Liege, in 1754, he
was sent to serve on the mission at Lincoln. He came
to Liverpool in 1759, and laboured in this town for seven
years. After the suppression of the society, in 1773, he
accompanied Father John Carroll, afterwards first Archbishop of Baltimore, to Maryland. He returned to England
in 1775; and served the missions of Shepton Mallet, Exeter,
Worcester, &c." Father Carroll, at an advanced age, met
his end in a very sad way, as the following extract from the
Gentleman's Magazine of 1794 will show :—" Death, aged
about seventy-four, Mr Robert (Anthony) Carroll, a Roman
Catholic priest. He had stopped at the end of Red Lion
Court, Fleet Street, to shelter himself from the rain, and
was followed by three men, one of whom gave him a violent
push, which turned him quite around. He then gave him a
blow which drove him across the pavement into the kennel
(*i.e.*, the *canal*, or gutter), and, falling on the edge of the
curb, he received a wound on the right side of his head,
which occasioned his death. Mr Carroll lay for some time
unobserved by the neighbours, but was afterwards seen near
the place where he fell, in company of three young men,
one of whom was observed to have hold of him by the arm,
upon which Mr Carroll did not appear to lean as if he stood
in much need of such support. They all passed down Fleet
Street together, and were no more seen by the spectators
near Red Lion Court. Where a coach was taken for him is
not yet known, but he was carried to St Bartholomew's
Hospital in one, with his head bruised, and speechless, and
continued speechless till one o'clock in the morning of the
6th (of September), when he died. The men who brought
him discharged the coach, and gave the nurse a small present,
then took leave, and have not since been heard of. A
letter in Mr Carroll's pocket led to a discovery of his
place of abode, which was at No. 33 King Street, Holborn.
He had been robbed of his watch, and, it is supposed of
what money he had in his breeches pocket, as none was

found therein : but, in a side pocket, the nurse found a purse, containing eleven guineas, and a single guinea wrapped in brown paper. Mr Carroll was a man of irreproachable character and some property, having left a will, in which he bequeathed about £500 to two nieces residing in Ireland, with some other legacies." The *Xaverian* adds—" Father Carroll found time to translate and publish four volumes of sermons of the great Jesuit preacher, Bourdaloue, under the title of 'Practical Divinity.' Apparently Father de Backer, in his great work, ' Bibliothèque des Ecrivains S.J.,' did not identify this book, for the only reference to it runs thus in the second volume, p. 84, under the heading *Bourdaloue : Traductions*, ' Sermons translated from the French, by A. C., 1776, in 12, 4 vol.'"

The Father John Carroll, afterwards Archbishop of Baltimore, with whom Father Anthony Carroll went to America, was cousin to Charles Carroll, of Carrolltown, one of those who signed the famous Declaration of American Independence.

From the *Xaverian* we also learn that there was another Irish priest who succeeded Father Carroll. It says— " Father Peter O'Brien, like his predecessor, Father Carroll, was a native of Ireland, where he was born, on March 28th, 1735. Entering the English province at Watten, September 7th, 1754, he was, in due time, professed of the four vows. He certainly laboured on the Liverpool Mission between the years 1760 and 1770, but the exact date and length of his residence cannot now be determined. Father O'Brien spent ten years in the West Indies, and in 1773 he was at Antigua. The climate affected his health, and returning to England, he was sent to Newhall, Essex, and there he died, February 28th or March 5th, 1807, in the seventy-third year of his age. He had renewed his vows in the restored Society."

Another account speaks of a priest at the old chapel, named Bryan, who had been an officer in the Irish Brigade, and afterwards went to Antigua. It is also stated that, " be coming heir to his eldest brother, he returned to England, and died at Newhall, in Essex." It is probable, from the similarity in the names " O'Brien " and " Bryan," and the incidents spoken of, that these two accounts refer to the same person.

From the days when Irishmen first took service in foreign armies until our own, the hope that has ever cheered their exile has been that some day they might draw their swords for Ireland. This hope they never relinquished—even in the darkest hour of Ireland's woe. After the failure of the Jacobite expedition to Scotland, the enemies of England were not slow to take advantage of this feeling. In 1759, Commodore Thurot sailed out of Dunkirk to ravage the shores of Britain, and to attack the strongholds of British rule along the coast of Ireland. In connection with this there is a memorable and significant circumstance. As the chapel of the Liverpool Catholics, in Lumber Street, was wrecked and burnt during the rising of Charles Edward, so was the building erected in its place, on the same site, attacked by a mob in the year of Thurot's expedition. This can scarcely be a mere coincidence, for, up to our own time, when anything has arisen to arouse British feeling into an outbreak against the creed and country of Irishmen, the fury of the mob has been invariably directed against the churches and chapels of the Irish Catholics of Great Britain. M'Gee, in his history of Ireland, tells us that Thurot was of Irish extraction, and that his real name was O'Farrell. After being driven about by storms, and losing one of his vessels, another having returned to France, he entered Lough Foyle, but did not land. On the 21st of February 1760, he appeared before Carrickfergus, and, effecting a landing at the head of his sailors and marines, carried the place by assault. "After levying contributions on the rich burgesses and proprietors of Belfast, he again put to sea." After this, as we learn from the *Annual Register* and other records of the time, he spread consternation along the coasts of England and Scotland. Relating the end of the bold Franco-Irishman's career, M'Gee says—"His ships, battered by the wintry storms which they had undergone in northern latitudes, fell in, near the Isle of Man, with three English frigates, just out of port, under Commodore Elliott. A gallant action ensued, in which Thurot, or O'Farrell, and 300 of his men were killed. The survivors stuck to their victors, and the French ships were towed, in a sinking state, into the port of Ramsey. The life thus lost in the joint service of France and Ireland was a life illustrative of the Irish refugee class among whom he became a leader. Left an orphan in childhood, O'Farrell, though of a good family, had been bred in France in so menial a condition that he first visited England as a domestic servant. From that condition he rose to be a bold and dexterous captain in the contraband trade, so extensive in those times. In this capacity he visited almost every port of either channel, acquiring that accurate knowledge which, added to his admitted bravery and capacity, placed him at length at the head of a French squadron. Lord Mahon said of him— 'The honour and bravery of this bold adventurer are warmly acknowledged by his enemies. He fought his ship until the hold was almost filled with water, and the deck covered with dead bodies.'"

It will be seen that all the "wild geese" exported from Ireland to the continent of Europe did not find their way into the armies of France, Spain, or Austria. Some elected to harass their ancient enemy on what has been considered her own element—the sea. The gallant O'Farrell graduated in the contraband trade. Some nine years later, we hear of other Irishmen who appear to have been following his example. Here is an account, from the *Annual Register*, of an action between these ocean rapparees and a British ship of war—"On October 26th, 1768, a very brisk engagement happened between his Majesty's cutter, the *Lord How*, Captain Cummins, commander, and two smuggling vessels from France, manned with Irish, off Milford. The action began in the afternoon, and lasted till night, when the smugglers, under favour of the darkness and a brisk gale, made their escape."

CHAPTER IX.

THE IRISH IN LONDON IN THE EIGHTEENTH CENTURY—
BURKE AND SHERIDAN—RELAXATION OF THE PENAL
CODE—SCOTTISH "NO-POPERY" RIOTS—THE GORDON
RIOTS IN LONDON — IRISH VICTIMS — THE UNITED
IRISHMEN IN ENGLAND—FATHER O'LEARY.

JUDGING from the frequent mention of Irish names in the *Annual Register* about this time, and from other circumstances, our countrymen must have become tolerably numerous in London—particularly in the neighbourhood of Drury Lane. Thus we have it chronicled that "the Irish giant, Cornelius M'Grah, who was 7 feet 8 inches high, and had been exhibited in a show at Bristol and London, died on the 16th May 1760, aged twenty-four." And, in February 1765, we are told that "there died lately in Maggard Street, St Giles, Mrs Farrell, who, by letting two-penny lodgings, amassed upwards of £6000." No doubt Mrs Farrell's customers would be chiefly her own countrymen, such as hawkers or labourers from Ireland, passing through London for the harvesting or Kent hop-picking. About the same time the death is recorded in Longacre, London, of one Philip Maguire, aged one hundred and five years. We hear of our fellow-countrymen outside the metropolis too. In August 1761, we read that—"a dispute happened between the farmers of King's Langley and the Irish reapers. The Royal Foresters, quartered at Watford, were sent for, and a great skirmish ensued, in which several were wounded. Six were taken and committed to St Albans jail, and the rest were dispersed." In the part of the *Annual Register* devoted to such matters, we learn that, in May 1766, "there is now living at Whitehaven one Peter M'Gee. He is about one hundred years old, and has been married to eight wives, who bore him twenty-eight sons and four daughters, the youngest of whom is now but nine years old." The much married Peter was, no doubt, a native of the north of Ireland, where the M'Gees are still a numerous clan. There has always been a considerable trade between Whitehaven and the various Ulster ports. This naturally brought an influx of our people—indeed the Catholic mission of St Begh, Whitehaven, dates from 1706. As might be expected, the Irish of Cumberland are chiefly from the northern province.

During the seventeenth and eighteenth centuries we have numerous proofs of the missionary character of our race, and of how the infamous penal laws had no terror for the good *soggarth*, who followed his humbler fellow-countrymen into England and Scotland, to minister to their spiritual wants. Thus we read, under the date of August 21st, 1767, that— "At the Assizes at Croydon, John Baptist Moloney was tried for unlawfully exercising the functions of a Popish priest and administering the sacrament of the Lord's Supper to divers persons, after the manner of the Church of Rome, when he was found guilty, and received sentence of perpetual imprisonment." But Britain had, by this time, met some serious reverses by land and sea, and, therefore, the penal laws, though not repealed, were becoming somewhat more mercifully administered; for, some four years later, we learn that Father Moloney "was brought before the Court of King's Bench and his Majesty's pardon read to him, on condition that, fourteen days after his enlargement, he will quit the kingdom and not return without leave, which he readily agreed to. He was bound, himself, in a penalty of £500, and two of his friends in penalties of £200 each."

At this time the Catholics and Irish had more to fear from the brutality of the British mob than from the Government, for, in 1768, St Mary's Catholic Church, Preston (dating from 1605), was pillaged and profaned. The rabble sought the life of the priest, but he escaped across the Ribble with the Blessed Sacrament on his person. All the registers of the church were burnt. Until very recent days the British mob became possessed, from time to time, with a no-Popery or anti-Irish mania. This feeling was particularly rampant as the Irish element gradually extended in this country, from about the middle of the eighteenth century until it culminated in the terrible Gordon riots of 1780. Sometimes it manifested itself in the wrecking of a "Popish" chapel, at others in the maltreatment of Irish harvestmen, or of Irish coal heavers in London, such as will presently be referred to. We know how, by studied insults to his creed and country, the hot-blooded Irish Celt is often made to appear the aggressor. In any case he is nearly always the greatest sufferer, for, even if he comes off victorious in the fight with his opponents, the law is pretty sure to claim him in the end as the chief victim.

We read of a terrible affray in London, on May 25th, 1768, between coal heavers and sailors. The coal heavers were mostly, if not all, Irishmen, for, even then, our people were beginning to form a large element in the river-side population of the metropolis. They were valued, just as they are now, because, as the *Annual Register* said—"It would be difficult to find men so adapted from strength, &c., to execute this laborious task of coal heaving as the Irish are." So desperate was the conflict referred to, that many lives were lost. A number of coal heavers were apprehended and brought to trial, but there is no mention of the arrest of any of the sailors. This happened about one hundred and twenty years ago, but the incident bears a strong family resemblance to what has occurred within the present generation in English towns, where the Irish were brutally treated, and had their homes and churches gutted. Yet, in the legal proceedings that followed, they often received the severest punishment. Two of the coal heavers, Murphy and Duggan, were brought to trial at the Old Bailey, on July 8th, and convicted for killing a waterman's apprentice. Three days afterwards they were hanged at Tyburn. On the same day that these two men were tried, we find that, "Seven coal heavers were capitally convicted at the Old Bailey, viz., John Grainger, Daniel Clarke *alias* Clarie, Richard Cornwall, Patrick Lynch, Thomas Murray, Peter Flaherty, and Nicholas M'Cabe, on an indictment for feloniously, wilfully, and maliciously shooting at Mr Green, the master of the Round-about-Tavern, in Shadwell. The trial lasted from nine in the morning till four in the afternoon." The men thus capitally convicted were, on the 26th of July, conveyed from Newgate in three carts, and executed in the Sun Tavern Fields, Shadwell. The *Register* says—"One, being a Protestant, went in the first cart, attended by a gentleman of Mr Wesley's persuasion, and appeared quite resigned, the other six, in the two following carts, who read with seemingly great fervour and devotion. They were all remarkably stout, well made men, and much excited the pity of an incredible number of spectators who were assembled in the streets. A guard of three hundred soldiers did duty about Wapping and Shadwell, but there was no need for their assistance, there not being the slightest attempt to rescue the malefactors. At the place of execution, M'Cabe declared he never fired off musquet or pistol in his life." In this the case of M'Cabe is curiously like that of Michael Larkin, executed in 1867, in connection with the attack on the prison van at Manchester. It will be remembered that a number of witnesses swore to having seen Larkin firing a revolver. It is well known that he never fired a pistol or other weapon in his life. There is no mention in contemporary records of the presence of a priest to administer the rites of the Church to the unfortunate Irish coal heavers who were Catholics. There was, probably, a priest in the locality at the time, for among the chapels wrecked in the Gordon riots, twelve years afterwards, was one in Virginia Lane, Wapping.

At an earlier date, probably, even than this, many of the Irish of London, as they do now, as well as from Ireland itself, went each year to the hop-picking in Kent. The present writer once met a very old Irishman in a remote Welsh village who was born in Kent, his parents having been hop-pickers. He spoke Irish with fluency. He said that for generations before his time the Irish had gone as "hoppers" into Kent. Some were London-born Irish, as at present—others came from Ireland and went back each year, mostly lodging, as they passed through London, in the neighbourhoods of Whitechapel, St Giles, and similar localities.

Of the Irishmen of genius who, in the seventeenth and eighteenth centuries, added a lustre to English literature, many, no doubt, sympathised with their country's nationality. Others were probably indifferent, seeking only the attainment of their own personal ambition, while not a few lent themselves to the enemies of Ireland.

Standing out boldly from the ranks of these eminent men,

there appeared upon the scene, during the eighteenth century, as prominent actors in the history of their times, two distinguished Irishmen, who are recognized not only as among the foremost of British statesmen and men of letters, but as sincere, indomitable, and able champions of the persecuted Catholics and of their suffering country. These were Edmund Burke and Richard Brinsley Sheridan.

The following details of their earlier lives are taken from the "Cabinet of Irish Writers," by Read and T. P. O'Connor. Edmund Burke was born in Arran Quay, Dublin, on the 1st of January 1730. His father was an attorney in large practice and good reputation. His mother was a Nagle of Castletown Roche, and held firmly to the Catholic religion of her family. Edmund was brought up in the religion of his father, who was a Protestant. Young Burke was taught reading and the Latin Grammar by a master, named O'Halloran, at the village school of Castletown Roche. At the age of twelve he was sent to a school kept by a Quaker, named Shackleton, at Ballytore in the county Kildare. When fourteen he entered Trinity College, Dublin, in front of which may be seen to-day two exquisite statues in bronze, which are not only noble monuments of Burke and Goldsmith, whom they faithfully represent, but of the genius of the Irish sculptor, Foley. In 1750, at the age of twenty, Burke come to London, and entered as a student of the Middle Temple. We next find him writing his celebrated work—"A Philosophical Inquiry into the Sublime and Beautiful." Doctor Johnson praised it highly, and Blair, Hume, Sir Joshua Reynolds, and other eminent men sought the friendship of the gifted author. In 1761 he went to Ireland as private secretary to William Gerard Hamilton, chief secretary to the Lord Lieutenant, but after a time he gave up the position as being inconsistent with his independence. In 1765 he became private secretary to the Marquis of Rockingham, in whose administration, eighteen years afterwards, he was Paymaster General, with a seat at the Council Board. In 1766 he became member of Parliament for Wendover. His first speech was on American affairs, and received the praise of Pitt. From this time the career of Burke formed a prominent part of the history of the day.

Richard Brinsley Sheridan was born in Dublin in 1751. He was descended from a family remarkable for their wit and genius—gifts which seem to have been the legacy of their descendants ever since. In his seventh year he was sent to the school of Samuel White, who was also the preceptor of the poet Moore. His education was continued at Harrow. Though he entered as a student of the Middle Temple, he did not follow up the study of the law, his taste evidently lying in the direction of literature. In 1775 he succeeded Garrick in the management of Drury Lane Theatre, which, no doubt, helped to direct still further his bent to dramatic literature. There is no writer, not even Shakespeare himself, whose works have kept such a constant hold on the stage up to the present day. They well deserve the honour, and it is generally conceded that his comedy, "The School for Scandal," is the finest in the English language.

Froude chooses to ignore a fact like this when he says that, though the history of Ireland is full of dramatic materials, she never produced a dramatist. He had a convenient memory at times, but never forgot anything which he could use to bring Ireland and the Irish into ridicule. As a matter of fact, some of the foremost "English" dramatists of the last two centuries have been Irishmen.

Sheridan afterwards entered the field of politics, in which he was a prominent figure all his life.

On March 22nd, 1775, Edmund Burke made an eloquent appeal for the American colonists against the exactions of England. It is a matter of history how such warnings as his were unheeded. The result was the American War of Independence, resulting in the recognition of the freedom of the United States of America by the Treaty of Versailles in 1783. Burke had never ceased to advocate the repeal of the penal statutes against Catholics. If he and other friends of the persecuted faith were more successful in this than in their efforts for the colonists, it was not so much that they had moved the sense of justice of the English Parliament and people, as on account of the embarrassments caused by the war with the Americans.

On the 28th of May 1778, the Royal assent was given to

"A Bill relieving His Majesty's Roman Catholic subjects from certain pains and penalties imposed on them by an act of King William." The *Annual Register*, in explaining the scope of the measure, says—" By this bill, for the relief of Roman Catholics, the clause in the Act of William III. for prosecuting popish bishops, priests, or Jesuits, is to be repealed; also the clause for subjecting papists keeping school for the education of youth, to perpetual imprisonment; also the clause that disables papists to inherit land by descent, and gives to the next-of-kin (being protestant) a right to inherit such lands; also the clause that disables papists from purchasing manors, lands, or hereditaments, in England or Wales; but leaves all lands in possession just as they were, and all causes in litigation as if this act had never been made; and the benefits arising from it are on condition of taking the oath of allegiance within six months after it passes into law."

The instalment of justice to the oppressed Catholics in England met with violent opposition from the British rabble. The no-Popery movement that followed commenced in Scotland, where the Irish had now settled in considerable numbers. There the bigots, fearing that the relaxation granted to the Catholics in England might be extended to Scotland, determined to prevent this if possible, and for a time succeeded. The *Annual Register* describes how the Catholics in Scotland and their property were molested by furious mobs, and thus details the proceedings in the Scottish capital :—

" *Edinburgh, Feb. 3rd*, 1779.—On Friday last copies of the following letter were dropped in the different streets and lanes in the city of Edinburgh :—

" MEN AND BRETHREN,—Who ever shall find this letter will take it as a warning to meet at Leith Wynd on Wednesday next, in the evening, to pull down that pillar of Popery lately erected there.

"A PROTESTANT."

" *Edinburgh, Jan. 29th*, 1779.—*P.S.* Please to read this carefully, keep it clean, and drop it somewhere else.—For King and Country UNITY."

"In consequence of this letter (continues the *Register*), a mob last night assembled at a house at the foot of Chalmers' Close, part of which was intended for a Popish chapel, but had not hitherto been occupied, the rest of the building being possessed by clergymen of that persuasion."
A description is then given of how the mob broke the windows and destroyed and set fire to the furniture, the inside of the house being reduced to ashes. They also attacked the chapel in the Blackfriars Wynd, and destroyed or carried off furniture and valuable books. They then wrecked the houses of Catholics, and intended to pull down the house of Principal Robertson, in the College Court, but the dragoons arrived in time to prevent this. The mob dispersed on being assured that all thoughts of bringing in a bill for the relief of the Catholics of Scotland had been laid aside. There were also no-Popery riots in Glasgow and other parts of Scotland.

The success of the violent outburst of bigotry in Scotland encouraged the "Protestant Association" to inaugurate a like reign of terror in England, where, owing to the gradually increasing immigration from Ireland, the hated papist seemed again as if becoming a power in the land. On Monday, May 29th, 1780, a meeting of the association was held in the Coachmakers' Hall, to consider the mode of presenting to Parliament a petition to repeal the Act passed for the relief of the Catholics of England and Wales. The notorious Lord George Gordon was the chairman of the meeting.

Following this, on Friday, June 2nd, at ten in the forenoon, several thousands of fanatics, whose numbers were increased enormously from the criminal population of London, assembled in St George's Fields. At eleven, Lord George Gordon arrived, and the multitude was set in motion. It was divided into three bodies, each of which crossed to the north side of the Thames by one of the bridges—London, Blackfriars, or Westminster—so as to gather strength on their way to the House of Parliament, where they arrived at half-past two, with their petition. Lord George Gordon harangued the people from the top of the gallery stairs, and denounced the friends of the Catholics who were opposed to the petition—particularly Edmund Burke, then member for Bristol. There was great rioting and intimidation of members of Parliament on their way to the House, where Lord George was allowed to bring up the petition; but his motion to have it taken into immediate consideration was rejected. The result exasperated the mob, which now dispersed, but only to gather strength for acts of violence.

On the same evening the dreadful rioting and conflagration commenced, which continued, almost without intermission, from that day, Friday, until the following Thursday.

Among the first places attacked and demolished was the Catholic chapel in Duke Street, Lincoln's Inn Fields, founded in the previous century as the chapel of the Sardinian embassy. The old Sardinian chapel was rebuilt after the riots, and still exists, as a reminder of what Catholics and Irishmen had to suffer in those penal days. Like others of our places of worship dating from that period, it is of modest exterior, as if shunning observation. It is plain, almost to ugliness, with its stuccoed front and circular-headed conventicle-like windows. Round it, and spreading westward, what was probably the first Irish colony in London was gradually increasing in 1780, and the fury of the no-Popery rioters was wreaked on their habitations. The Bavarian chapel in Warwick Street, Golden Square, was also attacked and destroyed; and the sky of London was lit up that night by the burning churches and houses of the persecuted "Papists."

On Saturday there was a lull in the rioting, but it commenced with renewed vigour on Sunday, when the mob attacked the chapel in Moorfield, and the dwelling-houses of the Catholics in the neighbourhood. They stripped the houses of furniture, and the church of the insignia of religion, and burned them and the church, leaving nothing but the bare walls.

On Monday the rioters paraded with the relics of their havoc, and burned them in the fields adjacent to Lord George Gordon's house. They also destroyed the Catholic chapels in Virginia Lane, Wapping, and at Nightingale Lane, East Smithfield. The existence of these chapels—

now no longer in the list of London Catholic places of worship—at this time, shews that the Irish population must have been considerable in these localities in 1780.

On Tuesday the mob appeared before Newgate, and demanded the release of the rioters arrested for the previous day's outrages. They set fire to the house of the keeper, and the flames communicated to the chapel and to the wards and cells of the prison. Upon this the prisoners—three hundred in number—four of them under sentence of death—were released. This accomplished, the rioters returned to their work of demolishing the houses of more of the unfortunate Catholics and those supposed to be their friends. In this way they destroyed the furniture of Sir John Fielding, and burnt the house, with its valuable contents, of Lord Mansfield, in Bloomsbury Square. They also broke into Clerkenwell jail and turned out the prisoners.

The reign of terror continued on the Wednesday, and so great was the dread of the citizens that the shops were shut and "no-Popery" chalked on them and on the houses. The King's Bench and Fleet prisons, and the toll house on Blackfriar's were burned, and there were conflagrations in every quarter. Though there were incessant conflicts in the streets between the military and the rioters, but little progress had as yet been made in checking the dreadful saturnalia.

Perhaps the most terrible scenes of all were in connection with the destruction of the distillery in Holborn, belonging to Mr Langdale, a wealthy Catholic. It was plundered and burnt, the loss sustained being in value nearly £100,000. "It is impossible," says the *Annual Register*, "to ascertain the number of unhappy wretches who lost their lives in the course of that dreadful night. Powder and ball were not so fatal to them as their own inordinate appetites. Numbers died from inebriation, especially at the distilleries of the unfortunate Mr Langdale, from whose vessels the liquor ran down the middle of the street, and was taken up by pailfuls and held to the mouths of the deluded multitude; many of them killed themselves with drinking non-rectified spirits and were burnt and buried in the ruins."

The unbridled passions of the rioters having exhausted themselves, the military at length got the upper hand, so that, on Thursday, the citizens began to recover confidence. By this time one hundred and seventy-three arrests had been made. One return gives the number killed and wounded by the troops as two hundred and ten. The entire number who perished from inebriation or in the ruins of demolished houses could not be ascertained, but must have been considerable.

In the trials of the rioters, at the Old Bailey, which followed, we get glimpses of the condition and location of the London Irish of those days. Among the victims of the rioters was Mr M'Cartney, a baker in Featherstone Street, Bunhill Row, whose house was demolished. Two men were convicted for pulling down the house of an innkeeper, Cornelius Murphy, who kept "The Sun," in Golden Lane. It is curious to note how the Gordon rioters displayed their zeal as orthodox champions of religion in exactly the same fashion as the Orange rioters of Belfast in our own day— by the plunder of "Popish" publicans. The sign of "The Sun" seems to have had an attraction for female rioters too. We find that at this same Old Bailey sessions one Elizabeth Lyons deposed that she did not see Susannah Clarke, then on her trial, do anything, but heard her say to Walters, one of the mob surrounding Murphy's house,—" They are Irish Catholics—if they are not, why do they keep Irish wakes?" Upon which, the witness said, Walters answered—"The house shall come down!" And come down it, accordingly, did, as poor Murphy found to his bitter cost. The woman, Susannah Clarke, got off on a technicality. Samuel Solomons, a Jew, figuring, no doubt, in the riots, as an orthodox Protestant, was found guilty of assisting in the demolition of the dwelling house of Christopher Connor, in Blackhorse Yard, Whitechapel. It would appear that the female rioters, in their orthodoxy, had an eye to substantial gain, for two women were convicted for stealing, while Connor's house was being wrecked, a feather bed belonging to that unfortunate Irishman. A boy was convicted for aiding in the pulling down of the house of John Lynch.

We read in the records of these trials that one "Jonathan Stacey was found guilty of pulling down the house of Mr

Dillon in White Street, Moorfields." The "Mr Dillon" here spoken of was the priest of the Catholic Church in Moorfields, destroyed by the rioters. A couple of months later we find the following reference to his death in the *Annual Register*—" Died, Rev. Richard Dillon, late of the Roman Catholic Chapel in Moorfields, where he had resided for thirty-six years, till it was destroyed by the mob in the late riots; at the same time his house having been totally pulled down, his books and household furniture burnt, without even a bed being left for him to lie upon; the shock he received from such barbarous treatment deeply affected his health and spirits, and is supposed to have hastened his death. He was a younger brother of an ancient family in the County of Meath in Ireland, and his character was universally respected and esteemed by a numerous acquaintance."

At these Old Bailey sessions thirty-five prisoners were capitally convicted and forty-three acquitted.

Among the Irish on the south side of the Thames who were sufferers by the riots were Thomas Connolly of Tooley Street, and Lawrence Walsh, whose houses were demolished. How great the devastation on the Surrey side must have been can be gathered from the charge to the Grand Jury by Lord Loughboro, at the commission at St Margaret's Hill. He stated that seventy-two private houses and four public jails had been destroyed. At this commission twenty-four prisoners were capitally convicted, and twenty-six acquitted.

Edmund Burke, in a speech at Bristol, thus speaks of the Irish Catholics of London and their clergy during the Gordon riots—

"What was the behaviour of the persecuted Roman Catholics under the acts of violence and brutal insolence from which they suffered? I suppose there are in London not less than four or five thousand of that persuasion, who do a great deal of the most laborious work in the metropolis, and they chiefly inhabit the quarters which were the principal theatre of the fury of the bigoted multitude. They are known to be men of strong arms and quick feelings, and more remarkable for a determined resolution than clear ideas or much foresight. But though provoked in everything that can stir the blood of men, their houses and chapels in flames, and with the most atrocious profanations of everything which they hold sacred before their eyes, not a hand was moved to retaliate or even to defend. No power under heaven could have prevented a general conflagration, but that their clergy exercised their whole influence to keep their people in such a state of forbearance and quiet as, when I look back, fills me with astonishment only. Their merits on that occasion ought not to be forgotten; nor will they when Englishmen come to recollect themselves."

The Catholics and Irish were, as we have seen, terrible sufferers by the Gordon riots, but in the end the cause of toleration was advanced by the feeling of horror occasioned by the outbreak.

Among the Irish in Britain towards the end of the last century we may class, for a short period, the distinguished patriot, Henry Flood. M'Gee, in his history of Ireland, says of him—"After the session of 1785, in which he had been outvoted in every motion he proposed, he retired from the Irish Parliament, and allowed himself to be persuaded, at the age of fifty-three, to enter the English. He was elected for Winchester, and made his first essay on the new scene on his favourite subject of representative reform. But his health was undermined. He failed, except on one or two occasions, to catch the ear of that fastidious assembly, and the figure he made there somewhat disappointed his friends. He returned to Kilkenny to die in 1791, and bequeathed a large portion of his fortune to Trinity College, to enrich its MS. library and to found a permanent professorship of the Irish language."

It has been said, and perhaps truly, that the Irish, as a race, are not fitted for conspiracies, but if ever there was a born conspirator it was Theobald Wolfe Tone, who, for a short time, seemed about to cast his lot on this side of the channel. In January 1787, he came to London, and entered his name as a student of the Middle Temple, but does not appear to have made any further progress there in the legal profession.

Edmund Burke was a vigorous opponent of the French

Revolution. This caused an estrangement between him and his former friends, Fox and Sheridan, who took the opposite side. Yet Burke was an undoubted lover of liberty, as was shown on many occasions by his advocacy of the rights of the American colonists, of his own countrymen, and of the persecuted Catholics. But in no act of his life did he stand out so pre-eminently as the champion of the oppressed, as in the impeachment of Warren Hastings. He did not accept the doctrine—which is the keynote in the writings of Froude and Carlyle in our own times—that the fittest object for the admiration of mankind is the successful pirate, robber, or murderer, providing the piracies, robberies, and murders are committed on a sufficiently colossal scale, and with sufficiently imposing surroundings. Burke, by his splendid eloquence, exposed to the world the crimes perpetrated by Hastings on the unfortunate Indian princes and people. Besides his own, there was a wonderful display of oratory during the course of this protracted trial, which lasted from 1786 to 1795. One of the most powerful speeches was delivered by Richard Brinsley Sheridan. Macaulay in his "Essay on Warren Hastings," says it was "a speech which was so imperfectly reported, that it may be said to be wholly lost, but which was, without doubt, the most elaborately brilliant of all the productions of his ingenious mind. The impression which it produced was such as had never been equalled." Of its effects on London society, Macaulay says—" The ferment spread fast through the town. Within four-and-twenty hours Sheridan was offered £1000 for the copyright of the speech, if he would himself correct it for the press." The trial ended in the acquittal of Hastings. No doubt those who had to give judgment felt that means such as he had used had largely helped to build up the fabric of British power. Yet, none the less, the splendid battle of Burke and Sheridan for humanity excited the admiration of the justice-loving world, and was not without good effect on the future treatment of India.

In 1794 Burke withdrew from Parliament, and on the 8th of July 1797, he died at the family seat of Beaconsfield. Macaulay pronounced Edmund Burke—"in aptitude of comprehension and richness of imagination, superior to every orator, ancient or modern." The great statesman, Fox, said—" If I were to put all the political information that I have ever gained from books and all that I have learned from science, or that the knowledge of the world and its affairs have taught me, into one scale, and the improvement I have derived from the conversation and teachings of Edmund Burke into the other, the latter would preponderate."

Previous to the insurrection of 1798, in Ireland, Arthur O'Connor, one of the leaders of the United Irishmen, was, on the 27th February, in the same year, arrested at Margate, while endeavouring to make his way to France. With him also were made prisoners, Father James O'Coigly, John Binns, John Allen, and Jeremiah O'Leary. They were brought to London on the 1st of March, in charge of Bow Street officers, in four post chaises, escorted by a party of light dragoons. They were examined before Mr King, and it was stated that they had been taken into custody on suspicion of holding a treasonable correspondence with the French government. At this examination it was stated that they had offered a Margate fisherman a hundred guineas as a security, in case they were taken by the French. From the evidence it appeared that they went from London on the previous Sunday by a Whitstable hoy. Arrived at Margate they put up at a little public house on the sands, where Father O'Coigly passed as Colonel Morris. They were suspected and arrested. They had in their possession sixty guineas and a large quantity of baggage, including fire-arms, cutlasses, &c. In the pocket of a great-coat, supposed to belong to Father O'Coigly, was found a paper purporting to be from a secret committee to the Executive Directory of France. The prisoners disclaimed knowledge of this, but otherwise declined to say anything, and were committed to the Tower. Following these arrests the *Annual Register* says, that, in consequence of information that Mr Arthur O'Connor had been seized at Margate, "in the actual attempt of taking his passage to France, with Quigley, the priest of Dundalk," there was a seizure of the papers and of the *Press*, O'Connor's newspaper, where it was printed, at 62 Abbey Street, Dublin.

On May 21st, at Maidstone, the judges tried for high treason the prisoners arrested at Margate. Arthur O'Connor, John Binns, John Allen, and Jeremiah O'Leary were found not guilty, and allowed to leave the country, with the exception of O'Connor, who was still kept a prisoner. Father James O'Coigly was found guilty. After the verdict, we find, from the report of the trial, that Justice Bullen, in passing sentence, addressing the priest, said—"he had conspired to destroy the sovereign, and overturn the constitution, crimes greater because inviting a foreign enemy to conquer the country. The prisoner (we learn from the report) listened attentively to the address and bowed respectfully to the court. He did not seem at all agitated, but, on the contrary, firm and serene."

On the morning of the 7th of June, Father O'Coigly was brought out of Maidstone prison, placed on a hurdle drawn by two horses, and escorted by a company of about two hundred Maidstone volunteers to the place of execution at Pennenden Heath, about a mile from the town. Arrived there, says the *Annual Register*, "he exchanged a few words with the Catholic priest who attended him, and prayed. He also sang a verse of the Psalms in English. He then made a very inflammatory speech, in which he protested his innocence, and reflected on the jury and witnesses. This he delivered in a steadfast and impressive manner." The board then dropped, and he was suspended for twelve or thirteen minutes. A surgeon took off his head, which was held up to the populace by the executioner, who said, " This is the head of a traitor." The head and body were put into a shell and buried at the foot of the gallows.

There is no doubt of the connection of Father O'Coigly with the insurrectionary movement of '98—indeed he gloried in it. In protesting his innocence, as described, he meant he had been convicted on wrongful evidence—the fate of many an Irish patriot since, when it became desirable for his enemies to have him put out of the way. Several eminent English judicial authorities declared at the time that the priest had been illegally convicted. It is more than probable that the compromising paper, which was the chief evidence against him, was placed in the pocket of his coat by one of the officers who arrested him. The records of the trial convey the idea that he allowed himself to be sacrificed to save his friends. Full justice has not been done to the memory of this noble-souled martyr for Ireland.

About this time many of the Irish "loyalists," in dread that a day of reckoning was coming for them, crossed the channel in hot haste. Their cowardice was strongly rebuked in a letter which the Duke of Portland wrote to Messrs Jordan & Bowen, of Haverford West. He says he received their letter about the influx of persons into their country from Ireland. He is "extremely sorry to observe that there are so many young clergymen and able-bodied men among them," and declares that their conduct exposed them to "dishonourable and disgraceful imputations."

Froude, on the authority of the "Report of the Secret Committee of the House of Commons, England, 1799," says there was a connection between the mutineers at Portsmouth and the Nore, and the insurrection of 1798 in Ireland. He says:—"Half the sailors and petty officers in the service were Catholics, and, in fact, it was discovered, when the causes of the mutiny were enquired into, that the United Irishmen had been busy instruments in inflaming discontent. Lee, who was one of the leaders, had been sworn into the society in Dublin, and had enlisted but a few months previously, probably to create the mutiny for which he was condemned. . . . The secret committee of the British House of Commons discovered that the crews had been largely sworn to be true to Ireland, to erect a Catholic government there, and to be faithful to their brethren who were fighting against tyrants and oppressors. There had been plans amongst them to carry different ships into Irish harbours, to kill the officers if they hindered them, and to hoist the green flag with the harp in the place of the British ensign, and afterwards kill and destroy the Protestants." Froude's theory (is that this was to be a diversion to allow of the landing of the French general, Hoche, in Ireland. That the United Irishmen had gained a footing in the British navy, just as a later Irish revolutionary movement did in the army, is most likely. Seeing, however, that most of the '98 leaders were Protestants, it is grossly improbable that there was any plot to "kill and destroy" their own co-religionists. The probability is that this evidence was given by some informer of the Titus Oates stamp, and was got up to order by those opposed to the further relaxation of the penal laws, to throw odium on the Catholic body.

A famous Irishman in London at this period was Father Arthur O'Leary. He was noted for his learning, wit, and eloquence. Many of his brilliant sayings are still preserved. Up to a certain period in his life he must have borne a high character for patriotism. On account of his powerful writings on behalf of the Irish Volunteers he was received with military honours in the Convention of that body which sat in Dublin in 1783. His name is chiefly connected in London with St Patrick's Church, Sutton Street, Soho, which mission he founded in 1792. The church is one of the remaining landmarks of the Irish during the last century in London, and indicates how they must have been gradually spreading into St Giles's and the adjacent neighbourhood. The edifice was not originally erected as a place of worship, it having been previously used as a fashionable resort for balls, concerts, and assemblies. It seems as if it had been formed out of a number of dwelling-houses. On entering Sutton Street, one at first sees nothing resembling a church, the most prominent objects being a couple of wooden porches, in shape like large cupboards or wardrobes, each surmounted by a cross. Otherwise the building to which they are attached looks like a warehouse, and is in striking contrast to the almost palatial structure of a well known sauce-manufacturer at the corner of the street.* Inside the church is a monument to Father O'Leary's memory, which tells of his "fervent piety, discreet zeal, and steady loyalty." Of this last quality he gave a striking specimen when he preached the funeral oration at the dirge for the repose of the soul of Pope Pius VI. In this, we learn from the *Annual Register*,

* Since the above was written, Father O'Leary's old chapel has been pulled down, together with the adjoining houses on the corner of the street, to get an enlarged site for a new church with a frontage into Soho Square. The foundation stone of the new edifice was laid on Thursday, June 18th, 1891. Cardinal Manning would have laid the stone had not the infirmity of his advancing years prevented him from being present.

that he "concluded by felicitating his flock on the happiness they enjoyed in this country, on which, and its constitution, he pronounced a glowing panegyric." Making all due allowance for the times, and for the rust of slavery having entered the souls of the pusillanimous and the venal, it is humiliating for the Irishmen of to-day to read this language — used while many of the penal laws were still in existence.

In the year previous to his speaking these slavish words, another Irish priest, Father O'Coigly, sealed his love for Ireland on the scaffold, at Pennenden Heath. To-day his memory is cherished among the martyrs for Ireland by all who estimate aright the patriot priest, Father O'Coigly, and the pensioner priest, Father O'Leary. Father O'Leary was also false to the reputation for patriotism he had made for himself as the champion of the Irish Volunteers, by his attacks on the United Irishmen who made such a noble stand for freedom in 1798. The pension he received from the Government until the time of his death is supposed to have been for services not altogether creditable to his memory as an Irishman.

The insurrection of 1798 was the most striking incident of the history of Ireland in the last century. The comparatively small Irish element then in Great Britain sympathised with the gallant struggle of their fellow-countrymen at home. Had the opportunity offered, who can doubt but that they would have shewn their sympathy as practically as have their descendants and successors in later days with the various national movements of the present century?

The enemies of Irish nationality used the rising of '98 as an excuse for the "Union" of 1800. The succeeding chapters will shew how the Irish in Britain have helped "the men in the gap" in their struggles to undo that hateful "Union" which has been a curse alike to Irishmen and to Britons.

CHAPTER X.

DISTINGUISHED IRISHMEN OF THE EIGHTEENTH CENTURY.

AMONG Irishmen, the three most distinguished ornaments of English literature in the eighteenth century were undoubtedly, Edmund Burke, Richard Brinsley Sheridan, and Oliver Goldsmith. Burke and Sheridan, having played a prominent part as statesmen in their own times, have been noticed already. Goldsmith was no politician, and for that very reason, probably, as well as for that lovable, improvident nature, which is supposed often to accompany genius, he seems to have won the sympathy of a far larger circle of admirers than either Burke or Sheridan.

Whether as a poet, a novelist, an essayist, or a dramatist, he certainly stands among the very foremost of the writers who have adorned English literature. Who has not read that most simple and charming story, "The Vicar of Wakefield," which has been translated into several languages? His brilliant comedy, "She Stoops to Conquer," is almost without a rival on the English stage; while his beautiful poem of "The Deserted Village," written, no doubt, from his early recollections of Ireland, touches us the more keenly, because it is as true to nature and to the condition of Ireland to-day as it was in Goldsmith's own times.

Not reckoning men like Dean Swift, who, being more connected with Ireland than this country, could scarcely be counted among the Irish in Britain, we have, in the eighteenth century, among a host of other distinguished writers, Thomas Parnell, the poet; Sir Richard Steele, whose writings were so much admired in the pages of the *Tatler* and the *Spectator;* Lawrence Sterne, famous among what may be termed the English classical writers; Sir Philip Francis, also a prominent statesman, and supposed by many to be the author of the "Letters of Junius;" Leland, author of a "History of Ireland;" John Boyle, Earl of Cork and Orrery, whose father had also been a distinguished writer in the Stuarts' reigns; and Edmund Malone, chiefly famous as a commentator of Shakespeare.

Among the dramatists of the last century, none, whether English or Irish, could compare with Sheridan or Goldsmith. Besides these there were many other brilliant Irishmen, including Andrew Cherry, who was also an actor and a poet. He wrote the ever-green "Dear Little Shamrock," a song which is, if anything, even more popular than Moore's exquisite song of "The Shamrock." There were, also, Hugh Kelly, whose first comedy was brought out by Garrick; William Congreve, a playwright much admired by Dr Johnson; Kane O'Hara, comic opera and burlesque writer; Thomas Southerne, Charles Molloy, Arthur Murphy, John O'Keeffe, an actor also; Owen M'Swiney, also a theatrical manager; and Thomas Sheridan, an actor and theatrical manager, and father of Richard Brinsley Sheridan.

Of famous Irish actors there were Spranger Barry, the rival of Garrick; Catherine, or Kitty, Clive; Elizabeth Farren, who became Countess of Derby; Charles Macklin (or M'Loughlin); James Quin, and Arthur Murphy, who was also a lawyer, dramatist, and editor.

James Barry, born in Cork, in 1741, attained great distinction as a painter, as did also Nathaniel Hone and other Irishmen. James M'Ardell was the most skilful mezzotint engraver of his day.

Bishop Berkely was famous as a philosophical writer, and Sir Hans Sloane, president of the Royal Society of England, was founder of the British Museum.

It will be seen, from a glance at the names of some of the distinguished Irishmen of the eighteenth century, that, despite the penal laws, which made learning a crime, Irishmen of the old Celtic race were far more numerous than in the preceding century in the ranks of every art and profession in which a naturally gifted people might be expected to excel.

BOOK V.

FROM THE UNION TO EMANCIPATION.

CHAPTER XI.

MARTIAL LAW—CATHOLICITY AT THE OPENING OF THE NINETEENTH CENTURY—THE FIGHT FOR EMANCIPATION.

WE have seen how the Irish had been, in gradually increasing numbers, settling in Great Britain during the eighteenth century. It is the present century, however, that has brought with it an immigration of such magnitude that it seems destined, after the lapse of ages, to be as fruitful of results for Britain as was the colonization from Ireland which founded the Scottish nationality and monarchy, and gave religion and civilization to the barbarous Picts and Saxons.

The immigration increased in volume with each decade of the first half of the century, until it reached its full flood during and after the terrible famine years from 1845 to 1849. After that, as we shall see, the stream slackened, not because better days had come for Ireland, but that the fountainhead of our race was drying up, and that our country, blighted by foreign rule, seemed, in all human probability, to be bleeding to death.

The union between Great Britain and Ireland added to the Irish in Britain those who represented or misrepresented Irish constituencies in the Imperial Parliament in London.

It was ominous of the evil days to come that, in 1801, among the first measures brought in was a bill for martial law in Ireland. These and other Coercion Acts, of more or less atrocity, have been the principal remedies for our

country's ills up to this moment. Arrayed on the side of
martial law at the commencement of the legislative connection between Ireland and Great Britain, we find all the
anti-Irish Irishmen of the day, while opposed to them, in a
gallant but ineffectual resistance, were Richard Brinsley
Sheridan—always the friend of Ireland and of liberty—Sir
Lawrence Parsons, and Sir John Parnell, who had been the
Irish Chancellor of the Exchequer. Sir John was descended
from the poet, Parnell, and was the great-grandfather of the
late Irish leader, Charles Stewart Parnell. He died December 5th, 1801, so that he did not long survive the extinction
of the Irish Parliament.

In connection with the insurrection of 1798, twenty of
the leaders, including Arthur and Roger O'Connor, Dr
James Macneven, Samuel Neilson, Thomas Addis Emmet,
and Thomas Russell, were imprisoned in Fort George, in
Scotland. In answer to a bigot of his day, who tried to
make it appear, as some of the enemies of Ireland do now,
that the insurrection was a "Popish Conspiracy," one of
the prisoners pointed out that, of these twenty, but four
were Catholics. On the 30th of June 1802, these Irish
prisoners, with the exception of Roger O'Connor, who had
been liberated on bail early in the previous year, were
embarked at Fort George, in a vessel of war, and were
landed, on the 4th of July, at Cuxhaven, on the coast of
Holland. Most of them rose to eminence in the lands they
made their homes. Arthur O'Connor and Dr Macneven
entered the French army, and we find frequent mention of
their names in the news-sheets of the day in connection with
Napoleon's projected invasion of England. O'Connor
attained to the rank of General in the French service, and
afterwards fought with distinction in the army of the Rhine.
He lived in France until the time of his death, April 25th,
1852. Thomas Russell, determined, if possible, to strike
another blow for freedom, threw in his lot with the revolutionary movement of Robert Emmet. The Government
was soon on his track, as we find from current newspapers.
Here is what one of them says of him, under date September
10th, 1803:—"Thomas Russell, the Irish traitor and
author of the rebel proclamation, for whose apprehension a

reward of £500 has been offered, was seen, about the middle of last week, in Scotland, and is supposed to be now in the neighbourhood of Newcastle, in order to take shipping; but the most active vigilance is employed for his apprehension." He was subsequently arrested in Dublin and conveyed to Downpatrick, where he was tried, and executed twenty-four hours after sentence of death had been pronounced upon him.

In reviewing the position of our people in Great Britain, in the early part of the present century, the religious statistics of the period will be of service.

Cardinal Manning gave, on official authority, the Catholic population of England in 1788 as 69,000. This, certainly, is not an over estimate. Indeed, when we find that of existing missions nearly one hundred were founded previous to 1788, it seems to be considerably below the mark. Allowing for the rapid increase of Catholics then going on, Cardinal Manning's figures are not inconsistent with those given by Bishop Gibson, who stated the Catholic population of Lancashire in 1804 to be 50,000. Of these, he said, 10,000 were in Manchester, where, fourteen years previously, there were, it was said, only 600. It is not probable that there was such an enormous actual increase as this. The apparent increase was most likely the effect of the relaxation of the Penal Laws, which allowed the more open practice of religion. This showed that there were many more Catholics than had been suspected. It must also be taken into account, in comparing Bishop Gibson's figures with Cardinal Manning's, that a large proportion of the Catholics of England were then, as they are still, in Lancashire. Their figures may be taken to represent pretty nearly the number of Irish, as the English Catholics might be balanced against the Irish Protestants.

The church statistics of some of the large towns will help in forming an estimate of their number in the various localities.

The missions now existing in London which date from a time previous to the commencement of the present century, are, the church of St Anselm and St Cecilia, Sardinia Street, Lincoln's Inn Fields (1648); St Mary's, Blomfield Street,

Moorfield; the Church of the Assumption, Warwick Street; St James's, Spanish Place, Manchester Square (1791); St Patrick's, Sutton Street, Soho Square (1792); and the French Chapel, Little George Street, Portman Square (1799). The register of the Church of St Mary and St Michael, Commercial Road, East, dates from 1773. St Ethelreda's, Ely Place, Holborn Circus, which was seized in the general spoliation at the time of the "Reformation," has only recently returned to Catholic hands. In a list of Catholic places of worship in London in 1804, we also find the following—Denmark Court, Crown Street, Soho; Prospect Place, St George's Fields; and South Street, Mayfair. The Church of St Anselm and St Cecilia (known as the Sardinian Chapel); of St Mary's, Moorfield; and of the Assumption, Warwick Street (the Bavarian Chapel), were wrecked during the Gordon Riots, as were also two more chapels, not in the above list—one in Virginia Street, Wapping, and the other in Nightingale Lane, East Smithfield. While some of the churches and chapels erected previous to 1800 still remain, we have, instead of others, larger and finer buildings. Thus—St George's Cathedral, Southwark, replaced a chapel in London Road. This mission dates from 1786, when, we learn from the *Universe*, the Rev. Thomas Walsh hired a room in Bandy Leg Walk (now Guilford Street, Borough) for £20 a year. Two years afterwards, the congregation had so increased that it was determined to build a new chapel in the London Road. It was opened on Passion Sunday (St Patrick's Day), 1793, by Dr Douglas, and the dedication sermon was preached by Father O'Leary. The chapel was built to hold 1000 persons, and, at the time, did actually afford more accommodation than any other Catholic church in London. At first the building was criticised as being too large and grand, yet in a few years it became too small for the congregation. In the same way the old church of St James, Spanish Place, has been recently replaced by a stately building not far from the old site. Touching were the words of Cardinal Manning in a sermon preached in the old edifice soon to be demolished. He said,—" It has fallen to my lot during the last thirty years and more to be present on the day when an old church, such as this, has ceased to be used as a church, and has been given up, and a new church has been opened. I have said Mass in the morning in the old church, and in the evening Benediction has been given in the new church, but I have never done so without a feeling of reluctance and regret. The old churches, which are the remnants of other days, built under the Penal Laws, or domestic houses converted to the use of a church, have about them something sacred and hallowed. This has been the Church of St James for over a hundred years—reaching back to the time of the Penal Laws, and the days when the offering of the Holy Sacrifice was a crime."

Edmund Burke estimated the Irish Catholic population of London at the time of the Gordon Riots as being at least from four to five thousand. As we shall see, Canon Toole's figures, which commence a little after the same period, show that the Catholic population of Liverpool trebled itself in about twenty-four years. A similar increase might be looked for in the metropolis. Twenty-four years after the Gordon Riots would bring us to 1804, when, according to these calculations, there would be from twelve to fifteen thousand Catholics in London. There is reason to believe that both these and Edmund Burke's figures are below the reality. The Penal Laws made it difficult to ascertain what was the Catholic population. Even up to the present time the vast wilderness of London is like another "dark continent." Every opening of a mission brings to light numbers of Catholics whose existence was previously unsuspected.

Liverpool has four Catholic missions dating from this time or previous to it—St Mary's, the history and vicissitudes of which have been traced in these pages; St Peter's, St Anthony's, which replaced the old "French Chapel" in Scotland Road; and St Nicholas's. Besides these there was formerly a Catholic chapel in Moor Street, just the kind of narrow thoroughfare in which one would expect to find a "Popish Chapel" in the penal days. For a short time, as we learn from the local directories of 1771 and 1781, there was a chapel in Chorley Street, the priest being the Rev. John Price, who, in 1788, built, at his own expense, another chapel in Sir Thomas's Buildings. Indeed, the last structure, though not in use, still stands, but is doomed, no doubt, to be soon swept away in the changes going on in the commercial parts of Liverpool.

Canon Toole, of St Wilfrid's, Manchester, has compiled the following very valuable tables, which help to show the proportion the Catholics of Liverpool bore to the general population in the years named.

Years.	Total Baptisms in Liverpool.	Catholic Baptisms in Liverpool.	Years.	Total Baptisms in Liverpool.	Catholic Baptisms in Liverpool.
1788-9	2332	260	1804	3348	531
1794-5	2527	309	1805	3482	528
1797	2540	312	1806	3831	584
1798	2677	367	1807	3912	583
1799	2909	391	1808	3713	571
1800	3033	459	1809	3702	593
1801	2767	412	1810	4001	764
1802	3123	487	1811	4183	803
1803	3293	485	1812	3889	667

Besides giving an idea of the proportion of Catholics to the general population, these figures show how rapidly they increased. They also enable us to form a tolerably accurate idea of the actual Catholic population. In 1880 the general annual birth-rate in Liverpool was a trifle over 37 in every 1000 of the population. Taking this to be the rate for the period covered by Canon Toole's figures, and assuming that the baptisms represented the births, this would give us a Catholic population in 1788 of 6916; in 1800 of 12,209; and in 1811 of 21,359.

Of the existing churches in Manchester, St Mary's, Mulberry Street, dates from the end of the last, and St Augustine's, Granby Row, from the early part of the present, century. Bishop Gibson, as we have seen, estimated the Catholic population of Manchester in 1804 at 10,000.

There are also Catholic churches and chapels in Leeds,

Sheffield, Birmingham, Wolverhampton, Newcastle-on-Tyne, Preston, Carlisle, Bristol, Whitehaven, Workington, St Helens, Warrington, Wigan, York, Norwich, Leicester, Bolton, and other towns, dating from the same time and previous to it.

The Scottish Catholic Directory shows but two of the present missions, both in Banffshire, which date from the last century. Besides private houses in which mass was said in the penal days, there must have been a number of other buildings used specially for Catholic worship, such, for instance, as those destroyed in the No-Popery outbreak in Scotland, which was the precursor of the terrible Gordon Riots in London. A considerable number of Catholic churches were built in Scotland in the earlier years of the present century, including St Mary's Cathedral, Edinburgh (1814), and St Andrew's Cathedral, Glasgow (1816).

By far the greatest development of Catholicity and the Irish element in Scotland has been in what is now the Catholic diocese of Glasgow. There is a singular fitness in this, for the ground on which stands the city of St Mungo—the name by which the Irish St Kentigern is often known—where the exiles from Ireland are so numerous, was once hallowed by the footsteps of that typical saint of our race—Columbkille. The Scots of to-day, in helping on the cause of Home Rule for Ireland, are but paying back a debt they owe to the countrymen of that great saint, for is it not part of the history of both nations how, from the sacred Iona, the saint returned once more to Ireland to advocate the rights of the Irish colony in Scotland, and how he won for them that self-government from which the Scottish nation dates its birth?

In the early part of this century Glasgow doubled its population in less than twenty years. This was, says a Scottish writer, "in a great measure caused by a continuance of that flood of immigrants which set in from Ireland and the Highlands through the neglect of both peoples by the Government. The landed aristocracy were permitted, just as now, to effect clearings, and to systematically starve and punish by tyranny a peasantry with a right equal with their own to live by the soil." Another writer, Mrs Johnson, refers to these clearances in the early part of the present century, which were principally, as now, in the north-west of Ireland. Speaking of the kindly feeling that prevailed towards the Irish previous to this wholesale immigration, she says—" Until the starving labourers and their families came over in such shoals as threatened to make the little lean morsel of our own poor leaner and less, there certainly existed a very kindly feeling towards the Irish over all the Western Highland and Western Lowland counties of Scotland."

Previous to the introduction of steamships, the small sailing vessels which brought our people over sometimes took several days to cross the channel. Bad as, up till now, the steamboat accommodation for deck passengers has been, it was far worse in those sailing vessels; consequently the poor harvestmen, in crossing backwards and forwards each year, often suffered great hardships. Considering that Ireland is so largely an agricultural country, it is surprising how few of its natives have taken to farming in England or Scotland. It is almost impossible to find one. As a rule, they have flocked into the larger towns and the centres of great industries requiring a large proportion of unskilled labour. Here their native wit and adaptability have had to carry them through the most difficult circumstances.

During the Peninsular war, and up to the time of the battle of Waterloo, in 1815, the Irish were probably more numerous in the army and navy of Britain than they have ever been before or since, if we except, perhaps, the time during and following the famine years. Of the troops led by Wellington and other British generals, fully half must have been Irish. In the navy, too, they must have been numerous, for the Irish fisheries were far more flourishing than now. The national decay arising out of the Union has been gradual, and it is only within the last two generations that we appear to be feeling its full consequences. The glimpses we get in the newspapers of the every-day life and surroundings of these Irish soldiers and sailors, are not always the most pleasing. The pictures are seldom painted by a friendly hand, and, as we are made to see them, they sometimes appear to have been a trouble to the well-regulated communities in which they have been quartered, by the exhibition of the pugnacity which is supposed to come natural to their race. But allowance must be made for the fact that if they were not out and out savages, it was no fault of British rule—all that lifted them from that position being the ministrations of the faith to which they had clung with a fidelity unexampled in the history of the world. We know, too, how a newspaper can exaggerate a case against an Irishman, particularly if he be in humble circumstances. We are, therefore, not surprised to hear of affrays, early in this century, in which soldiers or sailors bearing Irish names are prominent actors, while Ireland seldom, if ever, got credit for the deeds of her sons who had attained eminence in every walk of life.

The Catholics of Ireland had been told that their religious freedom would be the outcome of the Union. Those who believed this were grossly deceived, for it was twenty-nine years before Emancipation came. During the interval the struggle for religious liberty went on in and out of Parliament. Among the steadiest friends of the Catholics was that brilliant Irishman, Richard Brinsley Sheridan, who advocated their cause to the latest day of his life. His career has been traced in a previous chapter. His health gave way in 1815. His financial difficulties were so great that in his last illness he was actually arrested for debt in bed, and it was with great difficulty his removal was prevented. He died on the 7th of July 1816. For more than a century there has been a Parnell among the foremost defenders of Ireland and her people. It is deplorable to think that the latest of these, by his wicked and insane attempts to retain the leadership, threatened for a time to shipwreck the cause which he and his ancestors had done so much to serve.

Henry Grattan, having been elected to the British Parliament in 1805, found in Sir Henry Parnell an able supporter in pushing forward the Catholic claims. From then until the time of his death, June 4th, 1820, Grattan was the recognised champion of the Catholics in Parliament.

Meanwhile, Daniel O'Connell, one of the most striking figures in Irish history, was, year by year, coming more prominently on the scene. A thorough child of the Irish people, he was the first really great leader of their own race and creed for over a hundred years. The struggle for religious freedom carried on under his guidance is part of the history of Ireland. When the royal assent was given, on the 13th of April 1829, to the bill for Catholic Emancipation, O'Connell became the first Catholic to enter Parliament since the enactment of the Penal Laws.

BOOK VI.

O'CONNELL AND THE REPEAL AGITATION.

CHAPTER XII.

CATHOLIC PROGRESS—ORANGEISM—ACCESSION OF VICTORIA
—THE CHARTISTS.

CATHOLIC Emancipation was soon found by O'Connell and the Irish people to be a not unmixed good. It opened the way to power and position to a few Irish Catholics, but this, in too many cases, estranged them from the bulk of their fellow-countrymen in the struggle for Repeal of the Union between Ireland and Great Britain, which the Liberator, as O'Connell was called, afterwards initiated.

The Irish here had more than quadrupled their number from the commencement of the century to Emancipation—judging from the increase in some of the large towns. The account of a meeting held in the Copperas Hill Catholic Charity School, Liverpool, on Thursday, May 27th, 1830, to promote additional school accommodation, gives us an interesting glimpse of the extent of the Catholic population, and what was being done for the spread of education among them at this time. The Right Rev. Dr Penswick was the chairman, and amongst those who supported him were a number of traders and professional men—Irish and English—well known in Liverpool sixty years ago, and up to a more recent date. One of the speakers stated that the proportion borne by the Catholics of Liverpool to the whole population was more nearly one-third than one-fourth, but that not a tenth of the children of the town attending school were being educated by the Catholics. The number of

Catholic baptisms in the previous year had been, he said, 1890. Applying to these the same birth-rate per 1000 as to Canon Toole's figures, would give us a Catholic population in 1829 of over 50,000.

The Irish in this country, owing to the restricted franchise, were not, at this time, the political power they have since become. Coming as they did, they naturally formed the poorest of the population. Nevertheless they were successfully fighting their way upwards in the battle of life, until the great Irish famine, some sixteen years after this time, came upon them like an avalanche, sweeping away in its disastrous course much of the progress which had been made. For the Irish have carried with them here the kindly customs of their country. Chief of these has ever been the virtue of hospitality. How, then, could they shut their hearts or their doors against their famine and fever-stricken relatives and friends who fled here, and often dragged down those who gave them shelter to the same wretched level as themselves?

But there had already come from Ireland another plague —the infamous system of Orangeism. The Irish Catholic immigrant had a sufficiently bitter lot from the enmity that generally met him here in seeking for a livelihood, without the additional rancour stirred up by those who, coming from Ireland, were the deadliest enemies of Irish nationality. Some of the names dearest to the hearts of our countrymen, for over a hundred years, have been those of their Protestant patriot leaders, but no true Irishman can countenance Orangeism, which represents the subjugation and humiliation of his country. The Irish Orangeman seems to be the only being on the face of the earth who has no country. Surely the air of a free Ireland, where he can no more be allowed to have his foot on the neck of the "Papist" than the "Papist" can on his, will one day touch his heart and dispel the ignorance and bigotry of which Orangeism is the creation.

As a result of the appearance of the Orange system in Great Britain, there has been, during the last sixty years, much bloodshed—often attended by loss of life. This has generally arisen out of the annual procession, on the 12th of July, in honour of what the Orangemen term "the pious, glorious, and immortal memory" of King William III. In these displays they usually carried deadly weapons, deliberately prepared to take life in case of a conflict, which they often did their best to provoke. Orangeism has been strong in Liverpool, because those who originally brought the hideous system from Ireland inoculated many of the English working-men with their own bigotry. But what may be termed the Nationalist Irish have always been a far more powerful element. They have ever been intensely patriotic, and of the overwhelming mass of them it could be said that there was nowhere a more intelligent and orderly population. On more than one occasion, when they or their churches or homes have been threatened, they have shown that they were well able to give a good account of themselves. As a rule, the foolish and insulting Orange displays have been treated with silent contempt. But among the more unthinking and least educated of our people there have been sometimes a few who had not sufficiently acquired that self-restraint so necessary in men who aspire to be free. As a consequence, when the Orange match has been deliberately applied, the materials for an explosion were not wanting.

In 1835, the Orange anniversary was the cause of considerable tumult in Liverpool. Many of the Irish in the poorer streets of the town appear to have been roused to a state of exasperation, and to have swept all before them. There was rioting in Ben Jonson Street, Crosshall Street, and Park Lane. Some of the Irish were arrested by the police and lodged in Vauxhall bridewell, but their friends broke in the door and released them. This was on the 12th of July, but the disturbances were continued on the following day, and were only quelled when the military were called out and the Riot Act was read in Park Lane.

At this time a fair proportion of our countrymen in Liverpool, as in other parts of Great Britain, were making progress in life as mechanics, shopkeepers, merchants, and professional men; but the great bulk were in the ranks of unskilled labour—nearly all the dock labourers being Irish.

There has been a great similarity in the localities inhabited by our people in the large towns of this country.

THE IRISH IN BRITAIN.

In the centre you generally had the mercantile quarter, the public buildings, and the leading business streets. Immediately outside this area, in the least desirable and oldest residential parts of a town, was nearly always to be found what was termed the "Irish quarter." So it was fifty years ago in Liverpool, when it had about a third of the population it has now, and did not cover a fourth of its present area. As a consequence, particularly in the narrow tumble-down streets, it was overcrowded and unhealthy. The Liverpool Irish lived more together then than now. Before most of the streets leading off Vauxhall and Scotland Roads —where the Irish have since become so numerous—were built, they lived chiefly in the neighbourhoods of Tithebarn Street, Dale Street, Whitechapel, and Park Lane. As these and the streets branching out of them encircled the commercial parts of the town, they almost formed one compact district. Since then, town and railway improvements have driven through this like a wedge, so that now the part most largely inhabited by Irish forms the north end of the parish of Liverpool, while, cut off from this and spreading southward, and overlapping into Toxteth Park—once the stronghold of Orangeism—there is a smaller area, chiefly inhabited by our people, who, as will be shown later, are, at the present day, numerous in every part of the town. These changes in their location may in some cases have caused a loss of political power, but socially they have been satisfactory, as they show that many who were formerly living among squalid surroundings, are now in opener and healthier neighbourhoods.

Similar changes have been going on in other great towns. Thus, Cardinal Manning, a keen observer of such things, in a sermon preached some years ago, in the Sardinian Chapel, London, said—"This old church had once, perhaps, the most populous flock around it of any in London. It numbered thousands in times past. There, then, existing only the Church of the Assumption, in Warwick Street; St Patrick's, Soho; and this church itself: all the Catholics of London had to attend one of these three. The flock here must, therefore, have been very large indeed. In later years churches have sprung up in Islington, the Italian

Church, Ely Place, Great Ormond Street, and Maiden Lane; and the population of the parish has been seriously diminished. Another cause which has thinned their numbers was the pulling down of the homes of our poor. By this clearing away of courts, streets, and alleys, thousands have been taken away, and the erection of large dwelling-houses has not restored them to the parish. There are only some two hundred of the Catholic poor dwelling in these houses, the room being taken up by strangers from other parts. The annual register of baptisms in this church formerly numbered 550, whereas now it has fallen to 220, so that the population is reduced one-half."

In 1837 Queen Victoria ascended the throne of these realms. Her jubilee was celebrated a few years since. Englishmen rejoiced at the progress made by their country in wealth and population during the queen's reign. Many wondered that Irishmen did not rejoice with them, forgetting that the fifty years then passed had been the most disastrous in Irish history, forgetting that the Elizabethan and Cromwellian methods of exterminating the Irish by fire and sword, paled before the hypocritical and far more cruel Victorian method which slew our people by famine.

The Reform Bill, which had been passed in 1832, and which O'Connell aided by his powerful eloquence, encouraged the British democracy to agitate for more sweeping measures. Accordingly, what was known as the great Chartist movement arose. It took its name from what was demanded—"The People's Charter." This contained six points: (1) Universal Suffrage; (2) Vote by Ballot; (3) Annual Parliaments; (4) Payment of Representatives; (5) Abolition of the Members' Property Qualification; and (6) Equal Electoral Districts. These demands were considered at the time to be very revolutionary, but a great portion of the Charter has since become law, and the rest, or something better, will also, no doubt, in due time follow.

O'Connell did not seem to grasp, as later Irish leaders have done, the fact that a common enemy ground down the Irish and British democracies. But O'Connell never really had the true democratic instincts. He showed no friendly feeling towards the Chartists or their leader, Fergus

O'Connor, who came of a patriotic Irish stock. His father, Roger O'Connor, was imprisoned in Fort George for his connection with the insurrection of 1798, at a time when O'Connell, himself, as a member of the Lawyers' Corps, was prepared to make war on his patriotic fellow-countrymen, who were fighting for freedom.

Many of the Irish in this country, particularly in the large towns, joined the Chartists, who were determined, as far as in them lay, whether inside the constitution or outside of it, to gain their ends. In fact, in 1839, they appeared in open rebellion in the hilly parts of Monmouthshire and Glamorganshire, where these two counties meet, and marched in a body of some seven or eight thousand men—mostly miners, upon Newport. In the attack they there made upon the military, about twenty of the miners were killed, when the rest dispersed. Among a number of prisoners taken were the leaders—Frost, Williams, and Jones, who, in the January following, were condemned to death, but were afterwards reprieved, and their sentences commuted to transportation for life.

Up to 1840 there had been a steady increase in the Catholic churches, which now numbered between four and five hundred, in Great Britain. But this did not by any means keep pace with the increase in the Irish population. Thus, we learn that, in 1837, the chapel in London Road, which was afterwards replaced by the noble edifice which is now the cathedral church of the diocese of Southwark, had become far too small for the congregation attached to St George's mission. An appeal, in the form of a "Statement," was made, which said that between 1793 and 1837 the congregation had increased from 1000 to 20,000. This would then include almost the whole of the Catholic population of London on the Surrey side of the Thames. The statement, referring to the then existing chapel, said—" The free part of the chapel affords space for about 600 persons; that is to say, when they form one dense mass, crushed together without the power of moving, and with difficulty of kneeling; indeed, a third part of the dense crowd are forced back, and so pressed together, that they have not the power of kneeling. This scene takes place twice, at least, each Sunday—

viz., at the ten and eleven o'clock masses. Besides this distressing state of things, a crowd of poor persons, unable to force an entrance within the crowded chapel, remain outside and pray in the open air." It was the same elsewhere throughout the country. Those who are old enough will remember how, some forty or fifty years ago, and later, the "chapels," as they were then invariably called, were filled to overflowing at every mass. In all kinds of weather the people had to kneel in the porches, or out in the chapel yard, or in the street, content if they could but get a glimpse, through an open door or window, of the interior of the sacred edifice.

It was perhaps a relic of the old penal days that sometimes caused the English Catholic to append "Mr" only to the priest's name when speaking of or to him, as if he were a layman. The Catholic from the north of Ireland generally prefixed the title, "Priest," to the clergyman's name, a custom probably adopted from his Protestant neighbour at "home," as Ireland was always lovingly called. The immigrants from Connaught and Munster brought over the endearing and more respectful title, "Father," now universally used.

CHAPTER XIII.

THE CENSUS OF 1841—WHERE THE IRISH WERE THEN TO BE FOUND THROUGHOUT GREAT BRITAIN.

HITHERTO, in estimating the number of our people at any given period, we have been largely dependent upon such Catholic church statistics as were obtainable.

It is only when we come to the census of 1841 that we find ourselves on really solid ground. We learn from it, for the first time, by actual official enumeration, the number of *Irish-born* then in Great Britain.

The following table shows the Irish-born population in various parts of Great Britain, and the percentage they formed of the general population :—

1841.

The various parts of Great Britain.	Irish-born.			Percentage of whole.	Total Population.
	Males.	Females.	Total Irish-born.		
England,	148,151	135,977	284,128	1·9	14,995,138
Wales,	3,080	2,196	5,276	0·6	911,603
Scotland,	66,502	59,819	126,321	4·8	2,620,184
The Islands,	1,664	1,867	3,531	2·8	124,040
	219,397	199,859	419,256	2·2	18,650,965

In proportion to the general population, the Irish were considerably more numerous in Scotland than in the rest of Great Britain—amounting to nearly five persons in every hundred; while in England there were not quite two Irish-born in every hundred. The lowest proportion of Irish was in Wales. Of the 5276 Irish-born in the Principality, 3174, or considerably more than half, were in one county—Glamorganshire, where the proportion was nearly the same as in England. In the adjoining English county, Monmouth, where the population is almost entirely of Welsh extraction, there were 2925 Irish-born, being over two in a hundred of the general population.

Extending into both Monmouthshire and Glamorganshire, there is an important mining and ironworking district, which accounts, even so far back as fifty years ago, for the comparatively large number of Irish, who are always in greatest demand where the heaviest labour has to be done. Our national poet, Thomas Davis, whose local knowledge was always wonderfully exact, speaking of the spirit which ought to animate his Cymric kindred, exhorts them, in his noble ballad, "Cymric rule and Cymric rulers," to be—

"Prompt and true
To plan and do,
And firm as Monmouth iron."

Davis knew that, even then, his Irish fellow-countrymen

were making the hills of South Wales their homes, and, no doubt, wished to promote a feeling of brotherhood between the two branches of the old Celtic stock. So far as the Welsh were concerned, his efforts were, for a long time, in vain. They have, however, borne fruit at last, for, though Davis is dead, his spirit lives in millions of Irish breasts, and, now that they have come to know him, as they do to-day, the Welsh are almost as proud of him as we are.

It was these Glamorgan and Monmouth hills that furnished the fighting men in the Chartist insurrection, when the attack, already referred to, was made on Newport, in November 1839. There were, however, comparatively few Irish among them then.

It might be expected, from the Irish coming in such large numbers, year after year, for over a century, to reap the harvests in England, that a considerable number of them would be found settled in the agricultural counties. It was precisely in these that the smallest proportion of Irish were to be found, according to the census of 1841, showing that the labourers, as a rule, either returned to Ireland each year, or found employment in the mining and manufacturing districts, and the seaports of Great Britain. Thus there were, at this time, in Lincolnshire, a county much visited by Irish reapers, but 1244 Irish-born, or a percentage of 0·3 of the general population, while in Lancashire the Irish-born were 105,916, a percentage of 6·3 of the entire population, constituting more than one-third of the whole Irish-born of England. The great mass of these were in the large towns, particularly Liverpool, where, at this time, nearly all the dock labourers were Irish, who formed, indeed, nearly one-third of the population of the great seaport.

Up till now the typical collier was always an Englishman, and considered to be about the lowest type of a Briton—morally and intellectually. The Irish at this time, however, began to be employed in the collieries. Now they are numerous in the pits all over the country, and, whether they can claim any credit for the change for the better or not, it is an undoubted fact that the mining population of Great Britain are among the foremost in political intelligence, and, in every respect, compare favourably with any other class.

In all the ironworking districts the Irish were now beginning to get employment, which accounts for their being numerous in Cumberland, Durham, Northumberland, Monmouthshire, and Glamorganshire.

But it was in the larger cities and towns that they were to be found in the greatest numbers. London—as might be expected—had the largest population of Irish-born. They formed, as we have seen, as far back as the middle of the last century, a considerable element in the river-side population, and had been making their way in every walk of life. The same could be said of the other principal towns of Great Britain. In the great seaports they were employed largely in connection with the shipping, while they were gradually gaining a footing in the various industries of the manufacturing towns, particularly in Lancashire and Yorkshire.

Scotland, as we have seen, had a far larger proportion of Irish-born to the general population than England. They were chiefly from the province of Ulster. Lanarkshire, in which the great city of Glasgow is situated, had 55,915, or nearly half of the Irish-born in Scotland, the proportion to the general population being 13·1 per cent. Renfrewshire, containing the important towns of Greenock and Paisley, where our countrymen are numerous, came next to Lanarkshire with an Irish-born population of 20,417, and having about the same percentage to the general population. Then came Ayrshire, with 12,035 Irish-born, and percentage of 7·3. Edinburghshire, embracing the Scottish metropolis, where our people had been for a long time settled, had 7100 Irish-born, and a percentage of 3·2. Forfarshire, containing the flourishing town of Dundee, with a considerable Irish population, had 6476 Irish-born, and a percentage of 3·8. Wigtownshire had 5772, and the largest percentage of natives of Ireland of any county in Great Britain—14·7. Dumbarton had 4891 Irish-born, and 11 per cent. of the general population. It will be seen that nearly two-thirds of the Irish in Scotland were to be found on the banks of the Clyde—in Lanarkshire, Renfrewshire, and Dumbartonshire.

CHAPTER XIV.

OPENING OF THE REPEAL AGITATION—FATHER MATHEW—
THOMAS DAVIS.

WHEN O'Connell raised the standard of "Repeal," the Irish in Britain threw themselves into the struggle with characteristic ardour. At that time they had by no means the same political power, in proportion to their numbers, as now, nor were they so well disciplined. To make amends for this they subscribed all the more liberally to the funds of the Repeal Association.

Liverpool, among the great towns, as containing the largest Irish element in proportion to the general population, probably took the lead. The old Repeal Hall, in Paradise Street, was, every Sunday night, the scene of great activity. The flood of platform oratory was only equalled by the flowing in of the sinews of war, gathered Sunday after Sunday, amid hail, rain, snow, or sunshine, by the collectors, the best pillars of creed and country up to this moment — God bless them. How generously the warm-hearted exiles from the old sod contributed may be gathered from a letter, written to the Repeal Association by George Smyth, a Liverpool Irishman, who, in his day, made many sacrifices for his country. Enclosing a contribution of three guineas from Irish salt-heavers, he said that about £1000 in all had been sent from Liverpool in the year 1844.

We gather from the files of the *Nation* that the Irishmen of the metropolis, too, were well to the front. Among the localities from which contributions were regularly sent were Holborn, Chelsea, Drury Lane, Westminster, Soho, Gray's Inn, St John's Wood, Southwark, Bloomsbury, Lincoln's Inn, Finsbury, Rotherhithe, Saffron Hill, Kensington, Lambeth, and Shoreditch.

Other towns ran London and Liverpool very closely, and from Glasgow, Manchester, and elsewhere, large contributions were sent each week, as much as £100 being sometimes paid in as a single instalment.

During the Repeal agitation we find O'Connell taking

part in many liberal demonstrations in this country, and being received with great honour.

About this time Father Mathew, the famous Irish apostle of temperance, visited Great Britain, and administered the pledge of total abstinence from intoxicating drinks to many thousands of his follow countrymen. In London alone over 70,000 took the pledge. As in Ireland, this brought about a great social revolution. Though the effects were, in many cases, not so lasting as could be wished, there can be no doubt but that thousands of Irish families in this country can date whatever of happiness and prosperity they enjoy from the pledge administered by Father Mathew. The temperance movement helped the Repeal agitation. Besides enabling Irishmen to contribute more liberally to the national funds than ever before, it made them fitter for that freedom for which they were struggling.

The movement for Repeal reached its full flood in the summer of 1844, while O'Connell and other leaders were imprisoned. This aroused the national feeling to a higher pitch than it had ever reached before, and the Repeal Rent, as it was called, for the week ending June 22nd, 1844, reached the magnificent sum of £3389, 14s. 9d.

When, some three months later, the House of Commons reversed the judgment upon O'Connell and the other prisoners, there were great rejoicings for their liberation in all the large centres of population in Great Britain.

During the following twelve months, the Liberator launched his thunderbolts as vigorously as ever from the platform of Conciliation Hall. The agitation went on for a time with as great apparent vigour as before, but, nevertheless, O'Connell's imprisonment was a check from which it never recovered. Not that the spirit of the people was broken,—they would have followed him to death had he said the word,—but they saw it was useless any longer to look to him for that stern and vigorous action necessary for a leader of men aspiring to be free.

Ireland now suffered a loss which, coming when it did was irreparable. This was the death of Thomas Davis, on the 16th of September 1845. Though he never came into personal contact with them, no name has been more reverenced than his by two generations of the Irishmen of Great Britain. Among these are many thousands—some of Irish birth, others, born here of Irish parentage, many of whom have never seen Ireland—who have modelled their lives on the lessons he taught, and whose souls have been filled with patriotism by his undying songs.

BOOK VII.
THE FAMINE.

CHAPTER XV.

"GONE WITH A VENGEANCE."

IN the autumn of 1845 there fell across Ireland the shadow of one of the most appalling calamities the world has ever seen.

The potato crop, upon which the bulk of the people depended for food, was failing. The deadly effects, in Ireland, of the terrible famine which ensued have been described by many eloquent and forcible pens. Let us see how it affected the Irish here.

The panic-stricken people fled from their country, literally in millions, to America, to England—anywhere to escape from what seemed a doomed land. For though in the worst of the famine years, notwithstanding the potato blight, there was food enough grown to feed the whole people, under alien rule it was not for them. With a government in sympathy with the people, not a single human being in Ireland would have starved. The British government then, *ruling in spite of them*, stands charged with their murder. While not forgetting that many a noble soul in Britain helped the Irish people in this crisis, it is terrible to remember that in "Christian England" also, there was men who gloated with ghoul-like glee over what seemed to them the effectual settlement of the Irish question by the extermination of our race. This is no exaggeration of the language of the *Times* newspaper, in describing the probable effects of the calamity which had befallen Ireland.

We shall see how the fiendish hopes have been disappointed, and how one result of the famine has been to raise up a mighty power on the side of Ireland, which has baffled the machinations of her oppressors. Among those who, as described by the *Times*, had "gone with a vengeance," but who grew into forces, fighting for our country, none are more ardent in her cause than the Irish in Britain, many of whom, or their fathers, came here from Ireland at the time of the famine—not in a well-regulated emigration, but flung on these shores like the wreck of a routed army. Upon them it has left its indelible traces. If it has been a calamity and a weakness, it has also added enormously to their strength. Had they had the means, most of our people would have crossed to America at this time. Only a portion had enough to carry them so far. The rest sought refuge here, and we find the traces of these days in the wretched social condition of but too many of them and their descendants in the larger towns of Great Britain.

They suffered great hardships in crossing the Channel, for the accommodation provided for the deck passengers was, as a rule, not so good as that for the cattle. We can gather how they were sometimes treated from a case that came before the Cardiff magistrates, who fined the master of a vessel £20 for bringing from Ireland sixty-eight poor creatures, who were huddled together in such a way that, had bad weather come on, some of them must have perished.

In 1846 there was the old sickening story which had been so often repeated since the days of the Stuarts, of deputations coming to England seeking for the relief of Ireland's grievances and wretchedness — and all equally fruitless. One of these deputations was from the Corporation of Dublin to the Queen, at Windsor, asking her to use her influence towards grappling with the famine—needless to say, in vain. On February 19th, 1846, O'Connell appealed to Parliament for help—help which Ireland's own resources could have well supplied, had they not been drained to minister to the luxury of absentee landlords.

At first it was denied that there was any famine. When this could no longer be said, the relief given was often but a mockery, and mostly came too late. Ireland could, however, always get one remedy for her woes—Coercion—and this she now got with a ferocity to which she is but too well accustomed.

The fugitives from Ireland brought with them the famine-fever, of which many thousands perished here. Liverpool, being the principal emigration port, saw, in the most intense form, the horrible results. Day by day vast numbers of the famine and fever-stricken Irish landed on the quays. The enormous number of 13,470 of them received relief from the poorhouse in the week ending December 20th, 1846. We can gather some idea of the condition of Liverpool some weeks later, when the *Liverpool Mercury* writes—" Government ought at once to be moved to erect enormous sheds in Ireland, where, as in barracks, the destitute poor may have shelter and warmth and good air. All paupers leaving Ireland for England should be told that they will be immediately liable to be sent back again by the parochial authorities of Liverpool, Bristol, &c. We have no right to sit still and let pestilence walk in amongst us. At this moment the progress of the fever in the cellars and garrets of Liverpool is most alarming. The first flush of warm weather will spread disease and death into hundreds of streets. The wretched state in which the poor people arrive, and the shocking dark, damp, dirty places in which they herd—as many as thirty in a cellar—are the most certain constituents of malignant fever, and deeply shall we suffer in a few weeks by the loss of many of our valued townsmen and townswomen, if the evil now growing around us be no longer stayed." In the month of February 1847, the number of Irish poor landed in Liverpool was 26,348—being at the rate of over 300,000 for the year. By this time three of the parochial relieving officers had died of typhus fever, caught in the discharge of their duty. Though the steamship companies raised the fare for deck passengers, the stream did not slacken. There was a similar state of things in London, Bristol, and the other great seaports.

The inland towns also suffered from the awful visitation.

A Leeds newspaper, in describing the terrible condition of the poor Irish immigrants in that town, says—"In Upperhead Row, Swallow Street, and their yards and courts, there are a great number of Irish lodging-houses, where large numbers of our fellow-creatures are nightly herded in dark, damp, and ill-ventilated cellars, more like tombs than lodging rooms." An abstract is then given of the various lodging-houses, beds, and inmates, which cannot be read without a shudder.

The famine-fever prevailed to an alarming extent in Glasgow and Greenock. In the latter town the infirmary became so full, that additional provision had to be made for those who were daily being brought in. Towards midsummer, as had been predicted, the pestilence reached the ordinary inhabitants of the English and Scotch towns. The *Liverpool Courier*, speaking of the wretched places where the poor Irish were driven to take shelter, said—"It is lamentable to find that the contagion, generated in these places, has seized upon the middle class, and that the unenviable name that the influx of Irish immigrants and the consequent spread of contagion have acquired for the town, have prevented strangers from visiting us as usual in the summer season, and that the absence of these visitors has entailed a heavy loss upon the shopkeepers, in addition to having to maintain a population who ought to have been provided for in their own land." Nothing could be more true than this last statement of the *Courier*, which thus, unconsciously, bore testimony to the necessity for Ireland having the making of her own laws, and thus being able to provide for all her people "in their own land." By the end of June no less than eight of the Catholic priests of Liverpool had died of fever, caught in ministering to their perishing people. The position of a priest was then like that of the soldiers in battle. He stepped into the place left vacant by the death of his predecessor, with the consciousness that almost certainly the same fate awaited himself.

Though during the famine years the presence of our people in the larger towns was more apparent than elsewhere, they flocked also into the agricultural districts, particularly in the harvest time of 1846 and 1847, like an invading army. The *Lincolnshire Mercury* had a kindlier word for the poor people than they were generally accustomed to receive. It said—" A large number of Irishmen have already passed through Stamford on the way to the Fens, with the view of endeavouring to procure field work before the hay harvest commences. Some of the men give deplorable accounts of the scenes of deprivation they have quitted in their own country, and speak with a fervent desire to obtain immediate employment, in order that they may remit their savings to their distressed families." In the following year (1848) the *Liverpool Albion* thus bespeaks a kindly reception for the Irish reapers—" The Irish peasantry are coming over in considerable numbers to assist in the labour of gathering in the harvest. They have no weapons save their sickles, and we hope for these they will find full employment. We trust, too, they will be received throughout England without any prejudice in their disfavour, that their offers of service will be frankly met, and that none will be ungenerous enough to taunt them on account of the proceedings with which they, probably, have no concern." This refers to the rising of the Young Irelanders, which will be described in the following chapters.

BOOK VIII.

YOUNG IRELAND.

CHAPTER XVI.

THE *NATION* NEWSPAPER—THE YOUNG IRELANDERS—RIBBONISM — THE IRISH CONFEDERATION — THE YOUNG IRELANDERS IN GREAT BRITAIN—TERENCE BELLEW MACMANUS.

THE Young Ireland movement may be said to have dated from the foundation of the *Nation* newspaper by Charles Gavan Duffy, Thomas Davis, and John Blake Dillon. The first number appeared on the 15th of October 1842. From it sprang a genuine national literature, "racy of the soil," which has, ever since, been rapidly growing and fostering a spirit of manhood in the Irish people such as they never had before.

The more ardent spirits among the repealers thought that O'Connell would really appeal to arms under certain circumstances. Indeed his language would often imply that he had this idea in his mind. But with his imprisonment, after all the monster meetings and semi-military parades, came the disillusion. The cleavage between the two sections of repealers became daily more apparent.

Nowhere was the teaching of the *Nation* received with greater avidity than in Great Britain. As a consequence, when the physical force ideas began to gain ground in Ireland, there was a corresponding movement on this side of the channel. It was a policy of desperation, intensified by the appalling ravages of the famine. The British Government, while professing to relieve the distress, was allowing the people to die of starvation. This brought the crisis, and the Young Irelanders began to cry out, in very despair, that rather than our people should die in the ditches of starvation, they ought to die like men—even though the struggle were all but hopeless—fighting for freedom.

From the first the Young Irelanders were a thorn in the side of O'Connell. Much as they reverenced him for the services he had rendered to his country, they complained that he could not, and did not, take that independent action towards the Government which the supreme crisis in Ireland's fate demanded. He was upbraided for his leanings towards the whigs, and although he had never sought for favour or office for himself, it was charged against him that he had done so for his relatives and hungry hangers on. There was some very outspoken language in Ireland from Thomas Francis Meagher, Michael Doheny, and others, which was echoed back from the Irish here. This roused O'Connell's anger, and a number of repeal wardens were expelled from the Association in June 1846. Amongst these was George Archdeacon, of Liverpool, against whose warlike language, couched in somewhat extravagant terms, the Irish leader might have more effectually turned his great powers of ridicule than his wrath. Archdeacon's expulsion does not seem to have damped his martial ardour, for it landed him in gaol in 1848, while, some twenty years afterwards, we find him again in Liverpool, connected with a later Irish physical force movement. A number of the Manchester repealers were also severely dealt with by O'Connell. The Rev. Daniel Hearne had been removed from his mission in Manchester by the Catholic Vicar Apostolic of what was then the Lancashire district. A meeting of his fellow-countrymen was held on June 15th, 1846, to sympathise with him. It was stated at this gathering that he had been removed "for his firm and steady adherence to the interests of his native land." In the account of the proceedings there are some interesting statistics. An estimate is made that there were in Manchester, in 1846, 80,000 Irish and of Irish extraction. Reference is also made to the "4000 Catholics of Stalybridge, more than 5000 in Stockport, 3000 in Ashton, and 4000 in Hyde and district." At the meeting of the Repeal Association in Dublin, following this, a letter was read from O'Connell, condemning the Manchester repeal wardens for the manner of their opposition to the bishop, and asking that Mr Treanor of Stalybridge, and Mr Finnigan of Manchester, be struck off the list of wardens. The language used on this occasion by one of the speakers, Captain Broderick, in denouncing Father Hearne's sympathisers, would lead his hearers to think that these were in some way connected with one of the secret societies which have existed among the Irish at home and abroad under the general name of Ribbonism. In this he did an injustice both to Father Hearne and his supporters. That patriotic Irish priest had always strongly denounced Ribbonism—frequently speaking and writing in the press against it. Indeed, at the very meeting the proceedings of which O'Connell found fault with, Father Hearne, speaking of how he had combated Ribbonism in Manchester, said— "When he found Paddy M'Kewism introduced among them by designing knaves, he warned them against the frightful consequences of the system." It need scarcely be said that the Young Irelanders, the body with which Father Hearne's friends were in sympathy, never were in favour of secret societies of any kind.

As Ribbonism had at one time a strong footing in Great Britain, particularly in the north of England, it may be well here to give some account of its workings on this side of the channel. Captain Broderick, though wrongfully connecting Father Hearne's friends with Ribbonism, was undoubtedly right when he said—"I am perfectly aware, from having sat on committees to enquire into the working of Ribbonism, that many of the Ribbon pass-words come over here (to Ireland) from Manchester, and that Manchester was, in point of fact, the focus of Ribbonism in Ireland." Indeed Ribbonism, in one form or another, existed among the Irish here as long as it had done at home. Like the other "isms" which have appeared, it was but the inevitable outcome of oppression. We can readily understand how it got a footing here among Irish harvestmen, dock labourers, and others, who, finding themselves a kind of Ishmaelites in a hostile land, were absolutely driven into some kind of combination for mutual protection. The history of the Irish in Great Britain, for two centuries, is largely made up of the records of savage attacks upon themselves, their homes, and the temples of their faith, so that when Ribbonism was transplanted from Ireland it found here a congenial soil.

A. M. Sullivan, in his "New Ireland," says—"From 1835 to 1855 the Ribbon organisation was at its greatest strength. With the emigration of the labouring classes it was carried abroad to England and to America.

"At one time the most formidable lodges were in Lancashire, whither, it is said, the headquarters were removed for safety. Likely enough some kind of a combination was found to be almost a necessity of the labouring Irish at one stage of their existence in England."

In addition to mutual protection, the members appear to have been led to believe that there was a patriotic, and even a religious object. Mr Sullivan alludes to one, Jones, a clerk to a salemaster in Smithfield Market, Dublin, who was general secretary to the Ribbonmen. His letters refer to the organisation as being intended "to free Ireland," to "liberate our country," to "unite all Roman Catholics," &c. Writing on the 24th of April 1838, to an official of the society in England, he says—"Send us word immediately what is the determination of the friends belonging to the Hibernians in Liverpool. If they act for the welfare of their native land, they will join with those persons who wish to see their native land free." At this time the Hibernians in Liverpool were very numerous, and were generally supposed to be an ordinary benevolent society. They were a powerful body, and, for many years previous to and after this date, their annual St Patrick's Day processions through the streets of Liverpool were magnificent displays. The general body could hardly have been a secret society—at first at all events—as the Catholic clergy of the town and the children of the schools formerly took part in their processions. The Hibernians have, for many years, disappeared from public view. It is quite possible that Jones's letter was intended to draw them, or a portion of them, into a secret organisation, which they appear to have become in more recent years. The connection between the Ribbonmen in Ireland and Lancashire, referred to by Mr Sullivan, is mentioned in a letter sent by Father Hearne, in July 1843, to O'Connell. In this he speaks of a Ribbonman, named William M'Kenna, who had left Manchester for the County Monaghan. He said there were eight Ribbon lodges in Manchester, and that they were very strong in Liverpool, and always had been.

Some nine months after this letter was read in Conciliation Hall, a man named Hanlon, and others, were tried in the County Monaghan for attending meetings of the Ribbon Society, and having passwords. The evidence given at the trial showed the connection between the Ribbonmen in the north of Ireland and the north of England. An informer, named Thomas Gillon, swore that Patrick M'Kenna told Charles Kelly and himself not to delay away, for the "goods" were ready and would shortly be given out. The "goods" were, he explained, the passwords for the ensuing quarter. This informer also stated that Hanlon gave Kelly a printed card to go to attend a meeting in Liverpool on February 4th, and he did not go. Hanlon, he said, he had known for six or seven years. Another informer, Peter Gillon, described on his fingers the signs settled for the last quarter, and told what were the passwords. Hanlon only was found guilty. The following passwords were revealed at this trial. It will be seen that they take the form of question and answer, commencing with an ordinary salutation—

"How do you do, sir?"
"I am quite content."
"In what cause?"
"Our present laws."
"May all Irishmen truly agree!"
"Yes, and France will join us speedily."

This reference to France would seem to carry back the existence of these secret societies in Ireland to the days of the "Wild Geese," or the still later times when help for Irish freedom was expected from the first French Republic and from Napoleon Bonaparte. There was a body of Ribbonmen in the County Down called "Thrashers." They, no doubt, originated as a defence against Orangeism. Many of these crossed over to the north of England. They had salutations suitable to the season and the hour of the day or night. One of these was—

"It's a dark night."

If the person saluted proved to be a brother "Thrasher," the answer was—

"And so are our enemies."

Although understood to be condemned by the Church, they were very orthodox, at their convivial gatherings, in their toasts. One of these was—

" Here's youth and bloom
To the Church of Rome,
And the crown to its right owner!"

The last line would seem to show that some leaven still remained of the old Jacobite spirit of the last century, or it might refer to the "uncrowned king," as O'Connell had been called. If so, this would certainly be repaying good for evil, for nobody denounced the Ribbonmen more strongly than the Liberator.

Regarding the orthodoxy of the Ribbonmen, a distinguished leader in Ireland's latest revolutionary movement had a curious experience. The secret bodies in the north of England were bitterly opposed to the Irish Revolutionary Brotherhood, the history of which will be given later, because it was feared it would draw their best men from them. The gentleman, with a view to getting a more patriotic spirit infused into them, had a conference with certain leading spirits among the Ribbonmen. He told them the objects of his organisation, and how it was sought to accomplish them. They listened with great stolidity, considering they were Irishmen, to what he had to say. When he had finished, one got up as spokesman, "Tell me," said he, " Do you let Protestants into your society?" If so, they would have none of it. He was told that all good Irishmen, whatever might be their creed, were admitted, and the names were recited of the past Protestant leaders who had been in every Irish national movement. The Ribbonmen were unmoved by this, and so they remained unconverted. Another zealous missionary of the Irish Revolutionary Brotherhood, since dead, in pursuing his propagandism in certain towns, in the streets where his fellow-countrymen lived, found his path very often strewn, by the Ribbonmen, not with flowers, but with brick-bats. It has been said, too, that more than one poor fellow coming fresh from Ireland to work at the Liverpool docks, and expecting to be at least civilly treated by his fellow-workmen—who were, and are, mostly of his own nationality—has found himself cruelly deceived. If he did not know the grip or the password, the heaviest part of the work would, somehow, be thrown upon him, while occasionally he would even receive bodily injury.

Twenty years after Jones, the general secretary of the Ribbonmen, made his appeal to the Liverpool Hibernians, then apparently an open organisation, the Right Rev. Dr Brown, Catholic Bishop of Shrewsbury, in a sermon at Birkenhead, said—" All secret societies, such as the Hibernians, are strictly forbidden, and no Catholic can join them with a safe conscience."

It is curious to find in America the same uncertainty as to the character and objects of the Hibernians as here. There is this difference, however, that, while here—if they have not actually ceased to exist—they have disappeared from the public view, in America the "Ancient Order of Hibernians" comes out boldly into the light of day, and is a most powerful organisation. Opinions regarding it are most conflicting. The New York *Freeman's Journal* says: —" 'The Ancient Order of Hibernians' is but another name for Ribbonmen." It asserts that though the bulk of them may take no oath, "a secret oath, an oath condemned hopelessly by Catholic morals, is taken by a certain number of those who control the A. O. H." The Right Rev. Dr Gilmour, Bishop of Cleveland, U.S.A., says of the Hibernians :—" This is a society organised by nobody knows whom, nor how controlled. It is governed by some secret central power, has passwords and obligations greatly like an oath, is directed by parties unknown to the Church, who send orders here, there, and elsewhere. In several dioceses of the country this organisation has been condemned, and its members refused the sacraments. So far they have been tolerated in the diocese of Cleveland, but we must confess we do not like the organisation." Mr Timothy M. Healy, in describing the Irish in America, says :—" After the League, one of the most important Irish societies is the Ancient Order of Hibernians. It is a friendly benefit society, employing grips or passwords, something like the 'Foresters,' or 'Oddfellows,' and is confined—by the fact that the members must periodically approach the sacraments of the Church—solely to Catholics. In spite of its religious complexion, however, two bishops—one an Englishman and the other a German— have pronounced against it, and but for the fact that in some dioceses it is coldly looked upon by the Church, it would doubtless have spread into the greatest Irish organisation in America. . . . The Hibernians have political as well as benevolent objects, and state that their head-quarters are in Ireland; but what their precise political objects are, and what the nature of the communion is with the home country, remains, as far as outsiders are concerned, quite obscure."

Among our countrymen in South Wales and Monmouth there are in several places Hibernian Societies. The adoption of the name seems, however, to have been merely a coincidence. They are purely benevolent societies, having nothing secret about them, and being in no way connected with any secret organisation.

During the summer of 1846 the relations between the Old Irelanders, as those who adhered to O'Connell were called, and the Young Irelanders, became more strained than ever. The crisis was reached on the 28th of July 1846, when, in opposing a motion in Conciliation Hall, embodying the idea that the freedom of a nation was not worth the shedding of a drop of blood, Thomas Francis Meagher delivered his celebrated oration known as the "sword speech," and he, with William Smith O'Brien, Thomas Devin Reilly, Charles Gavan Duffy, John Mitchel and others, left the hall, and the Repeal Association, never again to return. It was not long before practical effect was given to Meagher's precepts, for, in the December of the same year, we hear of arms being purchased in Birmingham for use in Ireland.

The opening of 1847 saw the formation of an Irish party distinct from that led by O'Connell. On the 13th of January the Irish Confederation, as the organisation was called, was established. In the accounts of the proceedings we find that the Irish of Great Britain were represented by Terence Bellew M'Manus, George Smyth, and Dr Murphy, of Liverpool; and E. F. Murray, of London. The expelled Repeal Wardens flocked into the new organisation, and among other meetings which helped to strengthen it was one held at the Parthenium Assembly Rooms, St Martin's Lane, London. Here it was stated that, but a few months previously, upwards of forty meetings were held weekly in London, and as much as £50 frequently remitted to the Association in Dublin; whereas, now, there was scarcely one meeting being held in connection with the Repeal Association, and little or no money being collected. The chairman of the meeting stated that the Repeal Wardens of London had been condemned by the Association without being heard. "The oratory," he said, "against physical force was a mere pretence. It was raised by Whig force, but it was not in the power of Whiggery to stay the torrent of Repeal." These denunciations of the Whig proclivities of O'Connell's chief supporters were followed up in the *Nation* of January 23rd, which spoke in strong condemnation of the Irish leader's relatives getting Government situations.

But the voices of those who condemned O'Connell so strenuously were hushed, or only raised in sympathy, when the news of his serious illness became known. With the generous instincts of their race, they only wished now to remember all the good he had done, or striven to do, for his country. The London Confederates, while never relaxing that determination to hold aloof from English parties, whether Whig or Tory, were among the first to pay their tribute of respect and love to their old leader by passing an earnest vote of condolence with him, with hopes for his speedy recovery. O'Connell was the Moses of the Irish race. He had successfully led his people one stage on their journey, but, like his prototype of old, was never to reach, with them, the promised land of freedom. He looked upon the Irish people as his children. The terrible famine, which seemed to threaten their very annihilation, he might have grappled with had he been in his magnificent prime of life, but, with his once vigorous mental and bodily powers undoubtedly failing, the appalling calamity completely crushed him, and must have shortened his span of life. He died at Genoa, on the 18th of May 1847, and with him passed away the Repeal movement in its constitutional form.

Though the agitation nominally lingered on after his death, it had no real vitality. The Irish Confederation drew to it most of the active and ardent spirits. Organising meetings in connection with it were held, and clubs formed in all the chief towns of England and Scotland during the next twelve months. The Young Ireland leaders were in great demand for these gatherings. On Sunday, June 20th, we learn that Thomas Francis Meagher attended a meeting of the Liverpool Confederates. It was held at the George the Fourth Assembly Rooms, Hood Street, where there was an Irish national reading room open every Sunday, from an early hour, free of expense. Here he would meet that noble souled Irishman, Terence Bellew M'Manus, who became the most prominent figure among the Irish in Britain in connection with the '48 movement. In a lecture delivered after the death of M'Manus, this is how Meagher speaks of him—"You will easily conceive the feelings with which I this night relate to you, now that he is dead on the shores of the Pacific, the life of Terence Bellew M'Manus, one of the truest, one of the most generous, one of the most active, one of the most gallant, one of the most loving and lovable of the party. Standing close upon six feet high—bearing himself proudly erect—having all the dash and a good deal of the gay, rollicking swagger of the soldier—his large open features beaming with good fellowship, the enthusiasm of a guileless and elastic nature, and the fire of a quick and restless brain —a world of fun, kindliness and affection, hospitality, bold truthfulness and chivalry speaking from his glistening eye, as well as from his full, ripe, sensuous lip—with his two big hands outstretched to shake his friends into convulsions almost, his racy laugh ringing loud and strong, and all because he was so exuberantly glad to see them—there stands Terence Bellew M'Manus in the prime of life; busy, happy, prosperous, and beloved." This description refers to a time when M'Manus had been some years in Liverpool, having, Meagher said—"Started in boyhood from the little town of Monaghan, where he was born, to seek his fortune somewhere abroad; that being for the most part the destiny of his race." After describing the scenes of his early life in Ireland, Meagher continues—"With an imperfect education—having never in fact gone through a course of regular scholarship—but with a stirring brain and rapid conception, a bold and instant readiness of execution, which more than supplied the place of the philosophy and other acquirements of the schools, bidding good-bye to Monaghan, he dashed into business in the busiest city of the busiest country of the old world; and, after a short time, having won by his incessant diligence and proud honesty something deeper and warmer than the good-will merely of the great commercial people about him, he had as much profitable work as he could well attend to, and fully as much popularity as any one need covet. His commercial relations with Ireland were most extensive. The forwarding agent of many of the largest houses in the north and south of Ireland—houses importing the woollens of Yorkshire and the cotton goods of Lancashire—just at this very time, in the spring of 1846, merchandise to the annual value of one million and a-half pounds sterling passed through his hands. Prosperity, however, the realisation of a handsome income, the attainment of a high mercantile position, did not hurt the sweet, rich flowers of patriotism and pride in all that concerned Ireland which filled his fresh young nature with their beauteousness and fragrance in cloudier days and humbler circumstances. When it was announced, in October 1843, that O'Connell would assemble the people of Ireland on the plains of Clontarf, and there demand the restoration of the National Parliament with the voice of congregated hundreds of thousands, as he had already done at Tara, at Mullaghmast, on the Curragh of Kildare, and at Enniscorthy, within sight of Vinegar Hill—and when it was rumoured that Sir Robert Peel and his colleagues had determined to disperse this meeting by force, and occupy the plain with 20,000 British troops, in defiance of the vauntings of O'Connell, and to the opprobrious discouragement of his followers—the repealers of Manchester and Liverpool resolved to charter four steamers, cross the channel, and with their countrymen, on their own sod, share the fortunes of the day, whatever they might be. The repealers of Manchester were under the command of my friend, Bernard Sebastian Treanor, now a practising lawyer in Boston, and arrived in Dublin the morning immediately preceding the day the proscribed meeting was to take place. They numbered one thousand men, and their arrival furnished the authorities of the Castle with an additional reason for the adoption of military measures to suppress the meeting. The meeting was announced for Sunday, the 8th of October. The Liverpool repealers disembarked the morning after, their detention being caused by the seizure of the steamers they had chartered by the forcible employment of them by the Government for the transportation of troops to Dublin. Terence Bellew M'Manus commanded this second *corps d'armee* of incursive Irishmen. There was nothing generous or bold to be done where the rights and honour of Ireland were at stake that he was not the foremost and the boldest. His vexation on learning the turn which events had taken on the previous day was bitter and intense; for he was one of those who held that O'Connell should have stood his ground, believing that, had he done so, the foreign Government would have backed down; or that, at most, had the Government drawn the sword upon the right of petition and public remonstrance, the blood shed by them upon the plains of Clontarf would have appealed to the sympathies of Europe and the execration of America, whilst it inflamed the vengeance of the Irish race the world over, to an intensity which nothing could subdue and nothing could resist. From the time I first saw him—the time of the deputation to Smith O'Brien

—it was my happiness to meet M'Manus frequently for nearly two years. I had occasion to go to London six or eight times after I went there with this deputation, and I made it a point to stay a day or two in Liverpool, going and coming for the sake of the thorough enjoyment his frank, bright society afforded. On these occasions I invariably found him mounted on a tall, spindle-legged, black, leather-bottomed stool, in a dusky little room, in a gloomy, vast, overhanging sort of warehouse, forty or fifty feet above the level of the rumbling and blackened street, up to his eyes in business, at an old mahogany desk, all smeared with ink, sprinkled with blotting sand and otherwise blotched and mottled. There he was, dashing through letters, bills of lading, orders on Huddersfield, orders on Manchester, drafts, advices, railway receipts, invoices, columns of figures two feet in height, policies of insurance—a perfect labyrinth of business, enough to entangle and confound the shrewdest old chap—there he was dashing through that multitudinous business of his, at the rate of one million and a half pounds sterling in a year—radiant, hearty, full of pluck, teeming with brain, and having a fond, proud, dutiful, chivalrous thought for Ireland all the while. No wonder he had this beautiful and noble thought and that it never left him. On a shelf in that dusky little office of his (in North John Street) there was a large tin box painted in imitation of bronze, with the initials 'T. B. Mc.,' in white upon the lid. That box contained his green and gold uniform, a brace of pistols, and a rifle—the rifle of course disjointed as in a gun case. He never wheeled round on his tall, gawky, leather-bottomed old stool, without his eye flashing on that box; and as surely as it did, off went his bounding heart right into the romantic hills of Ireland—right into the thick of a tempest of fire and smoke—and he was blazing away, charging to and fro, cheering at the top of his voice for the freedom of the land that bore him, ringing out with reckless ecstasy—

" 'A soldier's life the life for me,
A soldier's death, so Ireland's free ! '

"With all his social impulsiveness M'Manus was a persistent drudge when there was drudgery before him, and it was his duty to keep to it. The business of the day over, his office and box locked up for the night, the vast and gloomy warehouse left to itself and the rats, he used to hurry across the Mersey to his little cottage on the beach, near Birkenhead, a mile or so from the fort, commonly known as Rock Fort, the accessible points of which, for ulterior purposes, he used constantly to study with the eye of a remorseless conspirator. It was a neat, old-fashioned, cosy little cottage —had a green door, a brass knocker, projecting eves, white muslin curtains to the low, square windows—and the shingly beach striking straight down to the water's edge, right in front of it. The evenings I spent with him in that old-fashioned cottage will ever be to me unclouded memories of pleasure."

CHAPTER XVII.

THE CONFEDERATES IN GREAT BRITAIN ORGANISE AND ARM THEMSELVES.

THE year 1848 was made memorable by the great continental revolutions which shook almost every throne in Europe. This and the diversion which the Chartists, who had been arming, were expected to make in England in favour of any revolutionary movement, raised the hopes of the physical force party in Ireland, and helped to precipitate the rising which took place.

The Chartist organisation was formidable, in point of numbers at all events. This must certainly have been the impression created on the mind of Michael Doheny, who came from Dublin to address a camp meeting in favour of the People's Charter, held at Oldham Edge, near Oldham, in March. Feargus O'Connor, the Chartist leader, addressed the meeting, which consisted of from fifteen to twenty thousand men.

An idea of the spirit of the Irish here can be gathered from the speeches delivered at a meeting held on the 26th of March 1848, at the Farringdon Hall, London. In answer to certain threats which had been made, every speaker who appeared on the platform declared his solemn determination to procure arms and to use them there—there in England, in case any butchery of the Irish people at home took place. It was quite plain, however inadequate the resources in their hands for such a gigantic undertaking as insurrection against England, that the men of these confederate clubs were in earnest—terribly in earnest. As a further indication of this spirit, which would have extended and intensified with the first gleam of success, we read that two Irish trading vessels, when outside the port of Liverpool, hoisted the Irish flag. This was considered so serious that a man-of-war gave chase and compelled them to lower their colours.

The Young Irelanders in the English and Scotch towns were arming themselves as best they could—mostly in a rude fashion. Dr Lawrence Reynolds opened, in April, an "ironmonger's shop," at 110 Leeds Street, Liverpool, for the sale of arms. Among these were what were described as cutlasses, but which were really a kind of cane-cutters. These were sold at the low price of 6½d. each. Dr Reynolds also had a stock of guns, which he sold at 12s. 6d. each, the price of a blunderbuss with bayonet being 15s. There were pikes, too, the favourite weapon of '98, for sale, some being fitted with handles from eight to ten feet long. The enterprising doctor, in addition to his ironmonger's shop, had a stable in the neighbourhood of Pickop Street, which he used as a store for arms. About the middle of May a shop for the sale of arms was opened at the corner of Gould Street and Rochdale Road, Manchester, by a shoemaker named Downey. His stock of weapons apparently consisted of but two kinds. One was a substitute for a sword similar to that offered for sale by Dr Reynolds. It might be described as a rude cutlass, with a blade about two feet long, fastened into a common wooden handle, without a guard for the hand. The other weapon was a pike-head, about two feet six inches in length over all. The socket, into which the handle of the pike was intended to fit, was six inches long and had two cheek pieces a foot in length which could be firmly attached to the staff with screws. The blade, which was about a foot long, tapered from a breadth of about an inch and a quarter to a point. The opening of Downey's shop created a considerable sensation in the neighbourhood. Weapons of the kind described were also obtainable in other places, and with these many of the Confederates were supplied. It was evident from this that they did not intend to confine themselves to mere declamation, but were determined either to cross over to Ireland, when the time came, to help the men in the gap, or to create a diversion in their favour on this side of the channel. When the news of the sentence of John Mitchel to transportation reached London, the Confederate clubs held meetings to arrange for the arming of their members. As they could not find weapons for all, raffles were held, and guns and pikes given to the winners; those who were unsuccessful having to be content with anything they could get.

Following upon this, towards the end of May, there were some extraordinary demonstrations, consisting of marching and counter marching through the streets of the metropolis, of large bodies of combined Chartists and Confederates.

In Leeds, Bradford, Halifax, Bingley, and other towns in Yorkshire the Chartists were, meanwhile, arming and drilling. There were desperate conflicts in the neighbourhood of Manchester Road, Bradford—which was the stronghold of the Chartists—when the police and special constables attempted to arrest some of the leaders and to search for arms. The Chartists made a determined onslaught on their opponents, who had to fly, many of them being dreadfully injured, before the infantry and dragoons came to their assistance and compelled the insurgents to beat a retreat. There were also disturbances at Manchester, Oldham, and other places, and many of the Chartist leaders were arrested.

There was a considerable Irish element among the Chartists, but during the whole of June new Confederate clubs, composed almost exclusively of Irishmen, were being formed, and members being enrolled. Thus Bernard M'Anulty, writing from the Club Room, Corn Market Newcastle-on-Tyne, on the 20th of June 1848, says:—"The friends of Ireland have formed a club here, called the 'No. 1 Newcastle-on-Tyne Felon Repeal Club,'" and announces that one hundred and twenty-four members were enrolled in about twenty minutes. Bernard M'Anulty is one of the best types of the Irish in Britain that we have, for he still lives at a green old age. Working his way by the sheer force of ability and integrity into the very front rank of life in the town of his adoption, there has been no more ardent champion of his native land for over half a century. A sturdy, large-hearted son of the northern province of Ireland, like so many of our people who have settled on the banks of the Tyne, his once powerful frame, bright cheery face, racy mother wit, and keen judgment, are familiar to all who have ever taken anything like a prominent part in the various Irish movements on this side of the channel.

During the month of July events followed thickly and fast upon each other in Ireland, including suppression of newspapers, arrests of leaders, the proclamation of Dublin, Cork, Waterford, and Drogheda, and the suspension of the *Habeas Corpus* Act. These incidents form part of the history of Ireland at this stirring period, and have been well described by able pens.

In Great Britain there was scarcely less excitement than in Ireland. The powerful Irish element in Liverpool was known to be in sympathy with the national movement, and, with a view to overawing it, a military encampment was formed at Everton. The preceding six months of 1848 had been a time of great activity among the Liverpool Confederate clubs. There were a number of meeting places—including the rooms in Hood Street, Paradise Street, Preesons Row, Circus Street, Bevington Bush, Great Howard Street, and Hurst Street. Among the most active spirits were Terence Bellew M'Manus, Dr Reynolds, George Smyth, Dr O'Donnell, Dr Murphy, and Patrick O'Hanlon. Michael Doheny came from Ireland to address a meeting in Queen Square, and there was a great demonstration at the Music Hall, Bold Street, and an open air meeting at the north shore, beyond the Clarence Dock, which was then the furthest north of the Liverpool docks. It was evidently the intention of the Confederates in England and Scotland to keep a portion of the troops engaged on this side had the rising met with any success in Ireland. M'Manus, at one of the meetings, said they had England in a state of siege, for the Government did not know at what point they would attack them, and Dr Reynolds advocated the raising of barricades. At the committee meetings arrangements were made for procuring arms from Birmingham and elsewhere. Drilling must have gone on almost openly, for we hear of the John Mitchel Club in Liverpool arriving at a place of meeting in marching order. Warned by these proceedings, the authorities made provision to cope with any insurrectionary movement that might arise. The police were exercised in the use of fire-arms, and strong extra guards were placed on the docks. A large body of special constables were appointed, about 500 dock labourers being subsequently dismissed from their employment for refusing to be sworn in. The ulterior intentions of the authorities with regard to the Confederate clubs in Liverpool were kept secret, but, on Saturday, July 22nd, two arrests were made for illegal possession of weapons. One of the men arrested, named Cuddy, was stopped in the streets carrying a bag full of formidable-looking pike-heads. On the Sunday night following this the various clubs in Liverpool and Birkenhead had private meetings to arrange their plan of action, and similar councils met in others of the large towns.

CHAPTER XVIII.

THOMAS D'ARCY M'GEE AND THE YOUNG IRELANDERS IN SCOTLAND.

IRELAND has no more patriotic children than those who have made their homes in Scotland. They were now rapidly increasing in numbers, as we find, on the authority of the City Chamberlain of Glasgow, that, a few years after this, out of a population of 391,400, within the Parliamentary boundary, considerably more than one-fourth of the inhabitants of that city were Catholics.

Many of them in this crisis were anxious to share the fortunes of their countrymen at home, however desperate these might be, in the impending struggle. One of the most brilliant of the Young Ireland leaders, Thomas D'Arcy M'Gee, has given the following stirring narrative, written some three years afterwards, of his adventures in Scotland, and what brought him there, in the month of July 1848:—

"Early on Saturday, July 22nd, I left my pleasant home in Cullenswood, near Dublin, to which I was never to return. On reaching the city I found a telegraphic despatch from London had just been published announcing the suspension of the *Habeas Corpus* Act. It was contended on all hands that the hour for action, or submission, or flight for the Confederates was now come. Of the 'Council of Five' there were then in Dublin but three members. One is now in Van Dieman's Land; the others were Mr Dillon and myself. We had a hasty meeting in the old council rooms of the Irish Confederation. They decided to proceed that evening to Enniscorthy to advise with Smith O'Brien, and (as I understood) to proceed with him to the district between the Suir and the Shannon, and to operate from that basis according to circumstances and their best judgment.

"A gentleman had arrived in Dublin that morning, with a proposition which decided my movements, and led me into some singular situations. He was a professional man, by birth an Irishman, who had resided a long time in Scotland. He had an only son, two rifles, and £120 in money, which he brought as his offering to the country. He informed me that several hundreds of Irishmen in Scotland had been all the year preparing for this event, that they had a good share of arms and ammunition, and that, if any plan could be devised to bring them into Ireland, they could be relied on for courage and endurance. I do not now mention this gentleman's name, because I do not know but he is still under the laws of England.

"We perceived on consultation that if it were possible to land four or five hundred staunch men in the north-west —say at Sligo or Killala—where the Government were completely off their guard (all their anxieties being centred on the south) an important movement might follow in Sligo, Leitrim, Roscommon, and Mayo. It would be like hitting the enemy on the back of the head. It would necessarily draw off some of the forces from Munster, through the valley of the Upper Shannon, which, with its continuous chain of lake, bog, and mountain frontier, would be a difficult ground for the movements of a regular army.

"It was necessary, as our informant said, that 'someone with a name' should go over and concert with the Irishmen in Scotland the mode and time of action, and I was the only person at hand willing for that service. For my encouragement Meagher assured me I would be 'as famous as Paul Jones' if I got the men out of the Clyde, and Mr Dillon suggested as a landing-place the old ground, Killala.

"That afternoon I left Dublin, and on Tuesday morning was in Scotland. I cannot give the exact particulars of my movements there. All who were in my confidence are still in Scotland, with the exception of Mr Peter M'Cabe, of Glasgow, now in the United States. I will only say that I visited and consulted our friends in four of the principal towns—Edinburgh included. I attended meetings of the clubs, and in each instance instituted committees. I obtained in a few days a list of nearly four hundred men, pretty well equipped, ready for the risk. A sub-committee surveyed the Broomielaw and the Clyde, and though their report was unfavourable to the attempt of getting out in one body, a gentleman, now in America, gained over the crew and officers of an Irish steamer, to take us as passengers from Greenock, where the tide in a few days would answer for the departure, about ten o'clock at night. The arms were to be previously shipped as merchandise or luggage, and the destination to be Sligo."

It was an exciting time among the Confederates in the English towns. These, like their brethren in Scotland, as described by M'Gee, were casting about for means of reaching the scene of action in Ireland, and a small number did actually succeed in getting over, among these being, as we shall see, Terence Bellew M'Manus. The great bulk, however, had to be content to hold themselves in readiness to create a diversion, if necessary, on this side. Allowing for all exaggeration, this would have been of a sufficiently formidable kind had the insurrection gone on in Ireland, for the *Standard* correspondent in Manchester wrote at this time—"The clubs here boast they can assemble 7000 men in an hour. Such measures have been adopted that they will find this utterly impossible. Troops are in constant readiness." This probably gives an over-estimate of the strength of the Confederate clubs in Manchester alone, but it must be remembered that Manchester is the centre of a circle of towns but a few miles distant, each containing then, as now, a large Irish population.

Meanwhile, to resume his narrative, we shall see how fared it with Thomas D'Arcy M'Gee and his friends in Scotland—

"These arrangements," he wrote, "occupied from Tuesday till Friday of the last week of July. In the meantime the London journals arrived with the news that O'Brien and his friends had been received with open arms in the south, and great excitement and suspicion of strangers arose in Scotland. In the reading-room at Paisley I read myself, in the *Hue and Cry*. One paper stated I was in Waterford, another said I was revelling among the clubs in the County Dublin. The *Times* did me the honour of coupling me with Meagher, calling us the two most dangerous men now abroad. No one suspected my real locality.

"On Friday I was in Edinburgh, intending to return to Glasgow, when Mr ——, accompanied by a friend, suddenly joined me. I saw they were a good deal agitated. They told me a Scotch mechanic, who had been formerly in Dublin, had seen me in the streets of Glasgow, opposite the Wellington statue, and that the news was all round the town ! They added that the magistrates were in secret sitting, and as the writ of *Habeas Corpus* is unknown to the law of Scotland, I would be certainly arrested and summarily imprisoned if I returned. They were instructed to advise me to go to Ireland through the north of England; to prepare our friends in and about Sligo, and that they would complete the project which they had begun, and which was now in promising forwardness. I complied, and Mr —— handed me a purse as a personal gift from the committee. The purse contained twelve or thirteen sovereigns, the only public money I received in this enterprise. After purposely driving to the West of Scotland depôt, we returned to the North British, and my friend saw me off a station or two on the way to Newcastle-on-Tyne. I slept that night in Newcastle.

"Between Newcastle and Carlisle the next day (Saturday), I had for a fellow-passenger the Rev. Thresham Gregg, who was on a lecturing excursion against the Pope in the north of England. I had been introduced to him a year or two before, and supposed he knew me. He certainly looked very hard at me from under his travelling cap, with his half-shut cunning eye. I had in my hand *Bradshaw's Railway Guide*, which he asked to see. At the wayside stations he kept constantly inquiring the distance to Carlisle, and I sorely suspected he meant to peach.

"In Carlisle I met at dinner two Dublin priests—one from Westland Row Chapel. They were bound on a pleasure trip to Loch Katrine and the Trosachs. They informed me I was 'proclaimed,' and seemed surprised at my returning. We parted very cordially, and that night I went to Whitehaven, where I had to wait over Sunday for the Belfast steamer. In Whitehaven I met (by accident) with Mr James Leach, the well-known Chartist, with whom I had some conversation. On Tuesday morning I arrived in Belfast."

By this time M'Gee would have found that events had so shaped themselves in Ireland that the sooner he got out of the country the better. The same circumstances put an end to the daring scheme of the Scottish Confederates. Otherwise there is no doubt but they would have contributed one of its most startling chapters to the history of the '48 movement.

CHAPTER XIX.

THE RISING — M'MANUS AT BALLINGARRY — ARRESTS IN ENGLAND AND SCOTLAND—ARREST TRIAL AND TRANSPORTATION OF M'MANUS—HIS DEATH.

MEANWHILE, as we have seen, Terence Bellew M'Manus, eager for the fray, left Liverpool to take his part in the struggle in Ireland. He sailed on Monday, the 24th of July, in the steamer for Kingstown, and landed on the following morning. A detective crossed in the same vessel to watch his movements, and to give information to the Irish authorities. M'Manus left after him in the packet in a tin case his green and gold uniform of the '82 club, which was afterwards described at his trial as a military uniform. This he was to have sent for, but as he soon discovered he was being watched, he did not do so. The detective from Liverpool accompanied him in the train from Kingstown to Dublin, following him to the *Irish Felon* office, which M'Manus found closed. He then went into a hotel close by, where he managed to shake off the detective, and, getting clear away, it was not long before he was in Tipperary. This was on the Tuesday, and from then until the collapse of the rising on the Saturday, at Ballingarry, M'Manus seemed to be ubiquitous. His coolness, sagacity, and daring, during the brief campaign, proved him to have been a born soldier.

On the Wednesday he was at Mullinahone, with Smith O'Brien, to whose humanity the Attorney-General afterwards paid a high tribute, because "he did not have recourse to the armed force under his command for the purpose of destroying the small body of constables." O'Brien was a chivalrous Irish gentleman, but too Quixotic for a revoluionary leader. He set his face against carrying on the war at the expense of the enemy, and as an army cannot exist without food and other supplies, the rising was thus doomed to failure from the very outset. From Mullinahone they marched to Ballingarry, where the people were being drilled. The leaders slept at the house of Mr Cavanagh, an armed guard being posted outside during the night.

On Thursday they returned to Mullinahone, and on the evening of the same day reached Killenaule, where they were received with great enthusiasm. Here they passed the night.

On the following morning, expecting the arrival of the military, M'Manus, whose activity was something marvellous, overtook, on the road, near Killenaule a decent farmer named M'Carthy (who afterwards could not be got to identify him) and pressed his horse into the service. Perceiving the approach of troops he returned to the town and assisted in throwing up barricades to resist their farther progress. Captain Longmore, who commanded the troop of cavalry which now rode up, having assured the people he had no warrant for the arrest of O'Brien, he and his force were allowed to proceed unmolested. O'Brien, M'Manus, and the other leaders brought their men back to Ballingarry the same night.

Saturday, July 29th, saw the end of the rising. A body of police, under Inspector Trant, marched out from Callan to arrest O'Brien, for whose apprehension a reward of £500 was offered. They reached Farrenrory, on their way to Ballingarry, between twelve and one o'clock. Here they found a barricade had been erected, with three or four hundred men behind it to dispute their progress. Instead of attempting to force a passage the police retreated and succeeded in taking refuge in a strongly built, slated house, known as the Widow M'Cormack's, which they barricaded before their pursuers could reach them.

M'Manus bore a gallant part in this, the closing scene of the rising. Meagher describes the daring manner in which he stood his ground under the fire of fifty constabulary carbines, and how with deliberate aim he returned their fire—also his attempt to set fire to the house, with the view to dislodging the police. This attempt failed, and it became evident that the police could not be driven out.

Father Fitzgerald, the priest of the parish, and Father Maher, the curate, now arrived, and used their influence to stop the hopeless struggle. Then, when it was evident that all was over, there was a dispersal of leaders and people in various directions.

In the affray at Ballingarry, the police, being under cover from first to last, suffered very little from the fire of their assailants. Two of the attacking party were killed and several wounded, including James Stephens, who received a rifle ball in the thigh. Wounded as he was, he managed eventually to escape out of the country, and lived to be the leader of a later formidable movement for the liberation of Ireland, in which many of the Irish in Britain bore an important share. Dillon, Doheny, O'Gorman, O'Mahony, Reilly, and other Confederate leaders also succeeded in escaping from Ireland.

William Smith O'Brien was captured by the police on Saturday, the 5th of August, and Meagher, O'Donoghue, and Leyne, on the 12th. As the days went on, and still no tidings were heard of M'Manus, it was thought he must have made good his escape from Ireland.

Meanwhile, in England and Scotland, there were seizures of papers and arms, and wholesale arrests and committals of the more prominent Confederates. A club in Blundell Street, Liverpool, was entered, and the papers carried off, while five hundred of Dr Reynold's cane-cutters were seized in a cellar at the corner of Atherton Street in the same town. Among those arrested in Liverpool, before and after the rising, were Edward Murphy, secretary of the Sarsfield Club, in whose house arms and papers were found when he was taken; Martin Boshell, who held a good mercantile position in Liverpool; Thomas O'Brien and Joseph Cuddy, arrested with pike-heads in their possession: George Smyth, a hatter in a good way of business, and for a time one of the ablest and most earnest propagandists of O'Connell's Repeal movement; Patrick O'Hanlon, a thriving woollen draper, who sacrificed his prospects for the Irish cause; James Laffan, Francis O'Donnell, and P. H. Delamere. These were in due course tried, and, with the exception of Delamere, convicted, receiving sentences of imprisonment varying from three months to two years.

On the night of Tuesday, August 15th, between ten and eleven o'clock, an imposing force of military, including infantry and cavalry, aided the police in making a raid on the Confederate clubs in Manchester. The club held at Whittaker's Hotel, Ancoats, was swept of its occupants, and elsewhere a number of the leaders were arrested. Among those captured were Thomas Rankin, engraver; Daniel Donovan, weaver, of Back Ormond Street, Oldham Road; John Joseph Finnigan, weaver, Meadow Street, one of the Repeal Wardens denounced by O'Connell; Patrick Devlin, glazier, German Street, Oldham Road; and Michael Corrigan, groom, Cheetham Hill. It will be seen, from the occupations of these men, that, as in a still later physical force movement, the Confederates drew their sturdiest recruits from the intelligent artizan class of the towns.

After this there were a number of other arrests of Liverpool and Manchester Confederates, including George Archdeacon, who, notwithstanding the fierce denunciation of O'Connell in 1846, still continued an incorrigible and unrepentant rebel; Bernard Sebastian Treanor, spoken of by Meagher as the leader of the Manchester expedition to Clontarf; George James Clarke, and Peter Feeney, who had attended from Manchester at the anniversary meeting of the Irish Confederation, held in Dublin at the commencement of the year. Against these and Donovan, Finnigan, and Rankin, captured in the raid upon the clubs, true bills were found at the assizes, and in the trials that followed they were sentenced to various terms of imprisonment. In their descriptions of these trials the newspapers frequently confounded the Irish Confederates with the English Chartists. Indeed, so much did they make common cause, that many were members of both organisations. An Irish artist, however, named William Dowling, who had been arrested in London, being described as a Chartist in the charge made against him of conspiracy to raise insurrection, objected to be so called, saying he was "not an English factionist, but an Irish nationalist, his object not being to disturb English society but to free his country." He was convicted, and suffered the usual penalty of militant patriotism.

Of the more prominent Liverpool Confederates Dr Reynolds alone escaped. This was the more singular, as from his boldness in the sale of arms, he seemed almost to court arrest. When the inevitable warrant was issued for his capture, and the police went to his house to execute it, they found he had disappeared, leaving behind a small quantity of arms and ammunition. Crossing the river to Birkenhead, he walked to Bebington, where he took train for Birmingham, the detectives being so closely on his track that they reached that town to find he had but just flown. By rail and coach he reached South Wales, where for some weeks he was housed and fed by Welsh friends. Notwithstanding the pursuit after him being so hot, he was able to take passage from Bristol for America. In New York he commenced as a surgeon, and entered upon a prosperous career. The gallant doctor died a few years since in America, at an advanced age. His military instincts and love for the old land never left him. During the great civil war he was attached to a portion of the Irish-American Brigade, the 63rd Regiment, in the capacity of surgeon. From a brief memoir in Captain Conyngham's interesting work on the Brigade, we learn that Dr Lawrence Reynolds was a native of Waterford. He was the author of several beautiful and touching national poems, and was endowed with great wit and humour. Captain Conyngham speaks of him as the poet laureate of the Brigade.

Terence Bellew M'Manus was not so fortunate as his friend Dr Reynolds in eluding his pursuers. He was supposed to be on his way to America, which was indeed the case, but unfortunately he was not quite out of the lion's jaws when, by the merest accident, he was captured. On Wednesday, August 30th, the police boarded an American vessel, the *N. D. Chase*, at Cove, as she was about to sail for Boston. They were looking for an absconding defaulter. Instead of the runaway they found M'Manus. He was recognised by the head constable, who had seen him in Liverpool, and arrested. It was a terrible and crushing blow to be taken thus—with freedom almost within his grasp. His trial for high treason opened at Clonmel on Monday, October 9th, 1848. There was scarcely an incident described in the evidence brought against him which was not at the same time a testimony to his high honour, his conspicuous gallantry, and the rare nobility of his nature. On the 23rd of October he was placed in the dock with Meagher and O'Donoghue to receive sentence. Their bearing was manly and unflinching. M'Manus, in reply to the usual question from the judge, said that, whatever part he had taken in the struggle for his country's independence, he was ready to abide with a free heart and a light conscience the issue of his sentence. He declared, standing as he did between the dock and the scaffold, that, however much he had felt the injustice of English rule in Ireland, he had never had any animosity against Englishmen, for amongst them he had spent some of the happiest and most prosperous days of his life. It was not for having loved England less but for loving Ireland more, that he then stood before his judges. Meagher and O'Donoghue having also spoken, the Chief Justice passed sentence of death for treason upon them. The extreme sentence was not carried out. The Confederate chiefs, including William Smith O'Brien, who also had been convicted, and sentenced to death, were transported to Van Dieman's Land.

Here we leave Terence Bellew M'Manus for a season, while we see how fared it with his fellow-countrymen in Great Britain, after the failure of the insurrection, which seemed to be the last feverish struggle of a nationality perishing of famine and pestilence. This done, we shall follow him into his exile, and join in the rejoicings that greeted his escape from captivity. We shall trace his life and struggles in America until the time of his death, and we shall join in spirit with the whole Irish race in that wondrous funeral procession, which — bearing the dead patriot's bones over continent and ocean to their mother earth in Ireland—startled the world with another proof that the spirit of Irish nationality is undying.

BOOK IX.

IRISH PROGRESS IN BRITAIN.

CHAPTER XX.

THE GREAT IMMIGRATION—LOCATION AND CONDITION OF OUR PEOPLE.

The Famine, as we have seen, caused an enormous immigration of the Irish into Great Britain. In 1841 the Irish-born numbered 419,256. The census for 1851 showed that there were then 519,959 in England, and 213,907 in Scotland —total for Great Britain 733,866.

Let us glance at the changes which had taken place in those fateful ten years, during which the Irish-born had nearly doubled. The numbers of the Irish peasantry who each year crossed the channel to reap the harvest in England and Scotland had enormously increased.

The men from Donegal landed mostly in Glasgow, while the hardy Connaughtmen generally passed through Liverpool on their way to the English agricultural counties. It was a sight to remember—the vast armies of harvest men, clad in frieze coats and knee breeches, with their clean white shirts with high collars, and tough blackthorns, who might be seen, some forty or fifty years ago, marching, literally in their thousands, from the Clarence Dock, Liverpool, and up London Road, to reap John Bull's harvest. We have shown how, in 1841, but few had then become permanent residents in the agricultural counties. In Lincolnshire, in that year, there were but 1244 settled natives of Ireland. In 1851 there were 2344. They had about doubled their number—

simply keeping pace with the total increase of Irish throughout the country; yet each year vast numbers of Irish came over for the harvest, for we find that in three or four days in August 1850, according to the *Stamford Mercury*, 12,000 of them passed through Liverpool from Ireland, on their way to the fens of Lincolnshire. The census figures show how few must have remained each year. It was the same in Kent. "Multitudes of Irish," said the *Spectator*, in September 1850, "have migrated to Kent for the hop-picking. Near East Farleigh and Barming some 2000 swarm about the road, and 'squat' on bits of waste land." In that same year two priests, from the London Oratory, went to minister to the spiritual wants of the hop-pickers; and their harvest, too, was abundant. A considerable number of the Irish hop-pickers must, from time to time, have settled in London, for of those who now go "a-hopping" each year, many are London-born of Irish parentage.

In 1851 there was in some of the agricultural counties about the same proportionate increase of Irish-born as in Lincolnshire, in others there was scarcely any, while in two cases there was an actual diminution. It will be seen, therefore, that the Irish labourers mostly returned home each year, or got employment in the mining and manufacturing centres, or in the construction of the new railways, then going on with extraordinary rapidity.

They were but the waifs and strays of the great frieze-clad army of harvestmen who remained permanently in such counties as Lincoln. In out-of-the-way villages there, and in other agricultural districts, you still occasionally come across a little colony—the remnants of the famine years. Of the old people who are left, some scarcely know any tongue but Irish, and you will sometimes hear from the lips of an old harvestman a story of the "black '47," told with simple pathos and unstudied eloquence, from which years of exile have not entirely driven the impress of his Connaught home. In some places the presence of our country people is due to another cause. You will find an Irish "navvy" who has settled down in a village, after working at the making of some railway. Often, in these places, if the original settler be gone, you find the second or third generation of his descendants, who mostly cling to the faith of St Patrick and the traditions of fatherland.

Lancashire, in 1851 as in 1841, still had the largest number of Irish-born, as well as having the largest percentage in proportion to the general population. The increase in Middlesex (including London) had gone on in a similar proportion. In Yorkshire, which comes next in point of Irish population, the increase was considerably above the average for the whole country. This would show that our people were finding employment in connection with the woollen manufactures of that great county. There was a still larger increase in several other counties. Thus, in Staffordshire and Glamorganshire there were about three times as many Irish-born in 1851 as in 1841, their chief employment being at the coalpits and blast furnaces. It was the same in Northumberland and Durham, where, in addition to these industries, they found a market for their labour in connection with the shipping industries along the banks of the Tyne, and at Sunderland and Hartlepool. The Irish-born had also largely increased in Derbyshire, where they became engaged in the mining industries along the eastern portion of the county, and the cotton manufactures in the north-west. The increase was considerably above the average in most of the Welsh counties as well as Glamorganshire. In Cheshire, Warwickshire, Cumberland, and Northumberland, having a considerable Irish population, and a number of other counties where the Irish were not so numerous, there was about the average increase. In Devonshire, Gloucestershire, and Somersetshire, and some of the agricultural counties, the Irish-born had but slightly increased, while in Berkshire and Suffolk there had been a diminution.

Turning to Scotland. As a whole the Irish had increased in about the same proportion as in the rest of Great Britain. Lanarkshire, as in 1841, contained nearly half of the Irish of Scotland, but the increase had not been so great relatively as the average of other Scottish counties. More than half the Irish of Lanarkshire were in Glasgow, and largely engaged in labour connected with shipping. Throughout the rest of Lanarkshire the chief employment was in connection

with the coalpits and blast furnaces. In Renfrew, south of
the Clyde, the next county to Lanark in point of Irish population, the increase had been comparatively small; while in
Dumbartonshire, north of the Clyde, the increase had been
even less. The Irish were chiefly engaged in connection
with the shipping industries on both sides of the river, and
in the staple manufactures at Paisley and other inland towns
and villages, some also being colliers, as in Lanarkshire. In
Ayrshire there was already a large Irish population in 1841,
as indeed there had been since the last century. There
was a considerable increase in 1851, but not so great as
the average for the whole country. In Wigton and Stirling
also the increase was below the average.

In Edinburghshire (including the Scottish capital), Fifeshire, and Haddingtonshire, the increase was considerably
above the average. The greatest increase was in Forfarshire (with the thriving town of Dundee), where the Irish
had trebled their number. The other Scottish counties in
which the Irish were not so numerous, and where there was
a considerable proportionate increase, were Perth, Roxburgh,
Selkirk, Peebles, Clackmannan, and Kincardine. In the
rest of the Scottish counties there was about the average
increase.

Taking a general survey of the Irish in Scotland in 1851,
it will be seen that, though considerably more than half of
them were still in the counties watered by the Clyde, the
proportion of the whole of the Irish of Scotland was less
there than in 1841. They were, in fact, getting more equally
diffused through the rest of the country, particularly along
the banks of the Tay and the Firth of Forth, as it will be
seen that the greatest increase was in the counties bordering
these—Forfar, Fife, Edinburgh, and Haddington. There
was a considerable increase, too, in the valley of the Tweed,
where the woollen goods called after the name of that river
are chiefly manufactured.

CHAPTER XXI.

"SPREADING THE FAITH"—THE WAR OF CREEDS AND RACES.

THE foregoing details give a rough idea of the various parts of Great Britain in which the Irish were located in 1851, and the increase or diminution in the various districts.

About half of them were in the large towns, where many sank into a condition of wretchedness it is appalling to contemplate. To an Irishman who loves his country, and would take away the stigma cast upon her by her oppressors of being the "beggar among the nations," it is hard to speak or write calmly on this theme. It is harder still to listen with patience to the drivel of those who maintain that it is the destiny of Irishmen to be driven forth over the earth in order to "spread the faith," never thinking that, amid their wretched surroundings in this country, many thousands of our own flesh and blood are lost—body and soul. This loss is directly attributable to the loss of Ireland's freedom. With a healthy emigration from a free Ireland, and not a panic-stricken flight from a land apparently bleeding to death, the missionary spirit of our country would have an unfettered and noble scope, for it would be unaccompanied by much that we are bound to admit is disedifying in the condition of many of our people here. That they have ever been a missionary race is certain. They have carried their faith and nationality with them wherever they have gone, and given a great impetus to religion. With all their shortcomings, to be expected in a race which has undergone ages of slavery, with all their wretched surroundings here, the schools and churches they have erected throughout the land, with the large and devoted body of priests and teachers, are the best testimonies that they still retain their old love for religion and learning.

The decade from 1840 to 1850 was a period of great railway development, and large numbers of Irishmen were employed in the construction of the various lines which seemed to be springing up like mushrooms all over the country. They were looked upon as interlopers. The bad feeling against them often developed into open violence, and in the early years of railway construction there were frequent desperate conflicts. The history of this war of creeds and races—for the Irishman's creed was as obnoxious as his nationality—has a tragic interest. Though they were numerous in some places, the Irish were, after all, but one in fifty of the British population, so that when an onset was at any time made upon them, they had fearful odds to encounter. These untutored Irish labourers often at these times displayed courage as great as was ever seen on a regular field of battle. Such conflicts had now been going on for about ten years, and mostly arose out of the rivalry between the Irish and English "navvies," as the labourers were called who worked on the railways.

One of these engagements, which occurred in October 1839, when the Chester and Birkenhead railway was being made, was described as a regular pitched battle, the weapons being pick-axes, shovels, and bludgeons. Encounters like these were of such constant occurrence that, in their efforts to gain a living, the Irish were literally fighting for their existence in more ways than one, in the midst of what was but too often a hostile population. The famine drove them here in such numbers as to glut the labour market, which would tend to bring down wages, and thereby rouse the animosity of the native labourers.

It would not be right to describe our people as having been on every occasion innocent of giving provocation, though they generally were. Their native pugnacity, particularly when roused by drink, sometimes provoked these quarrels.

This, however, even by the accounts in the English newspapers, was not the case in connection with some desperate rioting in and about Penrith, on the Lancaster and Carlisle railway, then in course of construction. These riots commenced on Monday, February 16th, 1846, and lasted for several days. According to the local newspaper, the rioting was commenced by the English navvies, who were unwilling to allow the Irish to work on the same part of the line. The Irish, on the whole, appear to have been fairly well able to hold their own. Some of them were attacked by their opponents in a lodging-house—probably one kept by an Irishman for the accommodation of his fellow-countrymen. It is quite a common thing to find in the smaller English towns in the agricultural districts, at least one lodging-house with an Irish name on the sign that offers "accommodation for travellers." These mostly date from the famine years, when there was more demand for them than now. Some four years after this affray a Catholic chapel was opened in Penrith, so that it would appear that the ubiquitous Irish Celt—the *Goban Saor*, the builder of churches of our own days—managed to hold his ground here after all, and is on good terms with his neighbours throughout Cumberland.

There was rioting in the same year, on other lines of railway, between the men of the two nationalities; and in the following year there was a savage attack in Walsall upon the Irish inhabitants.

The details of how our unfortunate people had to fight literally for their very lives during these years reads like the records of a nation in a state of civil war. The terrible famine which drove them from Ireland excited but little sympathy here—nay, it seemed but to intensify the hatred with which the Irish immigrants were regarded, and to bring about another attack of the "No-Popery" and "Anti-Irish" mania which periodically seized upon the British mob. This feeling was particularly strong in South Wales towards the end of 1848, and lead to an outbreak in Cardiff, in which the Irish of the town and their church and houses were attacked. There was also an attack on the Irish in Dunfermline in 1850. There certainly was not much of the boasted chivalry of the so-called great "Anglo-Saxon" race in their treatment of our people in this country during these years.

CHAPTER XXII.

CATHOLIC DEVELOPMENT—RESTORATION OF THE HIERARCHY IN ENGLAND—THE "PAPAL AGGRESSION" MANIA—TENANT RIGHT—"THE POPE'S BRASS BAND"—RIOTS AGAIN—TREASON OF THE SADLIER-KEOGH GANG—CATHOLIC DISABILITIES IN THE ARMY, NAVY, AND PUBLIC INSTITUTIONS—FATE OF SADLIER AND KEOGH.

THE enormous increase of the Irish in Great Britain from 1841 to 1851 meant a corresponding increase of Catholics. Cardinal Manning, speaking of this, says—"Such has been the influx from the pure, untainted fountain of the faith from Ireland, from the land where the pastors never ceased to feed their flock. They were martyred one after another, but the blood of the martyrs is the seed of the Church; when one was martyred another rose in his place. The episcopate of Ireland never ceased, and the succession of her pastors was never broken. Ireland, in the midst of all its poverty and sufferings, and under its Penal Laws, long since removed, has covered the face of the land once more with cathedrals and churches and convents, with seminaries and colleges, not in Ireland alone, but throughout the world. In North America and in Australia, Irish faith and Irish blood have spread and scattered broadcast the seeds of eternal life, which, taking root, springs up a hundredfold." The outward sign of the great impetus given to Catholicity in Great Britain by the immigration from Ireland was the restoration of the Catholic Hierarchy in England after a lapse of two hundred and sixty-five years, the ancient Hierarchy having ended with Thomas Goldwell, Bishop of St Asaph, who died in Rome, April 3rd, 1585. Pope Pius IX. addressed an apostolical letter, dated 24th September 1850, to the Catholics of England. This stated that owing to the great increase in the number of Catholics the time had come when the form of ecclesiastical government should be resumed in England, such as freely existed in other nations, where no particular cause necessitated the existence of Vicars Apostolic.

The Hierarchy was restored on the 29th of September

1850. England became an ecclesiastical province with an archbishop and twelve suffragan bishops, taking their titles from their own sees. A few years later, by a sub-division of existing sees, two more were added. The province of Westminster, comprising England and Wales, now consists of the archiepiscopal see of Westminster, and the fourteen suffragan sees of Birmingham, Clifton, Hexham and Newcastle, Leeds, Liverpool, Middlesboro', Newport and Menevia, Northampton, Nottingham, Plymouth, Portsmouth, Salford, Shrewsbury, and Southwark. Upon Dr Nicholas Wiseman, Vicar Apostolic of the London district, which then came to an end, was conferred the two-fold dignity of Cardinal and Archbishop of Westminster. As the increase in the number of Catholics, which caused the restoration of the Hierarchy, arose from the great influx of the children of the land of St Patrick, it was but fitting that the first head of the restored Hierarchy should also be the son of Irish parents.

Nicholas Wiseman was born on the 2nd of August 1802, at Seville, the capital of Andalusia, in Spain. His father, James Wiseman, was a merchant of Waterford and Seville. His mother was Zaviera Strange, daughter of Peter Strange, of Aylwardstown Castle, Kilkenny. He was brought to England in 1805, and thence to Waterford, where he spent the next two years of his life. When old enough he was sent to Ushaw College, in Durham. In 1818 he left for Rome, where he was entered as a student of the English college. In 1835, after an absence of seventeen years, Dr Wiseman revisited England. On June 8th, 1840, he was consecrated Coadjutor Bishop of Melipotamus; afterwards Coadjutor for the central district of England. On August 29th, 1847, he was translated from the central district, and, on the death of Bishop Walsh, February 18th, 1849, he succeeded as Vicar Apostolic. On the 6th August 1850, he was summoned to Rome by the Pope, and, as we have seen, was made Cardinal Archbishop of Westminster. On the 7th of October he issued a pastoral, "given from the Flaminian gate of Rome," in which he gave the details of the various sees, and directed *Te Deums* to be sung in rejoicing for the restoration of the Hierarchy.

Meanwhile, a perfect storm of indignation was raised throughout Great Britain against the "Papal Aggression," as the act of the Pope was called. It seemed as if nothing but the re-enactment of the Penal Laws against Catholics would satisfy the fury of the bigots. The key-note was given to the howl of indignation by the Prime Minister, Lord John Russell, on the 4th of November, in his famous letter to the Protestant Bishop of Durham. In this he agreed with the bishop in characterising what he termed the "Aggression of the Pope" as "insolent and insidious." He further said—"There is an assumption of power in all the documents that come from Rome—a pretension of supremacy over the realms of England, and a claim to sole and individual sway, which is inconsistent with the Queen's supremacy, with the rights of our bishops and clergy, and with the spiritual independence of the nation, as asserted even in Roman Catholic times." He then foreshadows the penal enactments he has in view. "I will only say," he continues, "that the present state of the law will be carefully examined, and the propriety of adopting any proceedings with reference to the recent assumption of power deliberately considered."

On the 5th of November—gunpowder plot day—the London populace gave vent to their "no-Popery" zeal, by making Cardinal Wiseman the "guy," and burning him in effigy. Later in November the Cardinal Archbishop arrived in London, and, finding the no-Popery agitation going on so fiercely, he wrote a powerful appeal to the people of England. It was of little avail, for John Bull, not so easy to rouse as a rule, was in one of his paroxysms, and the Press lost no opportunity of fanning the flame of popular wrath. The *Times*, as usual, led the "no-Popery" outcry with the malignity it has always shown when the nationality and creed of Irishmen had to be assailed. It was exceeded, if possible, by *Punch*, a periodical which, by its vile and brutal caricatures of the Irish and of their leaders, did so much to stir up hatred and contempt of our race among the English, and a corresponding bitter feeling among the Irish. It was on this occasion that the famous Irish artist and caricaturist, Richard Doyle, severed his connection with *Punch* on account of the insults offered in it to his creed and country.

Among those who joined in the howl against the "Papal Aggression" were certain "noble" English Catholics. Lord Beaumont and Lord Camoys protested against the Pope's action. The Duke of Norfolk, however, went further than either of these, for he felt himself so much of an Englishman, and so little of a Catholic, that he actually renounced his religion. It is understood, however, that he returned to the fold before his death. The present holder of the title has a reputation for piety which is only equalled by the bitterness of his hatred for the Irish cause. Yet these are the kind of men who have ever intrigued, and are still probably intriguing, at Rome against Irish nationality. Their conduct gained the approbation of the British mob, who cheered for Beaumont and Norfolk at their indignation meetings in some places, while in others, such as Cheltenham, they gave vent to their feelings by wrecking the Catholic chapel, and burning the effigy of the Pope.

At many of the meetings language was used that might easily have led to a repetition of the Gordon riots and other "no-Popery" ebullitions which have disgraced British towns. By the end of November the mania had risen to fever heat. In Birkenhead there might have been terrible bloodshed but for the influence of the Catholic clergy upon their people, who had been exasperated almost beyond endurance by the insults offered to their religion and its ministers. A meeting was convened by the bigots, ostensibly for the purpose of enabling the people of Birkenhead to express their opinion on the Pope's action, but, really, by packing the meeting, to get a resolution passed, in denunciation of the "Papal Aggression."

At that time the new docks in the rising town of Birkenhead, which were intended to rival those of Liverpool, were being constructed. As a consequence, a great number of stalwart Irish labourers were employed in the works. This was, as we have already seen, a time of great activity in the construction of railways, and of great public works like these Birkenhead docks, which gave employment to large numbers of the unfortunate victims of the famine who were strong enough for such labour. As we have seen, too, they wanted not only powerful bone and sinew for their daily toil, but courageous hearts to defend themselves, as they so often had to do, against the attacks of the enemies of their creed and race. Thus there were collected in Birkenhead all the materials for a terrible explosion, and it was not the fault of the "no-Popery" fanatics that their match missed fire through the devotion of the Catholic clergy and the loyalty of their flock. The conveners of the meeting announced that none would be admitted but ratepayers, but when the doors were opened only their own adherents were let in. Many, who were refused admission on the plea that they were not ratepayers, went home for their receipts for rates and taxes, but, on their return, were not only refused admission, but the indignant crowd which, as might naturally be expected, gathered, were assaulted by the police—a strong force of these having been drafted from Liverpool. This statement of eye witnesses might be taken as a partizan account, were it not fully borne out by the evidence of the police themselves at the trial which followed. There is a strong family resemblance between what happened at Birkenhead some forty years ago, and the infamous conduct of the police in provoking a riot at Mitchelstown, in more recent years. No doubt if the Liverpool police had been armed with deadly weapons like their Irish brethren, some of these Birkenhead Irishmen would have been butchered like the three men murdered by the police at Mitchelstown. Here is the evidence at the Chester assizes, as given in the English daily papers, of Superintendent Ride, of the Liverpool police. He said that—"At the time he had his men in front of the police court, all was quiet. The space where the people were gathered was open to the public. It was on his suggestion the people were driven off. After the crowd had given way altogether, the police force followed and struck them with their sticks, the people having yielded at the time. He noticed one of the officers following a man as far as the corner of Market Street. The people were driven across Market Street, which was a public highway. He heard complaints in the crowd of ill-usage by the police. This was at the time the Rev. Mr Brown was addressing them, and the complaints were pretty general." The priest, Father Brown, had actually succeeded in pacifying his people, who had, in answer to his appeals, given up their weapons. The *Freeman* correspondent, who cannot be charged with exaggeration as to the conduct of the police, as we have seen by the way his testimony was reluctantly borne out under cross-examination by Superintendent Ride, thus describes the sequel—"During this time several Catholic ratepayers were ignominiously ejected from the steps of the building where the meeting was being held. At length a well-known tradesman was knocked down, kicked, and trampled on by Inspector Birney, of the Birkenhead force. The pent-up insulted feelings of the people, amongst whom were a number of stalwart Irish 'navvies' from the dock works, could bear no more. In less than five minutes the building was gutted, and more than twenty policemen laid *hors-de-combat*—two so seriously wounded as to be pronounced in great peril. The police made a sally, but were again defeated, and another with like success." In the meeting all was consternation. "Where are the magistrates?" cried one. "Where is Sir Edward Cust to lead the police?" Search was made, and the valiant baronet, the Colonel of the Cheshire Light Cavalry, was found hid under the table. Mr Jackson (a magistrate), in great trepidation, exclaimed—"Oh! for God's sake, Mr Brown, appease the people—you only can save our lives."

Owing to Father Brown's exertions, peace was restored and the people were led by him to the chapel-yard, where he addressed them, attributing the disturbance to those who convened the meeting, and exhorting them to be peaceful. In the evening a committee of Catholics met and published an address to their townsmen, detailing the whole circumstances, and adducing facts to prove that the cause and incentives did not originate with them.

Threats were made to wreck St Werburgh's Catholic Church, but the people were up to defend it, and no such attempt was made. At the inevitable trial which ensued, the Irish were, as usual, the sufferers, as the police, who really ought to have been in the dock as the originators of the riot, would not, if they could help it, apprehend any else. The only punishment the police got was a severe censure from the judge, who sentenced three of those brought before him to twelve months imprisonment, and two to nine months. Less than a couple of months afterwards, however, they were discharged in consequence of a numerously signed petition presented in their favour to Government.

The "no-Popery" mania was so rampant that even the theatre was made the scene of its manifestations. "The revival of King John," says the *Times*, "on Tuesday night (December 10th, 1850) at the Haymarket Theatre, was the occasion of a strong anti-Papal manifestation on the part of a numerous audience. Scarcely had Mr Rogers entered in the dress of Cardinal Pandulph, than he was greeted with groans and hisses on every side, and it was with difficulty that silence could be obtained for Mr Macready's denunciation. But when the denunciation of the intruder did come —when King John declared—

' That no Italian priest
Shall tithe or toll in our dominions,'

the enthusiasm was tremendous. The audience, already knowing the tenor of the speech, anticipated the words, and the thunder rather preceded than followed the points."

Lord John Russell, in conformity with the intention expressed in the famous "Durham letter," brought into Parliament, on the 6th of February 1851, what was known as the "Ecclesiastical Titles Bill," which made it illegal for the Catholic bishops to assume the titles of the new sees created by the Pope.

Ireland was by this time somewhat recovering heart after the effects of the famine and the failure of the political action of O'Connell and the Young Irelanders, although wholesale evictions were taking place everywhere throughout the country—north as well as south. An agitation for the reformation of the land system in Ireland, therefore, now arose, and, in the ranks of the Tenant League, Catholic and Protestant Irishmen were to be found on a common platform, trying to raise the condition of their country. Among the leaders were Charles Gavan Duffy, one of the few prominent men of the '48 movement not transported nor in exile, the Government having failed to convict him when put upon his trial; William Sharman Crawford, who, even in O'Connell's time, had sought to bring about an agitation for the protection of the down-trodden Irish farmers; Dr Gray, proprietor and editor of the *Freeman's Journal;* George Henry Moore, a brilliant orator, who, though an Irish landlord, was one of the ablest champions of the rights of the tenant-farmers; and Frederick Lucas, a noble English Catholic convert, who threw in his lot with Ireland at this time—becoming, like the Geraldines, "more Irish than the Irish themselves." Lucas was proprietor and editor of the *Tablet*, which, in his hands, did splendid service for the Catholic religion and for the Irish cause. The *Tablet* has since become an organ of rampant Toryism, and one of the most rancorous enemies of Ireland, while still professing to be an orthodox Catholic newspaper. The Leaguers were well supported in the Press. In addition to the *Freeman* and the *Tablet*, they had the *Nation*, which, suppressed in 1848, had been revived by Duffy soon after his release from prison; the *Banner of Ulster*, edited by an able and honest Presbyterian, Dr M'Knight; the *Cork Examiner*, of which John Francis Maguire, a zealous defender of creed and country, was editor; and other journals. They adopted the policy of what was called "Independent Opposition." They pledged themselves to oppose any Government that did not deal satisfactorily with the demands of the Irish tenant-farmers. There were at this time as corrupt and venal a gang among the Irish members of Parliament as ever cursed any country. In their hearts, as after events showed, they were opposed to the independent policy, yet they had to appear to go with the stream until the time was ripe for the betrayal of their country. These were William Keogh, John and James Sadlier, Anthony O'Flaherty, and some others of the same stamp, who afterwards became famous, or infamous rather, in Irish history, whose objects were office and plunder. The independent policy of the Irish Tenant League was, therefore, gall and wormwood to them, and their aim was in some way to weaken or destroy it. The "Papal Aggression" mania and " Ecclesiastical Titles Bill" were a

Godsend to them, for these enabled them to pose as the champions of religion and the true friends of Ireland. Their eloquence and zeal in Parliament in opposing the Bill gained for them, from the Irish people, the title of "The Irish Brigade," while the English Press had for them the less complimentary designation of "The Pope's Brass Band."

Mr Gladstone, Sir James Graham, and others of the Peelites, opposed the Ecclesiastical Titles Bill, which became law in the same session it was introduced.

At the close of the session the "Brigade" received an enthusiastic welcome in Ireland from a multitude of unthinking people. Sadlier and Keogh and their friends felt, however, that they were the objects of suspicion by the Tenant Right leaders. They, therefore, affected to feel indignant at this. At a meeting, held in Cork on the 8th of March 1852, in connection with the election of a member of Parliament for a vacancy which had occurred, Keogh made his famous declaration of independence of all British parties. After an outburst of indignant eloquence, he exclaimed—"Let the minister of the day be who he may—let him be the Earl of Derby, let him be Sir James Graham, or Lord John Russell—it is all the same to us, and, *so help me God*, no matter who the minister may be, no matter who the party in power may be, I will support neither that minister nor that party, unless he comes into power prepared to carry the measures which universal popular Ireland demands." We shall see how Keogh kept that oath.

The "no-Popery" mania, caused by the "Papal Aggression," was further stirred up by a royal proclamation against Catholic processions. This was the immediate cause of a desperate riot at Stockport, on Tuesday, June 29th, 1852. The enmity against the Irish no doubt had some foundation in the fact that they were becoming numerous in that place, so that the effect of their competition in the labour market was feared. It had been the custom in the town for the Catholics to have an annual procession of the school children, "not," says the *Annual Register*, "a party or sectarian demonstration, but a display of the result of their educational zeal." When the royal proclamation appeared, it was a triumph for the ignorant and bigoted amongst the people of the town, who boasted they would see it enforced against the "young red-necked scholars," as they called the Catholic children. There is such a strong family resemblance between these outbreaks that it is not necessary to go into details; enough to say that in the riot, which broke out with great fury, two Catholic chapels were gutted, and everything within them taken out and burnt or otherwise destroyed. The Irish fought bravely for their homes and their churches, but were overpowered by the immensely superior number of their opponents. Many were severely injured, and one Irishman died from the terrible treatment he received. They were, as usual, made the chief victims of the law in the proceedings which followed. Judge Crompton, in passing sentence on the prisoners convicted of rioting, commented severely on the conduct of the police authorities for the partiality they had shown. In sentencing the three Englishmen who had been convicted, he said it was disgraceful that where a violent mob of three or four hundred persons had been guilty of such base outrages, there should be the least difficulty in bringing before the court many more persons than the three he saw before him. There had been no difficulty, he said, in taking one hundred and thirteen of the parties on the other side. "On the last occasion," he continued, alluding to the Gordon riots of the last century, "that similar outrages were committed, men like the prisoners answered with their lives for their crimes. They had assailed the persons and property of Irish Roman Catholics, denounced the Rev. Mr Frith, upon whose conduct there was not the slightest imputation of blame, they had insulted the feelings of Roman Catholics in every possible way, and trampled on the cross which they should have shrank from injuring."

At the general election of 1852, when the Derby-Disraeli Ministry went to the country, between forty and fifty Irish members were elected who had taken the Tenant Right pledge, some meaning honestly to keep it, and others to take the first opportunity of breaking it, when by so doing they could secure their own personal advancement. It is gratifying to find at this time how true were the instincts of the Irish of Great Britain, and how well they were able to discriminate between the blatant sham champions of "faith and fatherland," who only waited their opportunity to sell both, and the genuine lovers of their country. They showed their correct appreciation of the situation in Ireland, in their usual practical manner, by subscribing to the fund to secure the return of Charles Gavan Duffy for New Ross; meetings being held in various parts of London, and in Birmingham, Liverpool, Bradford, Glasgow, and other places, in furtherance of this object. At the Tenant Right conference, held September 8th, 1852, at which forty Irish representatives were present, the following resolution was proposed by William Keogh—"Resolved: That in the opinion of this Conference it is essential to the proper management of this cause that the members of Parliament who have been returned on Tenant Right principles should hold themselves perfectly independent of, and in opposition to, all governments which do not make it part of their policy, and a Cabinet question, to give to the tenantry of Ireland a measure embodying the principles of Mr Sharman Crawford's Bill." Seeing that there were at this time three parties, the Whigs, Conservatives, and Peelites, in Parliament, and that none of these was strong enough to carry on the government without external aid, there was every prospect of success for the Tenant Right cause, had the Irish party remained an unbroken phalanx.

The long looked for opportunity came, only to find Ireland betrayed once more. The Conservative Ministry went out of office on the rejection of their Budget, on Friday, December 17th, 1852. A new ministry was formed by Lord Aberdeen, and despite their oath and pledges, Keogh and Sadlier, and others of their vile gang, sold themselves for office. From that hour the Irish people—many of whom had been evicted for daring to vote for these men, believing them to be the purest patriots—began to lose faith in constitutional agitation. The great bulk yielded themselves to despair, or became so utterly demoralised as to condone the perjuries of Keogh, Sadlier, & Co., feeling rather proud of their gilded chains, and only seeing in the elevation of these scoundrels to office an honour paid to the creed of the majority of the Irish people.

As the years went by we shall see how the bolder spirits turned their thoughts once more to the pike and rifle; and, as they had seen the open movement of 1848 fail so signally, trying to break their galling chain by the methods of secret conspiracy. We shall see, too, how the never-failing Nemesis overtook the betrayers of their country.

In Great Britain, as elsewhere, where the sons of the Emerald Isle are to be found, the Feast of St Patrick is each year duly honoured in the Catholic Church services; there being frequently, also, eloquent panegyrics on our national Saint. In addition to this there were formerly processions in Liverpool and other places. Though generally creditable displays, they were sometimes the cause of rioting and intemperance. About this time the more rational way of celebrating the national festival, which is now customary, began to be adopted, and, instead of the processions through the streets, there were gatherings in public halls, in which the programmes consisted of selections of Irish national music and addresses by prominent Irishmen. Among the first of these was a celebration in Glasgow in 1853, presided over by the Rev. Dr Cahill—an eloquent religious, political, and scientific lecturer; and one in Liverpool, under the auspices of Father Nugent, the well-known philanthropist and temperance reformer. In still later years these annual gatherings have not only been pleasant re-unions of Irishmen and Irishwomen, but have become powerful means of helping the Irish national cause, through the able addresses of members of the Irish Parliamentary party and other more or less famous speakers.

The treason of the "Irish Brigade" dashed the hopes of the farmers for, at least, a generation, but the honest members of Parliament were still able to do some service for the Irish Catholics in the army and navy. Chief among the champions of Catholic soldiers and sailors was Frederick Lucas. The time was opportune, as England, in 1854, was engaged in the Crimean War, and therefore in a mood to make concessions to Irishmen—if not from a sense of justice, at least from motives of expediency. A review of the history of the previous hundred years will show that it was only when England was at war, and in some sore strait, that any concession was granted to Irishmen or to Catholics. Had the Tenant Right party not been shattered by the villainy of Keogh, Sadlier, and the rest, they, with a little pressure, could now have got all they wanted.

Though Catholics were supposed to be emancipated, this could hardly be said of those in the army and navy, for, besides the greatest inequality of treatment, their conscientious convictions were often grossly outraged. Among other matters which Lucas called attention to, and was instrumental in having amended, was the teaching of the Protestant catechism to Catholic boys in the navy, and the men not being allowed ashore when in port to hear Mass on Sundays. He also called attention to the inadequate pay of Catholic chaplains, who, while they had to minister to one-third of the army, only got one-seventh of the money granted. In one of his speeches in the House of Commons, he gave the following statement of the religious denominations in the army on the 3rd June 1853:

Protestants, . . . 74,330
Presbyterians, . . . 12,765
Catholics, . . . 41,400

128,495

The number of Catholics would give a fair idea of the number of Irish at this time. Lucas had no data as to the number of Catholics then in the navy, but said they could not be less than one-fourth of the whole. That the devoted clergy who ministered to their co-religionists in the Crimea required the aid of championship like his, was apparent from a letter from Father Molloy, a Catholic chaplain in the Crimea, detailing how he had been refused admission to the barracks, and treated with heartless cruelty by the British authorities at Scutari. The *Nation* of November 4, 1854, in denouncing this, says—" It is absolutely sickening to think that our brave countrymen are not only perilling their lives, but their immortal souls, for a Government which exhibits such coarse ingratitude."

The year 1855 was one of terrible depression in Irish politics. It saw the departure from Ireland of Charles

Gavan Duffy, who had kept the flag of nationality flying in the *Nation*, under the most depressing circumstances. He went to Australia, utterly disheartened at the political demoralisation which seemed to be eating out the very heart of Ireland. It also saw the death of the more than Irish Frederick Lucas, who, seeing how England was playing the old game of intrigue against Irish liberty, by trying to rule our country through Rome, appealed in vain to the Pope, and, while returning broken-hearted to Ireland, took ill at Staines, and there yielded up his pure and noble soul on the 22nd of October 1855. There seemed to be now no obstacle to the complete triumph of the treason of the "Brigadiers," yet was the vengeance of heaven surely, if slowly, overtaking them. Edmond O'Flaherty, who had been made a Commissioner of Income-Tax, finding his career of fraud was coming to an end, fled from justice. John Sadlier had acquired possession of enormous sums of money by means of the Tipperary Bank, of which he was the proprietor. The country people of the district had the greatest confidence in it, and it had thousands of depositors. The money of the bank was used by Sadlier in a number of speculative schemes of great magnitude, which, proving failures, he had recourse to all sorts of discreditable means to keep his credit good—including forgery. The inevitable end must come, and, as he saw it approaching, he made all kinds of desperate efforts to stave off impending disgrace. At length, appalled by the certainty of the ruin which he knew the failure of the bank must bring upon thousands of people, by the dread of the terrible exposure fast approaching, and the life of the convict that surely awaited him if he lived, he resolved, rather than face all these, to end his life by poison. With this desperate end in view, he left his house at midnight on Saturday, February 16th, 1856, and, on the Sunday morning, he was found lying dead on Hampstead Heath.

A year later, his brother, James Sadlier, being also guilty of fraud, fled from justice.

The vengeance of heaven seemed to have forgotten the greatest villain of the whole band—William Keogh. He was made a judge for his betrayal of the Irish cause, and, in that capacity, lived for many years, a bitter enemy of his country and of those who sought to help her. But length of years was, doubtless, the greatest curse that could have befallen him, if we are to judge by his state of mind in the closing scene of his wretched life. Being sent to Belgium for the benefit of his health, he there showed such symptoms of insanity as attempting to kill his attendant and himself. He remained in this mental condition, gradually sinking until the day of his death, at Bingen, September 30th, 1878. There are few characters in Irish history more execrated than Judge Keogh.

The fact that England was so hard pressed to keep the field with anything like credit during the Crimean War, made it politic to grant some concessions to the Irish in the army. The terrible "Indian Mutiny" also brought further instalments of justice. The *Madras Examiner* stated that, in 1858, while the struggle was going on, about half of the European soldiers in India were Catholics, and complained of their unfair treatment with regard to the education of their children. It seems that at this time "subsistence money," of five shillings for each child of a soldier, was stopped, where such child, if above four years of age, was not sent to the regimental school, which was conducted on Protestant principles. We read with horror how, in the attempt to force the "Reformation" upon Ireland, the heirs of noble Irish families were seized, and brought up in the "Court of Wards," to hate the creed and country of their fathers. We see how this was paralleled in later times. Bitter, indeed, was the fate of the unfortunate Irishman who was driven to take service under the British flag. If he perished and left little ones behind him, his last moments were tortured by the thought of the loss of their immortal souls, should his orphans be taken into one of the schools of proselytism connected with the army. Indeed, in reckoning up the losses to creed and country in Great Britain, account must be taken of influences like these.

John Francis Maguire, an able and honest Irish member of Parliament, accompanying a deputation to General Peel, the Minister of War, spoke strongly on the difficulties placed in the way of Catholic soldiers getting their children into schools where their faith would not be interfered with. Among other things, he complained of the extraordinary rule of the Hibernian Military School in Dublin, which limited the admission of Catholic children to one-third of the whole, and this while nine out of every ten men recruited in Ireland were Catholics. This was done with a view to getting widows of Catholic soldiers to sacrifice their consciences to their poverty, by entering their children as Protestants.

It was notorious that while such a large proportion of the British army was Catholic, out of five hundred orphan boys at the Duke of York's Military School (a national establishment) there were not a dozen brought up as Catholics, and indeed, children known to the authorities of that establishment to be Catholics had been intentionally educated as Protestants.

BOOK X.

FENIANISM.

CHAPTER XXIII.

JAMES STEPHENS AND THE PHŒNIX CONSPIRACY—JEREMIAH O'DONOVAN (ROSSA)—THE BROTHERHOOD OF ST PATRICK—THE M'MANUS FUNERAL—THE IRISH REVOLUTIONARY BROTHERHOOD IN ENGLAND AND SCOTLAND—INFORMERS AT WORK—SEIZURE OF THE "IRISH PEOPLE"—ARRESTS IN ENGLAND—THE LIVERPOOL IRISH VOLUNTEERS.

AFTER the Sadlier-Keogh treason came a period of apparently unexampled political prostration in Ireland.

Four years previously the "Young Ireland" movement had been broken up and most of its brilliant leaders imprisoned or forced into exile, so that it appeared to many that both moral and physical force had been weighed in the balance and found wanting. If anything further were needed to discredit constitutional agitation it was the shameful sale of themselves to England by the "Pope's Brass Band." The British Government, no doubt, now thought that at length the spirit of the Irish people was totally crushed, and that the reduced population it might be safe still to leave in the country could be used as the drudges of the empire. Green Erin might now become England's kitchen garden, and the viceroy patronizingly told an assemblage of Irishmen that the true destiny of their country was to be "the fruitful mother of flocks and herds"—in other words, that their great end and aim in life was to supply beef and mutton for their English masters.

But though the seed sown in 1848 appeared for a time to have sunk into barren soil, it was destined to fructify, and the generations growing up into manhood eagerly drank in the soul-stirring lessons in prose and poetry which were the legacy left them by "Young Ireland."

Millions of their relatives, too, who had fled from the famine, with vengeance in their hearts against the Government calling itself "civilised," which had allowed its "subjects" to die of starvation, found a home in free America. As a natural consequence, these, in their communications with their friends and relatives at home, became the means of spreading republican ideas in Ireland.

The disgust arising out of the treachery of the "Irish Brigade" helped on these ideas, so that many even who had been disposed to give moral force another trial, who had not sunk into the torpor of despair, and who still hoped to serve their country, swelled the ranks of those who thought that all that was left to them was to "watch and wait" for the hour when once more "England's difficulty" would become "Ireland's opportunity."

In this mood a number of ardent young men in the town of Skibbereen were found, in May 1858, by James Stephens, some ten years after he had been wounded in the attack on the police at Ballingarry.

With John O'Mahony he had spent some time in Paris after the collapse of the Young Ireland movement. This failure, after all the splendid oratory and the magnificent literature which had been brought to bear on the Irish people, seems to have caused Stephens and O'Mahony to come to the conclusion that, to perfect and carry out a successful insurrection, a certain amount of secrecy was required. They must, they thought, fall back upon the methods of the United Irishmen, which had produced, in 1798, an insurrection so formidable, that with more united action and better fortune it might have proved successful. Taking advantage of their stay in the French capital, they made themselves acquainted with the methods of the Continental revolutionists. Arrived in America, they laid the foundation of the Irish revolutionary movement known as Fenianism, this fanciful name being taken from the ancient Fenians, whose prowess is recorded in remote Irish history.

Stephens set himself to the task of spreading the movement in Ireland, and, hearing of the body of young men in Skibbereen who called themselves the "Phœnix National and Literary Society," he was not long in making their acquaintance. He found in them just the material he wanted; the most daring and enthusiastic spirit being a man who has since done and suffered much for the Irish cause—Jeremiah O'Donovan, better known as O'Donovan Rossa, the latter name being derived from the place to which his family belonged. It was not long before the inevitable informer appeared amongst them. A number of arrests were made. Then followed trials and convictions; but the Government, not wishing to make too much of the conspiracy, was satisfied to inflict but light punishment. And so the Phœnix conspiracy collapsed, but only to give place to a more formidable organisation, affiliated to the Fenian Brotherhood in America, and known to the initiated in these islands as the "Irish Revolutionary Brotherhood."

The firing of the first shot in the great American Civil War, on the 9th of January 1861, gave an overwhelming impulse to the Fenian organisation. Hundreds of thousands of Irishmen flocked into the armies engaged on both sides. They formed the backbone of the Northern armies, and without their aid the Union could scarcely have been preserved. Many took service, as Irishmen had done in foreign armies for over two centuries, hoping to use the military training so gained in fighting for freedom for their country. Among these the "circles" of the Brotherhood spread like wildfire.

In Great Britain, too, as well as in Ireland, these circles began to be introduced. In a secret conspiracy there is no absolute safety from a spy, for we have seen many instances where men in the service of a government have actually joined a revolutionary organisation to obtain a knowledge of its movements and to betray its members. But, if strictly carried out, these circles would have made the Brotherhood almost as spy-proof and safe from shipwreck as a vessel built in water-tight compartments. The chief recruiting ground of the Irish Revolutionary Brotherhood, the membership of which was secret, was an organisation having its movements so open that the accounts of the meetings of its branches were published week after week in the newspapers. This was the "Brotherhood of St Patrick," which had its ramifications in most of the provincial towns of England and Scotland. In an address, issued to the "Irishmen resident in London," in April 1861, it is stated that "the single object of the National Brotherhood of St Patrick is to compass the union of Irishmen for the achievement of Irish independence. The sole qualification of membership shall be honest devotion to Irish nationality, based on the conviction that no foreign power has any right to make laws for Ireland." The address concludes with the following significant passage — "A member of the National Brotherhood of St Patrick, by learning the use of arms, does not forego any of his social rights." The organ of this brotherhood was a newspaper, published in London, called the *Irish Liberator*.

During the next few years we read of meetings of branches of the Brotherhood at 27 Dean Street, Soho, in Finsbury, and in other parts of London; in Dewsbury, Sheffield, Bolton, Rochdale, Birkenhead, Stockport, Bootle, and other towns. In Liverpool and Manchester we come across the names of men at this time who were imprisoned for their connection with the Young Ireland movement. The Sarsfield branch held its meetings in Circus Street, Liverpool, one of the Confederate meeting-places in 1848; and the central Liverpool branch met in the Devon Street Hall, where the presence of the irrepressible George Archdeacon sufficiently indicated the character of the proceedings. We find another '48 rebel, John Joseph Finnigan, presiding at a meeting of the Manchester central branch, held at 50 Marshall Street, while other old Confederates were taking a prominent part elsewhere.

Just as the Civil War in America gave an enormous impetus to the Fenian brotherhood, the year 1861 witnessed an event in Ireland which showed that the national spirit had survived the betrayal of the Sadlier-Keogh gang, and was as intense as ever. This was the famous funeral of

Terence Bellew M'Manus, which brought many thousands of recruits into the ranks of the Irish Revolutionary Brotherhood in Ireland and Great Britain. We left M'Manus, thirteen years previous to this, under sentence of transportation to Van Dieman's Land. Thomas Francis Meagher, speaking of the years that followed, said of him—" Throughout all the scenes and changes—in prison—on that wearisome voyage of five months to a penal island—during his lonely exile there—M'Manus showed he possessed the same generous, courageous, glowing heart as ever." From Meagher's description of the every-day life of the '48 prisoners in the convict settlement, it would appear that they were treated after the manner of most civilized nations towards political prisoners, and not with the brutality which has since been shown to Irish rebels against British law. In 1851 M'Manus escaped from Van Dieman's Land, and, reaching California, settled in San Francisco, where he resumed his old business. In the following year Meagher also escaped to California, and received a hearty welcome from his old friend. M'Manus does not appear to have prospered in his business. He remained the same high-spirited, pure-souled patriot he had ever been. In 1860 he heard of a movement for an amnesty for him, and wrote to John Francis Maguire, saying he would refuse it, if offered to him. He would never, he said, return to Ireland, if he could not go without the consent of a foreign ruler.

He kept his resolve, for never again, as a living man, did he touch the soil of Ireland. In the following year he died. His bright spirit was free at last, and all that was mortal of him, it was determined by his friends, was to be sent home to the land he loved so well. The world has rarely seen such a funeral. Across the continent of America the body of M'Manus was borne, and, all along the route, myriads of exiled Irishmen came to show their reverence for his memory, as the mournful cortege passed through the great cities, until it reached New York—the capital of Irish America.

There the remains were placed before the high altar of St Patrick's Cathedral. A solemn requiem was sung for the repose of the soul of the dead patriot, and Archbishop

Hughes addressed the great congregation—assembled to do honour to the memory of M'Manus, and to pray for his eternal rest. The Archbishop dwelt on his love of country, and explained the doctrine of the Church as to when it became lawful to take up arms to resist oppression. Because, he said, M'Manus loved his country, he did not cease to love his God. He loved his Church, and died in her holy communion, and it was for this, besides the public honour his fellow-countrymen paid to his remains, that those remains were before the altar of God, and that every solemn rite was offered up for his eternal welfare.

The body, being conveyed aboard the steamer that was to take it to Ireland, was accompanied by the appointed members of the committee, the more distinguished of them, Meagher, O'Mahony, and Michael Doheny, having to remain behind, as the taint of treason to British rule was still upon them.

The ocean crossed, the remains were landed at Queenstown, on the 30th of October 1861. The funeral obsequies in Cork took place on Sunday, November the 3rd. A vast concourse of people attended, and afterwards followed the hearse to the railway station. From thence the body was conveyed to Dublin, where, previous to interment, it was placed in the hall of the Mechanics' Institute, as the Archbishop of Dublin, Dr Cullen, had refused to permit any lying in state or public ceremonial in any of the churches of his diocese. This deeply stung many whose orthodoxy was beyond question. To them it seemed that the Irish people and their cause were as nothing in his eyes, compared to the temporal advantages the Church might gain from the British Government. The action of the Archbishop of Dublin was, undoubtedly, instrumental in making more Fenians than the efforts of all the "centres," from James Stephens downwards, for they held that here was the fact plainly brought before Irishmen, that they were slaves in their own land. Here, they said, was a man of stainless life, whose career was worthy of the admiration of all lovers of humanity, whose remains and memory had, in a foreign land, been treated by the dignitaries of the Church, of which he was a faithful son, with the honour befitting them—here were those remains refused in his own land, lest it should offend the Government, the rites accorded even to the sinful and the erring. Truly, they said, the lot of the Irishman who loves his country would seem to be a hard one, if he is to be banned both here and hereafter, for, according to Dr Cullen, what was right and praiseworthy in New York, must be reprehensible in Dublin.

Thank Heaven! the reign of the "Castle Bishops" in Ireland is at length ended, and never were bishops and priests and people more united than now, while the love of Irishmen for their faith is as ardent as ever.

On Sunday, November 10th, 50,000 men followed the hearse to Glasnevin, where the body of Terence Bellew M'Manus was interred, amid the prayers of the people.

On both sides of the channel the ranks of the Irish Revolutionary Brotherhood became enormously increased by the excitement and enthusiasm created by the M'Manus funeral. Some idea of the number of its adherents may be formed from the circulation its organ, *The Irish People*, then had in England and Scotland. Mr A. M. Sullivan, in his "New Ireland," says of that journal—"Its existence enabled us in the *Nation* office—as, no doubt, it enabled the Government also—to ascertain substantially where Fenian and non-Fenian nationalism prevailed. It swept all before it among the Irish in England and Scotland, almost annihilating the circulation of the *Nation* in many places north and south of the Tweed."

Two of the most active of the first organisers of the I.R.B., as the Irish Revolutionary Brotherhood was often termed, in England, were John Flood and John Vincent Ryan. John Savage, in his "Fenian Heroes and Martyrs," says of Flood—"He is a fine-looking man, of large person, and frank, handsome features, adorned by an ample beard of a tawny colour. His bearing is upright and stalwart. He is (in 1868) about thirty years of age, and a Wexford man. . . . His companions speak of him as a man of great energy, who always stood faithfully to his work and was respected and relied on by the people." John Ryan was what was called a "Liverpool Irishman." His family were in comfortable circumstances, his father being a prosperous merchant of Liverpool. He received a good education. His favourite reading was the literature of the Young Irelanders. He was a proficient in all athletic exercises. Many of his old school-fellows, who followed his body to Ford Cemetery a few years ago, still speak of him as he was in his youth and early manhood, a splendid specimen of humanity—physically, mentally, and morally; one who would have been received by acclamation into the ranks of the ancient Fenians; for he had all the gifts necessary for admission into that band of heroes, whose prowess we read of in the ancient chronicles of Erin.

The Government had, through their paid agents—men of the Talbot and Le Caron type—and, indeed, from the desire for notoriety among incautious men of the I. R. B. itself, been long aware of the progress of Fenianism. During 1865 there were several informers at work in Ireland, figuring as red-hot patriots until they had got sufficient information for the Government to make a swoop. One of these was Pierce Nagle, an employe in the office of the *Irish People.*

There were Government spies and informers at work in England, too. Such was Francis Pettit, an army pensioner, who had been imprudently taken into their confidence by members of the Brotherhood in the north of England. On Saturday, 26th August 1865, according to his evidence at subsequent trials, Pettit was returning from Swinton, near Manchester, in company with a man named William Kenny, who worked at Longshaw's Cotton Factory, at Pendlebury. They conversed, among other things, on Fenianism, and Kenny, Pettit said, induced him to take the following oath or pledge:—

" I, Francis Pettit, do solemnly promise and swear that I shall be faithful and bear true allegiance to the Irish Republic now virtually established, and that I will take up arms at a moment's notice in defence of the same," &c.

There was more than this, Pettit said, but he could not recollect the rest of it. Three days after this, Kenny called at his house. After that, on Sunday, the 3rd of September, they went to a meeting at the house of Patrick Scally, in Salford. There, Pettit said, he was introduced to Scally and to a man named Thomas Quigley, a silversmith, of 26 Hollis Croft, Sheffield. This Sheffield Irishman, according to Pettit's story, told him that he had been travelling in Ireland, and that they had agents in every part drilling the people; that there was not a militia regiment in which they had not large numbers of men sworn in; and that in some regiments they had every man. In reply to Pettit's question, Where they were going to get arms and ammunition from? Quigley said they were getting plenty. They got rifles by contract in Birmingham at twenty-six shillings a piece, and they had twenty or thirty thousand rifles about Dublin, and large quantities of ammunition, besides what were in other parts of the country. Scally and Kenny heard this conversation, and Kenny turned to Pettit, and said, "What do you think of that? Are you satisfied now?" Then, taking Pettit by the shoulder, Kenny said, "Now, my boy! you will be a general yet. You are the boy can handle a regiment in style." It was then arranged that Pettit was to go over to Ireland as military instructor, and a letter was written by Quigley and given to him, addressed to Mr O'Connor, 12 Parliament Street, Dublin. He also received a second letter directed to the same place, signed "John Fottrell" and "Patrick Scally." When these letters were given to the embryo "military instructor," Fottrell was not in the same room, but in one below. Fottrell walked a short distance with Kenny and Pettit, and parted with them at the bottom of Blackfriars Street, Salford, saying there was to be a meeting that night at a certain public-house in Manchester, and that there would be about three hundred of "the family" there. Before they parted Kenny invited Pettit to a meeting at Eccles at 9 o'clock that evening. He did not attend, but he afterwards met Kenny, who said they would have raised money to send him over to Ireland had he been there. The money for this purpose appears to have been raised, for Pettit relates how, on the 8th of September, he left for Ireland. Previous to doing so, indeed as soon as he got the letters of introduction into his possession, he wrote to the War Office, and a Manchester police officer called on him in due course with the letters he had sent. Pettit then handed to him the two letters of introduction he had got. The officer, having copied these, gave them back to Pettit, who told him it was his intention to go over to Ireland and get all the information he could. Arriving in Dublin, he made his way to the office of the *Irish People*, and handed his letters of introduction to Mr O'Connor. He also saw O'Donovan Rossa. He was told to call on Monday. He did so, and was brought upstairs. There he again met Rossa, and told him he was a sworn member of the organisation, and had been engaged by Quigley as a military instructor. Rossa told him that the men in England from whom he had got the letters had no authority for what they had done. An effort was made to find him employment at a new Catholic church which was being erected in Thomas Street, and, in response to a letter from Pettit describing how he was stranded in Dublin, Scally of Manchester sent him a letter of sympathy, enclosing a remittance. Pettit's career as a spy was but a short one, for O'Donovan Rossa was convinced, at their first interview, that he was an agent of the Government. He appears to have done his best for his employers, and was very anxious for an introduction to Stephens. "The Old Man," as the "chief organiser of the Irish Republic" was sometimes called by his friends, was not by any means so anxious to see *him*, as we gather from the following letter found on James O'Connor when he was arrested:—

"*Friday.*

"MY DEAR FRIEND,—Mrs O'Shaughnessy and John Ryan of Liverpool met me with the others to-night. I gave Mr Quigley no authority to send over parties such as those in question. We have more than enough of them, and, even if otherwise, I will not have them put upon me. Settle the matter as best you can. I will not see this man or any coming in such a way.—Yours, J. P."

This was one of the signatures used by James Stephens. He sometimes also signed his communications "J. Power." For the moment no use was made of Pettit by the police, who kept him in reserve until they had struck a sudden blow at the organisation, which placed in their hands a vast mass of evidence in corroboration of what they already had from the informers.

This was the seizure of the *Irish People*, and the arrest of a number of the leaders, on the 15th of September 1865— an indication that the conspiracy was now to be grappled with in the open. Among those arrested at the time, or soon afterwards, were O'Donovan Rossa, John O'Clohissy, Thomas Ashe, Michael O'Neill Fogarty, Mortimer Moyniham, W. F. Roantree, Thomas Clarke Luby, George Hopper, John O'Leary, and James O'Connor—but James Stephens, the master spirit of the I. R. B., was not to be found.

The blow struck in Ireland was speedily felt here, for among the papers seized were many addresses of members of the Brotherhood in England, and other compromising documents. Pettit's information was used to supplement this, and many arrests were made. On the Thursday following the seizure of the *Irish People*, two detectives from Dublin arrested, at 52 Townsend Street, Sheffield, James Quigley, on a charge of treason. He had been employed as a travelling agent. Documents were found in his possession which showed his connection with the I.R.B., and which, with those seized at the *People* office, led to other arrests. He was remanded to Ireland for trial. The police were acting with great promptitude, for, on the same day, Dublin detectives arrested, in Salford, the two men who had given Pettit a letter of introduction—Patrick Scally, a bookbinder by trade, and John Fottrell, a porter employed in the Victoria Station of the London and North-Western Railway. Scally was taken at his house, 41 Chapel Street, Salford. Fottrell was found at his work. On searching his house, in Kidderminster Court, Chapel Street, Salford, the police found documents relating to the Fenian movement, and a quantity of arms and ammunition. He had been a Young Irelander, and had to leave the country in 1848, having only recently returned to England.

Certain documents, found, after the arrests, in Dublin and Sheffield, contained such information as determined the Irish executive upon making further arrests. Among those captured was the inevitable George Archdeacon. It will be remembered that in the Repeal agitation he was deposed from his rank as Warden, and expelled by O'Connell for his warlike propensities. He was an energetic Confederate in 1848, and an active agent of the Brotherhood of St Patrick in 1861. On the morning of Saturday, 23rd of September 1865, Sergeants Smollen and Dawson, of the Dublin detective department, arrived in Liverpool, bearing a warrant, signed by Lord Wodehouse, for the arrest of Archdeacon. He was then between fifty and sixty years of age, and, as we have seen, quite a veteran in the various Irish movements. At the expiration of his term of imprisonment received in 1848, he went to America, where he remained about seven years, becoming during that time a naturalised citizen. He returned to England about 1855, and for a short time took up his residence in London, afterwards removing to Manchester for a few months. In 1861 we find him in Liverpool, a prominent man in the Brotherhood of St Patrick. For some time after that, up to 1865, he resided at No. 11 Bidder Street, Islington, where he kept a small periodical shop and carried on a stationery business—a special feature of which was his agency for the *Irish People*. Here the Dublin detectives, in company with two of the Liverpool fraternity, found him. They called him out and charged him with high treason. He appeared surprised, and immediately said—"You have no right to touch me; I am an American citizen, and I have a paper in my pocket to show it." He was, however, taken to the detective office, and there he was again charged. He demanded to see the warrant, and it was shown and read to him. It charged him with, "having been connected with divers other parties in certain acts of high treason." He repeated that he was an American citizen, and produced a document to show this. After this his house in Bidder Street was searched, and a quantity of letters and other documents, tending to establish his connection with the Brotherhood, were found. There were letters from Sheffield, London, and various towns in Lancashire; also from New York, intimating that sums of money had been from time to time forwarded to him to enable him to visit the various towns and to forward the movement in this country.

There were traces of his having been to Burnley, Blackburn, Bolton, and other places in Lancashire, in furtherance of his mission, and in one of the documents he was designated as "the delegate representing Lancashire." A great quantity of copies of the *Irish People* were seized in Archdeacon's shop. In consequence of the suddenness with which the arrest was made, he was taken to the station without having an opportunity of communicating with his wife and daughter, who were in the house. Mrs Archdeacon complained bitterly of this, saying she had lost her father, her brother, and her son "by the English," and that owing to English laws she was about to lose her husband. Archdeacon was removed to Dublin by the steamer *Columbia*, which sailed from Liverpool at ten o'clock the same night.

It was considered important, in connection with statements which had been made relative to members of the I.R.B. being among the Liverpool volunteers, that, while the detectives were searching Archdeacon's house, two young men, wearing the uniform of the "Irish Brigade," a local volunteer corps, came in and asked for copies of the *Irish People*. There was a great scare in England at this time, particularly in places like Liverpool, where there was a strong Irish element. An uneasy feeling, consequently, prevailed as to the loyalty of the Irishmen in the naval reserve and the volunteers—particularly in the one distinctively Irish corps. Colonel Bidwill, who commanded it, and the other officers, strenuously maintained the loyalty of their men, and the authorities affected to believe this. Nevertheless, some time afterwards, the whole of their arms were removed to the storehouse of another corps, on the plea that the storehouse of the Irish corps was not strong enough to baffle any attempt to carry off the arms. Adjutant Graves, who was very popular among the men, could not but have had a shrewd suspicion, from the soldier-like bearing of the young Irishmen who were about this time joining the corps in such numbers, and the readiness with which they went through their exercises, that possibly they had been drilled before on the hills of Cork or Tipperary, by moonlight, or on the strand near Dublin. In the years from 1865 to 1868 the members of this Liverpool Irish Corps were undoubtedly men of a finer physique and higher intelligence than those who have been in it in later years. Not but that these last would make good fighting materials, too, for, though many of them have never seen the old sod, they come of the pugnacious Irish race. They seem, however, more like the types you meet about Scotland and Vauxhall Roads, and Marybone, who so largely form the rank and file of the Lancashire militia, formerly known as the "green linnets," from the colour of the uniform they wore some years since.

CHAPTER XXIV.

ARREST OF STEPHENS—TRUE STORY OF HIS ESCAPE, TOLD BY JOHN DEVOY, ONE OF HIS RESCUERS—DEVOY AND STEPHENS ON THE CHANCES OF A RISING IN 1865— MORE ARRESTS IN ENGLAND—ARMS FOR IRELAND.

THE authorities felt that they had accomplished but little while the head of the revolutionary organisation was still at large, so that the utmost vigilance was used by the police for the capture of Stephens. Their efforts were at length successful. On the morning of Saturday, November 11th, 1865, he was arrested at Fairfield House, Sandymount, where he had been living for some time as "Mr Herbert." With him were also taken three others of the Fenian chiefs —Charles Kickham, Hugh Brophy, and Edward Duffy.

The arrest and subsequent escape, early on Saturday morning, November 25th, of James Stephens, form one of the most exciting chapters in Irish history. The following graphic account of his escape from prison, and of the position of the revolutionary movement in Ireland at the time, is from the pen of John Devoy, who, as will be seen, was a prominent actor in what he so vividly describes—

"The principal actors in the affair are all now in this city (New York). Five of those who took part in it are dead. Another one is in Australia, and two only are still living in Ireland, so that there is no longer any reason for concealing the facts. They will serve to illustrate both the strength and the weakness of Fenianism, its power of commanding sacrifices from a large portion of the people, including men in the service of the Government, and its utter poverty of resources for the physical struggle with England which was the object of its existence.

"James Stephens was at that time unquestionably the most popular and powerful man in Ireland. He was hated by the loyalists as no man had been hated since the days of Daniel O'Connell, and if his influence over the masses was considerably less than that of the great agitator, it was all powerful with a very large class of the people. His will was law to an organisation numbering fully 80,000 men. The Irish in America regarded him as the predestined leader of a revolution.

"The movement inaugurated by Stephens first attracted outside attention on the seizure of its organ, the *Irish People*, in September 1865, and the arrests which culminated in that of the leader some weeks later. The arrest of Stephens, Kickham, Duffy, and Brophy at Fairfield House, and the seizure of the documentary evidence found there were naturally regarded by the Castle as the death blow of the conspiracy. It spread dismay among the rank and file of the Fenians. While this feeling was not shared by the leaders still at large, they could not help recognising the fact that their followers were much discouraged by the blow. They went on with their preparations, however, and those who know the facts are now convinced that had Mr Stephens remained in prison an insurrection of a much more serious character than that which was so easily suppressed in March, 1867, would have broken out.

"Stephens, on being brought before the magistrate for preliminary examination, made a defiant speech which caused his followers and the public to believe that he was backed by strong resources. He was credited with entertaining a confidence of ultimate success which, unless bereft of common sense, he could not have really felt. A few days later every one was satisfied that he knew all about the escape which afterwards took place, and that this knowledge justified his attitude of defiance. He has ever since encouraged this belief, but the simple truth is it was

ARREST OF STEPHENS.

utterly without foundation. Mr Stephens at that time knew nothing whatever of the possibility of escape, and the idea had not yet entered the mind of the man who afterward conceived and executed the plan which restored the Chief Organizer to liberty.

"Here are the facts: Among the officers of the prison were John J. Breslin, hospital steward, and Daniel Byrne, one of the two night watchmen. Both are now residents of this city, Byrne being on the police force, and Breslin in Commissioner Coleman's department. Byrne was a member of the Fenian organisation, having been sworn in by Captain John Kerwan, the ex-Papal zouave, now also of this city, but Breslin, although a man of strong nationalist opinions, did not belong to any organisation. All his brothers, however, were Fenians. One of them, who has since been Vice-President of the Land League in this city, was at that time an acting Inspector of the Dublin police, and clerk in the Superintendent's office, a station which enabled him to render most important service to the conspirators. Learning from a conversation with one of his brothers that the arrest of Stephens was regarded by the Fenians as a serious blow, and having been favourably impressed by some conversation with and observation of the man himself in prison, John Breslin determined to set him at liberty. Through his brother Neal he got into communication with Colonel Thomas J. Kelly, now of the New York Custom House, whose rescue by an armed band of Fenians in the streets of Manchester two years afterward led to the hanging of Allen, Larkin, and O'Brien. Kelly had almost from the seizure of the *Irish People* newspaper, two months before, been the actual manager of the movement, although everything was done in the name of the C. O. I. R. After the arrest of Stephens, General E. F. Millen had been elected to fill his place temporarily, and Kelly, who was not favourable to the new appointment, eagerly grasped at Breslin's proposal to release the chief whom all would recognise. Kelly was a man of great intelligence and force of character, who had resided many years in the United States, had served through a portion of the Civil War, had risen to the rank of captain in an Ohio regiment, and had been on the staff of General

Thomas. He entered into correspondence with Stephens, through Breslin, whose daily tour through the prison with the doctor gave him many opportunities for communicating with the prisoners. Breslin had, besides, several personal interviews with Stephens, and the details of the plan were easily communicated to the latter.

"The plan was very simple and effective, and was Breslin's in every detail. Stephens was placed in one of the hospital cells in a small corridor on the third floor. The only other occupants of the corridor were his colleague, Charles J. Kickham, the popular poet and novelist, who recently died in Dublin, and a regular jail-bird named M'Leod. The Governor, to provide against all possibility of escape, had a police sentinel placed on the other side of the door leading to that portion of the prison where O'Leary, Luby, Mulcahy, Roantree, and the other Fenian prisoners were quartered, while the other entrance to the corridor was secured by two doors, one of wood and the other of iron. M'Leod was in a cell between the cells of Stephens and Kickham, and had orders from the Governor to ring his cell gong on the first sound of anything unusual in the neighbouring cells. This would have at once given the alarm, and have effectually prevented escape. The police officer could not unlock the door between him and the corridor, and the iron door at the other end could only be opened by the pass-key, which was locked in the Governor's safe. The Governor's office, where all the keys were deposited at a certain hour every evening, was effectually protected from all attempts from the inside by a heavy iron gate, locked on the side facing the main entrance.

"Breslin had a latch-key which opened the door of the hospital where he slept, and that leading to the portion of the prison where Stephens was confined. To enable him to enter the corridor he must have a pass-key, and to open the cell door another key. He took impressions in beeswax of the regular keys in use in the daytime, and new ones were filed down to fit the impressions by an optician still resident in Dublin. Even at this early stage of the affair a hitch occurred which showed the lack of precision and promptness characterising the whole Fenian movement.

The bees-wax was not forthcoming at the time appointed. After waiting several days, Breslin was obliged to go out and buy it himself, thus running the risk of giving a clue to the police that might be the means of convicting him if brought to trial. The keys were finally in Breslin's hands, but even at the last moment he was obliged to do some filing on one of them, and to run some extra risk by fitting it to the lock of a door that Byrne, his colleague in the enterprise, could not open.

"The keys having been fitted, Colonel Kelly was notified, and arrangements were made to receive Stephens on the outside of the prison walls. Byrne was on the watch every second night. The 21st was chosen because that was one of his nights on duty, and for a more singular reason. Breslin had a superstition that the 21st was a lucky day for him, because nearly all his strokes of good fortune had befallen him on that day of the month.

"So sure were the authorities of the safety of the captives that no military guard was placed in the prison, but a regiment of cavalry and a battery of artillery were quartered at Portobello barracks, within fifteen minutes' walk. The only guard was a detachment of Metropolitan Police, four of whom were stationed inside the main entrance, and others at various points in the prison.

"At the inception of the plot Colonel Kelly sent for me, and told me the duty I was to perform. For two months the police held a warrant for my arrest, and my description was in the *Hue and Cry*. Like many others who were wanted by the police, I remained in Dublin waiting for the fight which we all confidently expected, and I could attend to no regular business. I had been placed in charge of the organisation in the British army. We numbered about 15,000 men, fully 8000 of whom were then stationed in Ireland. For that and other reasons I happened to be better acquainted with the local officers and rank and file of the Dublin organisation than any man then within Kelly's reach. He told me he wanted me to pick out from ten to twenty of the very best men I knew in Dublin for a special work requiring courage, coolness, and self-control. They all ought to know how to use revolvers, but were not to use

their arms even if fired upon, except ordered to do so.
They were to be capable of making a desperate fight if
necessary. I was to avoid as much as possible selecting
'centres,' or men filling other positions demanding constant attention. Kelly did not then tell me the exact
nature of the work, but I had no doubt it was a rescue of
'The Old Man.' A few days later, when I reported for
his approval the men I had selected, he told me it was to
act as a bodyguard for Stephens on his release by men
inside the prison: that there would probably be no need
for us, but we were to be on hand in case any accident
should interrupt the escape. A dozen men, he said, would
be quite enough, including himself and two others. These
two were John Ryan, the son of a Liverpool dry goods
merchant, a splendid type of man, mentally and physically,
and the optician. He told me I was to have charge of the
party under his directions, and I was to conceal them in
small squads in positions covering every avenue of approach
to the prison.

"I selected eight men, whom I considered to be the best
fitted for all the possibilities involved in the attempt.
Nearly all of them were wanted by the police, and many
afterward suffered imprisonment. Most of them had seen
some kind of service. All except one were powerfully knit
men of proved courage, and all knew how to handle both
rifle and revolver. Paddy Kearney, a Dublin blacksmith,
had served many years in the British army, and was a man
of exceptional courage and decision of character. He had
been somewhat of a tough in his younger days, but had a
strikingly handsome face and a splendid physique. He had
great natural military talent, and had he not been behind
prison bars at the time of the rising later on, Kearney's
Tigers, as the rough diamonds composing his circle were
called, would have given a good account of themselves.
Michael Cody, a friend of Kearney, was a low-sized but extremely powerful man, of great determination. He had a
weakness for punching policemen occasionally, but, like
Kearney, had a face which was a model for an artist. He
had served some years in the Dublin militia. John Harrison was a corn porter of magnificent proportions, who had

spent some time in the English navy, and seen service at Bomarsund under Admiral Napier. He had never had any difficulty with the police, but had knocked out the best men among the Dublin coal porters, who were at that time mostly anti-Fenians. Dennis Duggan was a young coach-builder, who had served in the English volunteers, and was noted for his courage and coolness. Jack Mullen was the son of a Dublin shopkeeper, and had led a roving life. When a boy he had enlisted in the English, and had later on served in the American navy, participating in some of the principal naval fights of the civil war. Matthew O'Neill was a Dublin stonecutter, who had never seen any service. He was centre in one of the most important circles in the city, and was a man of fine physique. Jack Lawler had never been a soldier, and was rather small, but was recommended as a man of great pluck. William Brophy was a carpenter and a strong civilian. These, with Kelly, the two men chosen by him, and myself, were the only persons outside the walls of Richmond prison that night.

"Colonel Kelly informed me that a supply of revolvers would be ready, so that each man would be fully armed and prepared. None of the men was informed of the nature of the work required, but Colonel Kelly confided the secret to a few of those around him, and they in turn revealed it to a few friends. In this way the story spread, until at least 200 men in Dublin knew that 'the Captain' was to be taken out. The subject had become a pretty general topic of conversation among the officers of the organization. This led to serious embarrassment. Scores of men, especially the recently arrived Irish-American officers, felt hurt because they were not chosen to take part in the affair, and they angrily remonstrated. One man, who heard the rumour just as he was leaving for the south, was so overjoyed at the prospect that on the very night of his escape he confided the knowledge to a soldier of the Fourth Royal Irish Dragoon Guards, then stationed at Ballincollig, County Cork, whom he wanted to swear into the conspiracy. The trooper refused to be sworn in, and immediately gave information to the authorities, who sent it to the Castle. It reached Cork Hill about the time the news of the escape was spreading dismay among the officials. Had the dragoon's story reached Dublin a few hours earlier, Stephens would have been sent to break stones in Portland prison with O'Leary, Luby, and his other lieutenants.

"At length the day fixed for the escape arrived. All was ready inside the prison, and the authorities had not the faintest suspicion of anything wrong. The same police guard did duty; no soldier was any nearer than Portobello Barracks, and the Governor retired as usual in full security, and without a shadow of suspicion. No movement either of troops or police indicated the taking of any precautionary measures, or the existence of the slightest misgiving for the safety of the caged Fenian chief. The crown lawyers and the Sheriff were busily preparing for the trials, and every partisan of British rule in Ireland looked hopefully forward to the speedy collapse of the conspiracy. A few striking examples were to be made; the prisoners of lesser note were to be let off with short terms of imprisonment, and panic and demoralisation could be trusted to do the rest. Ireland would relapse into the calm of despair, and the crowbar brigade and the emigrant ship would soon effect a final solution of the Irish problem. Dublin Castle slept tranquilly that night, with no warning of the panic and consternation that overtook it on the morrow.

"Toward midnight the little squad of men told off for a body guard dropped one by one into Lynch's public house in Camden Street, a short distance from the prison, and quietly awaited the word to move. But the promised revolvers were not forthcoming, and much disgust was expressed. Kearney, who had a hot temper, flew into a violent rage, and berated the leaders for their neglect. He was a born soldier, and expected soldierly precision and promptitude in such matters. 'If they mismanage a little thing like this,' he said, 'how is it going to be when the real work comes?'

"The men could have supplied themselves if they had known in time that the promised revolvers would not be on hand. Every man had some time previously been ordered to put his weapons away in safe keeping, and revolvers could not be got at short notice. We had been assured by Kelly that the weapons would be ready at a certain time and place that evening, but they were not there. The man deputed by Kelly to bring them had turned the work over to another, who in turn left it to a third, and the last man neglected or misunderstood his instructions. At a late hour in the evening we had to hire an outside car and apply to friends living in different parts of the city, and by midnight all but four of the men had revolvers. Two were brought to the spot where Colonel Kelly and a few of the men were stationed in a field opposite the prison, about an hour before the escape, by Nicholas Walsh, a well-known Dublin artist, who has since then died in Florence. Eleven men only had revolvers: one had a large knife, and a thirteenth man, whose name I have not mentioned and who came without orders, had no weapon whatever, and was sent home early in the night. Not a man refused to go to the ground, although some were unarmed when they started out. They fully expected a fight with police, warders, or soldiers, before the work was finished.

"The night was dark and wet, and the few policemen on duty in the lonely neighbourhood of the prison kept as much as possible under shelter. A thorough search was made of the Circular Road, on which the prison fronts, Love Lane, the bank of the Grand Canal, which runs at the rear of the prison, and a little lane running from the Circular Road to Sally's Bridge, which crosses the canal close to the prison grounds. One policeman was met sheltering himself under an elm tree on the canal bank, and another peeped out of a hallway on the Circular Road, near Clanbrazil Street, but a little conversation, enlivened by a swig from a flask of whiskey, revealed the fact that not a single extra man was out and that nothing startling was expected.

"The men arrived on the ground by different routes in small groups, and quietly took up positions previously assigned them. Kelly, Ryan, the optician, and Brophy were at a point opposite the prison wall, in a field on the other side of the Circular Road, keeping in the shadow of a high wall running diagonally inward from the road. Kearney, Cody, Mullen, and Lawler were placed under the shadow of a hedge at the gate of the field, directly opposite the prison gate. Harrison, Duggan, and O'Neill were in a little dark nook at the Love Lane end of the prison wall, between the latter and the wall of a cabbage garden that lay between the Circular Road and the canal. My instructions were to move from post to post, reporting at intervals to Colonel Kelly, till the time fixed for the escape, when I was to take my place with him. A low mud wall separated the field from the road, and in a hole on the inside of this wall John Ryan had, earlier in the evening, deposited a coil of stout rope, with knots arranged at about every two feet of its length, so as to make it easier to climb by when flung over the wall.

"Here the men waited in the drizzling rain for hours for the signal which was to tell them that Stephens had been let out of the prison, and was waiting inside the outer wall for the rope to be thrown over. He was to throw a stone over the wall as a signal that the rope was wanted, and the 'quack, quack,' of a duck repeated by Ryan was to announce that the moment was at hand. There was a genuine duck in a neighbouring garden that raised a false alarm once. The C. O. I. R. was an hour behind time.

"When the prison clock struck one, Breslin left his quarters in the hospital, and quietly opened the door leading to the corridor where Stephens' cell was situated. No one else was up but Byrne and Stephens, who was waiting in his cell dressed and ready to move. Ascending the stairs noiselessly, Breslin opened the two doors leading into the corridor as quietly as he could, but it was impossible to do so without making a slight noise. The policeman on the other side of the door at the other end might hear if he was listening, and if M'Leod was awake there would be trouble. Stephens heard Breslin turn the key in the cell door. He slid from the hammock, where he had been lying dressed. No superfluous words were spoken. Stephens, after receiving a loaded revolver from Breslin, followed the latter as noiselessly as possible out of the corridor and down the stairs. Here an anxious pause of a few moments was made. If M'Leod, the jail-bird, rang his gong, all was over, but no sound came from his cell. He afterward explained his silence by saying that the key which let Stephens out of his cell would also open his, and that had he given the alarm his throat would have been cut. Hearing no alarm, Breslin opened the door leading out into the prison yard. Between this yard and the Governor's garden was a very high wall, which had to be crossed before the outer wall could be reached. Breslin had been assured that the ladder used in lighting the lamps in the yard was long enough to enable a man to cross the wall, but on making the experiment now he found that a tall man standing on the top rung of the ladder could not reach within several feet of the top of the wall. This was a serious hitch. M'Leod might have rung his gong and alarmed the prison without Breslin being able to hear it, and not a moment could be spared. After a hurried consultation he decided to return to the prison, and with Byrne's help bring out two long tables from the lunatics' dining-room on which to place the ladder. There was an unoccupied sentry-box close to where they stood, and inside this he placed Stephens, for all he knew there might be a policeman stationed in the Governor's garden. So, assuring Stephens that Byrne and he would take care of anything between the sentry-box and the prison door, he told him to shoot any man coming from the other direction.

"The two tables were carried out as quickly as possible, and placed one on top of the other against the wall at a point where Breslin knew there was a tool shed on the other side, which would facilitate the descent. The ladder was then placed on the upper table and held by Byrne and Breslin, while Stephens ascended.

"As Stephens stepped on the ladder he turned round and handed Breslin the revolver. This left an unfavourable impression on Breslin which nothing could efface. If there should be a policeman in the Governor's garden he could easily stop the further progress of the fugitive, and the men outside the wall could do nothing to aid him. Stephens climbed up the ladder, and, although there was some glass on the top of the wall, easily got over it, and dropped down to the shed on the other side, and thence to the ground. He walked over to a pear tree indicated by Breslin, which grew close to the outer wall, and which would aid him in climbing it. Hearing no footsteps outside, he took a handful of sand and flung it over the outer wall into the Circular Road.

"This signal was at once recognised. It was only the work of a minute for the little party with Kelly to cross the road and fling one end of the rope over the wall. Four of us held it, and immediately we felt a pull on it. There was evidently some hesitation on Stephens' part about climbing, and, after waiting a moment or two, some of us cried out, 'It's all right; we'll hold this end while you climb.'

"In a second there was a strong tug at the other end, and we felt him struggling upward, till at last we saw his head and shoulders at the top of the wall about eighteen feet high. The whole party had by this time rushed to the spot, and 'The Old Man' was greeted good naturedly, but in muttered tones. He peered down as if doubtful as to who might be below, and was quite out of breath. After he had vainly tried to hitch the rope between two stones on the top of the wall, John Ryan told him to drop down with his back to the wall, and we would catch him. He did so, and Ryan caught his feet on his breast, the sand on the soles leaving the imprint of the shoes on his buttoned coat. It staggered Ryan, and as he was coming down I caught Stephens about the knees and let him slide to the ground. When he reached it his clothes were puckered round his body, and, as he had grown fat in prison, it made him cut a rather ludicrous figure. I felt him tremble as I let him down, and this fact, caused probably as much by the exertion as by nervousness, gave the first shock to the belief I had previously entertained in his coolness and self-possession. The boys gathered around him, and, shaking his hand with Irish fervour, gave vent to their satisfaction in characteristic fashion. To all this his only answer was in a husky whisper to Kelly, 'Come on : come on.'

"Stephens and Kelly at once crossed the road and turned into Love Lane, a long, winding street running through market gardens and having few houses. From Love Lane they turned into Brown Street. In this street was the house where the C. O. I. R. was to be concealed. Mrs Boland, a sister of Mr James O'Connor of *United Ireland*, and now a resident of Brooklyn, had undertaken to shelter him, and a bright boy of fifteen, who had acted as messenger between Stephens and Kelly before his arrest, was on the look out. He had marked the house by dropping a number of small pieces of paper in a line on the sidewalk, trusting to the rain to keep them in their places, but by the time the two conspirators reached the spot the rain had ceased and a gust of wind blew the bits of paper in front of the next house, where lived a bitter Orangeman. They were just about to ring the Orangeman's bell when the boy appeared and showed them into the right house.

"Breslin left the tables and the ladder as they stood when Stephens crossed the wall, and the false keys in the doors, so that there might be no mistake about the manner of the escape, and returned to his room in the hospital, which he reached a little after two o'clock. He wore a pair of patent-leather shoes, so that his ordinary ones might not be soiled, and after carefully wiping the sand and dust from them he put them away, and, brushing his clothes, got into bed and was fast asleep in ten minutes. Byrne continued to make his usual rounds, and found no sign of anything to indicate that the escape was known. At four o'clock he raised an alarm and reported that Stephens was gone.

"A scene of wild confusion ensued. The whole prison staff was aroused, and every nook and corner of the prison was searched for the fugitive. The Castle authorities were at once notified, and in a few hours the police were scouring the city, searching houses and watching trains and outgoing vessels of all kinds. The garrison was placed under arms. Similar precautions were taken elsewhere, and an utter panic prevailed among the loyalists. Landlords and magistrates were paralyzed with dismay, and fully expected the outbreak of a formidable insurrection. Had Stephens been ready to give the word then, he could have got ten followers for the one that would have answered to his call at any previous time. But there were not a thousand rifles in the organisation. A really bold conspirator, having the splendid material that Stephens absolutely controlled, with 8000 out of the 25,000 troops then in Ireland sworn members of the organisation, 150 Irish-American commissioned officers who had gone through the civil war, and the Irish masses in America at his back, might not have been able to separate Ireland from England, but he would have struck a blow at British power that would have forced England to concede a Parliament in Dublin. The opportunity came and went without being seized.

"The people were wild with delight. Men who had till then looked with open hostility or cold indifference on Fenianism were seized with a sudden enthusiasm. They shook hands with their Fenian acquaintances in the streets, and congratulated them on the victory. It was the one proud day of the Fenian movement. The Government had been beaten in their own stronghold, and not a man ever suffered the loss of a hair. It made Stephens a lion, and it turned his head.

"Byrne was arrested next day, and committed for trial; but two successive juries disagreed, and he was finally released and allowed to leave the country. Not a shadow of suspicion rested on Breslin, and he remained at his post for a whole year, when, finding that he was likely to be arrested, he quietly slipped on board the Holyhead boat at Kingstown, and was in Paris the following night.

"Neither Breslin nor Byrne contracted for or ever received a single penny for the work. It was a labour of love. Stephens remained many months in Ireland directing the Fenian movement, stopping a great portion of the time in the house of Mrs Butler, a fashionable dressmaker, almost in the face of the Kildare Street Club, the headquarters of Irish loyalty, and finally escaped in a fishing-smack to France, whence he came to this country. Mrs Butler's patrons being mostly loyalists, on hearing of her harbouring the Fenian chief, withdrew their custom, and she was ruined and died in poverty.

"Such are the facts of the most remarkable escape of a political prisoner that ever took place in Ireland.

"JOHN DEVOY."

The opinion of John Devoy, that the end of 1865 would have been the most favourable time for raising the standard of insurrection, was held by all who were best acquainted with the resources of the revolutionary organisation. Here is what Stephens himself said in connection with this, in a speech at Jones's Wood, New York.

"The organisation in Ireland during the last year (1865) numbered 200,000 men—50,000 thoroughly drilled, and 50,000 partially drilled. It would take England thirty or forty days to concentrate 35,000 men in Ireland. It would take her three months at least to concentrate 70,000. We could concentrate, on four or five given points, 100,000 men in twenty-four hours. This was the time of our greatest power in Ireland. If at any time between the 24th of November and the end of December you had sent to Ireland a small force, or even only a few superior officers, with the necessary war materials, I do believe as firmly as in my own existence that Ireland would be an independent country to-day."

It is singular that, in this estimate of the forces at his disposal, Stephens makes no mention of what the Government evidently regarded as the most dangerous to her rule—the soldiers in the British army who had been drawn into the ranks of the Irish Republican Brotherhood. John Devoy, who had charge of this department, gives his estimate of their number, and he is not a man likely to exaggerate, for he has proved himself one of the most practical and capable men that the organisation produced.

Towards the end of 1865 some of the most active among the Brotherhood in England were arrested. One of these, Thomas Hayes, described in the newspapers as the "London Head Centre," was sent over to Ireland to be tried at the Special Commission held in Cork. On New Year's Day he was brought before Justices Fitzgerald and Keogh, the latter the inciter to assassination in the palmy days of the "Pope's Brass Band;" and yet the stiff-necked Irish are always dissatisfied, and complaining of the instruments of British rule in Ireland.

The result of this trial was that Thomas Hayes was sentenced to ten years penal servitude. Several other prisoners were also dealt with at this Cork Special Commission.

The Dublin Commission was also going on for the trial of the principal Fenian leaders, most of whom were convicted and sentenced to various terms of penal servitude.

Judging from the number of seizures made in the months of January and February 1866, a considerable quantity of arms must have been sent into Ireland about this time.

Those seized would probably only amount to a fraction of the whole, for unless every box and package of goods coming into Ireland were opened and examined, it would be impossible to stop the importation.

It was notorious, too, that, in addition to the Irish-American officers who had crossed the Atlantic to take command of the revolutionary forces, a large number of Irishmen from various parts of England, including deserters from the army, were in Ireland, chiefly in Dublin, waiting for the signal for the fight.

CHAPTER XXV.

SUSPENSION OF THE HABEAS CORPUS ACT — STEPHENS REACHES FRANCE — GLADSTONE AND CARDINAL MANNING ON FENIANISM — FENIAN RECRUITS FROM THE ARMY—THE INFORMER CORYDON — MORE ARMS FOR IRELAND—RICKARD BURKE.

A BOLD measure was now determined on by the Government. This was the sudden suspension of the *Habeas Corpus* Act, which enabled the police to sweep all suspected persons into their net at one stroke. On Saturday, 17th February, the bill was introduced, without any previous notice ; but Lord Wodehouse, the Viceroy, anticipated its actual passing by commencing to make wholesale arrests on the morning of that day, so that by nightfall he had one hundred and fifty men in jail. This was, of course, done to prevent any chance of these crossing over to England or Scotland, when they heard of how the bill was being rushed through Parliament.

It was noticed that the steamers leaving the North Wall, Dublin, for England and Scotland, were unusually crowded ; the majority of the passengers being no doubt men seeking to escape the effects of the Suspension Act. The police narrowly scanned these passengers and detained all of whom they had any suspicion. Among those arrested from the steamers and in the neighbourhood of Francis Street, Usher's Quay, and Meath Street, were Thomas Connolly of Leeds, who belonged to the 5th West York Militia; Thomas Lawless of Leeds, discharged from the 1st Dragoon Guards in 1857; Mathew Regan of Liverpool, of no employment; Thomas Brien of Leeds, smith's helper; Patrick Myles, stay presser, of Rochdale; Edward Drummond, painter, of Greenwich; Thomas M'Mahon, labourer, of Glasgow; and Thomas Whelston of Greenock. It had been observed that considerable numbers of strangers, evidently Irishmen, though, judging from their accent, a long time resident in England, had been arriving in Dublin, where they remained without any ostensible means of support; and it was upon this class the police made the first pounce.

On Thursday night, February 22nd, the police made a raid upon Pilsworth's public house, 123 James Street, and a number of civilians and soldiers were arrested. The police expected armed resistance, and made their preparations accordingly. The house was surrounded, and each constable had directions to seize his man. They rushed in by both entrances, so that there was no means of escape. A determined resistance was made, many of the men being armed with revolvers. John Byrne of London, a reputed centre of the I.R.B.; James Doyle, also said to be a centre; Edward St Clair, and Stephen Kelly, an artist, from London, showed fight, but were overpowered. Amidst all the confusion occasioned by the sudden influx of the police, one man made himself most conspicuous. This was Corporal Thomas Chambers, of the 61st regiment. He had deserted nine months previously, and had then been about five weeks in Dublin, having crossed over from London for the expected fight. Before his enlistment Chambers resided in Liverpool, where he had many friends. When he was amnested from penal servitude he went to America, where he died in 1888. The inspector in charge of the police, finding a rapidly increasing crowd outside, and fearing that the prisoners would be rescued, sent off for reinforcements. Soon a strong detachment of military came up, and these, with the police, escorted the prisoners to Chancery Lane, a dense and threatening crowd following. Among those arrested were found several men belonging to line regiments, the rifles, and the dragoon guards.

Arms were still coming into the country, and seizures being made. On Saturday, February 24th, a box of hand grenades, which seemed as if intended for a street attack, was discovered on board of one of the steamers at the North Wall, Dublin. The box had been shipped in Liverpool, and was marked " hardware."

It was evident from the vigilance with which the police watched for these importations, from the suspension of the *Habeas Corpus* Act, and the numerous arrests of suspicious strangers, including so many deserters from the army, that the Government expected a formidable rising about this time, and were making preparations to cope with it. The Irish police, who form one of the finest armies in the world, were kept ready for action, and not only were the regiments of the line strengthened in Ireland, but the guards were sent over.

Meanwhile, the fact that Stephens, notwithstanding all their exertions, was still undiscovered in his retreat, must have added to the discomfort of the members of the Government, who fully expected to find him taking the field, though where or when they had not the slightest idea. The news, therefore, that he had safely reached the French capital, on Sunday, March 18th, 1866, although it must have caused considerable exasperation that their wily foe had now completely slipped from their grasp, was, on the other hand, a kind of relief, as it went to show that there was no immediate prospect of a rising, or Stephens would not have left the country.

Let us, at this point, see how it fared with him since the night of his release from Richmond prison, and his gaining a secure retreat in Dublin. The following incidents in connection with Stephens' escape from Ireland, through Scotland and England, to France, are from John Savage's " Fenian Heroes and Martyrs," and other reliable sources.

Stephens made no attempt to leave Ireland until more

than three months after his escape from prison. He remained in concealment in Dublin until the search for him had relaxed, and it was thought by the police and the Government that he had got out of the country.

"After all the ship searching," says Colonel Kelly, who accompanied him, "we started from the quays in the city of Dublin. Mr Stephens left his lodgings in an open car, and, on my honour, undisguised."

The craft in which he escaped was one of a fleet of fishing hookers which sailed from Kinsale and Howth. They were owned by a warm-hearted and patriotic Irishman, a fish merchant of Liverpool, the late Patrick DeLacy Garton, who during his lifetime took a prominent part in the national movement, and was for several years a member of the Corporation of the town of his adoption. He sat for Scotland ward, which is also now a Parliamentary division of Liverpool, and the only seat in Great Britain filled by an Irish Nationalist, in the person of Mr T. P. O'Connor.

Stephens and his friends had a rough time of it on the Irish sea. John Flood, one of the most active organizers of the Brotherhood in Great Britain, who assisted in making the arrangements for getting Stephens out of Ireland, was one of those aboard the hooker. Adverse winds blew her into Carrickfergus Bay with the loss of her tiller, and it was owing to Flood's knowledge of seamanship and experience, that the party were saved. He received a severe injury in the hand, letting go the anchor in the hurry to prevent their being driven too far into the harbour. They were altogether three days in the Channel before they landed in Scotland. They slept that night in Kilmarnock, rode in the mail train next day from thence to London, and, after sleeping in a hotel near Buckingham Palace, started by the morning train from Victoria Station for Dover. They got aboard the French mail steamer there about eleven o'clock on Sunday morning, and started for Calais, reaching Paris the same night.

The greatest of British statesmen, William Ewart Gladstone, was able at this time to take a more clearsighted view of what was going on in Ireland, and among the Irish in Great Britain, than most of his fellow-countrymen. The first lesson he received from the study of this led him to see the gross injustice of keeping an alien Church fastened on the shoulders of the Irish people. He, at least, felt bound to admit that there was some cause for Irish discontent. The following is what he said of Fenianism at a banquet in Liverpool a few weeks after the arrival of Stephens in Paris :—

" We have another strange, singular, and painful manifestation in the sister island. I advert to that which is known as Fenianism—a phenomenon which, no doubt, derives its force from a foreign agency and influence. But, gentlemen, when I say a foreign agency and influence, do not let it be for a moment supposed that I intend, directly or indirectly, to charge on the great and mighty people who inhabit the opposite shores of the Atlantic, the responsibility, or any part of the responsibility, of that deplorable and calamitous manifestation. I am deeply assured that our brethren in America, that the mass of those who form public opinion in America, regard the proceedings of those unhappy persons with the same feelings of grief, and the same judgment of condemnation with which you and I regard them. It is a sprinkling of persons in that great and gigantic community to whom these influences are owing. And, gentlemen, of these influences themselves what are we to say? It is impossible to contemplate them without the deepest pain. Acting upon those principles of general confession, which lie at the root of public affairs in this country, we cannot hesitate to admit that this deplorable principle, this deplorable power, would never have come into existence, had it not been for the record of past misgovernment and abuse. In the signs of providential retribution for the ills we have endured, for the errors we have committed, we derive these lessons—that in the future we must, even more carefully than now, endeavour to treat all our fellow-subjects and all our fellow-citizens, whether they be called Englishmen, Irishmen, or Scotchmen, upon principles of pure and equal justice; but that, in the meantime, we must, without hesitation, though not without grief, use every method, adopt every measure that may be necessary to maintain the authority of the law, and to preserve the peace of the country."

The last sentence in Mr Gladstone's speech meant in one word Coercion—the old, stupid, wicked remedy for Ireland. However justifiable, from a British statesman's point of view, this may have been at the moment, with an insurrection apparently impending, there has not been the same excuse for the Coercion that, since then, has been, over and over again, so ruthlessly applied to Ireland. It took Mr Gladstone twenty years to learn and to admit his error.

Cardinal Manning, an Englishman who loved his country as sincerely as we love ours, thus spoke of Fenianism—

"No greater self-deception could we practise upon ourselves than to imagine that Fenianism is the folly of a few apprentices and shop-boys. Fenianism could not have survived for a year, if it were not sustained by the traditional and just discontent of almost a whole people. Such acts of violence and rashness as have marked the last twelve months may be the work of a few, and those of no high or formidable classes; but they never would have been perpetrated, they never would have been possible, if it were not for the profound estrangement of a large portion of the people from British laws and British Government. This feeling is to be found nowhere more calm, deep, and inflexible, than amongst those who are in immediate contact with the land question, that is, in the occupiers and tenants, and in the labourers, whose lot is better or worse as the occupiers prosper or are impoverished. These are neither apprentices nor shop-boys, neither are they a handful, but a population, and a population in close kindred and living sympathy with millions who have tasted the civil and religious equality, and are thriving under the laws of the United States. Let us not deceive ourselves. Ireland is between two great assimilating powers — England and America. The play and action of America, if it be seven days slower in reaching Ireland than that of England, is seven-fold more penetrating and powerful upon the whole population. It is estimated that in the last twenty-five years £24,000,000 have been sent over by the Irish in America for the relief or the emigration of their kindred and friends. The perfect unity of heart, will, and purpose, which unite the Irish on either side of the Atlantic, cannot be more complete. Add to this, that the assimilating power of England, which has overcome the resistance of Scotland, and absorbed it into itself, is met by a stern repulsion in Ireland, which keeps the two races asunder. Add again, that the assimilating power of America is met and welcomed with gratitude, sympathy, aspiration; that the attitude of Ireland has long been, as Sir Robert Peel said in Parliament five and twenty years ago—

> ' With her back turned to England
> And her face to the West.'

"Four millions and a half of Irish in Ireland turn instinctively to five millions of Irish in America."

It is agreed upon all sides that whatever chance of success the Fenians had it was at the end of 1865 and beginning of 1866, when, as we learn from John Devoy and others, the Brotherhood had made so many proselytes in the army and militia. Devoy, whose particular department this was, had a number of zealous, if not always the most prudent, agents in England, engaged in this work. Some of these managed to carry on their propagandism unchecked; others—such they considered the fortune of war—fell into the hands of the enemy.

About this time there was recruiting going on for the I.R.B. among the Irish soldiers at Woolwich, by one of Devoy's most indefatigable lieutenants, who, like a number of others, had specially enlisted for the purpose. This was Peter Maughan, a young Irishman of Liverpool, who, in the last three months of 1865, sent a goodly number of soldiers, in civilians' clothes, over to Ireland, where they were kept, while awaiting the outbreak of the promised rising. Maughan was educated by that self-sacrificing and patriotic body of men to whom the Catholic religion and Irish Nationality owe so much—the Irish Christian Brothers. When he was a boy they had charge of several of the schools attached to the Liverpool churches, but as they steadily refused to place themselves under Government supervision by taking any grant, the financial exigencies of the various missions caused their places to be gradually filled by other teachers. Not a few Irishmen of Liverpool—some of them grown gray in the service of Ireland—speak with pride of having been school-fellows with Peter Maughan at St Patrick's. When old enough he learned the trade of a joiner, which he followed for a number of years, until he gave himself up entirely to the service of his country. Like a good many other active members of the I.R.B., he graduated in the ranks of the Brotherhood of St Patrick. He was of rather low stature, in fact just sufficiently tall to be enlisted in the British army, but was sinewy and possessed of great powers of endurance, being also a man that no danger nor hardship could daunt. For nearly three years he managed to evade the vigilance of the police, while constantly pursuing his mission among the Irish soldiers. He was, as might be expected, taken at last, and sentenced to ten years penal servitude.

During 1866 there were numerous arrests of soldiers for their connection with the revolutionary movement.

A number of the arms sent into Ireland were forwarded through Liverpool, which seems to have been made a depot for the accumulations of the sinews of war of the I.R.B., for shipment to Ireland. Alluding to this, the *Times* said—"Stephens has declared that he could, in spite of the British Government, get thousands of muskets conveyed into Ireland. The places of shipment vary, but there can be but little doubt that a considerable quantity has been taken to Ireland, *via* Liverpool."

In the month of September 1866, the notorious informer, known as John Joseph Corydon, began to give information, about these arms among other things, to the Government. The Irish name has been sufficiently disgraced by wretches of this description, but it is very probable that this man had no Irish blood in his veins at all. There are those in Liverpool who knew him in his youth, before he went to America, who say he was born, the son of an unfortunate woman of the town, in a low haunt, long since swept away by town improvements, called Spitalfields. The scenes of his boyhood seem to have had an attraction for him when he returned to England from America in connection with the Fenian movement, for at the subsequent trials of the victims he had betrayed, Isaac Butt, their

counsel, extorted from the foul wretch the admission that
he had been living with a woman of the town, in a house
of ill-fame, in the same street. Corydon, or whatever else
may have been his name, was at this time a young man of
smart appearance. At first sight he might be set down as
a third-rate actor or circus performer out of work. He
generally wore a frock coat, buttoned tightly, to set off a
by no means contemptible figure, and carried himself with
a jaunty swaggering air after the conventional style of
certain types of the "professional" actor. He was of
medium height and of wiry, active build. He had a
globular-shaped forehead, curving outward at the eyebrows,
very aquiline nose and lantern jaws. His red hair was thick,
and curled like a negro's, and he wore a tolerably heavy
moustache of the same colour as his hair. An American
newspaper explains Corydon's treachery by surmising that
he was driven to it by want. There is no doubt but that
many men in connection with the movement, who, according to the enemies of Ireland, where living on the earnings
of the Irish servant girls of New York, led a life of great
hardship and self-denial, which brought more than one of
them—like John Ryan of Liverpool—to an early grave.
But Corydon was not one of these. Whether or not he
had previously been known as a man of loose character we
have no evidence, but at the time he was betraying his
associates he was leading, according to his own confession,
an immoral life. It is therefore more likely he acted as he
did from a want of principle and a greed of gain. It is
a lesson that no man of questionable life should be trusted
in a great national movement.

Corydon served in the American army as a hospital
steward, and, during that time, became a Fenian. Up to
a certain point he appears to have been trusted by Stephens,
and the other leaders. When he started to give information,
he gave the names of people who were conveying arms
through Liverpool into Ireland, and caused a number of
arrests and seizures. He also kept the authorities posted,
so far as he could, in the movements of the Irish-American
officers, and had their meeting places watched by the police.
— The zealous and active agents of the Brotherhood not

only made their purchases of arms in Birmingham and on the continent, but actually seemed to have levied contributions on the military stores of Her Majesty herself, for among the arms and other materials found in possession of four men arrested in Liverpool, in September 1866, were a number of muskets which had been missing from the headquarters of the London Irish and other volunteer corps, and from the Tower.

Meanwhile, the shipments of arms from Liverpool and other ports into Ireland were going on briskly. On Thursday, November 21st, two cases consigned to John Daly & Co., of Cork, which had arrived by the previous day's steamer from Liverpool, were opened by the police and found to contain eighty rifles, bayonets, and bullet moulds. On the butt of each musket was stamped "Kynoch & Co., Birmingham." This Kynoch, who at this time was doing an enormous trade in furnishing arms to the I. R. B., was the same individual who, twenty years afterwards, offered to arm the Orange "ditch-liners" of Ulster against Her Majesty's forces, in case Mr Gladstone's Home Rule bill became law, and any attempt were made to enforce it on the "loyal" Orangemen of Ireland. A young man, named Tracey, who was in the employ of Daly & Co., was arrested, but admitted to bail and discharged.

The arms seized in Cork were but a portion of what had been sent into Ireland during the previous twelve months, by various devices and by many routes, through the agency of Colonel Rickard Burke, one of the ablest and most remarkable of the men that the revolutionary organisation produced. He was a graduate of Queen's College, Cork. In the American Civil War he was on the staff of General Lenham, and afterwards on General Woodbury's staff, and was a skilful engineer. He was at this time about thirty-five years of age, tall, and of fine physique and prepossessing address. He was an accomplished linguist, which was of great service to him in the many *rôles* he had to assume in the difficult and dangerous tasks he was intrusted with—tasks that required a man of resolution, of coolness, and of wonderful tact. Sometimes he was a Chilian officer, sometimes he was a student, and at others he was a commercial gentleman. In this latter capacity we find him in Birmingham, in December 1885, where, under the name of Edward C. Winslow, he opened negotiations with this same Kynoch & Co., whose names were stamped on the stocks of the rifles seized in Cork. He said he represented a house in New York, having branches in London, Paris, and other cities. He intended to conduct his trade in war materials in a thorough systematic and business like manner, and, on the 19th of December 1865, took warehouses and office at 64 George Street, Parade, Birmingham, at a rent of £25 a year. From that time, Burke and two assistants were engaged in receiving large parcels of arms in their depot. One of these assistants was Henry Mullady, who, being a carpenter, was useful in making packing cases for the safe conveyance of the arms. He was one of the Irish artisan class, who were the backbone of the Fenian organisation, and wherever active work was to be done he was never found wanting. After the first purchase, Kynoch introduced "Mr Winslow" to a gunmaker named Hill, from whom he bought a number of pistols. During December 1865 and January 1866, the amount Burke paid for arms was nearly £2000. He, of course, went to and fro to make his arrangements at the various ports of shipment for Ireland. During January and February great quantities of arms were sent to Liverpool, to be got into Ireland as the opportunity offered. As it was found advisable not to stay too long in one place, the depot in George Street was, after a time, given up, and new accommodation procured elsewhere, "Mr Winslow's" ready tongue and pleasant manner being always a good introduction to a stranger. From an address in London he afterwards wrote to Kynoch to send him quotations, and hoped soon to do a brisk business with him again.

The rifles seized in Cork in November 1866, addressed to Daly & Co., drapers, were shipped as if from Cook & Townshend, drapers, Liverpool. The packages were labelled "American cloth." It need scarcely be said that neither of these highly respectable firms would have ever known of the great trade they were doing in "American cloth," but for the suspicions of the police and consequent seizure. How much more drapery goods safely ran the gauntlet probably only " Edward C. Winslow " knew. He was in America at the end of 1866, but returned in time to assist in the preparations for the rising.

In the meantime, Stephens, having declared in America that the New Year (1867) would find him on Irish soil to open the campaign for liberty, numbers of Irishmen crossed the Channel to be ready to rally round at the upraising of the Irish national flag. Most got into Ireland safely, but some were arrested.

The Irish in England and Scotland were now closely looked after. " The Government, having become apprehensive," said the *Sunday Gazette*, " about Fenianism in Liverpool and Glasgow, is about to station a regiment in each town. It is not many months since one of the highest police officials in Ireland declared that Liverpool was one of the principal centres of the Fenian organisation." The *Gazette* further stated—" There is a powerful Fenian feeling among the Liverpool Irish."

CHAPTER XXVI.

NEW YEAR'S DAY, 1867—THE HOUR HAS COME, BUT NOT THE MAN — HOW THE FENIAN CHIEFS " SQUANDERED THE MONEY OF THE IRISH SERVANT GIRLS "— PREPARATIONS FOR THE RISING — THE PLOT TO SEIZE CHESTER CASTLE—M'CAFFERTY—FLOOD —DAVITT.

NEW YEAR'S DAY, 1867, had been looked forward to with great anxiety by some, with high hope by others, for had not James Stephens pledged his word in America that by that time he would be in Ireland at the head of his followers? The hour came, but not the man. Many execrated him for it, while others thought it was wiser of him to break the pledge than to make it.

But the ardent spirits in America, Ireland, and Great Britain chafed at it. Already a large number of Irish-American officers had crossed the Atlantic to be at their posts and take their respective commands when the word went forth. Others, too, came over to share in the fight, if fight there was to be, even though it were but a forlorn hope. Stephens having failed to keep his engagement in Ireland, the direction of affairs devolved upon Colonel Thomas James Kelly, who was then in America. He sent over Godfrey Massey, who is said to have been a colonel in the American army, with a considerable sum of money for the payment of the officers in Ireland and Great Britain, and also to make a military survey of the districts where the rising could be commenced with the greatest hope of success. Massey left New York on January 7th, 1867. In due time he reached this side of the Atlantic and entered upon his mission.

In the meantime, how fared it with the brave fellows, the Irish-Americans, who remained in these islands, or crossed over at the end of 1866 and beginning of 1867, for the fight? One of these afterwards wrote for the New York *Irish People* his "Personal recollections of the late attempted insurrection in Ireland." From this can be gleaned what truth there was in the statements made by the enemies and some of the so-called friends of Ireland—that these men lived in luxury and dissipation on the money of the organisation, a good deal of which was supplied, it was said, by the "Irish servant girls of New York." The following is the narrative, which was signed " W. S. H."—

"As I had opportunities of seeing how the American officers lived, and was constantly moving from one rendezvous to another, let the reader accompany me and see for himself the extravagant way in which General Burke and other 'Moffat Mansion Officials' live. We are in London and in the Regent Circus. Taking out a slip of paper we decipher the meaning of certain pot hooks and hangers, hail a cab and dash down towards Holborn. We would not be guilty of riding up to the house of a gentleman of extravagant habits in a common cab, but we haven't a carriage, so we dismiss the hansom near Great King Street, and turn down past Russell Square into a dingy street. We find the number of the house we are looking for very easily, and pull the bell. The handle does not yield gracefully like a knob accustomed to gentle fingers, but surrenders with a bang. The wire is broken, so Captain R—— B——, who joins us, raps with the butt of an instrument much worn by Irish-Americans at the time. There is no answer. R—— knocks again. Presently a shrill female voice sounds through the house and a man, whose name is John, emerges from a subterraneous passage. The female has irritated him. He blasts, blows, and damns his own sanguinary eyes, and opens the door so suddenly that R——, who was aiding the effort, nearly falls over him. We are requested to state 'what the 'ell we want?' We ask if Mr Webb is at home. John doesn't know, but if we go up to the top landing, turn to the right, and knock at the door, we may find him. R—— leaps up the stairs. There is no light, the stairs are in the last stage of consumption, and keen blasts of air striking us in the face tell of broken windows. At last we are at the door which is opened wide by General Thomas F. Burke. A word or two in whispers (walls have ears), a fraternal grasp of the hand all round, and we seat ourselves on an empty coal scuttle, kindly kicked over for our accommodation. There is no fire, though the night is cold, and a small piece of candle stuck in the bedpost gives all the light there is. The bed is occupied by Colonel —— from Missouri, who is suffering from fever and ague. His last sovereign was given for medical advice, and he is tortured with recommendations to eat plenty of nourishing food and to drink good sound port and claret. Burke owns half the bed, and will drag himself in beside his friend when we are gone. He is sickly too, and his wound is very painful. The General tells us that they were going out to supper when we came in, and invites us, with a grim smile, to accompany them. Two or three more gentlemen, who had been sitting quietly in a dark corner, got up and recognised us, and we all go out together. Those who listened to the 'message' of the President, or who read the magnificent calumny which the late Artemus Ward wrote to please the English, will expect to hear that our supper consisted of young ducks and early peas, washed down with champagne and medoc. I have been told by intelligent Englishmen that that was a standing dish with Fenian officers, and it was next to treason to doubt it. We will follow Burke into a coffee-house in the neighbourhood of his lodgings. The restaurant is one of those curious places maintained by the contributions of whimsical, mysterious old ladies, where cheap coffee of singular flavour and orthodox tracts are provided for all comers. A little bit of butter, a diminutive roll, and a text from Scripture, are given for two cents, and on special occasions soup and prayer are provided. On each side of the room are little boxes that look like pens. In these a miscellaneous crowd of labourers, bummers, and broken-down swells, dispose of the eatables, pay the reckoning, and read the religious paper. The arrangements for our supper are quickly made. Burke is nominated president of the mess, and sees that the sugar is properly divided. Colonel Irwin is detected in an attempt to 'squander the hard-earned money, &c.,' by ordering an extra roll. . . . It was a sight to make Englishmen stare. Six big, miserable, 'misguided Fenians' stinting themselves on bread and coffee rather than the money they had set apart to take them into the jaws of death should be diminished by a penny! But, to the honour of Burke and his associates, the picture is strictly true. The condition of other officers in Liverpool and Glasgow was not much better. The behaviour of the martyred O'Brien, who was in Liverpool during this crisis, was in perfect keeping with his heroic conduct afterwards on the Manchester scaffold. I happened to be better provided with money than my friends, and many true men would testify, could they but speak, that I did not hoard it. I had a better opportunity of knowing how Irish-American officers lived abroad than many, and can say, with profound thankfulness that it was so, that nothing could exceed the patient self-denial, economic foresight (when the case was interested) and sublime patience in the midst of want, and in the presence of a numerous and efficient police, which was everywhere shown by the Fenian officers. About the 1st of February, Colonel Kelly arrived in London, and was quickly followed by Massey. Money was distributed; next, orders were issued, and hope and confidence were inspired into all. The Chester affair soon followed."

Soon after Colonel Kelly's arrival in London, Massey reported to him in person the result of his mission in Ireland, and also in Liverpool, which was a chief rendezvous of the American officers. In London, concerting the plan of action with Kelly, were at this time General Fariola, a Franco-Italian, and General Cluseret, who afterwards figured as a leader of the Parisian Communists during the insurrection in the French capital which followed the close of the Franco-Prussian War. These officers were to proceed to Ireland to take command when the insurgents were fairly in the field. Colonel Kelly, while in London, in conjunction with delegates from Ireland and other leaders, drew up a proclamation detailing the reasons why they were about to fight for the liberties of their country—this to be issued simultaneously with the commencement of the insurrection.

All this time Corydon was giving such information as he could get to the authorities. He does not appear to have had a knowledge of Colonel Kelly's whereabouts, nor of that of Captain O'Rourke (known as Beecher), the paymaster, who were more than ordinarily astute men, and allowed but few to know of their movements. He, however, appears to have got upon the track of Massey, who again went to Ireland to make a military survey, returning to London to report to Kelly before finally setting off to be ready to be at his post in the south of Ireland at the outbreak of the insurrection. Corydon also made it his business to attend whatever meetings were being held in Liverpool at this time. Here he met, amongst others of the American officers, the two Burkes — Rickard and Thomas Francis, O'Rourke, Deasy, Michael O'Brien, M'Cafferty, and O'Connor, besides Flood, Ryan, and Mullady. In this way he became acquainted with the bold and startling scheme for the seizure of the weakly-garrisoned castle of Chester, with the large store of arms therein.

The plan was to bring from various points sufficient men, armed with revolvers, which they could easily conceal on their persons, to overpower the weak garrison and secure the arms. The telegraph wires were to be cut and the railroads not required for operations to be torn up. Should the initial movement succeed, and the arms be captured, sufficient railway carriages and wagons were to be seized to convey the Fenians and the war materials to Holyhead, where possession was to be taken of one or more steamers in which Ireland was to be reached and the standard of insurrection raised. It was considered that, if the field could be only kept with fair success for a sufficient time, the people would rally round, and the Irish in America would come across the Atlantic in overwhelming numbers to their assistance. The names most prominently identified with the Chester raid were those of John Flood and Captain John M'Cafferty. Flood has already been introduced. A correspondent of the *Nation* thus describes M'Cafferty, as he saw him in 1865 :—

"He has a dark bronzed face of a Spanish hue, oval in shape, with regular features, and large black eyes. His long black hair was parted in the middle, and thrown back behind his ears, flowing down upon his neck and shoulders. Well proportioned and strongly knit about the body, he looked, with his military cut and cool smile, just what he is described as having been, a resolute, skilful soldier, a bit of a 'free lance,' ready for a fight 'in any good cause at all,' and able to take his share of it when it came."

He was, in fact, a thorough type of a guerilla leader, as such, indeed, he had been, for in Morgan's bands, who fought on the side of the Southern States in the American Civil War, there was no more daring soldier than Captain John M'Cafferty. He was born in the United States, of Irish parentage. One of his first experiences of the land of his fathers was as an inmate of an Irish prison, for coming from America, at the end of 1865, to bear a part in what he expected to be a revolution, he was arrested on board the steamer at Queenstown. He was brought before the same Commission at Cork that sentenced the London centre, Hayes, to ten years penal servitude. He, however, was more fortunate, for the Crown prosecutors, not being able to prove any overt act of treason against him, he was discharged, along with Captain "Mackay" (Lomasney was his real name), another "Alien," on Tuesday, January 2nd, 1866. They both returned to America, and both eventually found their way back again to this side to be in the thick of the fray when it commenced.

It was a time of feverish yet hopeful expectation among the Brotherhood, who bore constantly in mind their oath to take up arms at a moment's notice for Ireland. Therefore, when the word went forth to move on Chester, and reached the men coming home from work on that Saturday afternoon—whether from the workshops of Birmingham and Wolverhampton, the coal-pits and blast-furnaces of the "Black Country," the factories of Lancashire and Yorkshire, or from the Liverpool docks and warehouses—it did not find them unprepared. Many who were at Chester can remember how stoutly the brave yet tender-hearted fellows bore the parting from wives and children, from father, mother, or others near and dear to them, not knowing if they would ever return. More than one good *soggarth*, too, could tell of the sterling piety of the poor fellows—men for whom, according to a Castle bishop in Ireland at the time, "hell was not hot enough nor eternity long enough"—who thronged the confessionals on that Saturday night and Sunday morning, to make their peace with God, satisfied, if need be, to give their lives for the holy cause of Irish Freedom.

At the time fixed upon, bodies of men were moved from the various points in the north of England and the midlands upon Chester. The plot might have succeeded from its very audacity, as there was but a small garrison in the castle, while there were many points at any one of which it might have broken down, even if the castle and arms had been taken. Many of the men selected for the expedition started from their homes on the night of Sunday, the 10th of February. The promptness and cheerfulness with which the order to move was obeyed showed wonderful discipline, for on the Sunday night and early the following morning not less than 2000 men were converging upon Chester.

On that same Sunday night, Corydon gave information. Some five years after this, General Cluseret, having stated that "it was owing to a mere chance that the Fenians failed to seize some 2000 stand of arms in Chester Castle," he was contradicted, in a letter to the *Times*, by Major Greig, who was Head Constable of Liverpool at the time of the raid. Here is his account of how he received and made use of Corydon's information—

"On Sunday, 10th February 1867, at half-past nine, I received sudden information from the informer Corydon, detailing a complete plan of the Fenian attack on Chester Castle next morning. At that time of night, with only a few hours to spare, and on so important a matter, I would not trust to a telegram. Fortunately, I did not do so, for the Mayor of Chester, with whom I would have communicated, I subsequently found, not only lived six miles from the city, but was from home at the time. I instantly despatched my second in command, Chief-Superintendent Ride, with a detective inspector, to Chester, with the utmost speed, with instructions not to rest until they had seen the Mayor of the city, the officer commanding the troops, and the chiefs of the police, city and county. They saw the deputy mayor, the officer commanding the troops, the ordnance officer (Captain Durnford) in charge of the arms, and the chiefs of the city and county police. During the morning of the very Monday mentioned by General Cluseret, instead of there being 700 Fenians present there was nearly double that number."

Soon after midnight on the Sunday, and while the raiders were still on the way, Superintendent Ride and Detective Carlisle of Liverpool, sent by Major Greig, as stated in his letter, arrived in Chester to warn the authorities of the impending danger. They roused up Mr Fenwick, the Chief Constable, and gave him information of what had been revealed by Corydon. The officers at the Castle were warned to prepare to resist any attack; arrangements were made to get the local rifle and artillery corps under arms without delay; and telegrams were despatched to the Quarter-Master General in London, and to the Assistant-Adjutant General in Manchester, for troops.

Captain M'Cafferty and other leaders had already reached Chester, a day or two in advance. Many Irishmen crossed over from Liverpool to Birkenhead by the late boat on Sunday night, and then started on their four hours' march by road to Chester. These dropped quietly into the city in various groups, during the early hours of Monday morning. The first considerable batch of Irishmen arrived at Chester station between two and three in the morning, and, at about four o'clock, "Some 400 suspicious strangers," said a newspaper correspondent, "arrived from Manchester and Birkenhead. They took possession of the waiting-rooms and slept on the floors." After this they kept arriving at intervals during the day, in company with one batch from Liverpool being Corydon, taking note of all he saw, with an eye to future contingencies. The leaders, finding they had been betrayed, managed to stop and turn back a considerable number coming into Chester and at Birkenhead and other points, while those already in the city got orders to leave without delay.

Amongst the contingents that arrived in Chester was one from a north Lancashire town, led by a tall, dark-complexioned young fellow who had lost an arm. "Unable to shoulder a rifle," says John Devoy, in his "Land of Eire," "he, with his single arm, carried a store of cartridges in a bag made from a pocket handkerchief." This was Michael Davitt, of whom more will be heard hereafter.

The astonishment and consternation among the citizens on that Monday morning, on hearing of the Fenian invasion, can well be imagined. The volunteers were got under arms as rapidly as possible, the Cheshire constabulary were drawn in from the various districts, and, in answer to the telegrams sent early in the morning, the regular troops arrived from Manchester at half-past two in the afternoon; so that, by seven o'clock in the evening, the hour at which it was understood the attack would be made, there was a formidable garrison in the castle and city.

Before that time, however, the bulk of the Fenians, being, as one of the newspapers said, "well officered and under control," had left the city. The later arrivals were also turned back, so that by Monday night the whole of the Fenians had disappeared as quietly and mysteriously as they came.

CHAPTER XXVII.

THE RISING IN IRELAND.

MOST of the Fenians who took part in the Chester raid returned to their homes, but a considerable number either left Chester direct by Holyhead for Dublin, or made their way to Liverpool, where they crossed by steamer the same night, anxious to be in Ireland for the impending rising. The alarm of the Chester raid put the police on the *qui vive*, so that many of those who crossed were arrested on their arrival, the whole force of the C. Division of police being stationed at the North Wall, Dublin, early on Tuesday morning, to receive them. Some few had an American appearance, others were evidently factory operatives or dock labourers, and they generally said they came looking for work, or to see friends. "With few exceptions," says the *Irish Times*, "they admitted what it would be useless to attempt to conceal, that they were born in Ireland."

A sharp look-out was now kept at all the ports in Ireland where there was steam communication with England or Scotland, and numerous arrests were made during the next few weeks.

For a time the police could hear nothing of the leaders of the Chester raid, but, on the 19th of February, M'Cafferty and Flood were traced to Whitehaven. On the following day they took their passage for Dublin, for the projected rising, in a coal brig, called the *New Draper*. Information of this was at once conveyed by telegraph and also by letter to the authorities in Dublin, who were thus put upon the alert. A watch was therefore set for the *New Draper*. At each side of the river police were stationed, and as the vessel sailed up they observed two men dropping into an oyster boat. The police gave chase in a ferry-boat and arrested the men as they got into a collier. Being questioned, they gave the names of William Jackson and John Philips, and described themselves as sailors, but would give no more information. The police, however, were not long in discovering that in "Jackson" they had secured the

Southern Guerilla Captain, John M'Cafferty, and that "Philips" was John Flood, one of the most active Fenian organisers in the country.

Another of the Chester leaders, John Ryan, was more fortunate. An old school-fellow of his, Richard Richards, a Liverpool-born Irishman, with the blood of the gallant Wexford croppies in his veins, was by profession an artist. He was then rapidly making his way to the front ranks as a painter. His pictures—landscapes chiefly—appeared in prominent positions in the annual exhibitions of the Liverpool Academy, and later still in the Autumn Exhibitions of the Corporation in the Walker Art Gallery, and were readily purchased at high prices. He was a good specimen of the Irish race in England—bodily as well as mentally. Like Ryan he was a trained athlete and a staunch Fenian to boot. After the Chester affair Ryan made his way to Richards and took counsel with him as to how he was to get to Ireland. They were both capital amateur actors, and it was determined that Ryan should "make up" as an artist, and that Richards should supply him with all the necessary "properties." The plan was carried out and Ryan got safely through the cordon of the police and into what he considered a sure retreat in Dublin. While here he got several letters from Richards and other friends in England, some written in a comic vein, but all as if to an artist in search of the picturesque, under difficulties, in the then disturbed state of Ireland. The friend in Dublin with whom he was staying was a member of the I.R.B., but not so prominent, it was considered, that he was likely to receive any particular notice from the police. This was a miscalculation, for one morning he was arrested in bed in his own house. Ryan, also being found there, was questioned by the police, and his "properties" and other belongings overhauled. Among the letters which the vigilant members of the C. Division inspected were some addressed to him—in a feigned name, of course—condoling with him on the prospect before him, should he attempt professionally to explore the Wicklow hills, of being impaled by the pikes of the outlaws or riddled by the bullets of the police. Everything was found so regular and complete that

P

with ample apologies from the police, the English artist was not molested. It can be readily understood, however, that Ryan at once looked out for safer lodgings.

A number of the Irish-American officers, too, succeeded in crossing from England. Among these was Colonel O'Connor, who appeared suddenly in arms among the Kerry Hills at the head of the Fenians of Cahirciveen and the district, on the 12th of February. That was the day originally fixed for the rising, but it seems that the news of the change of day, which had afterwards been made, did not reach this quarter. The consternation among the shoneens of Killarney and the district was most ludicrous, and was cleverly caricatured at the time by that racy Irish poet, T. D. Sullivan, of the *Nation*. O'Connor's Fenian bands soon learned their mistake, and quickly dispersed to await the day when the word to rise would be again sent to them.

As but few of the Brotherhood in Great Britain succeeded in running the blockade through the police, who kept such vigilant watch at every Irish port, the rising that followed forms more legitimately a part of the history of the Irish at home, than of the Irish in Great Britain. A rapid glance at the movements which now took place in Ireland will, however, be necessary.

Though it had come to be considered in the light of a forlorn hope, it was still determined to take the field, and accordingly, the rising was fixed to take place throughout Ireland on the night of Shrove Tuesday, March 5th, 1867. Corydon crossed over to Ireland as if to take part in the insurrection, but only to keep a better watch on the associates he was betraying. The military men who had been detailed to take command of the insurgents in the various districts found their way to their posts as best they could, and on the appointed night there was a rising in Dublin, Drogheda, Tipperary, Limerick, Cork, and some other places.

Irrespective of a considerable portion of the plan of the insurrection being betrayed by Corydon, it was at once evident that there was no hope of being able to make a successful stand against the armed constabulary and military. Added to this, the insurgents had hardly turned out when there came on such a terrible frost that it became impossible for them to keep the field, even if they otherwise had the power to do so.

The Dublin men left the city in several tolerably numerous bodies. General Halpin had charge of the rising in this district. As those who met him in England, as well as in Ireland and America, could testify, he was an able officer, a thoroughly scientific master of the art of war, and, with anything like a chance, would have given a good account of himself. In personal appearance, he was as different as possible from the ordinary type of dashing Irish-American officers. He was short in stature, and stout, and, with his close-shaven, placid looking face, looked like a comfortable Irish parish priest. The portion of his command under his immediate direction took the road which passes Kilakee House—which is about seven or eight miles south of Dublin—on the night of the rising; with him, as a staff, being John Ryan, of Liverpool, and some of the prominent Dublin leaders.

One of the parties which left Dublin was met at Tallaght and routed by the police, who took a considerable number of prisoners.

Another body of men that went out from the city met with better fortune, as they succeeded in capturing the police barracks at Milltown, Stepaside, and Glencullen. This party was led by Patrick Lennon, the son of an Irishman of Liverpool, one of the most remarkable and daring characters that the movement produced. The vanquished policemen themselves afterwards testified to his humanity at the taking of the barracks. Should the insurrection make any progress he was to command the cavalry, under General Halpin. He had been a soldier in the British army, having deserted from the 9th Lancers, taking with him his uniform, in which he rode down Broadway, in New York, in a procession of several thousands of Irishmen. After the rising he escaped to America. Returning to England, he travelled several times from London to Holyhead. Crossing to Ireland, he owed his long safety from arrest to his great facility for disguising himself and to the reputation he bore of being a desperate man. That he did not belie this reputation was shown by his shooting dead a policeman who attempted to capture him, wounding another, and getting clear off. He was, however, ultimately arrested and tried on the charge of treason-felony, and murdering the policeman. He was acquitted of the charge of murdering the policeman for want of proof, but was convicted on the other charges, and sentenced to seven years penal servitude.

In Drogheda the rendezvous was the market square, but the movement was here nipped in the bud.

The most formidable portion of the rising was expected to be in Munster. Here it was strangled in its birth by the treachery of Corydon. He had kept the police so well posted in the movements of Massey—who was to have had the chief command in the South—that he was arrested at Limerick Junction. The news of Massey's capture was a crushing blow for the Munster Fenians; nevertheless, they turned out in considerable numbers, and met with some successes, capturing the police barracks in several places and keeping the military flying columns well engaged.

CHAPTER XXVIII.

FENIAN ALARMS IN ENGLAND—ARREST AND RESCUE OF KELLY AND DEASY — "GOD SAVE IRELAND" — THE MANCHESTER MARTYRS—THE CLERKENWELL EXPLOSION.

ALTHOUGH the insurrection was speedily put down in Ireland, the most strict precautions were used by the Government and local authorities in Great Britain against any hostile movement of the Brotherhood, who were known to be numerous, particularly in certain large centres. There was a considerable amount of alarm in such places, as property to the value of many millions of pounds might, it was considered by its owners, be destroyed in case of any insurrectionary movement on this side of the Channel, which might be got up as a diversion, if the Fenians succeeded in making any headway in Ireland.

In no case was this scare greater than in Liverpool, with its miles of docks, filled with forests of shipping, "laden with golden argosies" from all ends of the world. The authorities made every preparation against surprise. Troops were kept ready in different parts of the town to be moved at a moment's notice, arms and ammunition were conveyed to safe places, and volunteer storehouses were strengthened, watched, and guarded day and night; as were also the banks, public offices, and docks; while the police force, detectives, and local corps of volunteers and pensioners were all kept on the *qui vive* for a threatened rising of the Liverpool Irish on St Patrick's Day. It was on the plea of the unsafety of their storehouse that the members of the Irish corps of Liverpool volunteers were practically disarmed at this time. Their arms were removed to the storehouse of another corps which was supposed to be stronger, but the probability is that the Government feared to trust the rifles in the hands of the "Liverpool Irish" at such a time. The idea of a rising in Liverpool on St Patrick's Day was, of course, absurd, but so great was the scare of the wealthy inhabitants and the local authorities that such was impending, that the Government sent round the steam ram *Wyvern*, which arrived in the Mersey on St Patrick's Eve. She anchored alongside of her Majesty's steamer, *Donegal* (just reinforced by 300 men), on board of which, no doubt, elaborate preparation was made for the bombardment of what would be regarded as the rebel quarters of Scotland and Vauxhall Wards, should the "desperate Fenians" succeed in getting these into their hands.

Corydon having now effectually done his work for his new paymasters, and his evidence being required for the conviction of the Fenians who had been captured, it soon became known to the world that he was an informer. This explained to Colonel Kelly and the other leaders who were still at large, how some of their best laid schemes had been in some way, that they could not understand at the time, thwarted. But there was a greater surprise still to come. Massey, in his prison cell, had become Queen's evidence. This shook confidence all round. He was a man of considerable address and ability, and, it cannot be doubted, up to a certain point, performed the work allotted to him faithfully. He was not, like Corydon, who sold him, a deliberate traitor, but, on his arrest, finding himself betrayed, he knew not by whom, he, in his turn, became a betrayer in order to save himself. With this and the other evidence it was not hard to secure convictions against the captured Fenians. Several were sentenced to be hanged, but their sentences were commuted to penal servitude for life, and others were condemned to various terms of imprisonment.

These circumstances, though depressing to the leaders who remained, did not cause them to abandon the struggle as hopeless. The rising had, however, proved one thing— that notwithstanding all the clever blockade running from Liverpool, Glasgow, and elsewhere, a very insufficient quantity of arms had been got into Ireland after all. A new plan was to be adopted. Those who were in the counsel of the leaders now heard that the flag was to be again raised in Ireland, and that a vessel, with a number of picked men and a plentiful supply of arms for the insurgents, was actually on the seas. A considerable portion of the Brotherhood in Ireland, owing to the circle system, was still intact, the American officers and organisers moving about amongst them to inspire them with fresh confidence. For the same purpose Kelly, Deasy, Michael O'Brien, Rickard Burke, Murphy, Condon, and other officers visited the various parts of England and Scotland.

Sure enough, about the middle of May, rumours of a mysterious vessel hovering about the coast of Ireland began to be heard. This was the brigantine *Erin's Hope*, formerly the *Jacnel*, which had got safely away from New York without suspicion. She reached Sligo Bay on the 20th of May. She had on board a number of Irish-American officers and five thousand stand of arms, three pieces of field artillery, and two hundred thousand cartridges. A lookout had been kept for her, and an agent went aboard and consulted with the Irish-Americans. The result was she left the bay and appeared off another point on the western coast, and again off Helvick Head, near Dungarvan. By this time the conclusion was arrived at that the landing of the arms had better not be attempted, as the chances of the success of another rising were but small. It was determined to take the vessel and arms back again to America to be used at a more opportune time. As her water and provisions had run so short that they were insufficient to supply the whole party for the return voyage, a number of the men were taken ashore in a fishing boat, but fell into the hands of the police.

The *Erin's Hope*, though so closely surrounded with British cruisers, ran the gauntlet through them, and brought back her cargo in safety to America. There was one thing proved by this remarkable voyage — the feasibility of throwing into Ireland sufficient weapons to commence an insurrection with, providing there was the necessary co-operation wherever the landing had to be made.

We have now arrived at the time when there occurred one of the most startling episodes in the history of the Irish in Britain.

As we have seen, several of the Irish-American officers remained in England after the rising. This would account for Colonel Kelly's presence in Manchester, early on the morning of September 11th, 1867, when he and Captain Deasy were arrested in Oak Street, near Shudehill Market. Two others who were with them made their escape. The policemen who arrested them as suspicious characters, from some observations they had heard from one of the party, took them to be burglars. At the police station Kelly gave the name of Martin Williams, and said he was a bookbinder. Deasy said his name was John Whyte, and that he was a hatter. When searched revolvers were found upon them, and this, with their Irish-American accent, caused them to be suspected as Fenians. After this the police were not long in fixing the identity of the prisoners, which was proved by witnesses when they were brought before the magistrates a second time, on Wednesday, September 18th. There were warrants against them for treason-felony, for their connection with the rising, and they were again remanded. Owing to a telegram from Dublin Castle warning the Manchester authorities of an intended attempt to rescue the prisoners, additional precautions were taken for their safe custody. Leaving the court the captives were conveyed through a double line of policemen to the prison van, which had several compartments, with a passage up the middle. Colonel Kelly and Captain Deasy were handcuffed, and the compartments in which they were placed were locked. These precautions were not taken with any of the other prisoners—three women and a boy. Sergeant Brett was the policeman in charge. He sat inside the van on a seat in the passage near the door. He was armed with a cutlass. The door being locked the keys were handed in to Brett through a grating. Twelve armed policemen in all guarded the van. Four sat in front with the driver, two rode on the steps behind, Brett kept guard inside, and four others followed the van in a cab. Leaving the court house on their way to Belle Vue prison, Hyde Road, they passed through some of the principal streets of the city, until they had gone some two miles, when they approached a point where the railway bridge (it has since been rebuilt) obliquely crosses Hyde Road, and where the houses were, at that time, thinly scattered, and the ground mostly devoted to brickfields. Just as they passed under the railway arch two men, armed with revolvers, barred the way. One of these, presenting his weapon, cried "Stop the van." The driver still kept on his way, when a bullet fired over his head and another into one of the horses effectually brought the van to a stand still. As if by magic, there now sprang from their ambuscade behind the walls that lined the road, and from the shadow of the abutments of the arch, a body of determined men, dressed, said the English papers, better than ordinary workmen, and armed for the most part with revolvers. The police fled panic stricken at the first volley of their assailants, who were evidently determined to accomplish their object, the release of the Fenian chiefs, without bloodshed if possible, for they fired over the heads of the defenders of the van. One portion of the men now formed an extended circle outside of the van, and, with revolvers in hand, kept the police, and the mob who had rallied to their assistance, at bay. Thus shielded from interruption, a second party of the Fenians set themselves to the breaking open of the van. The military precision with which the work was carried out showed the able direction of Edward

O'Meagher Condon, Michael O'Brien, and others who had commanded in many a fierce encounter in the American Civil War.

The most active of the assailants was William Philip Allen, who, being a carpenter, was one of those to whom was allotted the mechanical work of the daring enterprise —the breaking open of the van. Another who displayed great energy was Michael Larkin. Adopting the unscrupulous methods for securing the conviction of Irishmen on other occasions, as well as on this, several of the witnesses swore that he was one of the party who most freely used his revolver. As a matter of fact, which is now well authenticated, Michael Larkin never fired a pistol shot in his life-time. Every moment was bringing fresh reinforcements to the police and the mob, and the great object of the Fenians was, therefore, to force the van as speedily as possible. While engaged in this, the outer circle several times forced back the rush of their opponents, the Irishmen using their weapons rather to intimidate than to take life, for only two of their adversaries were wounded—one in the foot and the other in the thigh. Those who had ascended the roof tried to effect an entrance with crowbars, hammers, hatchets, and large stones, while others assailed the door of the van where the brave man, Sergeant Brett, stood on guard inside, refusing to give up his keys. At the commencement of the fray he opened the ventilator in the upper part of the door to see who were the assailants. Seeing them, he exclaimed, according to the account of Emma Halliday, one of the prisoners—"Oh, my God, it's these Fenians," at the same time endeavouring to close the ventilator, while one of the men outside tried to prevent his doing so. As the time was flying rapidly, something decisive must be done by the assailants of the van, before their opponents could gather sufficient force to overpower them. A shot was fired through the key hole into the lock, with the view of shattering it. Immediately a female voice was heard from inside, exclaiming—"He's killed." The bullet intended to force the lock had entered the head of Brett, and in a short time the wound proved fatal. Although the slaying of Brett was afterwards called murder (which in any case it certainly was not), the brave policeman's death was clearly an accident, which none more deplored than the man who fired the deadly ball. Another of the prisoners, Ellen Cooper, at the demand of the men outside, took the keys from the wounded man and handed them out. Quickly the door was opened, when the body of Brett fell out into the road. The Fenians rushed in and opened the compartments in which Kelly and Deasy were confined. Allen exclaimed, in the exultation and excitement of the moment, as he warmly greeted his chief, "Kelly, I'll die for you." His words proved prophetic, for Allen yielded up his life on the scaffold afterwards as a testimony of his loyalty to his country and his leader. The two rescued Fenian chiefs, still handcuffed, were at once hurried across the adjoining field and out of sight of the police and mob who were enraged at seeing their victims thus torn from their grasp. A few brave men stood their ground, sacrificing themselves to cover the retreat of their leaders. These were now hotly assailed by an overwhelming force. So closely was Allen pressed that he had not time to reload his revolver. When the brave Irishmen who formed the rearguard were satisfied that their leaders had got securely away, they retreated from the scene of action, followed up and being gradually surrounded by an overwhelming force. After being assailed in the most cowardly and brutal manner, Allen was captured at Beswick. Condon and some of the others, after being treated in the like brutal manner, were also taken and lodged in jail. The authorities, enraged at their power being set at defiance in the open day, resolved to have victims of some kind upon whom to wreak their vengeance. There was a reign of terror that night for the Irish of Manchester. Raids were made on the quarters where they lived, and about sixty Irishmen were dragged from their homes and flung into jail. On the same evening the two men whose liberty had been effected in such a daring manner, were seen by some brickmakers to enter a cottage near Clayton Bridge, handcuffed, and to quit it a few minutes afterwards with their hands free.

A large reward was offered by Government for their apprehension. All the efforts of the police to discover the retreat of Kelly and Deasy were unavailing, and no bribe could shake the fidelity of those who kept them in concealment. Colonel Kelly remained in a friend's house in Manchester for several months after his rescue. Seizing a favourable opportunity, he drove in a conveyance by road to Liverpool. Here he was taken aboard one of the steamers for America, not as an ordinary passenger, but boarded up in the bulk heading, where a friend kept him supplied with food and took down the boarding after they passed Queenstown. He reached America in safety, as did also Captain Deasy.

The news of the Hyde Road action, as it flashed on the wires to all parts, carried panic to the heart of England, and men asked each other where would the next blow be struck. The funds fell, for while rebellions in Ireland were regarded as a matter of course, the setting of England's authority at defiance in one of her great cities, was more than the wildest imagination could have possibly conceived. The Manchester police went about madly and recklessly among the Irish population, in search of other victims to wreak their vengeance upon, instead of those who had been torn from their grasp. When the prisoners were paraded for identification, there was no difficulty in finding witnesses to swear to any of them as having taken an active part in the attack on the van. In fact, so glaringly false was the evidence some of these witnesses were prepared to give, that the police thought it more prudent to let some of the prisoners go, lest there should be a breakdown through their witnesses discrediting themselves in the rest of the cases. The prisoners, when on their trial, too, complained of the scandalous way in which it was so managed, that individuals could be made so conspicuous as to be easily picked out by those who came to identify them.

The men bore themselves with dignity when brought before the magistrates on the day following the rescue. An English paper said of them—"All the men, particularly Allen, showed remarkable self-possession, old and young— some of them being heavy shouldered fellows, and others slimly built youths. They bore a striking resemblance to each other in their air of resolution, and what, for men in their station and in their present position, might be called consummate address." The prisoners were remanded for a week.

Meanwhile it appeared as if nothing but Irish blood would satiate the cry for vengeance, and in every quarter of the city fresh victims were sought out and thrown into prison. Strict search was made for the retreat of Kelly and Deasy, but it was of no avail. A house in Every Street, Ancoats, was suspected of being their hiding place, as well as the Fenian headquarters. Accordingly, a secret expedition to surprise this fancied stronghold was determined upon, and, on the night of Saturday, September 21st, a raid was made on the house by fifty picked men of the police force, armed with Colt's revolvers. They appear to have found a mare's nest, for only a man and two women were arrested, and against these no charge could be made.

On the following Thursday, September 26th, the prisoners, strongly manacled, were again brought up before the magistrates, who refused to yield to the indignant demand of the prisoners' counsel that the irons should be removed from their hands. After farther evidence the prisoners were again remanded and brought up from day to day until the sitting of the Special Commission appointed to try them.

The Commission opened on Monday, October 28th, before Judges Blackburn and Mellor. Twenty-six men were now placed upon their trial, the great bulk of those who had been so wantonly arrested having had to be discharged from time to time for want of sufficient evidence against them. The following are the names and ages, as given to the police, of those put upon their trial—"William Gould, 30; William O'Meara Allen, 19; Edward Shore, 27; Michael Larkin, 30; Charles Moorhouse, 23; Patrick Kelly, 35; Michael Maguire, 22; John Martin, 34; John Brannon, 40; John Francis Nugent, 22; William Martin, 35; John Carroll, 24; Michael Joseph Boylan, 37; Michael Kennedy, 28; Thomas Maguire (of the Royal Marines), 31; Henry Wilson, 27; John Bacon, 40; Patrick Coffey, 27; Thomas Ryan, 30; William Murphy, 25; Thomas Johnson, 30; Daniel Reddin, 25; James O'Brannon Chambers, 29; William Brophy, 26; Thomas Scally, 22; and Timothy Featherstone, 30. The grand jury, of which Sir Robert

Gerard, an English Catholic, was foreman, returned a true bill for murder against Allen, Larkin, Gould, Thomas Maguire, and Shore. Some of the names given to the police were fictitious, as for instance, Allen's second name was not O'Meara but Philip, while the men set down as William Gould and Edward Shore were in reality the daring Irish-American officers Michael O'Brien and Edward O'Meagher Condon respectively. On behalf of the prisoners an application was made for the removal of the indictment to the Central Criminal Court, on the ground that they could not have a fair trial in Lancashire. The application was refused. The trial of the five men singled out as the principal victims went on during Wednesday, Thursday, and Friday. During the trial the most contradictory evidence was given, the most glaringly false being that against Maguire, who was represented as having borne a most active part in the attack on the van, whereas it was plainly shown afterwards, even to the satisfaction of the Government, that the witnesses who swore against him—the same on whose evidence the other prisoners were convicted—had perjured themselves. Their swearing was so reckless, that they testified to a number of specific acts during the attack on the van, by men, afterwards proved beyond doubt to have been at work the whole of the day of the attack at Liverpool docks. The jury at half-past seven on the evening of Friday, November 1st, pronounced the five prisoners, Allen, Larkin, O'Brien, Condon, and Maguire to be GUILTY. On these being asked why sentence of death should not be pronounced against them, they each in their turn replied.

Allen was the first to answer, and even the English newspapers acknowledged that the brave youth bore himself with the spirit of a martyr as he spoke. He declared that he stood in the dock for the same offence that Emmet committed. No man more regretted the death of Sergeant Brett than he. He would die, he declared, as many thousands had died, for the sake of their beloved land.

The true-hearted, earnest artizan, Michael Larkin, then spoke. Thoughts of his loving wife and little ones at home no doubt flashed across his mind at this moment, but his courage never failed as he addressed the court. He, too, declared that no one could deplore Brett's death more than he did. He denied the truth of the evidence given as to his use of a revolver on the day of the rescue, but he admitted—and gloried in the act—that he was there that day to assist in the rescue of the Fenian chiefs.

Then came the turn to speak of the man of iron nerve, Michael O'Brien, who had often faced death in battle, and now feared not to meet it there in his country's cause. He commenced by saying that every witness who had sworn anything against him had sworn falsely. He was, he said, a citizen of the United States, and if Charles Francis Adams had done his duty to him he would not be in the dock that day. He then gave a long address on the right of Ireland to freedom, and of her sons to resist those who kept them in thraldom.

As the unfortunate man, Thomas Maguire, rose, and stated in simple words the reason why he should not be sentenced to death, even then the judge, jury, and witnesses must have felt that every word he spoke was the simple truth, and that he was really what he described himself, a soldier of the Queen, having no knowledge of Fenianism or its professors. But conscience must be drowned, and this innocent man must suffer, lest, perchance, the other prisoners, who had been convicted on the same evidence, should escape.

Edward O'Meagher Condon now spoke. He, too, said that the witnesses against him had sworn falsely. He did not, however, deny having assisted in the rescue, but justified it, saying that if Jefferson Davis, who had been president of the rebel states of America, had been so rescued in a northern city, there would have been a cry of applause through all England. He said they were not afraid to die for what they had done—"At least, I am not," he added. "Nor I," "nor I," "nor I," promptly and proudly cried his companions. He concluded by saying—

"I only trust again, that those who are to be tried after us will have a fair trial, and that our blood will satisfy the craving which exists. You will soon send us before God, and I am perfectly prepared to go. I have nothing to regret, or to retract, or take back. I can only say, GOD SAVE IRELAND."

The now memorable words had scarcely escaped his lips, when they were repeated by his companions proudly and defiantly, yet prayerfully. "God save Ireland!" they cried in that English dock, with the shadow of death already lowering over them.

Judge Mellor then expressed himself as fully concurring in the justice of the verdict which had been recorded against them, and pronounced on the prisoners the sentence of DEATH.

They never quailed as they listened to their doom, and as they were leaving the dock they greeted the few friendly faces they saw, saying—"God be with you, Irishmen and Irishwomen." As they passed from the dock they again raised the defiant cry—"God save Ireland." That cry went forth from England's court of law, and was breathed that night in many an Irish home in Manchester, ere it was taken up by stern men and tearful women through the towns of Britain. "God save Ireland," was wafted across the sea, repeated by millions of voices in Ireland, and echoed back by Irishmen in every land, until it has now become at once the watch-word and the prayer for their country's coming resurrection.

Of the twenty-six men put upon their trials at the opening of the Commission, five were, as we have seen, sentenced to death, fourteen were discharged, while the following seven were each sentenced to five years penal servitude—John Carroll, Charles Moorhouse, Daniel Reddin, Thomas Scally, William Murphy, John Brannon, and Timothy Featherstone. As a specimen of the kind of "justice" administered at this Commission, William Murphy, at the expiration of his sentence, told the present writer that *he was not present at the rescue.* No harm could then come to him by telling the truth, as he had paid the penalty for what he had *not* done. Besides, it would have been the proudest boast of his life if he could have said he had been there. Maguire, the marine, was pardoned, it being apparent, after the few days' delirium of the English people had subsided, that the evidence against him (which also helped to convict the other prisoners) was false. After this the life of Edward O'Meagher Condon was also spared, for no other reason, that anyone could see, but that he was an American born citizen. It was now thought that surely the other three men would never be executed on evidence that had so utterly broken down. It would seem, however, that the authorities feared to deprive the savage populace altogether of their promised feast of blood, and, therefore, *some* Irishmen must die. The last scene of the Manchester tragedy was accordingly fixed for Saturday, November 23rd, 1867, at Salford jail.

A strong military force was poured into the city, and on the eve of the dread scene the rabble began to take up their positions to be in time next morning to gloat over the death of the Irish martyrs, just as the Pagan Romans of old went to the amphitheatre to witness the dying struggles of the early Christians. Again and again was the stillness of the night broken by the brutal shouts and choruses which they chanted, as the Indian does the death-song of his victim tied to the stake.

Far different was the scene within the walls where the brave Christian patriots slept their last sleep tranquilly, like men who had made their peace with God. At a quarter to five in the morning they were roused from their repose to assist at the holy sacrifice of the Mass. At eight o'clock they were led forth to die, attended by the priests of the church to give them the consolation of religion in their last moments. They met their death like men conscious they were yielding up their lives for a holy cause. Allen was first led out on the scaffold in view of the rabble. After him came O'Brien, who tenderly kissed his companion and whispered in his ear what were no doubt words of encouragement. Larkin was now led on, and to him also O'Brien whispered in like manner. The three martyrs in the face of that multitude of foes, now offered up their last prayer—" Lord Jesus have mercy on us,"—when the fatal bolt was withdrawn and the sacrifice consummated.

Their DEATH, which was intended to strike terror into the heart of Ireland, was in truth the LIFE of Irish freedom, for even the coldest hearts now glowed with that spirit of patriotism which has never yet been subdued in our country and NEVER WILL, for—

"On the cause must go,
Amidst joy, or weal, or woe,
Till we've made our isle a nation free and grand."

After the attack on the prison van several of the revolvers used by the assailants were picked up on the scene of the encounter. These were identified by a Birmingham gunsmith as being of his make. This led to the arrest of Daniel Darragh—who went by the name of Pherson Thompson—and the same gunmaker identified him as having purchased the weapons from him. In connection with the same matter, the Birmingham police arrested, on Thursday, December 5th, at his residence in Bradford Street, a prominent Irishman of the town, William Hogan, for purchasing pistols for the attack on the prison van in Manchester. The newspapers described him as—"A married man, and in his appearance a stout, fine-looking Irishman, about the middle height," and as having held "an important position as one of the chief emissaries of the district." With Hogan, at the time of his arrest was a tall, broad-shouldered, deep-chested, handsome, genial-looking gentleman, wearing a full brown beard. He also was taken to the police station and questioned. He said his name was Jones, and that he was a traveller for a commercial firm in Liverpool. As he had his samples, address cards, letters, &c., which the police officials inspected, and as they telegraphed to his firm in Liverpool, and were answered that "Jones" was what he described himself, they let him go. In John Devoy's graphic account of the escape of Stephens he describes the originator of the plan for getting the C.O.I.R. out of Richmond—John Breslin, who died in America some time since. Speaking of Breslin's family, who were among the most capable men the I.R.B. produced, it will be remembered that Devoy says—"All his brothers, however, were Fenians. One of them, who has since been Vice President of the Land League in this city, was at that time an acting Inspector of the Dublin police and clerk in the Superintendent's office, a station which enabled him to render most important service to the conspirators." The person so described was "Jones"—otherwise Michael Breslin, then on a special mission to this country, and by far the most important member of the I.R.B. then in Great Britain.

Hogan was brought up in the Manchester police court with Darragh. In addition to the evidence as to the purchase of the weapons, several witnesses, the same disreputable characters that were proved to have sworn so falsely at the trial of the men for the attack of the van, swore that Darragh also was present on that occasion. It is a question, whether, otherwise, he could have been convicted. But for the fact that Hogan's whereabouts on the day of the attack was well known to the police, and that they knew he could prove beyond doubt that he was not one of the rescuers of Kelly and Deasy, the usual evidence of his having taken part in the attack would, as in the case of others, no doubt have been got up, and he, too, would have been convicted. He was just the kind of man the police would use all their ingenuity to get put out of the way, but in this case they could not manage it. It was proved that a pistol marked "Mortimer" was picked up after the attack on the van, and a Birmingham gunsmith at the trial identified it as being of his make. The counsel for Hogan asked to see the pistol, and it was handed to him. "Are you quite sure the pistol is of your own make?" asked the counsel, directing a pistol to be handed to the gunsmith. The latter looked at the marking on it, and swore that it was. This disposed of the case against Hogan, for it was proved that the weapon sworn to, another revolver substituted for the original one by the counsel, had been turned out by another maker, and that "Mortimer, London," which was engraved on the pistol originally sworn to, was a name frequently put upon their pistols by the less noted Birmingham gunsmiths; it being one of the "tricks of the trade" to engrave upon weapons the names of firms not then in existence, but which, in their time, had been in good repute. Hogan was, of course, acquitted. Darragh was remanded, and when he, in company with another prisoner, was brought up for trial at the Assizes, so clear was the *alibi* made out for his defence that the judge charged strongly in his favour. Notwithstanding this the jury found him guilty of wilful murder. He was sentenced to death, but this was commuted to penal servitude for life. He died of consumption in Portland prison, on the 28th of June 1870. Hogan, with touching reverence for the memory of his dead friend, conveyed his remains to be buried among his kith and kin at Ballycastle, in his native Antrim. William Hogan, himself, afterwards died in Liverpool, his remains being followed to Ford Cemetery by many of the prominent nationalists of the city.

On the 13th of December 1867, there occurred the most lamentable incident in connection with the Fenian movement. This was occasioned by the blowing up of the wall of Clerkenwell prison, by means of a barrel of gunpowder, with a view to the rescue of Colonel Rickard Burke, who had been arrested and was there awaiting his trial. It was supposed he would be taking his exercise on the other side of the wall, in the jail yard, at the moment the explosion was timed for. It so happened that none of the prisoners were there at the time, otherwise it is extremely probable that the man it was intended to rescue would himself, among others, have been killed. This would go to show that those who caused the explosion had no idea of the terrible consequences that would follow. The houses on the other side of the narrow street were destroyed, and twelve unfortunate people were killed. Michael Barrett was executed for the deed, although it is by no means certain that it was his hand fired the fuse, as was stated at the trial, as a strong *alibi* was put forward on his behalf that he was in Glasgow at the time of the explosion.

Colonel Burke, Henry Mullady, and Joseph Theobald Casey were brought up on Tuesday, 28th of April 1868, at the Central Criminal Court, London, before Baron Bramwell and Justice Keating, charged with an attempt "to depose the Queen from her style, honour, or royal name of the Imperial Crown of Great Britain," &c., &c. " by divers acts and deeds." Evidence from the informers Corydon and Massey was given, and also as to the purchase of arms for sending into Ireland. The charge against Casey was withdrawn before the conclusion of the trial. On Friday, May 1st, Burke and Mullady were found guilty, Burke being sentenced to fifteen years and Mullady to seven years penal servitude.

CHAPTER XXIX.

MICHAEL DAVITT.

As amongst the Irish in Britain during the Young Ireland movement one man, Terence Bellew M'Manus, stood out with unmistakable distinctness, so another Irishman, Michael Davitt, attained even more remarkable prominence in connection with Fenianism. He was little more than a youth when he took part in the Chester raid. He has since, after undergoing a sentence of penal servitude, attained a widely extended fame as the founder of another Irish national movement which has met with a remarkable amount of success. He has also become a recognized power among the British democracy.

He was born in the year 1846, in the townland of Straid, in the county Mayo. His family were evicted when he was about eight years of age, and the memory of this, no doubt, influenced the whole of his after life.

You will find the people from the various Irish provinces running in veins, so to speak, in particular parts of England, Scotland, and Wales. They form little colonies—one member of a family bringing over another, and his relatives and friends, until they stamp certain places with their own characteristics. In just such a locality, where the Irish are mostly from the Western province, is the little cotton-manufacturing town of Haslingden, in North Lancashire, where Davitt's father and family settled on their arrival in England.

Looking down upon the Rossendale Valley is the range of high brown hills over which they could ramble after Mass on the Sundays to enjoy the health giving breezes and look westwards towards the Irish Sea, that separated them from their homes. One could well imagine that the exiles who preceded the Davitts had pitched their tents there, because the place reminded them of their native Mayo. Truly their fervid Celtic imaginations might well have seen a likeness—and yet how unlike? The face of nature may have had similar features in both, but whereas in their western home native trade had been paralysed by foreign rule, here it flourished. From Bacup, at the eastern end of the valley, as you traverse the not unromantic road westward, getting as you go forward glimpses of the Irwell—here more like a mountain stream and considerably cleaner than at Manchester—you everywhere hear the busy hum of industry. It is the same as you pass along, for miles, through the almost continuous rows of the two-storied cottages in which the factory operators live—through Stacksteads and Rawtenstall, until you reach Haslingden, nestling among the higher hills that mark the western extremity of the Rossendale Valley. Here they will show you, in Wilkinson Street, the cottage, built like most of the others, of the stone of the district, where Martin Davitt, the father of Michael, and his family lived. The elder Davitt found employment as an assurance agent. Michael was, while a child, sent to work at a cotton mill, where an accident caused the loss of his right arm. Other employment was found for him with Mr Cockcroft, a bookseller and printer, who also kept the local post-office at the corner of the market place. Here he could snatch opportunities for reading and following out his natural bent for culture, and here the gentle, bright-eyed, manly Irish lad is still borne in kindly remembrance. As he grew up he read with avidity such Irish books and newspapers as came within his reach.

At length, among the little towns and villages of Rossendale, there appeared a silver tongued missionary, whose place in the national ranks now knows him no more, but who, in his time, journeyed to the most distant corners of the country to fire the souls of Irishmen with the most exalted patriotism. His meetings were necessarily small, as they generally had to be held in secret, but his witching eloquence drew Michael Davitt and many of his friends into the charmed circle of the practical physical force nationality of the Irish Revolutionary Brotherhood.

We have seen how Davitt led his men to take part in the Chester raid. Returning to Haslingden, he got his circle into working order again. He was soon afterwards selected as organiser for the north of England, and entrusted with the difficult and dangerous work which had been carried on by Rickard Burke — purchasing and sending arms into Ireland. Many Irishmen in the north of England must have met him at this time in company with Arthur Forrester, and would have noted the remarkable contrast between the two young men. Forrester was eloquent and a poet of no mean order, having, like his sister, Fanny Forrester, inherited the gift of song from his mother, whose "Irish widow's message to her Son" will be remembered as one of the most beautiful and touching poems we possess. Forrester did all the oratory, while Davitt sat, an unassuming young fellow, mostly listening, but from time to time throwing in a practical remark. Yet under that modest, placid exterior was one of those enthusiastic natures that, in all ages, have risen up to move the world. His figure is tall and commanding. Like many of the western Irish he has something of the olive skin and dark hair that are supposed to denote a partially Iberian ancestry. He has strongly-marked handsome features, lit up by dark eyes which glance fiercely when denouncing oppression, but are tender as a woman's when listening to a tale of suffering. If he has not the calm self restraint once so characteristic of Parnell, and which, with other gifts, marked him out as a leader, he has the more lovable Irish nature, for which John Mitchel, sturdy Ulster Presbyterian as he was, had such intense admiration. He might have had some such nature as Davitt's in his mind, in his "Life of Hugh O'Neill," where he says— "The writer does indeed acknowledge a strong sympathy with the primitive Irish race, proud and vehement, tender and poetical; with their deep religion and boundless wealth of sweetest song, and high old names, and the golden glories of tradition."

With the remarkable personality of Davitt, which made it so easy for the police to keep a constant watch upon his movements, it speaks much for his astuteness and caution that he carried on the work of organising and purchasing and sending arms into Ireland for about three years before he fell into the hands of the law.

He was arrested in London, on May the 14th, 1870, in company with John Wilson, an Englishman, a gunsmith of

Birmingham, on the platform of the Great Western Railway station at Paddington. He was brought to court and remanded from time to time, so that Corydon might have the opportunity for fully inventing the case against him. At the trial the police evidence was to prove the purchase of arms by Davitt in Birmingham, and their storage there and in other places for the purpose of being sent to Ireland, and for distribution among the Brotherhood in England and Scotland.

When arrested, Davitt had, it was stated, £150 in notes in his possession. Wilson had in his possession fifty six-chambered revolvers. The theory of the prosecution was that Wilson had come to deliver the arms to Davitt, and to receive payment for them. The Crown Prosecutor, when Davitt and Wilson were brought up at the police court, dwelt upon this as a suspicious circumstance, and said, in urging the charge of treason-felony against both the prisoners, that he could show they had been connected in carrying out the Fenian conspiracy, and that the arms were to be ultimately sent to Ireland for treasonable purposes.

That Davitt was purchasing and storing arms, and forwarding them to various places, was, no doubt, sufficiently proved, and though also there could be no doubt but that his object was that they should be used in a fight for Irish freedom, there was no legal proof of the use to which they were to be put. He was, therefore, remanded from time to time, so that Corydon might have ample opportunity to get up the case against him after he had "identified" him in prison—no difficult task, considering Davitt's well-marked personality. At the trial Corydon gave the usual evidence of the meetings in Liverpool, previous to the Chester raid and the rising, attended by the American officers and others, among these being, he swore, Michael Davitt. He also swore that Davitt took part in the Chester raid. This completed the chain of evidence required by the police to connect the procuring of the arms with the insurrectionary movement. Davitt is quite certain that the notorious informer never saw him before he was brought to identify him in prison. But this man who was dealing in arms was evidently a "dangerous character"—

a man to be got out of the way, and if there was not sufficient evidence to legally convict him, it must be manufactured. It was not the first time this was done, nor the last.

The result of the trial was that Michael Davitt and John Wilson were convicted of treason-felony. As sentence was about to be passed, Davitt made an earnest appeal to the judge, not for himself, but for the Englishman. He declared that Wilson never knew until he arrived at Paddington station that he, Davitt, was an Irishman, or that his name was not "Jackson." He would, he declared, cheerfully undergo any additional sentence that might be passed upon him, if Wilson would be spared, and his wife and family saved from the workhouse; and he begged that the Englishman's sentence might be added to his own. Davitt was sentenced to fifteen years and Wilson to seven years penal servitude.

Michael Davitt's prison door only closed upon one chapter of his history. While in penal servitude, notwithstanding the cruel treatment of his brutal jailors, he had time to think out another plan for the solution of the Irish problem.

CHAPTER XXX.

RETROSPECTIVE—CHURCH PROGRESS—THE IRISH IN LIVERPOOL—THE IRISH IN BIRMINGHAM—"NO-POPERY" RIOTS AGAIN.

THE previous chapters contain some of the most striking incidents connected with Fenianism. They have been grouped together and put into their due sequence that they might be the more readily grasped. The ten years just gone through witnessed some startling scenes, but what has been described constitutes but a small portion of the record of our people here during that time. Otherwise it would seem to the casual reader that their history was made up of a series of conspiracies and abortive raids and risings, of splendid heroism and falsest treachery, of arrests and trials —ending in the inevitable prospect that the Irish patriot would appear to have always had to look forward to, of penal servitude or the gallows. These pages have shown, too, how the dormant spirit of bigotry was from time to time fanned into a flame by the foul breath of some "no-Popery" lecturer, and, as a result—in one or other of the towns of Great Britain—our unfortunate people driven to bay, and having to fight for their homes, their lives, and the shrines of their faith.

Notwithstanding all this, they had made substantial progress in the period now passed through. They were steadily coming to the front in social life, and out of their earnings had reared many noble churches and schools, showing that they still retained their old love of religion and learning; and, though some became demoralised by their surroundings, it was abundantly proved that Irish intellect and bone and sinew could hold their own in the battle of life.

The re-establishment of the Catholic hierarchy in England was a striking landmark in the history and progress of religion. It roused a storm of senseless bigotry, which in due time passed away, for from the first the Ecclesiastical Tithes Act was a dead letter. Perhaps the most striking proof of this was given by Dr MacHale, when he was being examined before a committee of the House of Commons in connection with a petition against the return of George Henry Moore to Parliament for Mayo. There he described himself as the Archbishop of Tuam, without any of the pains and penalties provided by the Act being inflicted upon him. After some years the Act was repealed.

Allusion has been made to the struggle for perfect religious equality, which Catholic Emancipation in 1829 did not entirely give. It has also been shown that the disabilities of Catholic Irishmen in the army and navy of Britain were only removed, as had always been the case, when this country found herself confronted with some danger abroad, such as the Crimean War or the Indian Mutiny. It was only when the Irish soldier or sailor became indispensable, and it was necessary to conciliate him, that substantial concessions were made to his conscientious convictions. Good service was done in Parliament by Frederick Lucas, John Francis Maguire, and other Catholic members, in procuring better facilities for religious ministrations for Catholic soldiers and sailors, for the poor in the workhouses, and for such Catholics as were unfortunate enough to find their way into prison.

As showing the progress of the Catholic Church in England, Cardinal Wiseman, in a paper read at the Catholic Congress at Malines, said that in 1830 there were 434 priests and 410 churches and chapels, and that in 1864 these had increased to 1242 priests and 872 churches. In the following year, on the 15th of February 1865, Cardinal Wiseman died.

He was succeeded in the see of Westminster by Dr Henry Edward Manning, who was created Cardinal some ten years afterwards. He was a man of saintly and noble character, who saw that religion could be better served by appealing to the hearts and minds of the people than by State intrigues, and though not of our race, he was in sympathy with Ireland's national aspirations. Soon after entering upon his episcopal duties, we find him showing in a prominent manner his love for the poor and erring. He presided over a meeting on Monday, 22nd May 1865, for the formation of a Reformatory and Industrial School Association. At this meeting there were brought forward some statistics as to the criminal or semi-criminal population of Liverpool, showing, among other things, what an undue proportion of Catholics there appeared to be among the inmates of the borough jail. These statistics were compiled and presented by the jail chaplain, Father Nugent, a man distinguished for his ability and philanthropy. Before becoming jail chaplain he had for many years laboured successfully to break down the barriers of prejudice against our country and creed. He had also largely devoted himself to the culture and elevation of the Catholic youth of Liverpool, and many prosperous Irishmen in that city to-day owe whatever position and culture they possess to the means of improvement afforded them by Father Nugent at the schools of the Catholic Institute. When he became jail chaplain he saw that the main cause of almost all the crime among our people was drink, and that, without it, they would be as free from crime as in the most virtuous parts of Ireland. He, therefore, commenced a temperance movement in Liverpool, which has rescued thousands from destruction, and made many a happy home which before had been wretched. After a time, he began to see that the most effectual way to deal with intemperance among our people was to stop the evil at the fountain head by assisting in any movement which would make the Irish people happy and prosperous at home, and thus keep them away from the temptations of the great cities of this country. Those, therefore, who had most actively opposed his former well meant emigration schemes, were pleased to find that Father Nugent's organ, the *Catholic Times*, had become one of the most strenuous advocates of self-government for Ireland. Any statement from a man like Father Nugent was bound to attract attention, and his statistics regarding the Catholic prisoners in the Liverpool borough jail were much quoted by men of every creed and party at the time. Some reference to them will, therefore, be necessary here.

Catholic prisoners would mean, in most cases, Irish prisoners or those of Irish extraction. He is no friend of creed or country who would keep back the truth in a case like this, but if such statistics are not to be used to the detriment of religion and to cast a slight on the Irish race, it is necessary that the *whole* truth should be known. Unfortunately, these jail statistics, distorted to suit their own purpose, and every fact creditable to our creed and country suppressed, were the stock-in-trade of more than one no-Popery lecturer. A well-known north of Ireland Protestant minister constantly used them. He also dwelt on the number of Irish in the Liverpool workhouse, and he triumphantly pointed to the statistics showing the number of Catholic inmates of the borough jail. "Why," he would ask, "was this? Was it because they were Irish? No—the Irish were a bright, intelligent people—he himself was an Irishman. Then how was it? Ah! my friends," he would say, "here you find the demoralising influence of Popery on those professing it, for while in Liverpool they are but one-fifth of the population, they supply one-half of the paupers and criminals." Those who have carefully read the chapter on the Irish Famine in this book, and have seen how Liverpool was the gate through which most of our people sought to fly from the dread visitation, cannot be surprised that an undue proportion of Irish wretchedness choked up the outlet, could get no further, and sank into a terrible condition of destitution. They were surrounded by many temptations, and led a most precarious hand-to-mouth existence. The "No Irish need apply" of the British Pharisee shut the door against the poor Irish girl looking for domestic service, so that there was nothing for her but street hawking, as there are but few manufactures employing young people in Liverpool. In the same way the boy of Irish birth or parentage, not having sufficiently "respectable" connections to recommend him to an apprenticeship to some trade or a post in a shop or office, was also driven to some street calling until he got the bone in him to shoulder a hod or work at the docks. Of course there were many exceptions to this, and in no place more than in Liverpool has it been shown how, with "a fair field and no favour," an Irishman is bound to come to the front.

But lamentable as was the condition of many of our people in Liverpool, let us even take these jail statistics so dishonestly distorted by the no-Popery minister, and they show that, on the whole, the Liverpool Irish were no discredit to the land of their fathers. To begin with—instead of being one-fifth of the population of Liverpool we are almost, if not quite, one-third. This can be proved by the census taken in the various Catholic church districts and by the canvass made by the various Catholic and Irish organisations in connection with registration. These last know the number of Catholic and Irish voters, and those who ought to be voters. In the Liverpool School Board there are fifteen members, of whom the Catholics return six. Now, making all due allowance for the compactness with which Catholics vote for the School Board, one-fifth of the population could hardly do this. Granting you are one-third, or nearly so, it will be said, how is it that you produce half the criminals? The explanation already given as to the condition of our people when driven here, and their surroundings and temptations after their arrival, would be sufficient. But this is not all. When it is stated that half the criminals are Catholics, the general nature of their offences must be taken into consideration. Of the large number who in the course of a year appear as separate and distinct offenders, many are really the same people over and over again, sent to jail, often for some petty offence which is really no crime at all. Take the poor basket girl, born in Ireland, perhaps, but more frequently in some street leading off Marybone. If she came from Ireland, she has probably had little chance of training for domestic service, and, if brought up in one of our wretchedly poor streets in Liverpool, still less. This explains in many cases the "No Irish need apply" that used formerly to be the tail end of so many advertisements for domestic servants. The girls take to selling oranges or apples, fish, or rubbing-stones—often carrying basket loads under which a strong man would stagger. Should they loiter to rest themselves, or to sell their stock, they are often harried and harassed, and "chivied" about by the police. Should they give "cheek" they are "run in" to jail. Brought before the magistrate they may, by drawing on their "stock money," pay the fine. If not, they are sent to the borough jail at Walton, and in due time figure in the statistics, and in the mouths of the howling "no-Popery" preachers and lecturers as "criminals."

Before a Parliamentary committee a vindication of the Catholic and Irish girls of the street-hawking class came from an English Protestant lady, who, in her evidence, gave as her experience, as an official of a philanthropic association in London, that the Catholic girls she had come in contact with compared favourably as to their virtue and general conduct with any others. The same would apply to Liverpool and elsewhere. Mayhew, in his "London Labour and the London Poor," also bears testimony to the virtue of the London-Irish coster girls and lads, who seldom, he says, like others of their class, form illicit connections.

There are, it cannot be denied, amongst the most wretched of our people in the squalid neighbourhoods of the larger towns, a number of offences, chiefly of violence, arising out of drunkenness. It is not that they drink more than people of other nationalities, but that, being naturally demonstrative, they put themselves more in evidence when under the influence of intoxicants, where an Englishman would go and sleep off their effects. Drink is a danger to our people politically as well as morally. The moral aspect of the case can be best dealt with by the clergy and the sacraments of the Church, and need not be further touched upon here, but as to politics in connection with drink, and the places where drink may be had, something may be said. A couple of illustrations will serve to show the evils of the connection. Under the head of "Alleged Fenianism in Deptford," the newspapers had an account of a trial of some Irishmen for treason-felony. They were, it seems, frequenters of a public house called the "King William." The landlord appeared to give evidence in the case, and, in his examination, incidentally said—"Oh, I am entirely supported by Irishmen." Here is another case. Some years ago a very respectable and patriotic Irishman—since dead —had a public house in Liverpool, as decently conducted an establishment as you would find anywhere. As he was a generous, warm-hearted man, he had a good connection among his fellow-countrymen. One day, during the most stirring years of the Fenian movement, Major Greig, the Liverpool head constable—who had just been made a C. B. through the use he made of Corydon's information—sent for our friend. "They tell me," said the Major, "that you have Fenian meetings held at your house." This was strongly repudiated. There were, the publican said, benefit societies held in his house, but, so far as he knew, they had nothing of a Fenian character. If he found it to be so he would at once stop these meetings. "Not at all," replied Major Greig. "Don't do anything of the kind. By all means let them meet there." It was evidently the idea of Major Greig that he stood in little need of informers so long as he could send his men in plain clothes to such houses to listen to the foolish and incautious talk sometimes going on in them. Similar incidents are known to have occurred elsewhere. A constitutional organisation has nothing to fear from police spies, it is true, but the holding of meetings and attempts to carry on political work —for they can only be attempts—where drink is sold, are demoralising, and unworthy of a great and holy cause. The League of the Cross, founded by Cardinal Manning, is undoubtedly doing good work in stopping intemperance. It shows the powerful grasp he possessed of the drink question in connection with his people, that, while grappling with the evil as he found it, his strong sympathies were with those who would deal with the causes that are chiefly responsible for the evil. He saw that nine-tenths of the misery and faults of the Irish arose from the way in which they had been driven from their country, where, with all their poverty, those who are now but too often a scandal to creed and country here, would, if still at home, be living virtuous and happy lives. He did not, therefore, like some ecclesiastics, attempt to suppress the holy feeling of nationality among Irishmen. On the contrary, he saw what a powerful influence it was to keep them safe amidst dangerous and grovelling surroundings, but, above all, he would stop the evil of their condition at its source by giving Ireland self-government.

The appointment of Catholic chaplains for public institutions marked the progress towards religious equality. There cannot be a doubt but that the Catholic population of Great Britain—and, therefore, to some extent, the available Irish strength—would be much greater now had it not been that, up to a comparatively recent date, Catholic children in workhouses could not be educated in the religion of their parents. This proselytism, and that among the children of Catholic soldiers and sailors, accounts for the large number of characteristically Irish names borne by many who are lost to both creed and country. The number is even greater than would appear from this, as any ardent politician can see in going through the registers of voters, where he will find among those lost to us many bearing what were originally Irish names, but which have been Anglicised almost beyond recognition in the spelling.

On June 6th, 1866, there was serious rioting in Portsmouth, caused by the ribald and blasphemous attacks on the faith of Catholics by a no-Popery lecturer named Murphy. This wretched creature became during the next few years the cause of rioting and bloodshed in several towns.

Among the most formidable of the riots were those in Birmingham. A sketch of the position and history of our people in that great centre will here be interesting. It is not a cheerful thing to contemplate, either for Irishmen or Englishmen, for Catholics or Protestants, that so large a portion of this book should be taken up with accounts of no-Popery and Anti-Irish riots. It will be seen that as far back as 1687 we have had to record the destruction of a Franciscan church and convent in Masshouse Lane by the mob of Birmingham. After that came William of Orange and the Penal Laws, bringing with them dark days indeed for the professors of the old faith in the Midland metropolis.

Whether as regards the old Catholic diocese of Lichfield or the present diocese of Birmingham, there are memories and associations connected with the Midland District of England which are of the deepest interest to Irishmen, for its apostle and patron, St Chad, if not himself an Irishman, was connected with our country by many ties. He was partially educated at the monastery of Lindisfarne, by St Aidan, an Irishman, one of the successors of St Columbkille. The Reverend Alban Butler says of St Chad—" For his greater improvement in sacred letters and divine contemplation he passed into Ireland." He filled the see of Lichfield until the time of his death, 2nd March 673. He was buried in the church of St Mary, in Lichfield. From thence his body was removed to the church of St Peter. The relics were afterwards translated into the great church, built in 1148, under the invocation of the Blessed Virgin and St Chad, which is now the Cathedral, and there remained till the change of religion. Lichfield Cathedral, which has within late years been restored, is a grand old structure and the glory of the Midlands. In its library, besides several other treasures, is one of those magnificent illuminated manuscripts of that Irish school of art which flourished more than a thousand years ago. The gem of the Lichfield collection is the manuscript known as the Gospel of St Chad. Westwood thus describes it—" There is an ancient tradition that the volume was written by St Gildas, and some of the entries in the book are at least a thousand years old. It certainly possessed all the characteristics of the ancient Irish school. This will account for the connection of the volume with Llandaff and St Teilo, as recorded in the marginal entries; while other entries record events which occurred at Lichfield, of which St Chad, or Ceadda, was the first bishop, in the seventh century. St Chad, although a Northumbrian, was educated in Ireland, in the school of St Finan, as stated by Bede. It is not impossible that the volume may have been in the handwriting of the saint himself, and hence the popular designation."

The Rev. Father Greaney, in his "Guide to St Chad's Cathedral," gives some very interesting particulars of the progress of the church in Birmingham since the penal days. After the destruction of the church and convent of the Franciscans, at the end of the seventeenth century, they removed to Edgbaston. It is said that some time in the last century Mass was said in a private house, now a butcher's shop, in Smallbrook Street. The Birmingham Catholics were day by day dying out or leaving the place, but there must have been, after a time, a revival, probably caused by a gradual influx of Irish, for they were beginning to increase in London, Liverpool, and elsewhere about the middle of the eighteenth century; and the same might be expected in Birmingham. At all events we find that, in 1786, St Peter's, the oldest existing Catholic church, was commenced, and had to be enlarged some time afterwards. In 1806, while Dr John Milner, the famous controversialist, was bishop of the district, a room in which to say Mass, the entrance being by a flight of wooden steps, was procured in Water Street. This was afterwards found too small, and it was arranged to build a new chapel in Shadwell Street, near the site of the present St Chad's Cathedral, which replaced it. This noble building, which stands in Bath Street, was erected from the designs of the great reviver of Gothic architecture in this country—Augustus Welby Pugin. The foundation stone was laid on the 29th of October 1839. Bishop Wiseman preached, and the "Friendly Brothers of St Patrick" assisted at the ceremonials of the day. This was the first Catholic church built as a cathedral

in this country since the "Reformation." Father Greaney
describes the wonderful way in which the relics of St Chad
were discovered and placed in Catholic hands. On Sunday,
June 20th, 1841, these relics were translated from Oscott to
the new cathedral, and placed on a bier, surrounded by
lights, in the Lady Chapel, and watched night and day by
the brothers of St Chad's Guild. The cathedral was consecrated on Tuesday, June 22nd, 1841, by Bishop Walsh
and his coadjutor, Bishop Wiseman. After the relics were
carried in, the doors were thrown open and the spacious
cathedral filled. The relics are now nobly enshrined over
the high altar. To the minds of the Irishmen of Birmingham
these relics of St Chad have a solemn significance. They
form a sacred connecting link between them and their
forefathers; for the Irish immigration of to-day brings with
it the same faith of St Patrick and St Columbkille that St
Chad found when he visited Ireland in the seventh century.
There is another coincidence of the same kind in Birmingham. Just as St Chad went to Ireland "for his greater
improvement in sacred letters and divine contemplation,"
so, some fifty years ago, certain pious Catholic ladies of
Birmingham passed into Ireland to prepare themselves for
a religious life, under the direction of the foundress of the
Sisters of Mercy, Sister Mary Catherine M'Auley. Singular
and significant, too, it was, that a bishop of Irish descent,
Dr Wiseman, like another St Aidan, received these pious
ladies in Birmingham, the convent of the order being at
Handsworth.

During O'Connell's agitation for repeal of the Union the
Irish of Birmingham were not behind, and on one occasion
had the honour of receiving the great Liberator in their
town; the occasion being a public breakfast given to him
by the English Reformers, on March 9th, 1844. He visited
Birmingham again in 1846, when his fellow-countrymen
presented an address to him. During the Tenant Right
agitation we find that a sum of money was subscribed here
and sent to Ireland to assist in the return of Charles Gavan
Duffy for New Ross.

In the summer of 1856 there were some vigorously
written letters from a correspondent of the *Nation*, called

"The Irish in England." From a reference to these in his "New Ireland," it seems they were from the pen of the late A. M. Sullivan. His letters from the "Black Country," in particular, contain some graphic and picturesque touches. It will be interesting to compare Mr Sullivan's experiences of the places he visited nearly forty years ago with what one sees there now. He has not much to say about Birmingham. Speaking of it, he says, "Iron is to Birmingham what cotton is to Manchester." Of the Irish in it, he tells us "there is ample provision for their spiritual wants," and it struck him that there was an extraordinary contrast between the condition of our people there and of the Irish in Liverpool and Manchester. He says of the Irish of the midland capital, "They are poor to a man, and chiefly bricklayers' labourers." Though he probably only had time to make a hasty survey of the place, and spoke of our people as he found those he met, he was, no doubt, in the main, correct. This was ten years after the famine, when they were still for the most part in the ranks of unskilled labour. You find them now in every rank of life, and tolerably numerous in the various trades for which Birmingham is famous.

Five years after Mr Sullivan's visit his estimate of the position of our people in Birmingham was borne out by Father John Sherlock, one of the finest characters Ireland ever produced. No man—priest or layman—in England has done nobler service for the Irish cause and people than he. He has now retired from active work, but as the old war-horse is roused by the sound of the trumpet, so he, from time to time, comes back to bear his part in the fray, when duty to Ireland calls. Though over eighty years of age, he has a wonderfully vigorous frame. His sweet Celtic face gives you the idea of one of our old Irish saints. At the time of the famine a good many from the west of Ireland came into the "Black Country," and numbers of them could speak nothing but Irish. There are but few of these old people left now, but many of their children are there still, though they are getting away to America as fast as they can. Father Sherlock had been taught Irish in his infancy by an old nurse, and he could still remember it pretty well. It was all the better that he had learned it colloquially, as, with a little study, he was able to hear the confessions of his countrymen who could speak in no other tongue, when sent to the mission at Bilston, then a more thriving town than now, in the iron-working district near Wolverhampton.

In October 1861, the late Bishop Ullathorne made an appeal for a new Catholic church in Birmingham, in the centre of the town, where there were about four thousand Catholics; the entire Catholic population of the town being, at this time, estimated at about 25,000. For fifteen years, he said, this congregation had used for worship an old dilapidated workshop in Well Lane, off Park Street and Allison Street. The upper storey was a chapel, and the two lower floors were schools. A trap-door in front of the altar enabled those below to hear mass through the aperture. They had now bought a handsome Unitarian chapel, which had been built in place of Dr Priestley's, burnt by the mob in 1791. The burden, the bishop said, rested on the Rev. John Sherlock, who for many years past had struggled bravely through the difficulties of founding the mission. Father Sherlock himself, in making his appeal, gives also a description of his flock. He says—" The formation of a large Catholic population here dates from the commencement of the famine in Ireland. As the great majority of them on arriving here were destitute, they fixed their habitations where they could get them cheapest, and at the same time near their employment. The elder members of the family work at buildings, while the younger and the females are employed in factories."

Father Sherlock converted the Unitarian chapel in Moor Street into a Catholic church (St Michael's), and for nearly thirty years afterwards it was the scene of his labours.

In the chapters on Fenianism it will be seen that Birmingham was one of the most active centres of the movement, and there cannot be a doubt but that a considerable number of Irishmen there were enrolled in the Revolutionary organisation. It is probable that this raised against the Irish and Catholic population of the town, whether Fenians or not, a feeling of enmity. This was exactly that inflammable condition that suited the purpose of the no-Popery firebrand, Murphy, when he made his appearance in Birmingham in the summer of 1867. In the disturbances that followed, the mayor and magistrates had the very best intentions, but, up to a certain point, appear to have been unable to control, not merely the fury of the no-Popery rioters, composed chiefly of the scum of the town, bent upon plunder, but their own police. It is well known that on this as on other such occasions, but for the partizanship of the police, who assisted in attacking the Irish and demolishing their homes, the Catholic priests could and did prevent acts of aggression on the part of their flock, who, with the exception of a few foolish and reckless people, were simply defending themselves, their property, their homes, and their church against the combined ruffianism of Birmingham, and could have done so successfully but for the rank and file of the police assisting the rioters.

An eye-witness of the scenes in Birmingham gives some graphic descriptions of what he saw, in a letter to the *Nation*, headed—" How the Irish fought in Birmingham." "On Wednesday night," he says, "the robbers and police broke into the Irish houses, beat women, children, old men, and old women, stole their goods, their clothes, their food, and everything they had in the world, broke everything they could not take, and drove the people out into the streets almost naked. Whole sides of bacon were selling for two or three shillings. The convents had to be defended, and so had the churches. As it was, there was one church in Moor Street attacked, together with the priest's house."

It is a peculiarity of mobs of this kind that the intensity of their hatred for Popery is only equalled by their passion for plunder. It was, it will be remembered, the same in the Gordon riots, as it has been in more recent outbreaks in British towns. It seems that only Paddy will fight for a sentiment. John Bull must fight for something more substantial. The object of the war may be called by a more high sounding name—it may be in the interests of civilisation or of trade, or it may be for the acquisition of territory, but, after all, the end sought is not much different from the hams and sides of bacon of the unfortunate Irish of Allison Street and Park Street, the quarter which suffered most from the Murphyites.

Following this, the firebrand, Murphy, was the cause of terrible rioting elsewhere. His appearance in Rochdale caused an attack on the Catholic church, the school, and the priest's house, and also on the Irish houses in Mount Pleasant. He was the instigator of still more serious rioting at Ashton and Duckinfield. The mob, after his harangue, broke into the Catholic chapel off Astley Street, Duckinfield, split up the crucifix, tore down the ornaments, and did considerable other damage. At Bury his followers got rather roughly handled by about eighty or a hundred militiamen who were up for their annual training at the time. The Lancashire militia is largely recruited from the Irish neighbourhoods of the large towns, and though some of these poor fellows may not be the most edifying Catholics, they feel bound to make up for any shortcomings in that direction by being ready to fight to the death for creed or country, should either be insulted. The climax of the Murphyite riots appears to have been reached at Ashton under Lyne, on May 10th and 11th, 1868. When attacked the Irish fought with great heroism, but as they were but a handful compared to their opponents, they were in the end overpowered, and their houses, as usual in such cases, plundered and gutted, and young and old subjected to the most brutal treatment, of which one Irishman afterwards died. Altogether, about one hundred houses and two churches were destroyed by the mob before the authorities put forth any real effort to deal with the reign of terror that prevailed in Ashton. As usual the Irish were made the victims of the law as well as of the mob, and the Catholic body could not even get any redress for the destruction of their churches. It was no wonder, therefore, that Murphy was emboldened to carry the Civil War into other towns, the most serious consequence that happened to him being that from time to time he was bound over to keep the peace, which obligation he as regularly set at defiance. Riot and bloodshed everywhere followed in his track. Ultimately, in one of the disturbances he created, the wretched man received such injuries as caused his death.

BOOK XI.
HOME RULE—THE LAND LEAGUE—THE IRISH NATIONAL LEAGUE.

CHAPTER XXXI.

THE HOME RULE CONFEDERATION OF GREAT BRITAIN—ISAAC BUTT—AN ACTIVE POLICY DEMANDED—THE CONVENTION OF 1877—PARNELL SUCCEEDS BUTT AS PRESIDENT OF THE HOME RULE CONFEDERATION.

ON May 19th, 1870, five days after the arrest of Michael Davitt, another constitutional agitation was inaugurated. The new organisation was called the "Home Government Association of Ireland." The most hopeful feature in it was that it was not confined to Irishmen of any particular creed or politics. It numbered among its promoters Catholics, Protestants, Whigs, Tories, Nationalists of a moderate type, and even advanced Nationalists who had been members of the Fenian organisation. Some of the Protestant leaders of the movement, honestly convinced of the justice of Ireland's demand for home government, have faithfully stood by the Irish National cause ever since; others, who only joined out of pique at the disestablishment of the Irish Church, went back again into the ranks of the ascendency caste. There were still others, of various creeds and politics, who gave their adhesion, as the Sadliers and Keoghs might have done, with an eye to their own future advancement. However, as will be seen, the honest men of the party ultimately prevailed.

The leader of the new movement was Isaac Butt. He was born in 1812, at Stranorlar, in the County Donegal. In 1829 he entered Trinity College, Dublin, where he took high honours. He had strong literary tastes, and was one of the founders of the *Dublin University Magazine*. He commenced his political career as a Tory of the most pronounced type, and was the ablest champion his party could find to pit against O'Connell, in the famous debate in Dublin corporation, on the question of Repeal of the Union. But, in time, his genuinely Irish nature asserted itself, and when he entered the Home Rule movement everything pointed to him as its natural leader. The Irishmen of England, among whom his figure while he led the agitation was a familiar one, though not blind to the weaknesses of his character, still bear him in kindly remembrance. A Protestant of the Northern province, he was, to the inmost core of his heart, Irish of the very Irish, and his genial, lovable nature commanded the affections of his fellow-countrymen as powerfully as his eloquence and subtle intellect did their admiration.

As we have seen, Michael Davitt, then a comparatively unknown man, disappeared for a time from view just as the Home Rule movement was being inaugurated. In the following year a number of the political prisoners, who had been undergoing penal servitude for their connection with Fenianism, were amnestied on condition of leaving the country. It seemed, therefore, that the new organisation, working by peaceful methods, now had the field of politics to itself.

As they had done with the other political movements since 1840, the Irish on this side of the Channel began to fall into line, and during 1871 and 1872 Home Rule associations were formed in several of the large towns of Great Britain.

The first really great impetus was given by Mr John Barry, who may be considered the founder of the powerful political organisation which has existed here since 1873; for, whether under the name of the Home Rule Confederation of Great Britain, the Irish National Land League of Great Britain, or the Irish National League of Great Britain, it has had a continuous existence; its methods and chief object—Home Rule—being still the same.

The Manchester Home Rule Association, of which Mr

Barry was then secretary, invited Mr Isaac Butt to a demonstration to be held in the Free Trade Hall, on the 8th of January 1873. Mr Barry conceived the idea of a federation of the existing local associations in Great Britain. He thought the visit of Mr Butt to Manchester would be a good opportunity for bringing representatives from the various towns together. Accordingly, invitations were issued to the local associations to send delegates to a convention, to be presided over by Mr Butt, on the day of the demonstration. There were about twenty of these associations represented at this conference, which was the first of the Annual Conventions which have been held since in one or other of the large towns of Great Britain and twice in Ireland itself.

At this first assembly there was a very valuable interchange of opinions among the delegates, who also brought forward propositions to be put into the shape of rules for the guidance of the new organisation—these rules to be submitted to another meeting of delegates to be held in Birmingham at an early date. In the meantime the other local bodies not represented at Manchester were to be invited to send delegates to Birmingham. The following resolution was unanimously adopted:—"That, as representatives of the Home Rule associations of England and Scotland, we are of opinion that a thorough practical union of all the associations is essentially necessary for the furtherance of the objects in view." It was also determined to call the union of the associations the "Home Rule Confederation of Great Britain," and Mr Isaac Butt was elected the first President. At the great demonstration held on the night of this first Convention, in the Free Trade Hall, Manchester, the principal speaker was Mr Butt, the chairman being Mr John Ferguson of Glasgow. The delegates who had taken part in the Convention attended, and the great hall was filled by the Irish of Manchester, who came in such large numbers to show their appreciation of the impetus the movement had received by that day's proceedings.

Advantage was taken of the interval between the Manchester and Birmingham Conventions to find out such associations as had not been represented at the first gathering, and to write to them to send delegates to the adjourned conference. This was held in the Town Hall, Birmingham, on the 24th of February following. Mr Butt presided at the deliberations in the morning, and Mr A. M. Sullivan in the afternoon. Another member of the then Irish Parliamentary party, Captain Nolan, was also present, and there was a good attendance of delegates. The draft rules were then discussed, and adopted, amended, or rejected, as the case might be, and provision made for the carrying on of the work of the Confederation. The place for the next annual meeting was also decided upon. This, as is well known, is every year the last business transacted at the Convention, and causes the most intense excitement, as each town, through the voice of its most eloquent advocate, puts forward its claim for the honour. Conventions have been held—in several of the towns more than once—in Dublin, London, Liverpool, Manchester, Glasgow, Leeds, Birmingham, Edinburgh, Newcastle, and Cardiff. Mr Isaac Butt, Dr Commins, Mr Butt a second time, Mr Parnell, and Mr T. P. O'Connor have been, in turn, Presidents of the Home Rule Confederation, under its original title and those it has subsequently taken, and have generally taken the chair at the Annual Conventions during their respective terms of office.

On the night of the Birmingham Convention of 1873 there was a great demonstration in the Town Hall, presided over by the veteran Irish priest, Father Sherlock.

After the Home Rule Confederation was established the associations then existing became strengthened by contact with a common centre, and other towns were encouraged to form associations, so that there was at once a considerable development of the organisation.

The great bulk of the Irish population of England is in the north—considerably more than one-third of them being in Lancashire alone. Scotland has a slightly greater Irish population than Lancashire. The district north of the Mersey and Humber contains almost three-fourths of our people, and there has been the same proportion since the Irish immigration began to assume considerable magnitude. The only large mass of Irish south of this line are in London, and these are, geographically speaking, isolated from the great bulk of their fellow-countrymen. For these reasons, and seeing also that the movement for the confederation of the local associations emanated from that city, Manchester was chosen as the most convenient place for the headquarters. Here it remained for a couple of years, when it was removed to Liverpool, because the publishing office of the *United Irishman*, the organ of the Confederation, was in that town. Later still, for the convenience of the members of the Irish Parliamentary party, and that it should have the active direction of such of these as were really in touch with the national movement, the headquarters were removed to London, where they still remain.

During 1873 and 1874 numerous public meetings were held in furtherance of the Home Rule programme, and, for the first time, perhaps, in the history of the Irish people here, practical attention began to be given to the registration and organisation of the Irish vote.

On June 4th, 1875, the first number of the *United Irishman* appeared. It was the organ of the Confederation, and did considerable service during the time of its existence. From its columns can be best gathered the progress of the movement in Great Britain about this time. Its first editor was Mr Hugh Heinrick, since dead, who was one of the pioneers of the movement in this country, and materially aided it by voice, pen, and personal service. He was succeeded in the editorship by Mr Daniel Crilly, an able an eloquent young Irishman of Liverpool, who has since had a much wider experience of Irish newspaper literature, and is now a member of the Irish Parliamentary party.

The most important event in connection with Irish nationality in 1875 was the celebration, in Dublin, on Friday, August 6th, of the Centenary of the birth of Daniel O'Connell. An immense number of our people from all parts crossed the Channel and took part in the procession through the streets of Dublin to the spot where now stands the noble monument to O'Connell—the work of the gifted Irish sculptor, Foley.

Nearly every Parliamentary election is now decided on the question of Home Rule for Ireland. This is as true of elections here as in Ireland. Probably the first time that an Irish Home Ruler appeared, *as such*, to ask the votes of the electors of a constituency in Great Britain, was when Mr Lawrence Connolly became a candidate for the representation of Scotland Ward in the Liverpool Town Council. This was at the Municipal election of 1875. He was returned by a large majority, and has since sat in the Imperial Parliament for an Irish constituency.

On Monday, August 21st, 1876, the Annual Convention of the Home Rule Confederation was held in the Rotunda, Dublin. It was presided over by Dr Commins of Liverpool. Mr Butt was also present, together with Messrs Biggar and Parnell. There was a large attendance of delegates from the various British towns.

This Convention endorsed the so-called policy of "Obstruction," which had been initiated by Mr Biggar, and has since made such a revolution in British as well as Irish politics, in the following resolution, which was unanimously adopted—" That in the opinion of this meeting, before adopting a course of action that *may* become necessary—namely, withdrawal—it will be expedient for the Irish members to adopt a much more determined attitude in the House of Commons upon all questions in which Ireland is concerned, so that the British people may be induced to adopt the principle of division of labour in Government." A vote of confidence was passed in Mr Butt. It was also resolved to remove the central offices of the Confederation from Liverpool to London. The resolution passed at this Convention, that a more determined attitude of the Irish Members of Parliament was necessary, embodied the sentiments of most patriotic Irishmen, and Mr Butt, who was present, agreed with it in a general way. As subsequent events showed, he was not the man to put it into active effect, and, when driven to take sides, in the end actually opposed it.

It must be remembered that he had an exceedingly difficult part to play with the materials at his command. He had managed to hold the party together, as, perhaps, but few other men could have done, by his tact and geniality, and that lovable nature which drew the hearts of even corrupt men to him. So far at all events there was in the Irish party the *appearance* of loyalty to Ireland—but that was all. There were men in the party who had been quite ready to swallow the Home Rule pledge at the hustings, who were, in their hearts, dishonest politicians. They could see, by the manner in which the Irish question was being pressed and received in Parliament, that all they had to do was to take part, such of them as were orators, in the debate on Home Rule, and to vote for it, and nothing farther was likely to come of it. Both Liberals and Tories regarded it in the same way, so that a man might be a red hot patriot in his denunciation of the Government of the day and take office the first opportunity that offered. Unfortunately, as time went on, Mr Butt seemed to fall more and more under the influence of this section of his followers. The honest men of the party saw that whatever Ireland had to look for from Parliament was to be got through the policy known in the days of the Tenant Right agitation as "Independent Opposition." As long as members looked for personal advantage from either Tories or Liberals when in office, they could never be sufficiently independent to be of real service to Ireland.

Joseph Biggar was the first man in Parliament to put the active policy into operation, and in doing so encountered a storm of opprobrium. He had seen that, rather than offend its traditions and customs, Irish members who were honest enough in their intentions, had allowed their people to be starved to death and to be treated with the most brutal tyranny. These simply confined themselves to the routine methods of Parliament, not sufficiently recognising the fact that it was a life or death struggle in which Ireland was engaged, and that he who would effectually champion her cause must have little regard, if the occasion demanded it, for the traditions or feelings of the "House."

In Charles Stewart Parnell, Biggar found a man after his own heart, and together they pitted themselves against the whole force of the British Parliament, their most relentless opponents being often of their own party. Their action was called "Obstruction" by their opponents, and yet it chiefly consisted in using the forms of the House to insure the various measures being properly debated. Thus they showed, in the most practical way possible, that Parliament had not time to deal properly with Irish affairs, and that, therefore, these should be left to Ireland herself. Then, again, if Parliament could not or would not deal with Irish affairs as they ought to be dealt with, if all measures—like those of Mr Butt—introduced by Irish members were to be contemptuously rejected, not on their merits, but *because* they were brought in by those having the confidence of the Irish people, Biggar and Parnell determined, in return, to make British legislation as difficult as possible.

Denounced by their leader, they were even more bitterly assailed by the embryo Sadliers and Keoghs of the party, who saw with alarm that the frustration of their corrupt schemes for self-advancement would be sure to follow the success of the honest and active policy. But Biggar and Parnell were more than recompensed for their labours, and the hatred and odium they had incurred, by the unmistakable voice of their fellow-countrymen—particularly in Great Britain. From the various associations and branches throughout England, Scotland, and Wales, resolutions of encouragement were sent to them, and one branch in Liverpool, the example being speedily followed, took for its name the "Biggar and Parnell Branch." As yet these two courageous men had received but little co-operation—even from the honest members of the Irish Parliamentary party in Parliament.

After the close of the Parliamentary session, a meeting was held on the 21st of August 1877, in the Rotunda, Dublin, in support of the action of Messrs Biggar and Parnell. They met with a most enthusiastic reception, and their policy was emphatically endorsed.

But the portion of the Home Rule organisation in Great Britain had always been the most advanced ; and, at the Annual Convention of the Home Rule Confederation, held at the Adelphi Hotel, Liverpool, on the 27th of August, in the week following the Rotunda meeting, more decisive action was taken.

This Convention was one of the turning points in modern Irish history. Two policies seemed to be conflicting, two camps seemed rapidly being formed, and the minds of men were attracted with unusual interest to the struggle. The tension was too great to be sustained very long, and the way the question shaped itself in the minds of all was—Where would the issue be first tried, and which policy, the new one or the old, would be triumphant?

It is a matter of no little pride to Irishmen living in England and Scotland that it fell to their lot to give answer to these questions; that they first gave the stamp of approval to a policy which but to-day stood within reach—to all human appearance — of a mighty success. But, with heaven's help, we shall yet succeed, though it was the hand of Charles Stewart Parnell himself which sought to dash the cup of hope from Ireland's lips, after he had been followed by her people with a devotion and a loyalty such as leader never, perhaps, received before.

At this Liverpool Convention Mr Butt retired from the presidency of the Home Rule Confederation of Great Britain, and Mr Parnell was elected in his place. The incident is well known; its importance has frequently been the subject of comment by men qualified by their genius and their position to deal with the history of their country. But it will be found that, beyond the bare mention of the fact stated above, the newspapers of the day scarcely give any place to a record of the event. It may then be considered not undesirable, at this stage in our *onward* march—for ours is the cause of a nation and of no single man, and must *go on*—to look back over the intervening years, and give some account of this Convention, which marked such a decided change in the fortunes of our country.

Mr Butt still retained the nominal leadership of the Irish Parliamentary party, a post, indeed, which he held until his death, nearly two years afterwards. His influence, however, was rapidly passing away, and the election of Mr Parnell as its head by the recognised Irish organisation of Great Britain, was the handwriting on the wall that foreshadowed the sweeping away of a policy of weakness and stagnation, and its replacement by the more determined line of action of later years. These Conventions, of which this of 1877 was, up till then, by far the most remarkable, composed as they are of representative men from every district, are practically the annual Parliaments of the Irish in England, Scotland, and Wales. It can readily be understood, then, that they are looked forward to with great interest each year. To a person attending one of these conventions for the first time it might seem that the intense, and sometimes almost fierce, earnestness displayed by many of the delegates in advancing their views might lead to stormy scenes, but the admirable discipline of the delegates and the wise guidance of the chairman pilot the discussion over the stormiest waves. There is abundance of animation and enthusiasm, and as the various resolutions come up and are decided on, it is interesting to see the proof which is afforded of the thoroughness with which the Irish race has permeated every part of Great Britain. All the larger towns, and most of the smaller ones, are worthily represented, while some delegates come from districts so remote that they cannot be found either in railway guide or map. At these gatherings you get admirable specimens of the accents of every part of Ireland. Moreover, you get varieties and shades which are not to be found on Irish soil, for on the original brogue is often grafted the characteristic pronunciation of some part of Great Britain; and, in addition to this, you have a full English, Scotch, or Welsh accent, from one of the many Irishmen in this country who have been born out of the land of their fathers. Indeed, there are in Wales many efficient branches formed, not only of Irish-born men but of many sons of Irishmen whose *native* tongue is Welsh.

It was Mr Butt's part, as head of the organisation, to preside at the Convention of 1877, and, accordingly, he came to Liverpool for the purpose. It can readily be understood that, on the present occasion, this was a less pleasing task for him than it had ever been before. The relations between him and those of his colleagues who were present had been painfully strained, and he had in Parliament condemned and rebuked their so-called "obstructive" action. Yet, to the last, much as they differed from him, much as they detested the corrupt and dishonest men by whom he was surrounded and influenced, every man in that assembly in Liverpool could truthfully bear testimony to the love he bore to the brilliant and genuinely patriotic leader, with all his weaknesses, whose very faults leaned to virtue's side. This feeling was universal, but as universal and as strong was the sense that they owed a duty to their country which outweighed every personal consideration. It seemed only too apparent that Mr Butt's leanings were irrevocably in the wrong direction: it was equally obvious that the one man marked out by common consent for the future leadership was Charles Stewart Parnell.

Mr Parnell came of a patriotic stock, being great grandson of Sir John Parnell, who was Chancellor of the Exchequer in the Irish Parliament, and one of the most determined opponents of the Union. He was born at Avondale, near Rathdrum, County Wicklow, in June 1846. He first entered public life in March 1874, as a candidate for the representation of the County of Dublin in Parliament. But he was defeated, as, until the extension of the franchise gave the representation to the Nationalists, the County of Dublin had been a Tory stronghold. In the following year, however, being again brought forward by the Home Rule League, he was elected as the successor of John Martin, in the representation of Meath. He became one of the most active and efficient members of the party, and it was noted from the first, by those who came in contact with him, that he took a special interest in his fellow countrymen in Great Britain and bore a prominent part in the work of organisation on this side of the Channel. We have seen how manfully he seconded Mr Biggar in his policy of "Obstruction." Mr John Ferguson of Glasgow, a prominent and active member of the Confederation, was probably the first to detect in Mr Parnell the qualities of a leader which were afterwards acknowledged by friend and foe alike. So strong, however, is the feeling among Irishmen against the very shadow of disunion, or anything like the semblance of indiscipline, that many thought Mr Ferguson somewhat premature in indicating Mr Parnell as Mr Butt's probable successor.

There was a prevailing impression that Mr Parnell was a cold and passionless man. This probably arose from the estimate formed of him from the usual style of his platform oratory. This, as is well known, was not of the type that rouses the enthusiasm of the multitude. In listening to Mr Parnell you were impressed with the conviction that you had before you a man who simply sought to convey to his audience what was passing in his own mind in the fewest and most expressive words he could command. He visited various parts of this country on his first entry into Parliament, in company with Mr Butt. Those who then came into contact with him will remember their first impression of him. Under that young man's calm exterior could be discerned such burning enthusiasm, such terrible earnestness of purpose, that some said—Surely another Emmet has arisen for Ireland. But these passions—how powerful and terrible they were his latter days disclosed—did not then consume him, nor lead him into desperate undertakings. They simply went, when directed by his keen judgment and powerfully disciplined will, to make up the great strength of his character; which was formed still further by the sense of the responsibility of having a nation's destiny in his hand.

In 1877 the names of Biggar and Parnell were inseparable, so it need scarcely be said that, at the Convention, in company with Mr Parnell, was Mr Joseph Biggar, a man proverbial for his blunt, honest, common sense, who would never call a spade an "agricultural instrument," and who, if he thought a man a scoundrel, would not hesitate to say so without any weakening qualification. Only those who knew him intimately can form an idea of the loss his death has been to Ireland and the Irish party.

Conspicuous also at this gathering were Mr John O'Connor Power, and Mr Frank Hugh O'Donnell, both then in the odour of sanctity as Irish Nationalists. Among Mr Power's admirers present were some who had listened with eager delight to his wonderful eloquence when on vacation during his "college days" at St Jarlath's, and there are scores of Irishmen to-day who can tell how they were, in years gone by, led into the National fold by his teaching. Natural gifts like his are to be envied and admired, but many of his former friends think that John Power would be a happier man to-day if he were still a journeyman painter in the Lancashire town where so many of his younger days were spent. It is probably due to his excessive individuality that Mr O'Donnell's place in the National ranks knows him no more. At one time Mr Parnell had no more loyal follower, and a co-worker of his in a fiercely contested election in the north of England still recalls how manfully the then member for Dungarvan faced a howling and angry mob, and called for a cheer for his leader, Mr Parnell.

Messrs Butt, Parnell, Biggar, Power, and O'Donnell were the only members of Parliament present. Among the representatives of "Erin's sons in England" who were there that day were, however, some who have since entered Parliament and still represent Irish constituencies. These were Mr John Barry, Mr Timothy M. Healy, and Mr Daniel Crilly. In the Home Rule cause there was no more bright, cheery, and active worker than John Barry, and to him the credit belongs of being the founder of the Home Rule Confederation of Great Britain. Mr Healy, who now occupies such a prominent and honoured position among Irishmen, was then known as an ardent, self-sacrificing young man of culture, who, even as a boy, was the life and soul of the National movement in Newcastle-on-Tyne. Mr Crilly is a type of the young Irishman reared on the English side of the Channel. From his very childhood he was trained in the traditions of the *Nation*, and when Mr T. D. Sullivan offered him an appointment on the staff of that paper it may be imagined how congenial a sphere of labour he then entered upon.

Mr Butt, as the President of the Confederation, was the chairman of the Convention during the greater part of the day, and when the time came for the election of the officers for the ensuing year, he expressed his desire to say a few words. He had been reluctant, he said, to accept the office of President the previous year, and, if they were disposed to re-elect him there were some reasons why he should not be their President this year. He would rather, indeed, they would not think of him as President; he wished to hold an independent position. At the same time he thanked them for the great kindness they had shown him for several years. Next year they might be guided as wisely—he hoped more so—but he did not think they would be guided more honestly than he had endeavoured to guide them. He asked them, in conclusion, to allow him to leave the chair when the election of officers was over.

The few simple words of Mr Butt keenly touched the hearts of all present, and probably no one there was more capable of expressing their feelings, as well as their views, than Mr John Ferguson of Glasgow, who rose to speak. It was his intention, he said, to propose Mr Parnell as the head of the Confederation. At the same time he felt the greatest possible regret that their grand old chieftain, who had in trying times raised the Irish banner, who had so long guided them, and who had been with them in so many hard fights, was to retire from amongst them. They were grateful to Isaac Butt for leading them so far, but they were going to try a more determined policy, and Mr Butt held views different to those they would endeavour to carry out. He hoped, though, that he would take council with the true and earnest men of the party, and that after a time he would return to lead them at that side of the water.

Mr Biggar also spoke in a way which showed how deeply he was moved. He was supposed, he remarked, to represent the extreme section of the Irish party, but he could say that he was exceedingly anxious that Mr Butt should continue to act as the leader of the party. He asked him to allow the earnest men of the party, who faithfully represented the opinions of a large and active class outside, to be his friends, and not the half-hearted, insincere men who would desert their principles and sell their country and constituencies for Government situations.

At this point Mr Butt interposed, saying, "I don't think you could say I did that." Mr Biggar, continuing, again begged Mr Butt to put his faith in men who represented the opinions of earnest Irish people. He had always argued against withdrawing from the leadership of Mr Butt, and he now asked him to appeal to the opinion of men who had proved their earnestness. If he did not do that, those who were only nominally following him would sell him and their country and their God at the first opportunity. As is well known, Mr Biggar never spoke with the mere idea of gaining applause, but the spontaneous outburst of cheering that greeted this expression declared how accurately he had stated the sentiments of all present.

It was evident that Mr Butt wished to have the committee and officers elected, and to vacate the chair before any discussion on the policy of the party should be initiated. Mr Parnell, however, expressed the general wish when he rose to say that it was of the greatest moment that Mr Butt should give them his opinion before withdrawing from the Convention. He alluded to Mr Ferguson's intention to propose his name for the onerous position of President, and said that he felt entirely unable to fill such a position. He could not help thinking that if they were suffered to discuss the question in the presence of Mr Butt, they might, perhaps, be able to see matters in a way they did not see them at that moment. Mr Butt, after discussion, might not still adhere to his decision not to act as President. The future was entirely for his own judgment. If Mr Butt considered it undesirable still to lead the Confederation, of course they must bow to him. At the same time it was of the utmost importance they should have his presence and assistance in their deliberations that day. He asked him not to do anything on that day that would be looking back on the great responsibilities every man must know he had undertaken in leading the Home Rule movement.

Mr Butt thanked the three gentlemen who had spoken for the manner in which they had alluded to him, but again requested the Convention not to ask him to take any part in the discussion of the question agitating the country. He had not come to take any such part. He would wish to be guarded in anything he should say. He believed that his power to heal the differences that existed might be very much weakened by some expressions he might use that day, and he would take it as a personal compliment not to be asked. He looked forward to the day when they would all be re-united. He was obliged to return to London that night; in fact, if he had taken his doctor's advice, he would not have been there then. As he had said before, he would like to be present at the election of officers, but they must not ask him to be present at any discussion afterwards.

Mr John Barry declared, that while receiving with the

greatest consideration and respect any request that came from Mr Butt, he would re-echo what Mr Parnell had said. It was extremely painful to him to urge on Mr Butt to offer them this satisfaction, but he thought they were entitled to it from the faithful allegiance they had borne him in the past.

Mr Butt asked that before the resolution (calling for a National Conference in Ireland) was brought forward, he should be allowed to retire. It would be easy, he said, to give the reasons why he dissented from the course taken by some members. They would expect that he would endeavour to propose some plan by which differences might be avoided. He confessed he was not prepared to do that. He would be departing from his proper place if he were to enter into any premature discussion on this question.

Mr O'Connor Power said he would ask Mr Butt one question—assuming that he would leave the chair—What action he proposed to take in reference to the Council of the Home Rule League calling for a National Council, and how that council should be constituted?

Mr Butt said he would consult the Home Rule League when he went over, but he could not say how that conference should be constituted.

Mr Biggar pointed out that the question would naturally influence Mr Butt's future action, and appealed to him to stay there to hear their discussion. Everyone would understand that Mr Butt was not committed to any resolution or opinion expressed there. He would not need to give his own opinion unless he liked. He would ask him, as a favour, to stay there and hear their different opinions.

Mr Butt then said he would stay there as long as he could. He did not feel in a position to commit himself to any particular course. He had to get the opinion of a large part of the Irish people before doing so. They (the delegates present) might assume the opinions of the Irish people to be the one way—he did not assume that. He would like to test that. He did not wish to interfere with them, and he thought they ought to leave him free as to his own time to state his opinions.

After some remarks from various gentlemen, Mr Madden

(Liverpool) proposed the following resolution:—" That the Home Rule Confederation of Great Britain, fully conscious that the feeling of the Irish people in Ireland is in favour of a more active and vigorous policy on the part of the Parliamentary representatives, calls upon the Home Rule League in Ireland to summon a National Conference to settle the lines upon which the future policy of the Home Rule party should be promoted."

Mr John Ferguson seconded the motion, which was carried unanimously.

At this stage Mr Butt again expressed his desire to leave; and Mr Ferguson, in a few touching and eloquent words, conveyed the feeling of the meeting towards their departing leader. He said that he felt called on, before Mr Butt left the room, to express their deep feeling of regret that he should be compelled to do so. There was no use concealing the matter—there was a divergence of policy. He moved that the warmest thanks of that conference be given to Mr Butt for his distinguished services.

Mr Parnell, who was evidently deeply moved, in seconding the vote of thanks, said that Mr Butt's services to the Irish people in forming them into one solid whole for the purpose of obtaining self-government, were immeasurable, and ought never to be forgotton. It was not without the greatest hesitation that he (Mr Parnell) had entered upon the course of action he had done in Parliament; but he did so from nothing but the strongest conviction of what was his duty. He could not conceal from himself that the existing parliamentary action was tending to demoralise the party. There were those in it who must be a source of weakness to it or to any national party, and the action he spoke of was tending to demoralise those who might have been made earnest and active men. He must confess to not having Mr Butt's confidence in English justice and sense of right. It was not too late for him (Mr Butt) to see a way to deal with England that would obtain freedom for their country, a way that would show England that if she would dare to trifle with Irish demands it would be at the risk of endangering those institutions she felt so proud of, but which Irishmen had no reason to respect. To Mr Butt was due a debt of gratitude by the Irish people they could never repay, for he had taught them self-reliance and a knowledge of their own power. If he (Mr Parnell) had felt it his duty to put himself into antagonism with Mr Butt, he hoped he would forgive him. If he had said or written harsh things, he had never said more nor less than was due to the gravity of the occasion.

Mr O'Donnell, who expressed a wish that next session might find Mr Butt at the head of a united party, also supported the vote of thanks to Mr Butt, which was carried unanimously with all sincerity and depth of feeling.

Mr Butt briefly replied, saying that he would be ashamed of himself if he were unmoved by that vote and the manner in which it had been passed. He hoped that the wish expressed by Mr O'Donnell might be realised, and it would not be his fault if they had not a united Irish party in the House of Commons. After expressing his good wishes for the Home Rule Confederation of Great Britain, which he hoped might long continue to assert the power of the Irish people in that country, he took his farewell.

The election of Mr Parnell as the successor of Mr Butt to the office of President of the organisation then followed, and clearly showed to what quarter the Irishmen of England, Scotland, and Wales looked for future guidance and light. Two other important resolutions were passed. One was proposed by Mr Parnell, and in moving it he justified the action taken up in Parliament by Mr Biggar and himself. The resolution was worded as follows:—" That, pending the decision of the forthcoming National Conference, we, the delegates of the Home Rule Confederation, deem it highly desirable that the members of the Irish Parliamentary party should reserve to themselves full liberty of action on all English and Imperial questions, upon which the party may not have previously agreed to act as a party." This was seconded by Mr Peter Mulhall (Liverpool), and carried unanimously.

Mr Mulhall then proposed, and Mr Ryan (Bolton) seconded : " That the Convention of the Home Rule Confederation of Great Britain hereby endorses the vigorous policy pursued by the Home Rule Parliamentary party who are termed the 'Obstructionists.'"

This ended the business of the Convention.

In the evening there was an imposing public demonstration. The chair was filled by Dr Andrew Commins, barrister, of Liverpool, a gentleman of rare culture and varied attainments, who had been President of the Confederation during an interval when Mr Butt had ceased to fill the post. He has since entered Parliament. Messrs Biggar, Parnell, O'Donnell, and Power delivered stirring addresses to the Irishmen of Liverpool and the district, who attended in thousands and displayed the greatest enthusiasm in favour of the active policy.

Surely if any vindication were needed of the action of Biggar and Parnell it has been amply furnished by the stirring events that have taken place since 1877. The instinct of the Irish people at that time taught them that new men and new methods were wanted; with the need came the men, and the fruits of their work are rapidly ripening around us.

The policy of vigour, honesty, and independence holds the field to-day. This was never shown more forcibly than when Ireland's representatives deposed their leader, Mr Parnell, because, notwithstanding all his splendid services, he had at length proved himself unworthy. Notwithstanding the check he, and he alone, gave to our advancing cause, it is bound to triumph. No one man can ruin it to-day, for the chief strength of a leader is not in himself, however honest and capable, but that he is the embodiment of the unity that pervades the whole Irish race.

CHAPTER XXXII.

RELEASE OF FENIAN PRISONERS—THE LAND LEAGUE—THE GENERAL ELECTION OF 1880—OVERTHROW OF THE TORY GOVERNMENT—LIBERAL COERCION—GLADSTONE'S LAND BILL—IMPRISONMENT OF THE IRISH LEADERS—ATTEMPTED SUPPRESSION OF *UNITED IRELAND*.

AT the end of 1877 and beginning of 1878 a number of the Fenian prisoners were liberated, the few that remained being also set free not long afterwards.

Among the released Fenians was Michael Davitt. On Sunday, April 28th, 1878, he and Corporal Chambers, also one of the released prisoners, attended a meeting at the Adelphi Theatre, Liverpool. Dr Commins presided, and an eloquent address was delivered by Mr John O'Connor Power. This was probably the first large public meeting that Davitt had ever addressed. With a constitution on which prison life had told a tale, he was, consequently, somewhat nervous. Nevertheless his simple and pathetic story, without any oratorical adornments, made a thrilling impression upon the audience. He said he had been sentenced to fifteen years penal servitude because he had dreamed in his boyhood that he would live to see the independence of Ireland, and, on arriving at manhood, that he wished to see his dream accomplished. For six years he had been in the same prison with his poor friend, Chambers, and he had never been allowed to speak to him though the privilege of conversation had not been denied to others. He had been exceptionally treated—worse, in fact, than the common malefactors. No work had been too hard or repulsive for him, because he was a Fenian. He had been placed in harness in a cart, as they placed an animal, and compelled to draw rubbish, stones, everything, about the prison yard, with a collar across his shoulders. This occurred under the administration of Mr Gladstone, who had visited Italy, and drawn down the indignation of Europe against the Neapolitan tyrant. He had been placed in a bone shed on the brink of the prison cess-pool, and in the midst of summer had to break putrid bones. This kind of treatment had succeeded in debilitating his friend Chambers, in sending poor Charles M'Carthy to an early grave, and in planting the germs of heart disease in himself; but he thanked God they had never succeeded in breaking his spirit as a man. Chambers, who had been a corporal in the British army, and appeared to be in delicate health, said he had been treated worse than the worst of murderers then in the prisons of England.

That Michael Davitt was not exaggerating when he described the effects of prison treatment on his own health was proved the same day. The excitement sustained him during the meeting, but, almost immediately afterwards, he had a serious attack which caused much alarm to his friends.

This was a trying time for Isaac Butt. Indeed it cannot be doubted but that political added to financial embarrassments, from which he scarcely ever seemed to be free, shortened his days. A national subscription was set on foot for him, but the response was by no means adequate to meet the difficulties of his position. He was compelled, therefore, to resume his profession, which he had practically given up when he took the leadership. He had possessed a vigorous frame, but the double duty would have been a severe strain on even a much younger man. It was no wonder, then, that he succumbed to mental and bodily trouble. His health completely gave way, and, after a few months' illness, he died on May 5th, 1879, at the age of sixty-five. The Irish people mourned his death, but, as Mr Ferguson had said at the Liverpool Convention, while they were grateful that he had led them thus far, they were now going to try a more determined policy.

A deplorable circumstance—nothing less than the dread, caused by a succession of bad seasons, of another famine, like that of forty years previous—made the Irish people more than ever determined upon the new line of action. Providence might again send a period of scarcity, like that which now appeared to be setting in, but the people, with more manhood than their fathers, resolved that, so long as there was food enough grown in the country for all, they would have it. They felt that so far from it being a Christian duty to lie down and starve that they might pay unjust and exorbitant rents, they, in so doing, would be committing suicide and murdering their families. With this crisis in Ireland's fate came the man to deal with it—Michael Davitt. After his release from prison and his lecturing tour, he had gone to America, where he took counsel with some of his friends as to a policy of action that would suit the circumstances of the time. Returning to Ireland he found the country in a wretchedly distressed condition and rife for the movement upon which he had set his mind. There had previously been Tenants' Defence Associations in the country, but Michael Davitt was undoubtedly the father of the Irish National Land League, a movement which brought about what was nothing less than a revolution in Ireland.

The Land League may be said to have dated its birth from a meeting held at Irishtown, in the County Mayo, on the 28th of April 1879, just as Isaac Butt lay down on his bed of sickness to die; so that, strangely enough, the organisation of which he had been the head began at the same time to be eclipsed, and was ultimately absorbed, by the new movement. The Land League made way in the country, meeting opposition, however, from some, like the late Archbishop MacHale, from whom it might least be expected.

It received an enormous impetus by the adhesion of Mr Parnell, whose action in Parliament, in conjunction with Mr Biggar, had gained him the unbounded confidence of the Irish people.

At a meeting held in the Imperial Hotel, Lower O'Connell (then Sackville) Street, Dublin, on the 21st of October, 1879, the following were elected officers of the Irish National Land League:—Mr Parnell, President; Messrs Kettle, Davitt, and Brennan, Honorary Secretaries; and Messrs J. G. Biggar, W. H. O'Sullivan, and Patrick Egan, Treasurers. The following resolutions, embodying the principles of the League, were passed:—

I.—That the objects of the League are (1) to bring about a reduction of rack-rents; (2) to facilitate the obtaining the ownership of the soil by the occupiers.

II.—That the objects of the League can be best attained (1) by promoting organisation among the tenant farmers; (2) by defending those who may be threatened with eviction for refusing to pay unjust rents; (3) by facilitating the working of the Bright Clauses of the Land Act during the winter; and (4) obtaining such reform in the laws relating to land as will enable every tenant to become the owner of his holding by paying a fair rent for a number of years.

A resolution was passed asking Mr Parnell to go to America, in view of the prevailing distress and threatened famine, and Mr John Dillon was asked to accompany him.

Soon after this Messrs Davitt, Daly, and Killen were arrested for "seditious" speeches in connection with the Land League agitation. Meetings to protest against this were held in various parts of England and Scotland, where our people, as usual, took up the movement warmly. Branches were formed, some of them independently and others in connection with the branches of the Home Rule Confederation of Great Britain, which, after a time, changed its name to the "Irish National Land League of Great Britain." Previous to his departure for America, Mr Parnell, on Saturday, November 29th, 1879, attended an immense open-air demonstration in front of St George's Hall, Liverpool. There were not less than fifty thousand people present. There had been a threat on the part of the Orangemen of the town to break up the meeting by force, and there was a public intimation from their leaders to come in their thousands and do so. Whereupon the committee of the proposed demonstration considered they were justified in making all due preparation to resist such an attack. Arrangements were therefore made for this purpose, and some thousands of stalwart "stewards" volunteered to protect the meeting from violence. It had been the custom of the Orangemen of Liverpool to go forth armed with deadly weapons, when they used to be allowed to hold their annual processions, and prepared deliberately to take life. Then measures were studiously adopted to provoke hostile manifestations, the result being that, on several occasions, guns and pistols were brought into requisition for the slaughter of the unarmed Irish by the Orange banditti. But when the Brotherhood heard that the Irishmen of Liverpool were, not in defiance but in self-defence, determined to assert their right to public meeting, and were *prepared* for the Orangemen, it became quite another matter. A counter proclamation of the most pacific kind was therefore issued, calling upon all law-abiding Orangemen to remain at home on the day of the meeting.

The authorities of the town, however, prepared for the demonstration, for inside of St George's Hall, and out of sight of the meeting, a large body of the Liverpool police, armed with revolvers, were kept in readiness for any emergency. So complete were the arrangements of the Nationalists that the most perfect order was kept in the vast assembly, and, had the occasion demanded it, the well-disciplined stewards would have given a good account of themselves. Mr Parnell, who was by this time, in fact, if not in name, regarded as the leader of the Irish people, met with a tremendously enthusiastic reception. When he stood up to address the multitude, in order to show what an Irishman could say or do in England, but not in Ireland, and as a protest against the arrests made in Ireland for "seditious" speeches, he said he was going to make a "seditious" speech. He then urged the Irish here to help their fellow-countrymen in the struggle going on at home. On the same evening he addressed another large assembly in the League Hall, the proceeds being for the Land League.

The elaborate preparations for self-defence made by the Liverpool Irish that day must have caused the local authorities to come to the conclusion that there was something mysterious at the bottom of the defensive preparation. They must have communicated their views to the Government at some time or another since, for, some ten years later, when the Tory Government of the day were using the most vile machinations, under cover of the *Times* newspaper, backed up by perjury and forgery unequalled since the days of Titus Oates, to blast the reputation of Mr Parnell, he was, when a witness before a commission, intended by its authors to secure his condemnation, asked about these Liverpool meetings. The names of those of the prominent Irishmen of Liverpool who were on the platform were gone through, and he was asked about these, one by one, if they belonged to the Fenian organisation, and as to their antecedents generally—questions which he answered with admirable tact and coolness. How this villainous attempt to ruin a nation through its leaders recoiled on the heads of the conspirators themselves, forms, it will be seen later, what is probably one of the most startling chapters in the history of the Irish here.

In due time, after the Liverpool meeting, Mr Parnell, accompanied by Mr Dillon, proceeded to America. They were everywhere received with honour and substantial sympathy as the ambassadors of Ireland.

On the 9th of February 1880, there was a bye-election in Liverpool, the result of which emboldened Lord Beaconsfield to dissolve Parliament within a month afterwards. The Liberal candidate was Lord Ramsay, an able and genial young Scottish nobleman. It was thought that the Irish vote could be secured for him by a vague reference to his being in favour of some arrangement of local government for Ireland that would not interfere with " the integrity of the empire." This was not considered sufficiently explicit by the local Home Rulers. Ultimately he agreed to vote for Mr Shaw's motion for an *enquiry* into Ireland's demand for self-government. From this some idea may be gathered of the advance which has been made since that time, when all that was asked from a candidate for Parliament was a pledge for *enquiry* only, yet few could be got to go even so far as this. The Irish of Liverpool, on getting the required pledge, supported Lord Ramsay with enthusiasm—in fact their enthusiasm was probably too exuberant; for there is no doubt it drove many who would be Liberals, if there was no Irish question, to the opposite side.

The defeat of Lord Ramsay in such an Irish centre as Liverpool by a majority of 2221, emboldened Beaconsfield to go to the country, in hopes of a similar success all round. Seeing how effectually the latent bigotry of Liverpool had been appealed to, he issued a bitterly anti-Irish manifesto when he dissolved Parliament, hoping to ride triumphantly into power again with such a battle cry.

But this had not the effect he anticipated in stirring up the bigotry of the country in general, while it roused the Irish vote against him with decisive consequences. The news of the dissolution brought Mr Parnell home from America. He landed at Queenstown on the 21st of March. With the small resources at his command, he worked wonders in Ireland, but for want of time and means to properly fight the electoral battle, many of the old corrupt school again found seats among the sixty-eight members returned as Home Rulers. Mr Parnell also infused new vigour into the Irish ranks in great Britain.

The Tories suffered an overwhelming defeat at the polls. The Liberals came back to power with a majority so great that it enabled them to be entirely independent of the Irish vote. Had this been foreseen more discrimination would have been used in supporting certain candidates, or otherwise, and in this way the balance between the two parties might have been held by the Irish vote, and greater pressure could thus have been brought on the party in power to yield justice to Ireland.

Mr Parnell had been, even before Mr Butt's death, recognised by most Irishmen as the real leader, but it was not until a meeting of the Home Rule members, held in Dublin previous to the opening of Parliament, that he was formally elected to the leadership of the party by twenty-three votes, against eighteen given for Mr Shaw. Some few of those who voted for Mr Parnell afterwards "went wrong," while, on the other hand, some who voted for Mr Shaw now went with the majority, and supported Mr Parnell's leadership. Later still, the Home Rule party became more palpably split into two sections, when it had to be decided where the Irish members should take their seats in the House of Commons. Mr Shaw and his friends decided to sit on the Ministerial side of the House, now the Liberals had come into power, and were supposed to be friendly to Ireland. On the other hand, the section which acted with Mr Parnell maintained that it was their duty to hold themselves absolutely independent of all British political parties, as, even with this apparently friendly Government, the occasion might arise when it would become necessary to give it the most strenuous opposition. Indeed, it was not very long until they had to do so, when the Government resorted to the old method of governing Ireland by coercion. They, therefore, showed their foresight as well as patriotism by taking their seats on the Opposition side of the House.

Although the Land League and other agencies were at the moment administering charitable relief to half a million of famishing people in Ireland, the Queen's speech at the opening of Parliament had not a word of reference to the distress, while it dealt fully with matters in every part of the world. Mr Shaw and his followers adopted the old tactics of not wishing to be disagreeable to the Government. Mr Parnell's party felt that they owed a stern duty to their famishing fellow-countrymen, and demanded that legislative action should be taken to save the lives of the people. Mr Parnell brought in a bill for the suspension of evictions, and, after some fierce discussion, the determined attitude of the Irish party drove the Government into taking up the question as one of the utmost importance and urgency. Mr Forster's Disturbance Bill was practically the same as Mr Parnell's. During the debate, Mr Gladstone said—" It is no exaggeration to say, in a country where the agricultural pursuit is the only pursuit, and where the means of the payment of rent are entirely destroyed for a time by the visitation of Providence, that the poor occupier may, under these circumstances, regard a sentence of eviction as coming, for him, very near to a sentence of death." The truth of this was so keenly felt that this expression has been often quoted since, and has become famous. The Disturbance Bill was carried in the Commons by a large majority, but was defeated in the House of Lords. This contemptuous rejection of the bill was allowed to passed unchallenged. The saving of the lives of the Irish people was evidently not a matter of sufficient importance for the Government to risk an appeal to the country against the decision of the hereditary chamber.

The Irish people and their leaders now, therefore, saw that they must look to themselves alone, and acted accordingly. The principal weapon they depended upon was combination, like that of a trades' union. The force of public opinion was brought to bear upon anyone who would take a farm from which another had been wrongfully evicted. The people were also encouraged in their resistance against landlord tyranny by the relief extended to those evicted from the funds of the League—the Irish-Americans being the principal contributors. During one week a sum of over £4000 was subscribed—a larger amount than the "Repeal Rent" ever reached in the palmiest days of O'Connell.

T

The year 1880 did not end before the shadow of coming coercion fell across the country. The Government that could not pass remedial legislation, on account of the House of Lords blocking the way, could always rely on getting measures of repression through that chamber. There was, therefore, all the greater temptation for the Government, in casting about for means of dealing with Ireland, to have recourse to these. One of the first indications of a resort to the bad old policy was the arrest of Messrs T. M. Healy and Walsh in the south of Ireland. They had gone to remonstrate with a land-grabber—the name given to a person taking a farm over the head of another—and were charged, under one of the Whiteboy Acts, with intimidation. A vacancy having just occurred in the borough of Wexford, Mr Healy was returned unopposed, as an answer to this Government prosecution. He and Mr Walsh, when brought to trial, were acquitted.

A prosecution was also commenced against fourteen of the prominent leaders for carrying out the policy of the League. The trial was entered upon on the 29th of December 1880, and on the 25th of January 1881 the jury were discharged, being unable to agree to a verdict. It could not be shown, therefore, that Mr Parnell and the other leaders had committed any illegality, and, as the ordinary law could not apparently touch them, it must be overborne, to deal with what was described in the Queen's Speech at the opening of Parliament as "an extended system of terror" in Ireland. Besides coercion, the speech also promised that the land question would be dealt with. On the 24th of January Mr Forster introduced his Coercion Bill, which met from the Irish party the most determined opposition at every stage.

There was one leader who could be reached without waiting for the passing of a Coercion Act. This was Michael Davitt, whose ticket-of-leave was withdrawn. He was arrested in Dublin on Thursday, February 3rd, 1881, brought over to England, and imprisoned in Portland. During the term of his incarceration he was visited by Mrs A. M. Sullivan, Archbishop Croke, and others, who found him well treated ; indeed, it is but right to say that he himself states that, but for the deprivation of his liberty and having to wear the convict garb, the year he spent in Portland was not the most unpleasant of his life, and during the time of his imprisonment he wrote a most interesting book on prison life.

When, on the day of Davitt's arrest, in answer to the question of Mr Parnell in the House of Commons if it were true, he was told it was, there was a perfect storm of applause, as if some great national achievement had been accomplished. The manner in which the Irish party made their protest against the arrest led to their suspension. The Coercion Bill was read a third time on February 25th, 1881, and an Arms Bill—the Peace Preservation (Ireland) Bill—on March 11th. On both occasions Mr Forster, in expressing his exultation at the triumph over the Irish party, declared, as subsequent successors of his have done under like circumstances, that this legislation would relieve Ireland from the tyranny of the League, and that the Irish members did not represent the people, who really wished to throw off their yoke. It is singular with what persistency such impudent and ridiculous assertions have been persevered in by Irish Chief Secretaries, notwithstanding the fact that the "terrorised" people, though having the security of the ballot to protect them, invariably cast overwhelming majorities for their so-called tyrants.

On the 7th of April 1881, Mr Gladstone introduced his Land Bill, the effect of which, when ultimately passed, was to establish land courts, to fix fair rents, to give greater security of tenure, and some facilities for establishing peasant proprietorship. The very fact that these land courts, though not as a rule constituted of men having the popular confidence, made great, and, in many cases, enormous reductions in the rents, showed how the landlords had been robbing the people, who could not have full justice unless the arrears incurred in attempts to pay impossible rents were reduced or wiped off as circumstances might require. In fact it would be nothing less than strict justice if, in many cases, not merely should the arrears be wiped off but the landlord compelled to make restitution of all he had received in past years above what the Land Court declared to be a fair rent.

The Land Act was inadequate in other respects, but there was no want of thoroughness about the Coercion Act, which was put in force against the people and their leaders with the utmost brutality. Under it great numbers of Irishmen were arrested and kept in prison without trial, and in several cases the police stabbed and shot down inoffensive people. On the 13th of October 1881, Mr Parnell was arrested and sent to Kilmainham prison, where he and other leaders and a great number of the active spirits of the League were imprisoned for several months.

Attempts were also made to suppress *United Ireland*, the organ of the League. The history of that newspaper, and those it succeeded, may be found interesting. When, in 1865, the organ of the I.R.B., the *Irish People*, was suppressed, the *Irishman* to some extent supplied its place among those holding advanced principles. It originated in Belfast, where it first appeared as the *Ulsterman*. It was afterwards published in Dublin, where the change of name took place, and ultimately fell into the hands of Richard Pigott, of infamous memory. As a rule the articles in it displayed ability and high-toned nationality, as, from time to time, a number of talented and patriotic Irishmen contributed to its columns. Like the *Irish People*, its principal circulation was on this side of the Channel, and chiefly in the north of England, where Pigott—whose name appeared as publisher—was highly thought of by many, who associated his personality with the politics and general tone of the paper, knowing nothing of the man's real character. But the tone of the paper was part of his stock-in-trade, and was frequently made to serve his vile personal ends. There cannot be a doubt but that, in addition to being flagrantly dishonest, he, from time to time, was giving to the Government such information as he could get about the doings of the secret organisation. It was felt by those who knew Pigott best that his connection with Irish journalism was a disgrace to it, and a danger to the national cause. As he was always in the market the leaders of the Irish Home Rule Confederation of Great Britain were in treaty with him in 1875 to purchase the *Irishman* and two other publications connected with it, but the negotiations fell through.

The *Nation* and other Irish newspapers had done splendid service up to the time of the Land League agitation. It was felt by the leaders, however, that a special organ for the League was necessary. With this end Pigott's newspapers and plant were purchased from him, and, if no other good resulted from it, the field of Irish literature was cleared of one noxious weed in his person. From that time he dragged on a wretched existence by using, in return for the pay of the enemies of Ireland, such literary ability as he possessed, in hashing up for publication any information he had managed to get during his connection with the *Irishman*. When it was taken out of the hands of Pigott, this newspaper was, after a short time, discontinued; but the most important change was the substitution of *United Ireland* for the *Flag of Ireland*, one of Pigott's papers. The new journal was established as the organ of the Land League, and Mr William O'Brien, a powerful and brilliant writer on the staff of the *Freeman's Journal*, became its editor. So fearlessly and eloquently did *United Ireland* advocate the cause of the tillers of the soil and of Irish nationality, that from the first it was marked out for the vengeance of Mr Forster and the Coercion Act. First Mr O'Brien was arrested, and then, one after the other, the rest of the staff. Finally, the office of *United Ireland* was entered by the police, such copies of the paper as they could find were seized, and the publication on the premises stopped, so that Mr Forster no doubt thought that he had successfully grappled with and stricken down once and for all the chief disseminator of "sedition" in Ireland. This brings us to the Christmas of 1881. But Mr Forster's rejoicings at that festive season were rudely disturbed by the news that *United Ireland* was not dead after all—for it was actually coming into the country from England, printed simultaneously in London and Liverpool. A quantity of the papers printed in London were seized, but the whole of the Liverpool edition ran the blockade safely, and, in spite of every effort of the police, was, in a day or two, in circulation in every part of Ireland. For several weeks this went on. The paper seemed ubiquitous. Sometimes it was printed in London, sometimes in Paris, sometimes in

Liverpool. Twice, when the police were keeping close watch in the latter town to trace it to Ireland, where it could be seized, it was printed in Ireland itself—once in Derry and once in Dublin. From time to time seizures were made of parcels on their way to various places in Ireland, but the utmost ingenuity of the police, backed by fines in Ireland and England, and imprisonment in Ireland, could not stop its production and circulation, until, ultimately, it was allowed to be brought out as before at the publishing office in Abbey Street, Dublin. There cannot be a doubt but that the knowledge that the organ of the League could not be suppressed then, prevented the attempt being made to suppress national journals under a later coercion *régime*.

During the early part of 1882, while the police were conducting the war against *United Ireland*, the Land League made great progress in Great Britain—among the most active agents in its promotion being Miss Anna Parnell, sister to the Irish leader. For a time the Home Rule Confederation and the Land League went on side by side —in some places an old-established branch of the Con federation becoming also a branch of the League, in others separate branches of the new organisation being formed. At length one organisation became merged entirely into the other as the Irish National Land League of Great Britain, which, still later, became the Irish National League of Great Britain.

CHAPTER XXXIII.

ABANDONMENT OF COERCION AND A RELAPSE INTO IT—THE TREDEGAR RIOTS—THE IRISH IN SOUTH WALES—A. M. SULLIVAN.

ONE of the first indications that the Government had found coercion in Ireland to be a failure, and that a more conciliatory policy was about to be entered upon, was the fact that *United Ireland* was allowed to be published in the ordinary way at the office of that paper, after having been three months on the *shaughraun*, with the police unable to prevent its production, whether in or out of Ireland, and its circulation in Ireland. What was taken to be another indication of the same tendency was that on Monday, April 10th, 1882, Mr Parnell was liberated for a few days from Kilmainham, on parole, to attend the funeral of his nephew in Paris. On Saturday, April 15th, Mr William O'Brien was set free, several of the staff of *United Ireland* having been previously released. Finally, the Government, having now fully recognised the fact that, as might have been foreseen, disorder increased and continued so long as the men were kept in prison who might have held it in check, Messrs Parnell, Dillon, and O'Kelly were, on May 2nd, released, and Michael Davitt and a number of others were liberated soon after.

Mr Forster, considering this a condemnation of the policy he had been the chief instrument in carrying out, and being still of opinion it ought to have been persevered in, seceded from the Cabinet.

But the message of peace intended for Ireland was met by the frightful butchery of the man who was practically the bearer of it, Lord Frederick Cavendish, in Phœnix Park, Dublin, on the 6th of May. This was but the terrible fruit of the Coercion policy, which had, by the imprisonment of the responsible leaders, left the field open to the forces of anarchy; and it seemed as if these were resolved not to be driven from it without at least striking a blow. It was afterwards known that Mr Forster's own life was aimed at, and that it was by the merest accident he escaped. There cannot be a doubt but that he was a well meaning man, and took the direction of affairs with the very best intentions towards the Irish people. It was only when he came in contact with the permanent officials of Dublin Castle that their influence diverted his good intentions into the old, blind, wrong-headed, brutal policy of repression— the only instrument with which, with but rare exceptions, successive British Governments have ever attempted to rule Ireland. Mr Forster having withdrawn himself from the scene, the chief of the permanent officials of Dublin Castle, Mr Burke, was marked as a victim. It was his life that was sought and taken in the Phœnix Park, when Lord Frederick Cavendish, who happened to be with him at the time, in loyally standing up in defence of his comrade, shared his fate.

It was a crushing blow for the Land League, just as it seemed on the point of success. A new reign of coercion was inaugurated. In Great Britain the anti-Irish feeling became roused to fury, and, in several quarters, scenes were enacted like those of the Gordon riots and subsequent outbreaks. Looking back at the history of our people here during the last and present centuries, the steady progress they have been making in numbers, social position, and political power, is from time to time overshadowed by the records of what seem to be struggles against stupendous odds for the mere right to live. Driven forth from their own soil, they have but too often found themselves the Ishmaelites of Great Britain—with every man's hand against them. Although the feeling against the creed and nationality of the Irish has almost always been present, it has generally been when the fierce breath of some strong political or religious excitement has swept over the land that they have felt the full fury of the British mob. So it was at this crisis.

There was an anti-Irish outbreak at Brighouse, in Yorkshire, on Monday, May 8th, when a number of our people were maltreated and their houses nearly demolished, this being accompanied, as usual, by an attack on the Catholic church.

At Stalybridge the low Orange element threatened an attack on the Irish and their church. But as the outrages committed fourteen years previously were still vividly in the minds of the Irish population, they silently and determinedly gathered round the church and schools on the evening of the threatened attack. Some remained on guard the whole night. Needless to say, the Orange rabble, finding the Irish prepared to meet them on equal terms, did not make their appearance.

The most terrible of these riots occurred at Tredegar, in Monmouthshire, just on the South Wales border. The momentary passion against the Irish undoubtedly precipitated the attack, but the feeling against them was of longer standing, and was intensified by other causes. To thoroughly understand these it will be necessary to glance at the position and history of the Irish in South Wales, of which Monmouthshire is practically a part.

The district lying along the north shore of the Bristol Channel, in parts of which the Irish are to-day so numerous, has for us a tragic interest, since it was here that Diarmid M'Murrough, when he was compassing the treason that ultimately cost our country her liberty, bought the swords of the daring and unscrupulous adventurers who formed the vanguard of the Norman invasion of Ireland.

Probably the largest Irish community to be found in Wales is in Cardiff, which has many interesting memories for Irishmen. But for its cosmopolitan character it might be almost looked upon as the metropolis of Wales. Indeed, in ancient times, it was the capital of the kingdom of Gwent. Following in the track of the banditti brought over by M'Murrough, Henry II. himself, in 1172, passed through Cardiff on his way to Ireland. The English kings, John and Richard II., also came this way with their troops intended for the completion of the conquest of Ireland; which, after all, has not been conquered yet.

From the statistics of the Catholic church and other sources it will have been seen that the Irish have been crossing in considerable numbers and settling in London, Liverpool, and other places for about two hundred years. But there are no Catholic statistics of this district extending so far back as that, for in no part of Britain did the faith more utterly die out than in Wales.

From the time of the evil-omened visit of the false Leinster king there was little or no communication between Ireland and South Wales, until about sixty years ago. Bristol, however, which is not far distant, has been, since the earliest times, a place where Irishmen were to be found, on account of its trade with the various Irish ports. It was also on the track of our people from the south and southeast of Ireland on their way to London and elsewhere. Some have also for a long time been coming over by way of Milford. A convenient halting place between here and

Bristol is Chepstow, which would probably account for the first Catholic chapel in these parts in the present century having been built there in 1827. After that you find people from Cork, Waterford, and other southern counties, coming direct to Cardiff, Newport, and Swansea, suffering considerable hardships in the small sailing vessels which brought them over. Indeed some few still come to Swansea in the same way in the small craft that bring ore from Berehaven, and which are frequently several days in crossing.

A calamity almost as great as Diarmid's treason, the Irish famine, drove the Irish here in great numbers. Their presence and competition in the labour market were resented from time to time by the native population in the fashion to which our countrymen had become only too well accustomed. In 1848 there was an attack on the Irish in Cardiff, and on their houses and church. As will have been noticed, the feeling that prompted these outbreaks was always more active at the time of any great political or religious excitement, and no doubt the action of the Young Irelanders in 1848 helped to increase the unpopularity of their fellow-countrymen here.

After the rising a sterling Irishman, who has since done good service amongst the Irish in Britain, made his first appearance on this side of the Channel. Let us here explain how he came to visit Cardiff. Arising out of the 1848 movement was another slight revolutionary attempt of which but little mention has been made in current Irish history. The name of Fintan Lalor was connected with it. Some of the active spirits had to fly the country. Among these was James Francis Xavier O'Brien, who, in 1849, reached Cardiff from Dungarvan in a small coasting vessel belonging to his father, and remained away from Ireland until the storm blew over. He was but a youth at the time, but his ardour for revolutionary enterprise was by no means damped by this first failure, for nearly twenty years afterwards, in the Fenian rising of 1867, we find him in company with the daring Fenian chief, Lomasney, better known as "Captain Mackey," capturing the police barracks at Cappoquin. With others he was arrested and put upon his trial, when the judge paid a high tribute to his humanity and courage in causing, previous to the attack, the removal of the women and children who were within the barracks. The jury found him guilty of high treason, and he was sentenced to be executed. This sentence was, however, commuted to a term of penal servitude, which he passed in Irish and English prisons. It is so far creditable to the Irish jail officials, that even among these he found some who, in their treatment of him, did not altogether forget they were Irishmen; whereas, in the English jails he fared worse than those guilty of the most abominable crimes. His treatment was a kind of barometer of what was passing in the outer world, its severity being relaxed or intensified according to the political movements of the day. He is a man of transparent honesty and has since visited Cardiff in connection with a later movement in which the Irish of Britain have borne their share, and in the direction of which no man has been more earnest and active. Indeed, in the late terrible crisis, brought about by the repetition of M'Murrough's crime, no one did more to marshal the Irish hosts in Britain in the almost unanimous and magnificent stand they made for Ireland against the further leadership of the man who had proved unworthy of the high trust placed in him.

Cardiff and Newport are rising towns, being the chief outlets of the coal and iron districts of Glamorganshire and Monmouthshire. In these towns, as in the east end of London, our people are chiefly employed as dock labourers. Theirs is hard work, and they are frequently able to earn good wages at it. It must be said, however, that they have not been as thrifty as they might have been, otherwise more of them and their children would be in better positions than we now find them. They have also been more careless —often from circumstances beyond their control—of their sanitary surroundings and personal comfort than their fellow-workmen. It must also be said that drink, more than poverty, has been the curse of the Irish here and elsewhere in Great Britain. It is not that they drink more than their neighbours—probably on the whole they do not drink nearly so much—but theirs is a more excitable temperament, and it tells more upon them. More than this, the Irishman does not so often use drink as the Englishman does, as an article of food and along with his food. The consequence is, and medical men, like Dr Mullin of Cardiff, can bear testimony to the fact, that where an Englishman falls sick he will often pull through, from the greater care he has previously taken of himself, the Irishman, even though naturally of a superior physique, often succumbs on account of his more careless way of living, added, probably, to the previous hardships he has undergone. It is not pleasant for an Irishman to hear that, amongst certain portions of our people in Cardiff, many of them living under such conditions, the death rate is considerably higher than their birth rate. If this state of things were anything like general it would not be a hopeful outlook for the future of Catholicity and nationality in this country. Happily there are brighter prospects before us than this, although there are yet similar districts to those spoken of in Cardiff, in several other towns— notably London, Glasgow, and Liverpool. Better accommodation is now, however, being provided, while, in addition to this, as the condition of our fellow-countrymen improves —and it is steadily improving—they are, in all the large towns, getting into better surroundings; whilst the rookeries formerly known as the "Irish quarters" are gradually disappearing, so that not one-tenth of the exiles from Erin and their descendants now live in such localities.

Cardiff and Newport remind you of Liverpool on a smaller scale, for while, as in Liverpool, you have a number of Irishmen in tolerably good positions, the employment of most is in connection with the shipping. This is, to some extent, the case also in Swansea, where, in addition, they are engaged at the iron, copper, and tin works, and also at the coal-pits near the town. In the district stretching from Swansea to Cardiff you find considerable numbers of our fellow-countrymen at Neath, Aberavon, Maesteg, Bridgend, Barry Dock, and elsewhere. Indeed they are to be found in most of the towns and villages of Glamorganshire.

Should you for the more perfect enjoyment of the scenery be travelling on foot through South Wales—say in the month of August, when Nature's mantle shows its most varied hues—you will come across your fellow-countrymen in the most remote villages. You may reach some sequestered spot where there is no Catholic chapel and no priest; though the name of the place, being that of some old Celtic saint—as often as not an Irishman—with the prefix "Llan," shows it was not always so. Even here you will generally find a handful of the ubiquitous Irish race.

But though the Faith died out in Wales from sheer want of priests, the people are still eminently religious in their own way, and though, as you pass along the road, you do not so often find, as of old—

" ———— the cross-tipped steeple,"

you meet with their little chapels, called by some Scriptural name,—" Moriah," or " Zion," or " Bethesda."

If, in addition to a taste for scenery and antiquities, you have also a passion for politics, you will be sure to notice at this particular time of the year, just as in England, a list of those entitled to vote nailed to the chapel door. It is well known that these lists are not always placed in the most accessible positions, but this does not deter you from further investigation; so that, even though you may not be so young as you once were, you will not hesitate to climb over a high railing to get at such treasures as these. They speak of the joy of the gold digger lighting upon a nugget amid a mountain of quartz. This can bear no comparison with the feelings of the patriotic Irishman in some out-of-the-way Welsh village, when, amid the wilderness of Jones's, Jenkins's, and Evans's that crowd the list, his eyes are gladdened by an occasional name with the true Munster ring, such as Donovan, Driscoll, or Sullivan—with or without the O'—but all racy of the "old sod."

Going back to Cardiff as your centre, if you go in search of more of your fellow-countrymen, and take the road which leaves the noble old cathedral of Llandaff to the left, you will find yourself following the course of the river Taff, and passing through some pleasant scenery. You are not long in reaching Treforest, between which village and Ponty-pridd you find a Catholic chapel and schools—a sure sign that some of those you are in quest of are to be found in the neighbourhood. Pontypridd is a quaint and lively little town, situated at the junction of the river Rhondda with the

Taff, and at the entrance to a valley which, hemmed in by rugged and barren hills, must at one time have possessed a grandeur and a beauty of its own, before Nature's temple became deformed by the industry of man. This is the Rhondda Valley. From Pontypridd to Ton-y-Pandy, you have for several miles—along the river, road, and railway, which sometimes run parallel to, sometimes cross each other—almost continuous rows of cottages, varied by blast-furnaces and coal-pits, with the ugly-looking cinder-heaps which always accompany them.

If you would meet the Irish dwellers in the Rhondda, the best place is at Ton-y-Pandy, where there is a little Catholic chapel, and the best time is Sunday morning at and after Mass, to which they come from all parts of the valley for many miles around—this being the only chapel in the district.

Retracing your footsteps to Pontypridd, and again going northward along the Taff Vale for about ten or a dozen miles, you find yourself in Merthyr, and in close contiguity to a number of other towns and villages where the exiles from Erin have in great numbers made their homes. Indeed, if you leave out the Irish in the seaports of Newport, Cardiff, and Swansea, the densest mass of our people in South Wales and Monmouth is to be found in and about the towns and among the hills within a radius of little more than ten miles east, south, and west of Tredegar, which may be said to be the centre of the iron and steel working district. It is situated in the north-east corner of Monmouthshire, having the Glamorganshire border a few miles to the west, and Breconshire, in which there are but few Irish, a couple of miles to the north. Round about here, then, is the region where you strike the richest vein of the true Irish metal—here among the barren, health-giving hills, which only afford grazing for the small Welsh ponies and sheep. Except where blasted by the unlovely surroundings of the coal-pits and iron-works, these hills have a certain picturesqueness, and through the intervening valleys, running for the most part north and south to the Bristol Channel, flow the rivers Neath, Taff, Rhondda, Rhymney, and Sirhowey. Besides Tredegar, the Irish are most numerous in Merthyr, Dowlais, Aberdare, Mountain Ash, Blaenavon, Brynmawr, Abersychan, Pontypool, and Cwmbran. In the vicinity of most of these places are immense heaps of cinders, the refuse from the mines and other works. These smoulder for a long time, and at night the flamelets of various hues, bursting forth here and there, present a singular appearance. Then, as in the Black Country in the Midlands, the whole district is lit up by the weird-like glare of the blast-furnaces, which work night and day. In and around some of these hill towns the cinder heaps, when cooled and solidified, have been built upon, and the many different levels neither improve the symmetry nor the sanitary arrangements of these towns and villages. At the iron-works the Irish are at the hardest labour, which neither Englishman nor Welshman can nor will do, and if you go into the works you cannot but admire the strength and dexterity with which they draw out the huge bars at white heat into the rollers which shape them into iron and steel rails.

They pay generously to support the cause of creed and country. They have in some parts of the district a plan for raising money for the support of the priest and church, which, however well it may act in some cases, is not without objectionable features. This is that, at the various works, money—about a shilling a month—is stopped from the pay of the Irish Catholics for the support of their church. The men, it is said, do not object, and it is urged that more is got in this way, because many who don't go to church at all, or but seldom, would not be likely otherwise to contribute. It is doubtful if the system acts towards the advancement of religion. It certainly tends to lessen the self-respect of both priests and people, for though the priest is simply drawing his own money, contributed by his own people, at the office of the works, it places him in a kind of dependency upon owners or managers, who sometimes expect political support in return, should any of these become candidates for public positions. This custom of stopping the priests' money out of the men's wages prevails to some extent in Scotland also, and probably in some other places.

As a rule there are not many inter-marriages between the Irish and Welsh. They are most frequent where the Irish have been born in Wales, and speak the language of the country as their native tongue, as they often do—particularly among the hills. In this way you get good Irish nationalists and Catholics bearing Welsh names, while, on the other hand, it seems incongruous to find names which are common—

"Where the Lee and Shannon flow,"

borne by men to be found at the Nonconformist places of worship on Sunday, and who are for all practical purposes Welshmen. Such cases generally arise where the father, an Irishman, has died while his children were in their infancy, and these have been reared by the Welsh mother in her own creed and among her native surroundings.

What has told most against our people has been their demonstrativeness when under the influence of drink. As a rule they have been courteous and careful not to give offence, but when the drink demon gained possession there were sometimes foolish boasts of their prowess, which often led to encounters, in which, although the physical superiority of the Irishman might give him an advantage for the time, he was bound to be the sufferer sooner or later. It must be said, however, that in the bulk there are nowhere more sterling, warm-hearted, and generous Irishmen than in South Wales ; and of none are the words of T. D. Sullivan more true—

"We've heard their faults a hundred times,
　The new ones and the old,
In songs and sermons, rants and rhymes,
　Enlarged some fifty-fold.
But take them all, the great and small,
　And this we've got to say:
　　Here's dear old Ireland !
　　Good old Ireland!
　　Ireland, boys, hurrah !"

The jealousy against the Irish which culminated in the terrible riots at Tredegar was greatly increased because many of the native population had been thrown out of employment, for in the making of rails iron was becoming superseded by steel, which was being rapidly turned out in large quantities by the Bessemer process. There being less hands required to work the new system, some one must go, and the Welsh were determined that, so far as in them lay, it was the Irish who must suffer. The correspondent of the *South Wales Daily News*, speaking of the aversion with which the Irish were regarded previous to the Tredegar riots, said—"The Phœnix Park and other outrages intensified this feeling, and it had been an open secret for some days that an outbreak was contemplated and inevitable."

The impending outbreak was not entirely unknown to the Irish. Many of them, particularly the younger generation, knew sufficient of the Welsh tongue to catch the muttered threats of vengeance let fall in public-houses and elsewhere by the native population, when none but themselves were supposed to be near. The whole of the Irish population, not only of Tredegar but of the other towns among the hills, were to be cleared out. Heaven knows their lives were not spent among the most cheerful surroundings, but their way of earning their daily bread was the only one known not only to the original settlers from Cork or Kerry, but to the generations of Irish parentage born here. Let us take a brief glance at their position in such places as Tredegar. Naturally there could not be a healthier locality, but the smoke and grime of the works are ever present. In Tredegar, as in other of these towns, the houses chiefly inhabited by the Irish, such as those in Iron Row, which face the works—some of which were attacked and burnt in the riots—were, and are, wretchedly poor places. They were mostly run up at slight cost by the iron masters, for the convenience of their work people, and to get out of them the greatest possible profit for the smallest possible outlay. Many of these being, as at Merthyr, actually built on the cinder-tips, the levels are irregular, so that the uneven surfaces become receptacles for refuse and stagnant water. Enter one of these dwellings and you will occasionally find but a single room on the flagged and damp ground floor, with a sleeping loft above, not high enough to stand up in. When added to the discomfort of these dwellings —inside and out—you have the thick, murky atmosphere engendered by the blast-furnaces, working night and day, it can well be imagined that homes like these have little attraction beyond what the light-hearted Irish nature can give to the most dreary abode. It is not surprising that some are driven to drink and to the usually brighter surroundings of where it is sold. Two generations of our people have been born and have grown up in these Welsh hill-towns. You will hear the racy Munster tongue of the original immigrant, while the accent of his children and grandchildren is undistinguishable from that of their Welsh neighbours, whose vernacular they speak; indeed you will find some who can converse in all three tongues—Irish, Welsh, and English. It is no uncommon thing to find a man of Irish extraction born in Rhymney or Tredegar, while his wife may have been born in Merthyr, and his children at Dowlais or elsewhere; yet they are all regarded by the natives, and by themselves, as being as much Irish as the original settlers who came in the famine years or still earlier.

With the exception of a few of those born of intermarriages with the native population—and some of these consider themselves good Irishmen too—they are, indeed, as a rule, as Irish in heart as though born in Cork, or Waterford, or Tipperary.

Indeed it is cheering to find, among so much that is calculated to depress you, how many of the domestic virtues which are the glory of the island of saints, how many of the kindly old customs of a warm-hearted race, and how much genuine patriotism you find here.

Go among them, go to Red Lion Square or the Iron Row, where the fiercest attacks were made on the Irish, and ask the origin of the terrible riots of 1882, and you will get a far clearer view of what then took place than you can gather from the newspapers of the day. When men are bent upon hostility and outrage it is easy to make the victims appear the aggressors. In nine cases out of ten this has been so in connection with the periodical outbreaks against the Irish, whether directed against their creed or nationality, or both, during the last hundred and fifty years. So it was in Tredegar.

Here, as in many places in this country, there were a number of people belonging to what is known as the "Salvation Army," one of those hysterical religious developments of which there has been such a plentiful crop, ever since those who consider themselves such a levelheaded, sensible people, left the old faith. In the early part of 1882 there came to lodge at one of the Irish houses in the Iron Row, Tredegar, an old soldier, who professed to be an Irishman and a Catholic. The only sort of employment he could get in Tredegar was of a very laborious kind, and he had probably acquired in the army a taste for a lazy life. As he was a fair scholar, and had the fluent tongue of an Irishman, he saw an opening for his peculiar gifts in the "Salvation Army," of which he became a recruit and a shining light. He made a great display of zeal, and created bad blood among the other lodgers, who, knowing his motive, did not hesitate to express their contempt for the renegade. In one of the "army parades," some of the Irish children pelted the "turncoat" with flour. This was how the Irish became the "aggressors"—this was made the immediate excuse for the explosion which was bound to come. This was on the Tuesday night previous to the outbreak, and during the week the processions of the "Salvation Army" kept up the excitement, and were the cause of disorderly scenes. There is no doubt but that the Salvationists were made use of at Tredegar, as they have been at Birkenhead and other towns, where disturbances have arisen, to excite and provoke the Irish into becoming the aggressors. The special correspondent of the *Freeman* said :—" On Friday night there were ominous knots of Welsh and Irish in the streets, and in the evening, when the Salvationists were holding a service in the 'Paddy Quarter,' as it was called, the 'Converted Irishman' was exhibited among the proceedings. A little hooting and the throwing of some flour over the converted one gave a pretext for the next night's attack."

It was not until the following evening, Saturday, July 8th, 1882, when the week's work was done, and men's passions were inflamed by drink, that the Civil War—for it was no less—broke out. Hostilities commenced by the smashing of the glass in many of the Irish houses. Then a large mob proceeded to attack one of the places in which they lived—Red Lion Square. At this time there do not appear to have been many Irishmen present to defend their homes, for one who was amongst the defenders states that when the mob attempted to enter the square it was held against them by but a couple of men and four women, and that these would actually have succeeded in keeping out their assailants until more help arrived, but that the police broke through, by way of affording protection to the people of the square, and let the mob in to do their work of pillage and destruction. Among the few who held the square was an old soldier named O'Meara, who, finding his dwelling attacked, armed himself with a scythe and stoutly defended himself against a host of assailants. He was eventually overpowered and severely treated. He was arrested and afterwards put upon his trial for his vigorous defence of his own and his neighbours' lives and property. At the trial of the Irish and Welsh prisoners, the prosecuting counsel displayed a singular amount of ignorance, or unfairness, or both, in stating the case against O'Meara. In describing the attack on the Irish quarter, he said:—"A number of persons assembled in a thoroughfare known as Red Lion Square." Now this would convey the impression that, this being what he termed a "thoroughfare," these people might have assembled there for an object which might have been quite legitimate, and that they might have been passing on their way to some other place when they were attacked, single-handed, by this Irishman, for he said, "he could not but regard O'Meara as the originator of what afterwards occurred." A brief description of the scene of the rioting will show how unjust to the old soldier was this way of putting the case against him.

About the middle of the town of Tredegar is a large open space, called from its shape "The Circle," where the Salvationists chiefly held forth. The Circle is crossed at right angles by two thoroughfares. The street leading southward towards the ironworks has the Iron Row, an Irish locality, crossing it at the bottom. The main thoroughfare of Tredegar cuts the Circle, running eastward and westward.

Leaving the Circle behind you, and going along eastward for a few hundred yards, if you turn off it to the left you will find yourself in Red Lion Square, which is not a "thoroughfare" in the ordinary sense at all. It does not lead to or from any place in particular, and, as a rule, few would think of entering it unless led by curiosity or having some special business in the place itself. Now the mob did not "assemble" there by accident, but actually burst violently into the place with the view to demolishing the Irish houses and turning out the inhabitants. These driven out and not daring to reappear, all the witnesses at the trial were on the one side, and the scene of savagery in Red Lion Square was afterwards all put upon the head of the unfortunate O'Meara, who, in defending himself, it is said, cut off the nose of one of his assailants.

By the time this is said to have occurred there were some five thousand Welshmen in and about Red Lion Square, and the houses of the Irish were attacked with the utmost fury.

They made a resolute stand for their homes and their families. But what could they do against such overwhelming odds? Doors and windows were broken in, furniture and bedding were tossed out into the square and a bonfire made of them; while the unfortunate people, after being brutally treated and rendered homeless, had to fly to seek shelter wherever they could. Some found it for the night about the coal-pits or out on the bleak, open hills, where they remained huddled together under severe showers of rain; while, according to the terms of a question, based on reliable information, put in the House of Commons by Mr T. P. O'Connor, not only were these poor people left homeless and their furniture destroyed, but, owing to the robbery of their provisions and money, a number of women and children were without food for twenty-four and some for forty-eight hours. Others of the victims stayed not until they had put many miles between them and the scene of the outrage, while fathers, mothers, and children got separated in the flight, and heard nothing of each other for many days.

A number made their way to Cardiff, Newport, and elsewhere, and some families even found their way to Ireland. Nothing less than the immediate clearing out of the whole Irish population would now seem to satisfy the mob, and the attacks on Irish houses and their inhabitants were carried on during the second day of the rioting—Sunday. The fury of the mob made no distinction between those who had come from Ireland and those of Irish parentage, who were actually natives of the place. All were equally obnoxious, as, amongst others, John Power, a Merthyr-born man, who kept a general shop at the corner of Iron Street and Iron Row, found to his cost. On that Sunday night the howling rioters came down Iron Street from the Circle in a body so dense that, in the words of an Irishman who described the scene, "You could walk on their heads."

Power heard their yells, and then a shower of bricks and large stones came crashing through the windows, and to this day the deep dents left by these are visible. He rushed to the door, and no sooner opened it than he was felled by a blow from a sling-shot or some iron instrument, he knew not what, for he was knocked insensible. The house was filled, upstairs and downstairs, in a minute, and everything breakable was smashed and thrown into the street. The other Irish houses in the row got the same treatment. The furniture and bedding thrown out were made a bonfire of, and one house was completely burned down.

In too many cases our people are not so thrifty as they might be, and do not always use the opportunities for advancement that come in their way. In Tredegar, as elsewhere, there were exceptions to this. One of these was a contractor, named Fitzgerald, who employed about 150 hands. He accumulated money, and, like a sensible man, bought a few houses on the pleasant part of the hill-side, lying some distance from the smoke and squalor of the town. In one of these houses he lived. Red Lion Square, Iron Row, and other places inhabited by the Irish, were eyesores to their enemies, but nothing more excited their envy and ill-will than to see what the Irishman, Fitzgerald, had been able to do from the fruits of his own industry. He, too, was therefore marked out for attack, and for two hours on the Sunday night his house was the scene of indescribable violence and tumult. He defended it as best he could. Two shots were fired from the house, one of which wounded a man among the mob. The shot that took effect was not, it is believed, fired by Fitzgerald himself, but by his wife, who bravely stood by him in defence of their home. The shooting of one of their number increased the fury of the mob, who broke through doors and windows, and, sweeping in, cleared out and demolished the furniture and everything within the place. Fitzgerald himself was so badly injured that, when he was carried into the police barracks close by, his life was for some time despaired of. As, according to the counsel for the prosecution at the trial which followed, the old soldier, O'Meara, was responsible for the atrocities in Red Lion Square, so it was with Fitzgerald. He said of him—"On Sunday again, in consequence of the action of a man who was not then present, but who came out of his house and fired a gun, another severe riot took place, and a great attack was made on house property, and windows were demolished." This sagacious lawyer evidently seemed to think that, when a violent mob threatened the lives and property of Irishmen, it was a criminal act for them to resist. Fitzgerald's house was even more out of the ordinary track than Red Lion Square. He did not invite the mob to come. They came just as they did to Red Lion Square, and for the same purpose. They could have had no object in assembling there but a hostile one, and yet Fitzgerald was made responsible for what followed. He must have considered himself fortunate that he was not put upon his trial for acting in self-defence—the authorities being unable to protect him and his fellow country-men—and that he was not severely punished for having his property destroyed and being nearly beaten to death.

At length it seemed as if the mob had nothing left to exhaust its fury upon, for the Irish who had not been previously driven out, finding the authorities gave them no protection, left the place almost *en masse*, so that out of a population estimated at from 1500 to 2000, there were only about 100 of them left. Such was the reign of terror, that

the benevolent Welsh people who assisted the destitute Irish families were threatened with attack also. It was feared, too, that the Irish in the other towns among the hills would suffer, so that many left these places to seek safety elsewhere. Although the bulk of them were able to return when the storm of passion had subsided, the uprising against them materially checked whatever progress they were making; particularly in connection with the younger people who were learning trades.

It was only on the Monday, when all the damage had been done, that the police, who had not been able to cope with the rioting, were sufficiently reinforced, and the military arrived on the scene. In the House of Commons Sir William Harcourt was severely brought to task by Mr Parnell and Mr T. P. O'Connor, as to why the rioting was allowed to go on unchecked, and why the additional police and military were so late in arriving on the scene.

At the Monmouthshire Assizes, on Wednesday, August 2nd, Mr A. M. Sullivan appeared for two Irish prisoners, Long and O'Meara, when they and four Welsh prisoners, on the recommendation of their counsel, pleaded guilty to the minor offence of riot, and each received a sentence of three months imprisonment, with hard labour. It is possible that the Irish prisoners might have been found guilty of some technical legal offence if their cases had been gone into; but it was monstrous that those who belonged to the party who had been the victims, and who had been acting in self-defence, should receive the same punishment as the men who had taken part in what was notoriously a preconcerted attack. Mr Sullivan no doubt, however, used good judgment, taking into consideration all the circumstances, not only on behalf of his clients, but in the interest of the Irish population who still remained or were gradually coming back to their homes. No man could feel more for his fellow-countrymen than he—none would more quickly resent an injury to those whom he regarded as literally his own flesh and blood. Yet here he felt himself placed in a trying position. While he was determined that justice should be done to them, he had to remember that most of them had, for better or for worse, cast their lot here;

many had been born here and knew no other way of making a living than in the industries of the district. He considered it his duty, therefore, to smooth the way for them, and no doubt his conciliatory tone towards the Welsh, when advocating the cause of his fellow-countrymen, had much to do with the more amicable feeling that has since prevailed.

There are few Irishmen who have rendered better service to our country. With his brother, T. D. Sullivan — the Irish poet-laureate—he kept the flag flying in the *Nation* when, so far as constitutional agitation was concerned, public opinion had become demoralized, and patriotism had apparently fallen to its lowest ebb. A. M. Sullivan had all the finest qualities of our race—the warm and exuberant fancy of the southern Celt, eloquence unsurpassed, an intellect quick to grasp whatever came within its scope, and an almost electric vitality; with a ready sympathy with the suffering and oppressed—a sympathy which could be as quickly turned into fiercest wrath against the oppressor. As in his later years he largely identified himself with his fellow-countrymen here, it is but right he should have a prominent and an honoured place among the Irish of Britain. The scenes of his childhood gave a colouring to his life. Reared by the romantic shores of Bantry Bay— upon whose bosom, open to the embraces of the Atlantic, fleets might ride, and through whose portals commerce might pour upon the shores of Ireland the wealth of distant climes—he saw but a waste of waters where even the hardy fishermen in their frail craft became fewer as each year went by, under the blight of foreign rule. In his later years, his sympathies seemed to have broadened to embrace all humanity. It may be said that while a man's household is perishing the misfortunes of others have small claim upon him, but, while ever ready to lend a helping hand where needed to men of every race, no one could deny that the warmest love of Sullivan's heart was for Ireland. Though some may have thought he ambitioned the *rôle* of a British statesman, they cannot say he ever ceased to be an Irish patriot; for even those whose ideal of Irish freedom is total severance of the British connection, would be willing to accord to him the latter title, if only in what they would consider a limited sense. Those Irishmen who believe in constitutionalism would, no doubt, rather have seen him more closely linked with the Irish Parliamentary party, but they must admit that he sometimes did service which the more extreme members could not have accomplished, and often, when the party were in what threatened to be a serious complication, likely to end in discomfiture, he would dash in to the rescue, and, with that ready tact which was so characteristic of him, bring them off with flying colours.

Mr Sullivan's visit to South Wales to defend his poor fellow-countrymen was one of the last acts of a life devoted to the cause of Ireland. Had he lived a few years longer he would have rejoiced to see the dawn of a better day for the Irish in South Wales.

CHAPTER XXXIV.

THE IRISH NATIONAL LEAGUE OF GREAT BRITAIN — THE 1885 ELECTION—THE BALANCE OF POWER—SUPPORTING THE TORIES.

SINCE the formation of the Home Rule Confederation of Great Britain in 1873, at the Convention held in Manchester and Birmingham, the organisation representing the Irish of Great Britain has gone on uninterruptedly, under the various names which the agitation for the time being has assumed.

The annual conventions were held regularly, the most important being that in Liverpool in 1877, where Charles Stewart Parnell succeeded Isaac Butt in the Presidency. Mr Parnell held the office until 1883, when, at the convention held in Leeds, he was succeeded by Mr T. P. O'Connor, who may be regarded as a typical Irishman of Britain, as he has taken up his abode here, and, during the greater portion of his political career, has identified himself with his fellow-countrymen on this side of the Channel. Those who had come into contact with him previous to the Leeds Convention felt satisfied that Mr Parnell, in proposing him as

President, sought to place the chief direction of the Irish National League of Great Britain in firm and able hands. Subsequent conventions and the way in which the League has prospered confirms this estimate of Mr O'Connor. Some have thought he might have been more conciliatory at these conventions, but let any one imagine the work he has to do. It has been said that these annual gatherings are the Parliaments of the Irish people here, and so they are. Imagine the debates at St Stephens to be confined to a single day in the year; imagine the assembly, instead of being largely composed of stolid dead-heads, who come to vote at the word of command, to be entirely formed of a race with whom eloquence is a native gift; imagine that each of these has come charged with a most important mandate from his constituents, which he is bound to deliver, and where is the Speaker could manage them? Only one of the same quick-witted race as themselves, who has the necessary tact and firmness, who from a wilderness of words can get straight at the point and deal with it promptly, who can at once sum up the whole merits of a case with great rapidity and generally more correctly than one of Her Majesty's judges would, after reserving his decision for several days over some knotty point requiring the utmost deliberation. During the Liberal Coercion days nobody could more mercilessly pulverize an opponent than Mr) O'Connor, but now that the "Grand Old Man," Mr Gladstone, has spoken the word, and the Liberal party have, practically, come on the Irish platform, no one is in greater demand among those who had many a time felt his scathing power as an opponent.

Up to the time of this Leeds Convention the Executive had been composed of the most prominent and trusted men of each district, men like Mr P. J. Foley, of London; Mr John Barry, who resided in Manchester in the earlier years of the Confederation; Dr Commins, of Liverpool; Mr Bernard M'Anulty, of Newcastle-on-Tyne; and Mr John Ferguson, of Glasgow. Besides these there was a large representation from the various parts of the north of England, the district where the Irish are most numerous. When the Confederation was directed, first from Manchester, and then from Liverpool, there was no difficulty in getting a sufficient number of the Executive to attend to do the required business. But when, following the resolution passed at the Dublin Convention of 1876, the seat of government was transferred to London, the distance was so great from the bulk of the Irish population in Great Britain, that it was but seldom the provincial members could attend. A plan was adopted by which those who could attend in London co-opted others to make up a sufficient number. At the Leeds Convention, on the proposition of Mr Parnell, the Executive was formed from members of the Irish Parliamentary party, who, being in London during the session of Parliament, and some of them residing there all the year round, could more conveniently attend than members from distant parts of the country.

The organisation, originally founded as the Irish Home Rule Confederation of Great Britain, in 1873, following the changes in the National movement at home in Ireland, had now became the Irish National League of Great Britain, and, as in Ireland, there was far more vitality in the new movement than in that led by Isaac Butt.

While the Franchise and Redistribution Acts of 1884 and 1885 placed the Parliamentary representation in the hands of the people of Ireland, they also added greatly to the political power of the Irish here.

The Franchise Act gave the same household suffrage to the counties which had previously been enjoyed by the towns. Thousands of Irish householders thus obtained votes, where formerly, under the restricted franchise, such a thing as an Irish county voter was almost unknown.

As the Liberal Government still pursued with great severity the policy of Coercion in Ireland, the Irish members opposed them with equal vigour, and on the 8th of June 1885, on a momentous division, they enabled the Tories to overthrow the ministry.

When the Tories came into office, they, in return for the support of the Irish party in turning out the Liberals, at once dropped Coercion. The new Viceroy, Lord Carnarvon, found Ireland much easier to govern by the policy of conciliation than by the now discarded method of r sion. The celebrated interview between him and Mr Parnell, in Dublin, and other circumstances, show that it was understood that Ireland was to get some measure of self-government, although, afterwards, it became convenient for the Tories to repudiate any such idea. Previous to the general election of 1885 neither Liberals nor Tories knew how the Irish vote would go—nor indeed had the Irish leaders themselves made up their minds, for they felt the value of the weapon they held in their hands, the Irish vote, too much to use it without due deliberation on one side or the other. It was not until a few days before the first of the elections that the word was finally given to support the Tories. The Irish in the country had, as a rule, hitherto voted for the Liberal party, and, therefore, it can readily be imagined how much it now went against their grain to support the Tories. The mandate had, however, gone forth, exceptions being made only in the cases of a very few Liberal candidates who had always been staunch friends of Ireland in Parliament; and loyal obedience was given by the great mass of the Irish electors of Great Britain.

Every one will remember the state of intense and eager expectancy in which Irishmen waited for the "word" which was to decide how their votes were to be cast. Their highly strung excitement could not have been greater if they had been preparing for an armed rising. In a few hours after the issue of the famous "manifesto" by the Irish leaders, hundreds of thousands of copies of it were placarded all over the country, while it was scattered broadcast in millions in the shape of leaflets and handbills, by the Tories, who felt that now at length they had got their most potent weapon with which to fight their Liberal opponents.

Liverpool being the chief Irish centre, and the Scotland division of that city, the only constituency in Great Britain able to return an Irish Nationalist against all comers, and Mr T. P. O'Connor being the candidate as well as the head of the Irish organisation on this side of the Channel, he naturally, as he states in his " Life of Charles Stewart Parnell," made his headquarters there during the 1885 election. Much to his surprise, as he tells us in the same book, Mr Parnell also made Liverpool his headquarters, though it might naturally be expected his presence would have been more essential in Ireland than in connection with the three seats being contested by Irish Nationalists in Liverpool, in only one of which was it possible to win. In Exchange division of Liverpool, for some reason, Mr Stephens, the official Liberal candidate, had been replaced by Captain O'Shea, who got the full support of the Liberal party. Following instructions from headquarters, the Irish Nationalists had denounced in no measured terms the candidates put forward by the Liberal party, which, when recently in power, had so brutally coerced Ireland; and Captain O'Shea was lashed more unmercifully than any of them on account of being a renegade Irishman. When Parnell himself came on the scene as a candidate for Exchange division, O'Shea was denounced more fiercely than ever. Mr Parnell, however, withdrew on the nomination day, and nobody doubted but that the Irish vote would now go to the Tories, as originally directed. On the same night there was a great demonstration in the League Hall. It had been called to support the candidature of Mr Parnell in the Exchange division, Mr O'Connor in the Scotland division, and Mr Redmond in the Kirkdale division; the latter being put up apparently to draw off votes from Mr James Samuelson, the Liberal candidate—a quite unnecessary precaution, as the Tory got more votes than Messrs Samuelson and Redmond combined. Mr Samuelson was a candidate, among a number of others, in whose favour many Irishmen considered the rule against supporting Liberals ought to have been relaxed, for he was thoroughly sound on the Irish question, and had been a courageous champion of the Liverpool dock labourers, most of whom are Irishmen. The astonishment at Mr Samuelson being opposed was all the greater when, at the last moment, Mr Parnell made an exception in Exchange division in favour of a man who had been justly regarded as a renegade from the Irish Parliamentary party. At the League Hall meeting, on the night of the nomination, there were many who had been present at Mr Parnell's *debut* on the same platform, some years previously, in company with Isaac Butt, and who remembered his extreme nervousness and awkward, hesitating speech. On the present occasion, when he came to speak of his own retirement from the contest in Exchange division, it could not but have struck the most thoughtless observer that he was even more ill at ease than on the night of his first appearance amongst them. But their wonder at his demeanour became intensified when he asked them to support Captain O'Shea, chiefly on the ground that "in no case was he ever found in the lobby in favour of coercion," and that the Tories ought not to have opposed him (Mr Parnell) in Exchange division when they were getting the Irish vote elsewhere. As he proceeded, the dead silence that followed every word that he spoke, and the amazement and consternation in which men looked into each other's faces and into his, evidently cowed even Parnell's audacious spirit. He only partially recovered himself when a few faint cheers, given from the force of habit, and because they seemed to be expected, greeted him as he finished, by saying, " If you desire to vote for Captain O'Shea, as an Irishman and a Catholic, I see no reason why you should not do so." We now know the reason of this man's confusion in face of the honest Irishmen of Liverpool—this man who had been trusted as leader never had been before—who, like another M'Murrough, was jeopardising the cause of Ireland by a guilty intrigue. At the close of the meeting numerous groups outside discussed the situation, many in anger, but all with feelings of apprehension.

On the day of the election Parnell worked unceasingly for O'Shea, even to the extent of taking away the canvassers from the Scotland division committee-rooms to assist in the return of his nominee, persisting in this notwithstanding the expostulations that in so doing he was risking the return of Mr O'Connor. It must be said, however, that though, in deference to the pressure of their leader, many went to help in O'Shea's committee-rooms, their honest instincts almost invariably prompted them to find their way back to Scotland division, where the real battle of Ireland had to be fought.

Parnell's clever strategy, in swinging round at the last moment a considerable portion of the Irish vote in Exchange division to the side of the Liberals, brought O'Shea within a few votes of winning. Few Irishmen regretted his defeat, particularly as they had won an overwhelming victory in Scotland division by the election of Mr T. P. O'Connor, the first, and as yet the only man, ever returned as an Irish Nationalist for a British Parliamentary constituency.

Such of the Tory candidates in the 1885 election as alluded to the Irish question pledged themselves to support some extension of local self-government to Ireland, and as being opposed to Coercion. At the commencement of the campaign it appeared as if, aided by the powerful Irish vote in the boroughs, the Tories would be returned to power by a considerable majority. This seemed at one time so certain that it became a question with the Irish leaders whether it was a desirable thing to give the Tories such a preponderating majority, and whether in the elections yet to come some relaxation should be made in favour of certain Liberal candidates. But those who knew the country best pointed out that the bulk of the county elections had yet to come, and that the recent legislation, which had assimilated the household vote in the counties with that which had prevailed in the boroughs, had enfranchised a large number of people, the majority of whom were likely to be Liberals. Hitherto the farmers and people in comfortable circumstances had formed the bulk of the county voters, but vast numbers of the labouring population in the smaller towns and villages, and in the outlying suburbs of the larger towns, were now called upon for the first time to exercise the franchise, and there was every probability that the bulk of these would vote for the Liberal party. No alteration was, therefore made in the arrangement already decided upon, and the Irish steadily voted for the Tories until the end of the elections.

The result showed that they were not able to counterbalance the newly enfranchised county voters. At the close of the General Election the members returned to Parliament were—Liberals, 333 ; Tories, 249 ; Nationalists, 86 ; Independents, 2. Tories and Nationalists combined had, therefore, only a majority of 2, or reckoning the Independents, 4 votes, over the Liberals. As the Tory leaders could not hope to gain the support of the more bigoted members of the party for any measure for the amelioration of the condition of Ireland, this bare majority was not sufficient to enable them to carry out any legislation in that direction, even if they were so inclined. Had the Irish vote been sufficiently strong to place them in power with a considerable majority, and yet not so great but that, thrown on the Liberal side, it might turn them out again should the occasion demand it, there most probably would, as a matter of policy, have been some legislation for Ireland in the direction of local self-government, and there would have been no Coercion. But, with a shameless disregard of election pledges, the Tory Government now announced their intention to introduce Coercion in Ireland and to suppress the National League. Their career was but short, however, for on an amendment to the Queen's Speech at the opening of the Session of 1886, they were thrown out of office, and Mr Gladstone again came into power.

CHAPTER XXXV.

MR GLADSTONE A CONVERT TO HOME RULE — HIS DEFEAT IN PARLIAMENT AND AT THE POLLS.

THE short interregnum of the Tories had given Mr Gladstone time for reflection, and he came to the conclusion that Coercion having been tried for ages against Ireland and found wanting, it was no use any longer to attempt to rule the country against the wishes of her people.

The extension of the household franchise to the counties had at length enabled Ireland to speak with her true voice. This she at once did by returning 85 out of 103 members of Parliament pledged to national self-government. This also was recognised by Mr Gladstone, who came to the conclusion that, Ireland having now demanded by an unmistakable majority the right to make her own laws, that right could no longer be, with safety, withheld from her.

It was understood, therefore, on his coming into office, that he was preparing a scheme of Home Rule for Ireland which would end the strife of centuries, and win for him a greater glory than any statesman had ever achieved before.

He introduced his Home Rule bill on the 8th of April 1886. But the great Liberal chief had failed to carry with him a considerable portion of his party, including Chamberlain, Hartington, and other prominent men, so that when the division on the second reading of his measure was taken, on June 7th, he was defeated by a majority of thirty votes.

The large Irish vote in many English, Scotch, and Welsh constituencies having been used with such decisive effect on the Conservative side in 1885, it was thought that, in the General Election which followed the rejection of the Home Rule bill, the turning over of this to the Liberal side might enable Mr Gladstone to come back to power.

But the lowest depths of anti-Irish and no-Popery bigotry were stirred up by so-called Liberals as well as by the Tory and Orange factions. As a result, Mr Gladstone's defeat at the polls appeared to be even more crushing than in Parliament. At the close of the elections the members returned to Parliament stood as follows :—

Tories	316
Dissensionist Liberals	78
	394
Liberals	191
Irish Nationalists	85
	276

Majority against Home Rule 118

As a result of the election, Mr Gladstone resigned, and a Tory Government came into office.

CHAPTER XXXVI.

THE BYE-ELECTIONS—"THE FLOWING TIDE"—THE LEAGUE PREPARES FOR THE NEXT ELECTION—OUR MUSTER ROLL.

JUDGING from the number of men sent to Parliament for and against Home Rule, Mr Gladstone's defeat seemed overwhelming. But when the votes given for the candidates on each side were summed up, it was surprising what a comparatively small number of these had given such a large majority in Parliament to the enemies of Irish freedom. Out of about two and a half millions of votes given, the "Unionists"—as the Tories and Dissensionist Liberals styled themselves,—had a majority of less than 80,000 at the polls,—in fact, about the voting strength of one large borough, such as Glasgow, Birmingham, or Liverpool. Added to this, hundreds of thousands of Liberals abstained from voting, some on account of the vile misrepresentation used by the "Unionists," others because they did not yet understand the nature of Ireland's demands.

Mr Gladstone was, therefore, by no means disheartened at the result of the general election, and as the British people became educated on the Irish question, bye-election after bye-election proved triumphantly the truth of his famous saying that the "flowing tide" was carrying the cause of Home Rule on to victory.

The fact that a great British statesman—the greatest, perhaps, who had ever lived—had taken up the cause of Ireland, effected a marvellous change in the position of our countrymen here. These pages have shown that for two centuries their history seemed to be but the record of one continuous struggle for existence. But now Mr Gladstone had spoken, a change came about, which seemed almost miraculous. The arguments Irishmen had used in putting forward the legitimate claims of their country had been almost universally treated with contempt, but once the great Liberal leader had taken his stand on their side, a large and daily increasing portion of the British public were willing to listen and to be convinced by the arguments for Home Rule which before they had scouted. As an example of the better feeling which now arose—in certain districts in South Wales and Monmouth from which our people had to fly for their lives but a few years before, Irishmen were now allowed to live in peace, and became respected, while no public men were more welcomed than Michael Davitt and other Irish leaders.

In every generation the Irish here have responded to the call of their fellow-countrymen at home when action had to be taken. So it was at this crisis. Never before were the Irish in England, Scotland, and Wales so well able to help the old cause; never before could their strength be used to such advantage. Ireland herself had spoken in no uncertain tones, and Mr Gladstone, in reply to the opponents who charged him with inconsistency in not having taken up the Irish cause before, pointed out that never before, owing, of course, to the restricted franchise, had Ireland made it clear, through the voices of the great majority of her representatives, that the one right she prized above all others, and which she was determined to have, no matter at what sacrifice, was the right to self-government.

But if instead of eighty-five members being for Home Rule, every man of the hundred and three returned from Ireland were in favour of it, she could not win it by constitutional means without the aid of her children on this side of the Channel. At first sight it might appear that the Irish here could do but little, since, although they and their immediate descendants are equal in number to fully one-third of the people at home, they could only send one representative to the British Parliament by their own unaided votes. Then, again, they had not been able to contribute to the national exchequer anything equal to the princely sums which their compatriots in America and Australia had sent to sustain the Home Rule struggle.

But though not able, apparently, to help the cause so effectually as the Irish at home and abroad, they found that they could really do far more, for, even with Mr Gladstone's powerful aid, it can scarcely be expected that Home Rule can be won without the Irish vote here. In about a hundred constituencies in Great Britain, the friends of Ireland could not be elected without this vote. It is true that at the General Election of 1886 the Irish vote did not counterbalance the Liberal abstentions—the chief cause of Mr Gladstone's defeat. The Liberal dissensionists, who then ranged themselves on the Tory side, of course counted for something, but not nearly so much as Mr Chamberlain, Lord Hartington, and other deserters from Mr Gladstone expected. Every bye-election showed that they were leaders with a comparatively insignificant following, and that the next General Election would probably wipe them out as a party altogether. The active Irish politicians of Great Britain realized the significance of the narrow majority of votes by which Mr Gladstone was defeated, and how much they themselves could do to turn that defeat into a victory on the next occasion. It was pointed out to the Irish here by their leaders, that even if British public opinion remained as it was in 1886, the Irish, if properly organized, could, *of themselves*, probably make all the difference at the next General Election. It was shown to them that the winning of freedom for Ireland rested in their hands, and that, in the contest now being carried on, the weapons with which they were fighting were *votes*. What had, therefore, to be done was so to increase the Irish voting power as to give Mr Gladstone the 80,000 votes he was short of in 1886.

The Irish of Great Britain—meaning those of unmixed Irish blood, whether born in Ireland or here—have generally been reckoned at about two millions, which may be taken as a tolerably correct estimate.

Now, the population of Great Britain in 1881 was 29,703,856. There are about five millions of voters. A great number of these are on the Register more than once, having qualifications in two or more constituencies. This is not the case to any great extent with the Irish voters. If these had the franchise in the same proportion as the general population, there ought to be about 340,000 Irish votes. It is quite certain that we have nothing like that proportion—particularly in the large towns. It is generally reckoned that on an average a proportion of about one in ten of the Irish population are voters. With close attention this can be largely increased, showing the necessity for keeping in good working order an organisation like the Irish National League. There are various reasons why we are not so strong on the Registers as we ought to be. In some places it may be from the unusual proportion of young unmarried men who have been drawn to some great industrial centre. These are scarcely ever householders, and the lodgings they occupy are seldom, except in London, of sufficient value to qualify for the lodger franchise. Of course the chief cause of our not appearing so well on the Registers is the comparative poverty of our people and the consequent overcrowding, which produces a small percentage of Irish votes in proportion to the population. This book has been written in vain if the poverty of our people here requires any explanation. It frequently causes the poor rate, which qualifies for a vote, to remain unpaid, and the receipt of parish relief, which disqualifies. Then, again, we have a large proportion of unskilled labourers, and as these frequently have to move about in search of employment, they are often left off the Register when really entitled. In most of the smaller towns we have a fair proportion of Irishmen, fully up to the average of their neighbours, who are voters. It is in the large towns we suffer the greatest loss. To these, the poorest, the most wretched, and the most helpless of our people flock in the hope of getting employment, and many of them sink into a very miserable condition. Where this state of things exists it has been found in some few places that not more than half our people, taking the ordinary proportion of voters to population, were upon the Register. It was in places like these that the Irish National League found its chief work, for most of these votes could be saved by close attention. A spirit of practical patriotism had to be infused into the people, taking their latent love of country as a basis. Men who over a glass were prepared to die for Ireland had to be taught that, at this crisis, Ireland wanted them to *live* for her, and to practise sufficient self-denial to gain for themselves the right of citizenship, which would enable them to strike an effectual blow for their country. It was pointed out in this way to Irishmen all over the country that they had it in their own hands to give Mr Gladstone the 80,000 votes which would enable him to win Home Rule for Ireland. The rapid extension of the League, and stricter organisation, gave promise of such an increase of Irish voting power as would make Mr Gladstone's success at the next General Election a certainty.

While estimating those of purely Irish blood in Great Britain at two millions, it cannot be any exaggeration to say, when we reckon how for many generations our people have been coming here, that fully double that number must have an admixture of Irish blood in them, and, therefore, naturally, more or less of Irish sympathies. It is astonishing, since Mr Gladstone took up our cause, and the Liberal party made Home Rule a plank in their platform, how many people you meet with who find they had an Irish father or mother or grandfather or great-grandfather; people who would never mention such a fact when the Irish were a despised and persecuted race—the Ishmaelites of the empire. We can now count on the votes of these. Besides this, there is no doubt but that the genial Irish nature makes itself felt in the neighbourhoods in which our people live, particularly in the poorer quarters of the large towns. This is not so apparent, perhaps, in places like Glasgow or Liverpool, where the Irish Orange element has done so much to poison the working classes against our cause, as in London and many other places. In the metropolis there are hundreds of thousands of the people who profess no religion, who are under no moral restraint of any kind. Amongst these, the Irish of the first, second, and third generations are settled and have a powerful influence. Mayhew, while he speaks of their faults, bears testimony to their good qualities, considering their dangerous surroundings, and says that in certain callings they seem to be the only people possessed of any idea of religion or morality. It is a well known fact that, among the London costermongers for instance, the Irish and "Irish Cockneys"—as the London-born Irish are called—have considerable political influence, and that in numerous cases they can get the English "costers" to vote for the candidate who is most favourable to the Irishman's creed and country. All these are influences which must be reckoned up in estimating the forces fighting for Ireland.

Let us now see how Mr Gladstone's "flowing tide" was working in 1887. Mr Goschen, who had been nominally a Liberal, having joined the Tory government, it was necessary to find him a seat in Parliament. The Tories of Liverpool were so confident that they had the seat practically in their hands, that they actually offered him the representation of the Exchange Division. The illuminations were all ready on the night of the election, January 26th, 1887, to celebrate his victory. There was rage and consternation in the Tory camp when it was found that he had been defeated by seven votes. The death of Mr Peter Rylands, one of the deserters from Mr Gladstone, caused a vacancy in the representation of Burnley. He had won the seat in 1885 as a Liberal by 687 votes. In 1886, when he fought the seat as a "Unionist" and got all the Tory votes, his majority sank to 43. On the 19th of February 1887, the election of his successor took place, when the Liberal won by 545 votes, or within 142 of the Liberal majority of 1885, when there was a united party. This was a crushing blow for the so-called "Liberal Unionists," for it showed that, as a party, they were almost non-existent in Burnley; it also showed the power of the Irish vote, without which the victory could not have been won. Burnley was, in this respect, a sample of about a hundred other constituencies.

These were among the signs of the "flowing tide," which both friend and foe could see. Added to this, the British mind was now becoming enlightened on the Irish question, so that many of those who had hesitated to vote in 1886, from want of knowledge, once more ranged themselves under the banner of the great Liberal leader.

CHAPTER XXXVII.

THE "TIMES" FORGERIES—THE "FLOWING TIDE" STILL SWEEPS ON—WILLIAM O'BRIEN.

THE enemies of Ireland now resolved that something must be done to check this movement in the minds of the English people, and to crush out the national spirit in Ireland. Notwithstanding all the pledges given to the contrary, it was determined that the old worn-out, wicked policy of Coercion should be applied. In order to carry this and to drive back the people of Great Britain into their anti-Irish prejudices, wretches as base as the infamous Titus Oates were rewarded for their services in trying to bring about the ruin of the Irish cause and its leaders. In Parliament and the Press, too, the enemies of Ireland were most active.

On March 7th, 1887, the *Times* newspaper commenced a series of articles under the title of "Parnellism and Crime." The object of these was to hold up the Irish people to odium as being so steeped in crime as to be unfit for self-government, and to connect Mr Parnell and the other leaders with every outrage which had been committed in Ireland since the formation of the Land League in 1879. That there had been crime and outrages during that period was undoubtedly true, but many of these were due to the fact that the people had been driven to desperation by landlordism and coercion. But, even so, taken at its very worst, Ireland would compare favourably with any nation on the face of the earth in this respect.

But the Tory Government had got to carry its Coercion Bill, and, therefore, day by day, Ireland and her leaders had to be discredited and vilified in the *Times*. These articles were, it was admitted, deliberately timed to reach their climax at the precise moment when they could do the most injury to the Irish cause,—the day fixed for the second reading of the Coercion Bill in the House of

Commons. That morning, April 18th, 1887, the following announcements appeared on the placard of the *Times*—

THE PHŒNIX PARK
MURDERS!
Facsimile of a
LETTER FROM MR PARNELL
EXCUSING HIS PUBLIC
CONDEMNATION OF THE CRIME.

Under the usual head of "Parnellism and Crime," an article appeared in the *Times* of the same day, calling attention to a facsimile reproduction published in the same issue of a letter supposed to have been written by Mr Parnell, which it was proclaimed would " bind still closer the links between the 'Constitutional' chiefs and the contrivers of murder and outrage."

The following was the letter, which, it was suggested, was written to Mr Patrick Egan :—

" 15/5/82.

"DEAR SIR,—I am not surprised at your friend's anger, but he and you should know that to denounce the murders was the only course open to us. To do that promptly was plainly our best policy.

"But you can tell him and all others concerned that though I regret the accident of Lord F. Cavendish's death I cannot refuse to admit that Burke got no more than his deserts.

"You are at liberty to show him this, and others whom you can trust also, but let not my address be known. He can write to House of Commons."

Then on the outer overleaf was appended the signature thus :—

" Yours very truly,
CHAS. S. PARNELL."

That there might be no mistake about the immediate object for which the appearance of the letter was timed, the *Times* leading article of the same day said :—

"We place before our readers to-day a document the grave importance of which it would be difficult to over-estimate. It is a facsimile of a letter from Mr Parnell, written a week after the Phœnix Park murders, excusing his public condemnation of the crime, and distinctly condoning, if not approving, the murder of Mr Burke. It needs no further words to recommend this document to the serious consideration of the public, and especially of members of the House of Commons. At the close of to-night's sitting, the division will be taken in the House on the second reading of the Crimes Bill."

The letter startled the world, and succeeded in securing the immediate and avowed object of its publication—the passing of the Coercion Bill.

The letter was plausible enough, but it proved too much. Anyone who ever received a letter from Mr Parnell knows that he wrote as he spoke—without any unnecessary words. Were he capable of writing such a letter he would have conveyed his meaning in a few lines, without mentioning the names of any persons or making the elaborate statements contained in the afterwards famous forged letter. His enemies might affect to consider him a knave, but they never would think of calling him a fool, as the writer of such a letter would undoubtedly have been.

The present writer, on first reading this literary bombshell, without hesitation named the author of the forgery, and at least a dozen of his friends, whom he met from time to time afterwards, had, he found, come to the same conclusion as he had done. In fact, so notorious was the character of the wretched man, that, as a person goes to a baker for bread or to a butcher for meat, knowing that he can get from these for money what he requires, it would be just to a man like this that anyone would go who wished to buy such articles as the famous forged "facsimile" letter and the others which followed.

Mr Parnell, of course, at once denounced the letter as an infamous forgery, but, because he did not immediately rush into the trap set for him and initiate a prosecution against the *Times*, he was proclaimed a criminal by the anti-Irish faction. But he was the last man in the world to gratify his

enemies by any hasty action. He could see that there was
a devilish plot which it would require time to unravel, and
he was determined not to be forced into any premature
action in vindicating himself. There cannot be much doubt
but that if at this time the matter of the forged letter had
been brought before a London jury, with the first experts
of the day to swear to the genuineness of the handwriting,
what would amount to a verdict of guilty would have been
found against him.

Confident that Mr Parnell and his friends feared to have
the matter investigated, Sir Charles Lewis, a Tory member,
determined to force their hands, while professing to be
interested in their reputation. He moved in the House of
Commons that an article from the *Times*, which he read,
be taken as a breach of privilege of the House. To his
astonishment and the consternation of the Government, the
Irish members took up the challenge, and moved that, as
they were members of the House of Commons, the honour
of the whole body should be protected by the appointment
of a Committee of the House to investigate the charges.
This was the very last thing their enemies wanted, as, day
by day, since the publication of the forged letter, the Tory
party and their Dissensionist Liberal friends had been using
every form of innuendo, and taunt, and insult against the
Irish members. "Curses, not loud but deep," must have
been showered on the head of Sir Charles Lewis by the
Government for his maladroitness, in exposing their trickery.
Of course the enquiry demanded by Mr Parnell and his
friends was refused, but, to save appearances, the grotesque
proposal was made that the Attorney-General be instructed,
on the part of the Government, to prosecute the *Times* for
the Irish members,—as if these were such idiots as to give
the materials for his brief to one of their bitterest enemies.

So, for a time, it appeared as if the matter were to be
allowed to remain as it was, and no language too vile or
ruffianly could be used against the Irish party by men who
proclaimed they could do this with impunity, as the Irish
members feared an investigation. Now, surely, they thought
and said, Mr Gladstone's "flowing tide" of British public
opinion would be stemmed and turned back upon him

and the Irish party, with a fury that would overwhelm them.

But though there still remained a vast amount of prejudice against Ireland and Irishmen throughout Great Britain, and these *Times* articles and the production of the forged letter had intensified it, the enemies of our cause must have felt that, after all, they had failed to move the great mass of the people. Nay, in the breasts of all right-minded men, their action only roused a warmer feeling towards the members of the Irish party, who were received with enthusiasm wherever they went. Instead of Mr Gladstone's efforts being checked, as was anticipated, every bye-election that came seemed but another and a stronger wave in that flowing tide which he prophesied would carry the Irish cause to victory. The forged letter appeared on the 18th of April. On the 1st of July a bye-election took place at Spalding, in Lincolnshire, a purely agricultural constituency. There was no Irish vote to help on the Liberal candidate. Outside of Boston, which is a borough in itself, there were probably not more than a dozen Irish electors, although each year thousands of Irish labourers come, as they have been doing for over a century, to gather in the crops, returning to Ireland with their earnings when the season is over. Even these poor fellows, by their good conduct and native eloquence, became, in their own humble way, missionaries of Irish nationality. The Lincolnshire men, who had known them and their fathers before them, knew that they were the true types of Irishmen rather than the pair of Belfast Orangemen, of glib and rancorous tongues, who had been imported to help in disseminating the poison of "Parnellism and Crime." In 1885 the Tories had won Spalding with a majority of 78 votes; in 1886 they won it by 288 votes; and now they felt sure that the *Times*' forged letter would win it for them by at least 1000. What was their consternation to find that not only had the Liberals wiped out the majority of 1886 but topped the poll by 747 votes? In fact, so unexpected was this, that most people thought, when they first heard of such a majority, that it must surely be on the other side. A bye-election was going on at Coventry at the same time. Here there was a considerable Irish vote, which enabled the Conservatives to win the seat in 1885, although it was not strong enough to counter-balance the Liberal abstentions in 1886, when there was a Tory majority of 405. But the flowing tide swept this away, and left the Liberal candidate at the head of the poll with 16 votes. The very smallness of the majority at Coventry proved how effectually the Irish here could aid their country's cause. On the other hand, it showed those who were inclined to be apathetic, that, in the crisis through which Ireland was passing, she could not afford to lose the help of a single one of her children.

"Parnellism and Crime" having palpably failed in its aim, was again brought prominently into public view in rather an unexpected way. Mr Frank Hugh O'Donnell, an able writer, and a speaker of considerable power, had been a member of the Irish Parliamentary party. But he had become so erratic, and so little amenable to discipline, that, at the General Election of 1885, he did not contest any constituency, well knowing he would not have been elected. On the grounds that in libelling the Irish party it had libelled him, he brought an action against the *Times*. The trial took place in July 1888. For the defence it was denied that Mr O'Donnell was one of the persons aimed at in "Parnellism and Crime," and advantage was taken of the splendid opportunity he had given to go over the whole ground again—the object being, of course, to prejudice British public opinion against the Irish cause. Conceiving it could now be done with impunity, the most truculent abuse was heaped on the heads of the Irish party as if they were the basest of mankind and already in the felon's dock. To back up the original forged letter, others of the same character, purporting to be from Mr Parnell, Mr Patrick Egan, and others, were produced and read in court. The Government showed its sympathy with the forger and libeller by allowing the Attorney-General to be counsel for the *Times*. He got a verdict for his clients. The incidents of the trial made it evident that decisive action must be taken in Parliament, by the Government, because they thought the time had now come to utterly crush their opponents, already covered as they were by such a weight of odium; and by the Irish party, because the audacity and recklessness of their unscrupulous opponents had at length placed in their hands the clue to unravel the foulest plot in all British history. Although there were numbers of people who knew the man only too well, who had no moral doubt of the identity of the forger of the original *facsimile* letter, there was not, at first, an atom of proof against him. Indeed, but for his cupidity and utter want of conscience, and the blind fury of his paymasters, who would stop at nothing to crush the Irish leaders, it is possible that the original forged letter would have gone down to posterity as one of those things the authenticity of which had neither been proved nor disproved.

But in the additional letters produced at the O'Donnell trial Mr Parnell and his friends at length had the irresistible proofs that their original suspicion as to the identity of the forger was correct. In these letters they recognised certain sentences and parts of sentences which had undoubtedly been used by them in correspondence, and they suspected that these had been traced or copied by the forger and interwoven into his forged letters to give them a greater appearance of genuineness. After investigation and events showed the correctness of their supposition.

Mr Parnell demanded a Parliamentary Committee of Inquiry into the charges made by the Attorney-General. He also commenced an action for libel in Edinburgh against the *Times*, but the managers of that journal, who had all along been challenging him, with all manner of taunts and jibes, to prosecute them, shirked the action by a technicality. The rabid Unionists in the House of Commons, imagining, after the result of the O'Donnell trial, that Mr Parnell was now completely at their mercy, demanded his expulsion.

Pressed in this way on the one hand, and by Mr Parnell on the other, the Government ultimately decided to establish a Special Commission, consisting of three judges, to deal with the charges contained in "Parnellism and Crime." Could the Government have foreseen the result of the Commission, it would never have been granted. Its object was to condemn, not to vindicate, the Irish members. Sir

William Harcourt, speaking at Derby, said of it, "It is quite a new plan—this question of the Special Commission. It was invented by the First Lord of the Treasury with the concurrence of an old friend of his (this refers to Mr Walters of the *Times*) and with the advice of Her Majesty's Attorney-General, who happened to be at the same time the first law adviser of the Crown and counsel for the *Times*. Of course the Attorney-General must have vouched the authenticity of these letters, or you may depend upon it that Commission would never have been constituted."

During the passing through Parliament of the bill constituting the Commission, attempts were made to provide that the judges should confine themselves to dealing with whatever specific charges there might be against the Irish leaders, chief of these—indeed, the only thing to which the country attached any real importance—being the authorship of the letters. But the object of the Government was to discredit and, if possible, ruin their opponents, and, just as the *Times* had done in "Parnellism and Crime," and the Attorney-General in the O'Donnell trial, they provided for still another re-hash, in this Special Commission, of whatever outrages had been committed in Ireland during the previous ten years. This was intended to still further poison, if possible, British public opinion against Ireland's demands, and to heap all the odium possible on the Irish members before the real issue would be reached. Accordingly, with the mechanical majority at the command of the Government, the bill constituting the Commission was passed exactly as the *Times* people wanted it, seeing that the Attorney-General, their paid advocate, as the highest law adviser of the Crown, had practically constituted the court before which he was to plead. Then, to make matters secure, the jails were ransacked to see if some unfortunate Irishmen, condemned to life-long imprisonment, could be tempted by the offer of their liberty to swear against the Irish leaders. The "Invincibles" were approached, but, to the eternal honour of these unfortunate men, who had themselves been betrayed by creatures of the Government, one only could be found to do the base work required of him. This was Delany, a man, as he himself confessed, of notoriously bad character, a convicted burglar, who had probably ingratiated himself into the ranks of the Fenians and of the "Invincibles" in order to betray them. He did his best, or his worst, for his paymasters, and got his reward, for, after the collapse of the conspiracy against the Irish leaders, he was liberated. With the dice thus loaded against them it seemed as if nothing short of a miracle could bring Mr Parnell and his friends safely through the ordeal.

For some eighteen months—that is, from the first appearance of the articles on "Parnellism and Crime" in the *Times*, until the opening of the Commission—the stream of calumny was poured out upon the reputation of the Irish leaders and the cause they championed. Let us see with what result.

In times past rioting and bloodshed and civil war had been carried into the homes of the Irish by far less incitement. But now, to the astonishment of their enemies, our people went on unmolested; quietly and persistently strengthening and perfecting their organisation in every part of England, Scotland, and Wales where a handful of Irishmen were to be found—always keeping steadily in view the 80,000 votes which had to be made to ensure the victory of Mr Gladstone at the next General Election.

If the Irish leaders were at this time passing through a terrible ordeal, it was a scarcely less trying time for Mr Gladstone, for the conspirators against Ireland did not hesitate to charge him with complicity with assassins. But the magic of his great name won the masses of the British people to the side of truth and justice, and at many a great public demonstration throughout the country none were more welcome than these "assassins," as the Irish members of Parliament had been called.

With the exception of Doncaster, not a wave went back of the "flowing tide," which still swept majestically onward. Besides, as a rule, lessening the majorities of the Tories where they were still able to hold their seats, with the one exception stated, whenever, at a bye-election, there was a change in the character of the representation of any constituency, the seat fell to a follower of Mr Gladstone.

The Commission was formally opened on the 17th of

Y

September 1888, before the three appointed judges—
Hannan, Day, and Smith. The first regular sitting was
held on 22nd October. The chief advocate for the *Times*
was the Attorney-General, Sir Richard Webster, while the
leader for the Irish party was their fellow-countryman, Sir
Charles Russell, whose admirable management of the case
for his clients wonderfully increased his already brilliant
reputation. Sir William Harcourt speaks of him as "a
man who by the greatness of his ability and the strength of
his sympathy with freedom will deserve to take a place in
the noble profession to which he belongs, with Erskine, as a
man who is willing and capable to do battle against fraud and
injustice, and vindicate the principle of truth and freedom."
Fifty-five of the Irish members of Parliament, together with
a number of other persons, were charged with being guilty
of crime or advocates of treason, sedition, assassination,
and violence. Why fifty-five out of the eighty-six members
should have been singled out as special criminals was not
apparent. It is probable, however, that the names of
certain members were put forward to give an air of reality
to the proceedings, so that it might be inferred that there
were certain specific charges against all of those mentioned
which could not be brought home to the rest. It is worthy
of note, as showing that even their enemies really considered
the authenticity of the *Times* letters, the main subject of
enquiry, that Mr Chamberlain said, in the House of
Commons, on Tuesday, July 24th, 1888, "If these letters
are shown conclusively to be base forgeries, the whole of
the rest of the case would be so prejudiced that the public
would not attach much attention to anything else."

Instead of the pith of the charges being got to as quickly
as possible, the whole of the ground was, day by day, gone
over again as in "Parnellism and Crime" and in the
O'Donnell trial, with the resources of the Government at
the disposal of the *Times*, the object being to blacken the
Irish party, and to raise prejudice against them. Speaking
of the assistance the Government gave to the enemies of
the Irish leaders during the Commission, Mr Gladstone,
in the House of Commons, said, "They had not only
placed at the disposal of the accusing party all their

stipendiaries, and the whole force of the police, and the whole machinery of the Government in Ireland, but they had even opened the cell doors of the dynamitard and the like, that they might give evidence against the Irish members." Week after week, policemen, magistrates, landlords, agents, informers, and emergency men from Ireland were brought forward to recapitulate, what the public had already read in the newspapers of the previous ten years, every outrage, real or imaginary, which had occurred in Ireland during that time. The jails in Ireland and England were scoured, too, for witnesses, and we can readily imagine what a temptation it was to some of the unhappy Irish prisoners there confined to bear testimony against the Irish leaders—for there can be no doubt but that some consideration, either prospective freedom or other advantage, was held out to these men. And so the Commission went on day by day until what had at the onset been regarded with the most intense interest began to get utterly wearisome to the public. It was hoped that the tales of horror told at the Commission would influence the bye-elections, but the result of these only showed how far the Government had overshot the mark. When the Commission reopened, after a short vacation at Christmas, the Govan election was going on, and what had been a Tory seat was won on the 19th of January 1889, by a Liberal majority of over 1000.

The associates and paymasters of assassins, as they had been called, the Irish members, were in great request at these bye-elections and were always heartily received. Mr David Sheehy did good service at Govan. A couple of days after the election he was arrested in Glasgow on two warrants for one of the numerous offences created by the Coercion Act. He was visited at the police station by the newly-elected member for Govan and some of the most prominent citizens of Glasgow, who paid the utmost honour to this Irish "criminal." There were also large meetings held to show the sympathy of the people of Glasgow with him, and a great demonstration was organised to bid him farewell as he left for Ireland in charge of his captors. His arrest under the Crimes Act brought the Coercion *regime* home to the doors of the people of Scotland, and greatly increased the effect of the Govan election. It proved that the men who had been hounded down by the Government and its instruments as the vilest of mankind were not only loved by the great bulk of the Irish people but honoured by millions of the people of Great Britain.

The British people soon afterwards received a striking object lesson of the same kind in the arrest of another Irish "criminal," William O'Brien, in Manchester. No man has given up his whole being to the service of his country more entirely than William O'Brien, or has so moved the hearts of our people to their utmost depths. They appreciate him accordingly, and none is more loved, more idolized than he, as is shown in any Irish assembly, where the very mention of his name brings forth the most spontaneous enthusiasm. This was just the sort of man upon whom the vengeance of the Government was sure to fall, so that he has had a very varied experience of the interiors of Irish jails at one time or another, for when once out of prison, it was seldom that the law, as administered in Ireland, was not weaving anew its meshes around him.

This is how his arrest in Manchester came about. On Thursday, January 24th, 1889, he was brought before a court at Carrick-on-Suir, constituted under the "Criminal Law and Procedure (Ireland) Act." As usual, he received an enthusiastic greeting from the people on his way to the courthouse, and there was the usual bludgeoning and other violence on the part of the police. During the proceedings there was some applause in the gallery while Mr Healy, who was Mr O'Brien's counsel, was speaking. Mr Bodkin, one of the "removables"—as the magistrates appointed under the Coercion Act were called by the people—ordered the gallery to be cleared. Mr Healy protested that his client should be tried in open court, and that if there were any clearance of the court they would go out with the people. Mr O'Brien said that he, too, would go out in that case. To the astonishment of the magistrates, and before they had time to realize what was taking place, Mr O'Brien, Mr Healy, and several other friends proceeded to leave the court. The police caught hold of Mr O'Brien and attempted to stop him, but he struggled on, and, aided by his friends, got clear away from the court-house. It was nearly dark when he and his friends got outside. Just at this moment the police were charging the unarmed people with fixed bayonets up and down the square. All was, therefore, confusion and excitement, so that by the time the police realized the fact of his disappearance the prisoner was gone as completely from their grasp as if the ground had swallowed him up.

Five days after this, on the following Tuesday night, there was a great meeting held in the Hulme Town Hall, Manchester, at which Mr Jacob Bright was to address his constituents. The meeting was preceded by a procession of the members of the Irish National League branches. Long before this Mr O'Brien had promised Mr Bright that he would be present at this gathering, but when it was known he was to be brought before the "removables" at Carrick under the Coercion Act all idea of his coming to the meeting was abandoned. Then came the news of his audacious, astounding escape. But, even so, it could not be expected that he could pass from the heart of Ireland to the heart of England, under sentence of four months' imprisonment, and with a warrant out for his arrest, without falling into the hands of the police. But, so far, he had not been arrested. He had promised to attend that meeting, and, for some reason they could not explain, there was a belief on the part of the people that he would be there. During the day it was rumoured that he had arrived in Manchester. The building in which the meeting was held was therefore crowded to its utmost capacity, while outside there were thousands of people. There was great disappointment when Mr Jacob Bright and other gentlemen appeared on the platform, but no William O'Brien. While the chairman was speaking loud cheering was heard in the street and roused the expectation of the audience to the highest pitch. Outside the enthusiasm was terrific as a cab dashed up and the crowd made way. A tall figure in a great coat came forth and struggled to get into the building, The police came forward, and it seemed as if, after passing through so many adventures by land and sea to keep his appointment, William O'Brien, like his namesake "Shamus," was to be

"——taken at last!"

But to the astonishment of the police and the group of people immediately surrounding, the tall, spectacled, muffled-up figure turned out to be, not William O'Brien, but Daniel Gauley, a patriotic, earnest, and energetic Irishman of Manchester. The people, though they could not help being amused, were cruelly disappointed, and the police were disgusted, when a ringing cheer inside proclaimed that something extraordinary had happened. Extraordinary indeed, for the same William O'Brien who had disappeared from view on the Thursday evening previously in Carrick-on-Suir, as if by magic, had made his appearance on that Manchester platform to keep his engagement with Mr Bright. Thanks to the ruse so cleverly carried out by honest Dan Gauley, he was able to run the gauntlet through one door while the attention of the police was taken off at another. At his sudden appearance, pale and tired and out of breath, the audience leaped to their feet, and their pent-up feelings found vent in a perfect hurricane of cheering, the first wild outburst being taken up again and again during several minutes, while William O'Brien, deeply moved by the scene, was being warmly greeted by Mr Jacob Bright and other friends on the platform.

A few words as to how Mr O'Brien had managed to keep his appointment that night. On leaving Carrick he drove to Wexford, a distance of ninety miles. Here he embarked on a collier, and landed at Porthcawl, in Glamorganshire, on the Sunday morning. From thence, with the captain, a young Irishman, whose heart was in the enterprise, he drove to Bridgend. Here he heard there was a good friend of Ireland, Father Ward, a man who believes that the more an Irishman really loves his country the more he clings to his creed: as a consequence, the Irish cause has staunch adherents among the members of his flock, which is widely scattered over several square miles of Glamorganshire. Going along the street in which his little chapel is situated, Father Ward met the conveyance containing the escaped " criminal " and the captain of the collier. Mr O'Brien, seeing the priest, got down and made himself known to him. It need scarcely be said that he got a warm *cead mile failthe* from the good *soggarth*. In Father Ward's hospitable home they were soon refreshed and rested, and, after having attended benediction, Mr O'Brien took the night mail passing through Bridgend for London. From thence he made his way to Manchester, in time for the meeting, as we have seen.

When the storm of cheers which greeted Mr O'Brien had subsided, and the chairman and Mr Bright had addressed the meeting, Mr O'Brien stood up to speak, and again there was another outburst of enthusiasm. He then gave a vivid description of the condition of Ireland, of his being brought before the "removables," and the circumstances of his escape and appearance there that night.

At the close of the meeting the warrant against Mr O'Brien was executed. As he was conveyed from the hall, marching in the middle of a strong body of police, preceded and followed by an immense torchlight procession and greeted by the enthusiastic cheers of the multitude, he was more like the hero of a triumphal march than a criminal being conveyed to jail. For fully a mile and a half from Hulme there was the same scene until he reached the Manchester Town Hall, where accommodation was provided for him for the night by the Mayor. On his way to Ireland on the following day he met with a cordial reception at Chester and Holyhead.

Mr Balfour, the Irish Chief Secretary, who was largely responsible for the cruel and contemptible way in which the Coercion Act was being carried out in Ireland, represented East Manchester in Parliament. He, also, had a meeting in Manchester, which was a striking contrast to that attended by William O'Brien. Balfour's meeting was very select, and there was no popular demonstration such as that which greeted the Irish leader. Had such been attempted he would have met with a reception the reverse of flattering. Accompanied by his detectives he got into Manchester and out of it as quickly as possible.

CHAPTER XXXVIII.

THE FORGERIES COMMISSION AGAIN—THE BRITISH SPY "LE CARON"—PIGOTT THE FORGER—EXPLOSION OF THE CONSPIRACY—FLIGHT AND SUICIDE OF PIGOTT.

LET us now look in again at the Commission, which has, meanwhile, been dragging its slow length along, like some huge reptile, leaving its slimy trail behind. Even the judges began to cry out against the iteration of ancient history, and the President hinted that, if it went on as it was going, life would not be long enough to see the end of it. While William O'Brien was receiving an ovation from the citizens of Manchester, extracts from his paper, *United Ireland*, consisting principally of speeches of the Irish members, were being read before the Commission. This and the re-hash of ancient history, spun out from day to day, was, we can now see, a device to gain time; as the revelations which subsequently came out showed what an amount of trouble his employers must have had in bringing up their principal witness to go through the ordeal of appearing in the box.

Until this chief actor could be brought upon the scene, the *Times* was able to produce rather an exciting interlude. On Thursday, February 5th, there came forward a really sensational witness, who, for the moment, revived the public interest in the Commission. He was a man who, according to his own evidence, had, since 1865, been a prominent member of the Irish revolutionary organisation in America, while all the time a spy in the service of the British Government. He gave the name of Major Henri le Caron. He had introduced himself into the ranks of the Brotherhood in America as of French origin, but he was an Englishman, a native of Colchester, and his real name was Beach. In his evidence he described how he had, by giving information to the Canadian Government, been the chief cause of the failure of both the Fenian raids into Canada. He also gave a description of what he professed to have known of the revolutionary organisation in America and on this side of the Atlantic. He stated, too, that he had had a conversation with Mr Parnell in 1881, in the lobby of the House of Commons in which the Irish leader said to him—"I have long ceased to believe that anything but the force of arms will ever bring about the redemption of Ireland." That he may have been introduced to Mr Parnell in the House of Commons is not unlikely, as many Americans coming to this country were introduced to him —people he had never seen nor heard of before, and probably would never meet again. In this way he may have met Beach, though he could not remember having done so, but that he had the conversation alleged he denied. It is grossly improbable that a man of Mr Parnell's sagacity, would, even if he held the views he had been credited with by the spy, communicate them in the way stated to a man he had never seen nor known before, no matter by whom introduced. This and other evidence of Beach was an attempt to connect the Irish National League with physical force organisations. Incidentally, in speaking of men sent from America to England to undertake dynamite explosions, Beach mentioned that one of these was William Francis Lomasney, who never returned, and that the organisation in America was then supporting his family. The Attorney-General added to this—"It is believed he perished in the London Bridge dynamite explosions." Lomasney, better known as "Captain Mackay," was one of the most daring and capable leaders of the 1867 rising in Ireland.

Beach's examination lasted for several days, and on his withdrawal from the scene the old wearisome programme of reading of speeches and recitals of outrages was again gone through. But this could not go on for ever, and on Thursday, February 14th, the first indication was given that the question of the forged letters, the only matter in which people were at all interested, was about to be entered upon. This was the appearance in the witness box of Mr Soames, the solicitor for the *Times*. In the course of his evidence, he stated that the letters had been supplied to the *Times* by the Secretary of the Irish Loyal and Patriotic Union, Mr Houston, who had obtained them from Mr Richard Pigott.

All who had ever known this wretched man now felt sure that the last scene of this exciting drama was close at hand. Those who, when the first forged letter appeared, connected the name of Pigott with it without any actual proof of the fact, but simply from their knowledge of the man's character and of his opportunities for doing mischief, were now certain that their surmises were correct, and that one of the most hideous conspiracies recorded in history was about to be exploded. Long before this, however, the proofs of the man's guilt were in the hands of the Irish leaders and their legal advisers.

The evidence given by Soames, of M'Donald, the manager of the *Times*, and of Houston, was astounding. After all the parade in the *Times* that those connected with that paper had in their possession proofs of the genuineness of the letters, it turned out that the only evidence they had, in addition to that of the actual forger, was that of an expert in handwriting.

Edward Caulfield Houston, who appeared in the witness box after Soames and M'Donald, deserves a few words of notice. He was then on the staff of the *Times*. He had previously been an occasional contributor, having written for that journal, among other things, a descriptive account of the trial of the "Invincibles." In 1885 he became secretary to the Irish Loyal and Patriotic Union, which he described in his evidence as a kind of Anti-Land League. About that time Lord Richard Grosvenor, then one of the Liberal whips, received from Pigott an offer to unmask, for a consideration of course, the Irish leaders, who were then supposed to be contemplating a kind of alliance with the Tories. Houston at this time professed to be a Liberal, and, being informed of Pigott's offer, visited him, and arranged to pay him £60 for 5000 copies of a pamphlet called "Parnellism Unmasked," to be distributed throughout the country in order to damage the Tories, and counteract the influence of the Irish vote at the General Election. When Mr Gladstone declared for Home Rule Houston transferred his services to the other side, and again sought the aid of Pigott to overthrow and ruin the Irish leaders. From his evidence, we learn that Houston asked Pigott for "compromising documents connecting the Parnellite movement with crime all over the country." It also transpired that Pigott at first told Houston that he thought such evidence could not be procured. Pigott would not probably, as a rule, do wrong for the sake of doing wrong, but it was his misfortune to have had no moral principle. Those who ever came in contact with him know that he appeared to think it the most natural thing in the world to lie or to cheat if it would procure him the means of self-indulgence, or would put money into his pocket, or save him from a loss. He was, as usual, in desperate straits for money, and when Houston returned he found that Pigott had thought better of the matter. It was accordingly arranged, as shown by the evidence at the Commission, that for "procuring" documents proving the complicity of the Irish leaders with crime and outrage in Ireland, Richard Pigott was to have a guinea a day, all travelling expenses, and special payment for every document.

Houston was submitted to a severe cross-examination, which disclosed the extraordinary pains he appeared to have taken to avoid any knowledge of Pigott's method of procuring the letters, and the persons from whom he was supposed to have received them. His evidence also showed how, in their vindictive endeavours to crush the Irish leaders, the *Times* people also appear to have deliberately shut their eyes, having paid to Houston up to the time of his appearing in the box, over £2900 for letters, without any proof of their genuineness beyond the opinion of a single expert, and the testimony of the forger.

At length, the forger himself appeared in the witness box, the unfortunate wretch being conscious, no doubt, that he was now in the toils from which there was no escape. His paymasters were, however, determined to make him the instrument of heaping as much odium as possible on the Irish leaders. The Attorney-General, therefore, questioned him as to the connection of certain prominent Irishmen with the revolutionary movement. He was then asked as to Houston seeking him out, and the work he agreed to do. These particulars had already been given by Houston himself. He then gave an account of his various journeys to

London, Paris, Switzerland, and America in search of documents.

This had been pleasant and profitable work for Pigott, for while he was engaged in "procuring" the documents— we now know how—the guinea a day and expenses were going on, and he would, no doubt, spin out the job as long as he could. His journey to London was, he said, fruitless, as, of those from whom he expected to get information, "some were dead, some were gone to America, and some were in prison."

The Government had evidently given every assistance in this vile work, and it was not their fault if Pigott got no information from Irishmen in prison. One of these was John Daly, who had always been a fierce and determined opponent of the constitutional agitators. He was then a convict in Chatham prison, where he was receiving the most brutal treatment. His friends in vain demanded a proper public enquiry into his case, but his prison door was readily opened to Pigott, who, judging from his own base nature, thought Daly would be glad of an opportunity of injuring the Irish constitutional leaders. Pigott had formerly known Daly, who no doubt thought the visit a friendly one. We can imagine the lofty scorn with which the advances of the tempter were spurned.

The following is the substance of the first portion of Pigott's evidence, as given in his examination by the Attorney-General. It need scarcely be said that the reader must use his judgment as to how much or how little of it to believe.

Early in 1886 he visited Lausanne, in Switzerland, to see Eugene Davis, a former contributor to Pigott's paper, the *Irishman*. Davis was understood to be a man of Fenian proclivities, and Pigott thought it was likely he could get some information from him. At first he was unsuccessful, but, being again sent to Switzerland by Houston, Davis told him that, "he had seen a letter in which Mr Parnell said that while admitting Burke got no more than his deserts, he regretted the accident of Lord Cavendish's death." This letter he believed to be still in existence. It was supposed to be in Paris, and Pigott was sent there by Houston in quest of it. There he met a man named Maurice Murphy, who told him he was in Paris on the business of the Clanna-Gael society, a secret organisation in America. Murphy had not heard of any such letter as that spoken of by Davis, but would make enquiries. After some days Murphy informed Pigott he had found this, and another letter of Mr Parnell's, and some of Mr Patrick Egan's in a black bag. He asked £1000 for them, but after some discussion, came down to £500. Murphy brought the bag to Pigott, who made a note of the contents. The letters submitted to him in court by the Attorney-General were, he said, some of those he then saw. Returning to Houston, who agreed to the terms, he was sent back to Paris, which he reached on the 20th of April 1886. Here a new difficulty had arisen. The heads of the Clan-na-Gael had ordered the refusal of the letters unless somebody went to America to get the necessary authority, and Murphy said that Pigott must go himself. Houston, after consultation with those behind him, agreed to this, and Pigott set off at the end of April or beginning of May. Arriving at New York he saw John J. Breslin, from whom he got, in a sealed letter, the authority to get the letters contained in the bag in Paris, which he reached in July. Houston afterwards crossed over and received the letters, paying for them the sum stipulated, £500 of which was to go to Murphy, and £105 to Pigott as his "commission." After this Murphy and his associates wanted to get the letters back, offering to return the money for them.

Such was the first part of Pigott's ingenious story as told in the witness box. The trips to Paris were very convenient, as they enabled him to make his purchases of the indecent pictures in which, it afterwards turned out, he had been doing a large trade. The negotiations with "Murphy," it would not do to close too soon, as the guinea a day and expenses would then come to an end. He was equal to the emergency, and the America trip was brought about. He displayed considerable ingenuity in fixing upon John Breslin as the person he saw in New York, that famous Irishman having died previous to the trial, so that there was nobody to contradict him. Pigott's representation that

" Murphy " wanted the letters back was an ingenious device of the forger to enhance their value and give an air of reality to the business.

Leaving the wretched man in the box, it will here be necessary, in order to throw light upon the incidents of the trial, to give an account gathered from the proceedings in court, and from various other sources, of certain incidents in connection with the forged letters which had occurred since their purchase by Houston.

Up to October 1886, Pigott had received in all £1080 for the letters and his expenses. By this time £1780 had been disbursed by Houston, who on getting possession of the letters, entered into negotiations with the managers of the *Times* for the sale of them, and the letters having been submitted to an expert, who pronounced them genuine, the purchase was made.

We now know how, after this, Pigott, having learned that the letters were likely to be published, became alarmed, and, with a view to save himself in some way from the consequences of his villainy, and also, possibly, to make a further sum of money from the other side, began a correspondence with Dr Walsh, Archbishop of Dublin. This was in March 1887, just before the commencement of the articles on " Parnellism and Crime " in the *Times*. Hinting at the existence of the letters, he proposed that the Archbishop should place him in communication with Mr Parnell, " to enable him either to stop the publication or to defend himself, to establish they were forgeries if he could." No doubt the theory Pigott expected Dr Walsh to accept, was that he was not the forger, but had got the letters from certain individuals who gave them to him as genuine. When at length the famous *facsimile* letter appeared on April 18th, 1887, Pigott wrote in alarm to Houston, complaining of it as a breach of the conditions on which he had parted with it. But when the first excitement had subsided, and months had gone by, and the threatened danger to himself appeared to have passed away, Pigott's cupidity impelled him to try his hand again at the forgery business, for which he had found such a good market.

Finding he had not been successful in making Archbishop

Walsh a medium through which he could blackmail the
Irish members and get from them a sum of money to enable
him to leave the country, he turned his attention to his old
employers—Houston and the *Times*. Accordingly we are
not surprised to learn from his further examination by the
Attorney-General that, at the commencement of 1888, he
had heard of more letters to be had in Paris. He had
found the business so profitable that for some months he
"procured" letters with great rapidity, varying the process
somewhat by furnishing, in addition to the letters ascribed
to Mr Parnell and Mr Egan, others from Michael Davitt
and James O'Kelly. These Houston was only too glad to
pay handsomely for, then hand them in at Printing House
Square, and receive the cash, and so the game went merrily
on.

Some of the letters, Pigott said in his evidence, he had
obtained in Paris from a perfect stranger to him, named
Brown—"Tom Brown" he added, amidst the laughter of
those in court, as if to give greater reality to this creature
of his brain. He further described how, in July 1888, he
procured other letters from persons whose names he did
not even give. He was no doubt emboldened to proceed
in his work by the result of the O'Donnell action against
the *Times*.

But the appointment of the Special Commission to
investigate the charges in "Parnellism and Crime" must
have caused him some trepidation, which was not lessened
by his receipt, on the 22nd of September, according to his
statement to the Attorney-General, of a subpœna to attend
the Commission as a witness, from Mr Lewis, the solicitor
for the Irish leaders, who now held in their hands the fullest
proof that he was the forger. It will be remembered that
the Commission was formally opened on the 17th of
September, the first sitting being held on October 22nd.
It must have been a time of fearful mental torture to Pigott.
He had interviews with Mr Parnell, Mr Labouchere, and
Mr Lewis, which he described in his examination, alleging
that Mr Labouchere had promised him £1000 if he would
confess to having forged the letters. About the same time
the *Times* people were putting pressure on him to get him

to testify in the witness box to the genuineness of the letters. He made statements at this time to Mr Labouchere and Mr Lewis which were partial confessions of his complicity with the forged letters. But there was no statement, however solemn, he made, which he would not again retract if it suited his purpose—in fact, as the *Pall Mall Gazette* said, he exuded lies at every pore.

At length his cupidity and the hope of getting £5000 from the *Times* if he could prove his case, caused him to determine to brazen it out and go into the witness box as we have seen.

When Sir Charles Russell commenced his marvellous cross-examination of Pigott, he had in his hands the fruits of the most patient research of the Irish party and their friends—clearly tracing the authorship of the forged letters to the vile wretch now about to undergo the torture of the damned.

Pigott must have felt a kind of uneasy wonder at the singular opening question of Sir Charles, who, handing him a blank sheet of note-paper, said—

"Mr Pigott, would you be good enough to write some words on that sheet of paper?"

"Yes."

Pigott then sat down and took up a quill pen to write.

"Write," said Sir Charles Russell, "the word 'livelihood' and leave a blank, then write 'likelihood' and leave another space. Then write your own name. Also write 'proselytism,' and finally write the names 'Patrick Egan' and 'P. Egan' underneath. You might also write the word 'hesitancy' with a small 'h.'"

The words were written as directed and handed back to Sir Charles Russell, having been first inspected by the Attorney-General and Sir Henry James. On that simple sheet of note-paper in the hands of the great advocate the forger had with his own hand woven more closely around himself the meshes from which there was no escape. He was then asked about certain letters he had received from Mr Parnell and Mr Egan regarding the sale of his papers. He was also confronted with the various letters, statements, and confessions he had made to Archbishop Walsh, Mr Lewis, and Mr Labouchere, some portions of which, he said, were correct, while others he endeavoured in a shifty, confused manner to explain away. The more he tried to extricate himself the deeper he sank into the morass of perjury and prevarication.

When he appeared in the box on the second day of his examination, Friday, February 22nd, 1889, he was questioned by Sir Charles Russell with regard to his correspondence with the Archbishop of Dublin. The various letters written both before and after the publication of "Parnellism and Crime" and of the "*facsimile*" letter were read. Pigott said that he had written to the Archbishop that he might be brought into communication with some of the leading members of the Irish party, perhaps with Mr Parnell himself, with the object of inducing them to provide him with means to leave the country. This was probably the nearest approach to the truth that he had yet made. It can readily be imagined that he would have felt more comfortable if he could by any means get "Parnellism and Crime" and the "*facsimile*" withdrawn. He therefore made such representations to Dr Walsh as to his knowledge of a plot against the Irish leaders, without admitting that he was the actual forger, as would, he said, enable him to point out how the designs against Mr Parnell and his friends might be "successfully combated and finally defeated." The following extract from one of Archbishop Walsh's letters to Pigott will show the position he took up in the matter.

"I do not know Mr Parnell intimately, and from what I do know of him I should be slow to undertake to put before him, as you suggest, the proposal that he should do anything with the view to prevent the continuance of the publication or of securing the withdrawal of those already published, or an apology for them. As regards the famous *facsimile* letter, no withdrawal would be worth looking for which did not candidly avow the letter to be a forgery and secure the handing over to justice of the forger. If those responsible for the publication cannot do this it is not worth while treating with them. If they can do it, but decline, except on certain conditions to be imposed on Mr Parnell, they are plainly persons with whom neither he nor any other honourable man could afford to treat."

z

This was written on the 12th of May 1887. As showing the veracity of the *Times'* witness, Sir Charles Russell, when he had got Pigott into a corner, extracted from him this admission—

"I may as well say at once that the statements I made to the Archbishop were entirely unfounded."

"What?" exclaimed the President in amazement.

"Entirely unfounded, my Lord," said Sir Charles Russell. Pigott then explained—

"My object was to put the matter as strongly as I possibly could, in order to induce his Grace to interfere, because I felt he would have a strong objection to do so; therefore I did not hesitate to write in that way."

So completely was Pigott riddled by the cross-examination, and so limp and helpless did he become in the hands of Sir Charles Russell, that in answer to the query—

"Which of the Parnell letters did you believe not genuine?" he replied—

"Well, all of them."

"You believed none of them to be genuine?"

"No," he answered, although, almost immediately afterwards, he denied having stated he did not believe the letters to be genuine.

He was also asked about certain correspondence of his, some years previously, showing how he endeavoured to blackmail Mr Patrick Egan, by stating that, unless he received a certain amount for his silence, his necessities would compel him to accept the offer of a reward from two mysterious emissaries of Dublin Castle for publishing certain matters in his paper intended to injure the Land League.

Most Irish politicians could well remember how Mr Egan turned the tables on Pigott by publishing the correspondence in the *Freeman*. Neither he nor anybody else believed in the mysterious romance of Richard Pigott, which simply proved that he was willing to betray to Dublin Castle for money any information that might be in his possession. Indeed, during this terrible cross-examination, Sir Charles Russel was able to elicit from him that he had, as far back as 1873, and afterwards, communicated such information as he could get about the Irish revolutionary movement to

Earl Spencer, the Lord-Lieutenant; and to several Irish Chief-Secretaries. One of these, Sir William Harcourt, has said, "He wrote to me when I was in office, over and over again, offering to sell me everything and everybody."

Sir Charles Russell came again to the matter of the negotiations for the sale of Pigott's paper to the National leaders, and the letters written by himself and Messrs Parnell and Egan at that time. After a good deal of prevarication, he was compelled to admit having received from these two gentlemen the various letters referred to. It will be seen how necessary it was for the great advocate to prove from his own lips that these letters had been in Pigott's possession.

Sir Charles at length unmasked his battery which it had taken months of patient preparation to perfect. Pigott was asked to explain how it was that certain sentences in the forged letters were exactly word for word the same as were to be found in the various genuine letters of Messrs Parnell and Egan, of which copies had fortunately been kept, and which Pigott had been obliged to admit having received. As the various extraordinary resemblances between the genuine and forged letters were pointed out to him he made a desperate effort to explain them away, from time to time, however, being completely driven into a corner for an answer.

Sir Charles Russell then called his attention to the way in which he had spelled "hesitancy" at the commencement of his cross-examination.

"You have spelled it 'hesitency.' That is not the recognised spelling," said Sir Charles.

"I believe not."

Everybody in court must have been satisfied that Pigott was the forger, but Sir Charles Russell continued to ply him as a skilful angler would a fish.

"Have you," he asked in his most suave manner, "noticed the fact that the writer of the body of the letter of the 8th January 1882—the forged letter beginning 'Dear E'—spells it in the same way?"

Pigott was now almost in a state of collapse, and utterly helpless in the hands of his tormentor. The forging of the letter was evidently present before his mind when he said—

"I have heard that remark made long since about the letter, that there was a word misspelled in it. My explanation of my misspelling is—having that in my mind, I got into the habit of spelling it wrong."

Sir Charles asked significantly—

"My Lords, did you get the last answer?"

Pigott wriggled like an eel on the hook as "coincidences" of the same kind were pointed out to him, but there was no escape for him.

Turning from this portion of the case, and in order to show what manner of creature Pigott was, as painted by his own hand, Sir Charles Russell caused begging letters he had sent to the late Mr Forster, formerly Chief Secretary for Ireland, to be read in court, together with that gentleman's replies. These showed the utter baseness and treachery of the grovelling creature in the box, who would, no doubt, have preferred the torments of the rack to the way in which his foul life was being exposed to public view.

At four o'clock Sir Charles Russell sat down, but immediately again rose to address the judges. It was thought that he was going to apply for the safe custody of Pigott, who, evidently, by the terrified, hunted look that appeared on his face, had the same idea on his mind, until the counsel for the Irish leaders commenced to speak. He merely had an application to make, that Mr William O'Brien and Mr Edward Harrington, then in prison, should be allowed to see copies of their newspapers, and accounts of the proceedings before the Commission.

It is to be regretted that Sir Charles Russell did not make an application for the safe custody of the witness, as no doubt had Pigott again appeared he would have wrung from him some clue to the conspiracy he afterwards spoke of as being behind the young man Houston.

The court adjourned to Tuesday, and many felt that in this long interval Pigott would have full time to realise his position, and fly, if he possibly could, from his impending doom.

Early on the following day (Saturday) Pigott went uninvited to the house of Mr Labouchere, to whom and Mr George Augustus Sala, he volunteered a confession, which was taken down by Mr Labouchere.

In this he confessed that he had made a number of false statements, and that he had fabricated the letters attributed to Messrs Parnell, Egan, Davitt, and O'Kelly. Describing the manner in which he had produced the forgeries, he said—" I grieve to have to admit that I simply fabricated them, using genuine letters of Mr Parnell and Mr Egan in copying certain words and phrases, and the general character of the handwriting. I traced some of the words and phrases by putting the genuine letter against the window, and placing the sheet on which I wrote over it." As will be seen, Mr Parnell and his friends had already discovered his method of producing the letters for which he had found such a ready market.

A Dublin solicitor, named Shannon, one of the *Times* jackals, called on him on the same day, and, at his suggestion, Pigott made still another statement, the correctness of which Shannon got him to vouch for, by making an affidavit on the Monday. In this, while admitting that he had forged some of the letters, he maintained that others, including the famous *facsimile* letter he believed to be genuine. This Shannon appears to have stuck to the wretched man like a leech from the time of the rising of the court on the Friday until within a short time of Pigott's flight on Monday. What passed between them it is hard to say, but the telegram sent to Shannon by Pigott when he was a fugitive from justice—" Please ask Mr S. to send me *what you promised*," indicated that he expected money.

Of course little credence could be attached to any statement of Pigott's after all the twistings and turnings, the confessions and recantations, he had made. Fortunately the forged letters themselves were complete evidence that he spoke the truth when he said he had traced portions of them on paper placed over the genuine ones. The forgeries having been photographed, it was found that the writing had first been traced in pencil and inked in afterwards. Traces of the original pencilling could be made out under the ink, which had a blurred appearance wherever the erasures had been made. Then, again, the signatures were exact reproductions of each other, so that when photographed on pieces of glass one covered the other exactly. Besides this, Pigott habitually and instinctively, as was shown at the Commission, spelled hesitancy "hesitency," as in one of the forged letters.

There was even a still more striking proof that the famous *facsimile* letter was a forgery. By magnifying the signature until it was nearly five feet long, it was clearly seen that the pen of the forger had stopped and begun again over twenty times. In Mr Parnell's genuine signature, magnified in the same way, the pen had only stopped twice. With all these, and numerous other proofs in the hands of the Irish leaders, it is not surprising that, when the confession to Messrs Labouchere and Sala was placed in the hands of Mr Lewis, he wrote to Pigott on the Monday morning, saying—" Mr Parnell has instructed me to inform you that he declines to hold any communication with you, directly or indirectly, and further instructs us to return the confession."

On Tuesday morning, February 26th, 1889, the Commission re-opened. At half past ten the judges entered.

"Bring in the witness," said Mr Justice Hannan.

Being told by the usher of the court that the witness was not there at present, the President turned somewhat sharply to the Attorney-General to ask for an explanation of Pigott's absence. The halting, confused reply ended with the statement that Mr Soames had sent to Pigott's hotel and found that he had not been there since eleven o'clock on the previous night.

So, then, Pigott had fled, as many expected. The news, of course, flashed all over the country. There was rejoicing among all honest men at the collapse of the conspiracy, mingled with regret that Pigott had been allowed to escape, while the discomfiture shown by the *Times*' advocates in Court was reproduced among the Tories all over the country. They were so utterly cowed that at Burnley, where a Parliamentary election was to take place, they had not the heart to enter upon the contest, and let the Liberal candidate in unopposed.

Sir Richard Webster, with cowed looks and tremulous accents, asked the Court for time to consider their position. Sir Charles Russell then rose, and said—"Whatever course my learned friend may think right to adopt, we shall pursue the same course, and insist upon the whole matter being gone through." Then, speaking rather as the champion of his country than as a professional advocate, he, in impassioned accents, proclaimed—"We deliberately charge that behind Pigott and Houston there has been a foul conspiracy."

The Court was then made acquainted, so far as they could be ascertained, with Pigott's various movements since the adjournment on Friday. He had not been seen after about four o'clock on Monday. The last person known to have been in his company was Shannon, the Dublin attorney, who was with him up to ten minutes past two the same afternoon.

At the sitting of the Court on the following day, a letter was produced which had been sent by Pigott from Paris to Shannon. This was opened, and found to contain the written confession which Mr Lewis had returned to the forger. There was nothing for it now but for the Attorney-General to apologise on behalf of the *Times* for the publication of the forged letters. The matter and manner of the apology, and that which appeared in the *Times* on the following day, were not such as an honourable opponent would make in admitting he had done a grievous wrong, but rather that of the foiled and discredited bravo, still willing to strike if he dared. Sir Charles Russell, in characterising the inadequacy of the apology in Court, said that his clients would not only go into the witness box, but ask the assistance of the judges "to enable them to see whether the young man Houston, the alleged journalist, the Secretary of the Loyal and Patriotic Union, went into the venture on his own account solely." During this and the sitting of the Court two days afterwards, Messrs Parnell, Davitt, O'Kelly, and Campbell went into the witness box and severally declared the letters attributed to them to be fabrications.

Meanwhile, what of Pigott?

For a couple of days nothing could be heard of him. On the Thursday morning it was found that he had arrived in Madrid by the Paris express. He had no luggage but a small hand-bag, and engaged an interpreter to show him about. He spent the day and part of Friday in seeing the sights of Madrid, while awaiting an answer to the telegram he had sent to Shannon, asking for the money which had been promised. His telegram was handed to the police in London, and at 5 o'clock on Friday afternoon, March 1st, a Spanish police-inspector called at his hotel and asked to see "Roland Ponsonby," the name Pigott had given. The fugitive was in his bedroom on the first-floor, to which the interpreter and police officer ascended. Entering the room the interpreter told Pigott of the visit of the police officer. He turned deadly pale and seemed to lose his nerve completely, but, recovering himself, said he would "see the gentleman." Muttering something about his luggage he stepped back, and, opening a small hand-bag, took out a large revolver. The inspector rushed forward, but was too late to prevent Pigott from placing the revolver in his mouth and blowing his brains out.

Thus retribution fell upon one, who, bad as he was, was by no means the worst of those who sought the ruin of the Irish leaders.

Everybody expected that the *Times* would have had the decency to withdraw from the case, now the forgeries had been exploded. Not so. With the most unblushing effrontery, the old re-hash of ancient history to blacken the character of Ireland and her leaders was opened up afresh.

Sir Charles Russell had asked the assistance of the judges to find who were the conspirators behind Houston, and, with that object, demanded the production of the books of the Loyal and Patriotic Union. Pigott being dead, this seemed now the only way of getting at his accomplices. The same Court which had ordered the production of the Land League books refused this simple act of justice to the much-maligned Irish leaders. This was too much. They would play with the loaded dice no longer, and retired from the case. Many of their fellow-countrymen thought they should have retired on the exposure of the forgeries, but they had faith in the judgment of Mr Parnell and the other leaders. Perhaps it was as well that the country should see what sort of justice Irishmen might expect from a Court made to order by the friends of the *Times*.

BOOK XII.
THE FALL AND DEATH OF PARNELL.

CHAPTER XXXIX.

PARNELL'S SIN—HIS DEPOSITION—THE IRISH IN BRITAIN REJECT HIM—IRELAND CONDEMNS HIM AT THE POLLS—KILKENNY—SLIGO—CARLOW—DEATH OF PARNELL—FREEDOM STILL IN SIGHT.

"We used to be united. Who has brought disunion amongst us? We used to be formidable alike to the foreign foe and to the domestic oppressor. What has shorn us of our strength? We have been the wonder of Europe and the admiration of America. Why are we to-day disowned by the one and a laughing-stock to the other? The reason is that we have had a traitor in the camp. Our general has betrayed us. For his own miserable gratification he has sold the pass, preferring an ignoble and licentious life in London to the liberation and advancement of his too confiding countrymen. This is he whom bad men support for evil ends and good men are deluded by throughout the country. This is the man who has wrecked our hopes, broken our serried ranks, who is striving to discredit the heads of our national church, to alienate the flocks from their pastors, and to decry, and thus humiliate, the very persons who, up to six months ago, he was used to refer to as models of generosity and patriotism."—*Speech of the* ARCHBISHOP OF CASHEL *at Thurles, on April 25th,* 1891.

MR PARNELL had emerged so triumphantly from the ordeal of the *Times* Forgeries Commission, that when, on December 28th, 1889, it was announced that Captain O'Shea had filed a petition to be divorced from his wife, and had cited the Irish leader as co-respondent, it was assumed by most of his friends that this was only another blow aimed at the Irish cause through him—a new plot which would end, as the other had done, in the confusion of his enemies. So, for nearly twelve months, there was but little uneasiness in minds of the Irish people as to the result of the charge against him.

For a long time he, who had once been a familiar figure at the gatherings of his fellow-countrymen in Great Britain, had not been seen amongst them, and when, in the summer of 1890, he emerged from his retirement to attend a meeting in the Westminister Palace Hotel, he met with a hearty reception from the representative Irishmen of London. Some were present who had been thrown much into contact with him when, some sixteen years previously, they first met him, a young man under the wing of Isaac Butt. These had not seen him for a few years, and were deeply pained at the change in his appearance. Everyone is familiar with the refined and intellectual features of the Charles Stewart Parnell of a few years ago—features that even the artists of the comic papers failed to caricature in any other way than by giving them a certain Mephistophilean cast. He had been ill, and it had even been rumoured that he was not likely to recover. There was a marked physical deterioration, and, though still a comparatively young man, he now looked old and haggard, and his voice had a harsh and hollow sound which those who now heard him after a long interval, had never observed in it before. There was the deepest sympathy with him, but scarcely a thought—even with the inevitable divorce proceedings impending—that he, who had been made by his only-too-loyal followers the idol of the Irish race, would in a few months be a self-disgraced man—not repentant for the crime he had committed, but standing up, unblushing and audacious, determined in his selfish pride to maintain to the last his claim to the leadership, reckless of the risk of ruin to the cause of Ireland.

The trial of the petition was commenced on Saturday, November 15th, 1890, and Mr Parnell did not appear to answer to the charge made against him. Evidence was given, and the jury returned a verdict that he had committed adultery with the wife of O'Shea. The sordid revelations at the trial came as a stunning blow to his fellow-countrymen. Apart from the actual crime of which he had been convicted, the evidence showed such treachery, meanness, and falsehood on his part, as stamped him one not fit to be trusted in the most ordinary transaction of life—much less with the control of a nation's destiny.

Sir Charles Gavan Duffy's theory seems to be that the exposures of the Divorce Court were but the revelations of Parnell's real character. Those who knew him best will tell you this is not true, and that he did once possess a noble nature, burning with an ardent desire to right the wrongs of his country. It was like plucking out their very hearts for the Irish people to cast forth their cherished idol, and many of them, hoping that he would at least show some sign of repentance for his sin, still clung to him.

Indeed, difficult as it is to imagine such credulity, there were even some, notwithstanding the decision of the Divorce Court, who still believed him to be innocent, and who were not convinced to the contrary until his so-called marriage with the wife of O'Shea—after the six months following the trial had expired, and he was *legally* free to form this connection. The formality at the Registry Office fully accounted for the continued absence of any sign of contrition for his sin, or the denial of it, which many of his only-too-faithful followers had looked for, and proved not only that he had committed the crime of which he had been convicted, but that he had, all along, deliberately determined to persevere in it.

The Irish Parliamentary Party met on Tuesday, November 25th, 1890. Mr Richard Power, the senior whip, presided. Previous to the vote being taken—appointing the sessional chairman—Mr Jeremiah Jordan arose and addressed Mr Parnell in a few kindly and considerate words, urging him to retire gracefully, and thus ease a situation of great peril to the Irish cause. Then it was that the Irish Party committed what most people considered the grave error of judgment of re-electing him chairman. It should be stated, however, that most of them thought he would be guided by Mr Jordan's words of warning, and, indeed, had been actually given to understand that, after they had paid Mr Parnell this last tribute of regard for what he had been, he would voluntarily retire. He soon made it evident that he had no such intention. In answer to Mr

Jordan he condescended to refer vaguely to what was in all men's minds—saying that in a short time he would put such a complexion on the case that he would be able to hold his head higher than ever before in the face of the world. Had he stopped here he might be taken to mean that he would prove his innocence of the crime of which he had been convicted in the Divorce Court. Some twelve months afterwards, when this incident was brought to light by Mr Donal Sullivan, Captain O'Shea, in a letter to the press, said in reference to it—"Mr Parnell seems to have had a very high opinion of the credulity of his audience." Their credulity would indeed have been great if they believed in his innocence on hearing the conclusion of his speech. He said he had been accused of betraying his friend. He had not, he said, had "bit or sup at his expense," he had not abused his hospitality, and he had not broken up a happy home. He further stated that of the twenty-three years of O'Shea's married life, he had spent but 400 days in his own home. Parnell's reference to O'Shea's neglect of his wife was evidently in palliation or justification of his own most grievous sin. The other matters he mentioned he appeared to regard as the most serious charges against him, for if he could prove he had done none of these things, and thought he could hold his head up higher than ever before, his language meant that he considered the adultery no crime—seeing that he made no attempt to deny what had been proved on that head in the Divorce Court, and which was subsequently placed beyond doubt by his so-called marriage with the divorced wife of O'Shea. Mr Parnell was understood to belong to some Christian denomination, and might, therefore, be supposed to be bound by some code of morality. If he did not consider himself so bound in connection with the offence he had been convicted of, why, then, his was a case for society to deal with? Even a Pagan community would be compelled, for its own preservation, to protect itself against any who broke up the family ties, the foundation of civilized society, as he had done; for savagery lower than that of the brutes would ensue, if such a condition of things as these offenders would create were tolerated.

A sickening feeling, as described by Mr Sullivan, came

over the bulk of those present, who saw plainly that the man they had helped to make the idol of the Irish race now stood a self-revealed, shameless profligate, and that they had been tricked into re-electing him. At the close of the meeting steps were taken which ended in his deposition from the leadership.

When it became known that the party had re-elected him, it seemed to many, who did not then know the whole of the circumstances, that they were showing him a cruel kindness —a kindness he afterwards cynically threw in their teeth. So also was the action of a considerable portion of the Irish people at this time a misfortune for Parnell. These, remembering only what he had done for their country, declared, with thoughtless generosity, that he should still be their leader. So demonstrative were these protestations of continued allegiance, that to a casual observer it might seem, at first, that the voice of Ireland was for retaining him. Though a great portion of these expressions of opinion had been manufactured, much of the feeling was genuine. It was most deplorable that all this afforded an excuse for the wretched man's determination to cling to his position.

Though many—notably Michael Davitt—at once pronounced against his continued leadership, the great bulk of thoughtful and patriotic Irishmen, reluctant to dethrone the man who had led them so ably, preferred for the moment to keep their own counsel. When they looked the situation fairly in the face, they came to the conclusion that a man capable of acting as he had done could no longer be trusted, and that his retention as leader meant the ruin of the Irish cause. The letter from Mr Gladstone to Mr Morley, which appeared on Wednesday, November 26th, in which he said that Mr Parnell's continued leadership would be "productive of consequences disastrous in the highest degree to the cause of Ireland," but voiced the feeling that the great bulk of Irishmen were reluctant to speak. By them it was not taken as "dictation," but as the candid advice of a true friend—one who had tried to coerce Ireland and had honestly admitted that he had failed, and was now devoting the remaining years of his life to the cause of their country.

Many of those whose generous enthusiasm for their leader

had at first caused them to cling to him, hoping that at least he would show some sign of repentance for his crime, began to feel that Mr Gladstone would be right in refusing to come into contact with a man who had so disgraced himself. These could not but feel that, after all, the medium of communication between the Irish people and Mr Gladstone—representing his own fellow-countrymen — should be, at least, for the credit of a virtuous and manly nation like ours, a man of ordinary cleanly life, whose word could be trusted, and whose hand might be grasped by any decent man without a sense of defilement. Such Charles Stewart Parnell certainly now was not; and as Home Rule could not be won on constitutional lines without the aid of a majority of the British people, he had become the one impossible leader. In this light the majority of the Irish members of Parliament began to look at the situation, and a second meeting of the party was called. At this Mr Parnell, with the effrontery which afterwards characterised him, took the chair, as if the meeting had to deal with some matter perfectly indifferent to him, and not with his own misconduct. After some hours' discussion the meeting was adjourned till the following Monday, December 1st. In the meantime, Mr Parnell's famous "manifesto" appeared on Saturday, November 29th. This, even more than his misconduct, opened the eyes of the majority of the Irish people and of the Parliamentary Party to the folly of retaining as leader the man capable of making such an audacious and unscrupulous pronouncement. In it there was not one word of his own crime—the *sole* cause of the terrible state of things which had arisen. Indeed, it would almost appear from his language that not he, but Mr Gladstone and his colleagues, had been guilty of some fearful delinquency.

On the second reading of Mr Gladstone's Home Rule Bill, June 7th, 1886, Mr Parnell said in the House of Commons:—" I now repeat what I have already said on the first reading of the measure, immediately after I heard the statement of the Prime Minister, that we look upon the provisions of the bill as a final settlement of this question, and that I believe the Irish people have accepted it as such a settlement." After this he had, on other occasions, professed himself satisfied with the desire of the great Liberal leader to give an adequate measure of Home Rule to Ireland. But the proceedings in the Divorce Court must have changed all this, for Mr Gladstone and a number of his own followers were now, he declared with astonishing contempt for the intelligence of Irishmen, no longer to be trusted. To obscure the real issue, and playing upon the feelings of a high-spirited people, he raised the cry of "dictation" on the part of Mr Gladstone. Still later, to blind the Irish people, if possible, to the fact that his leadership was the *only* question upon which there was any difference between Nationalists, he and his followers posed as the party of "Independent Opposition." It will be remembered that this was the policy of Duffy and Lucas, who opposed *every* party which did not do justice to Ireland, whereas Parnell's "Independent Opposition" was only against the party which was pledged to give Ireland justice. In this way he gained the support and encouragement of every enemy of our country, as was clearly shown in the bye-elections which followed, in which the Tory and Orange vote was invariably given for Mr Parnell's candidate.

The Irish members met on Monday, December 1st. The world is familiar with what took place during the week that followed in Committee room No. 15 of the House of Commons. Day by day, as men read the accounts of these proceedings, they were as much astonished at the patience of the majority of the Irish party as at the obstruction and trickery of Parnell and his followers. Seeing that it was his own misconduct that was under consideration, a sense of decency might have caused him to allow somebody else to preside. It soon became evident that he occupied the chair with the deliberate intention that the motion for deposing him from the leadership *should not be put.*

On Wednesday, December 3rd, the Hierarchy of Ireland met, and, basing their decision on the circumstances revealed in the London Divorce Court, declared that Mr Parnell was no longer fit to be the leader of the Irish people. This strengthened the hands of the Nationalists in room No. 15, where, meanwhile, the week was passing away in vain discussions.

Saturday came and still found Mr Parnell in the chair, as determined as ever to baffle those who sought his deposition. On the previous Monday Mr William Abraham had moved—" That, acting upon an imperative sense of our duty to our country, we, the members of the Irish Party, do declare that Mr Parnell's tenure of the chairmanship of this party is hereby terminated." Mr Parnell, with cool assurance, ruled him out of order. On Saturday, December 6th, after a week of weary and sickening debate, Mr Abraham moved the same resolution, *and again Mr Parnell ruled him out of order.*

It was quite evident that, as long as he remained in the chair, the proposition for his deposition would never be put. After a dignified protest from Mr Justin M'Carthy, that there was no possibility of their being allowed to bring the question to a test, he asked all who thought with him at that grave crisis to withdraw from the room. His son, Mr Justin Huntly M'Carthy, who had previously favoured Mr Parnell's leadership, then declared that, as the majority had decided, he would go with the majority. Forty-five members then adjourned to the Conference Room, and passed a resolution deposing Mr Parnell and electing in his place Mr Justin M'Carthy as sessional chairman of the Irish Parliamentary Party. The following are the names of those who took part in the deposition, and of those in America and elsewhere who remained true to Ireland—besides Sir John Pope Hennessey, elected afterwards :—

NATIONALISTS (53).

Member.	Constituency.
M'Carthy, Justin (*Chairman*),	Derry City.
Abraham, William,	Limerick Co., West.
Barry, John,	Wexford, South.
Chance, P. A.,	Kilkenny, South.
Commins, A.,	Roscommon, South.
Condon, T. J.,	Tipperary, East.
Cox, J. R.,	Clare, East.
Crilly, Daniel,	Mayo, North.
Deasy, John,	Mayo, West.
Dickson, T. A.,	Dublin, St Stephen's Green.
Esmonde, Sir T. H. G.,	Dublin Co., South.

Member.	Constituency.
Finucane, John,	Limerick, East.
Flynn, J. C.,	Cork, North.
Foley, P. J.,	Galway, West.
Fox, J. F.,	King's County, Tullamore.
Gilhooly, J.,	Cork Co., West.
Healy, Maurice,	Cork City.
Healy, T. M.,	Longford, North.
Hennessey, Sir John Pope,	Kilkenny, North.
Jordan, Jeremiah,	Clare, West.
Kenny, Mathew J.,	Tyrone, Mid.
Kilbride, Denis,	Kerry, South.
Knox, E. F. V.,	Cavan, West.
Lane, W. J.,	Cork, East.
M'Cartan, Michael,	Down, South.
M'Carthy, J. Huntly,	Newry.
M'Donald, P.,	Sligo, North.
M'Neill, J. G. Swift,	Donegal, South.
Molloy, B. C.,	King's County, Birr.
Morrogh, John,	Cork, South-East.
Murphy, W. M.,	Dublin, St Patrick's.
O'Brien, J. F. X.,	Mayo, South.
O'Brien, P. J.,	Tipperary, North.
O'Connor, Arthur,	Donegal, East.
O'Gorman Mahon, The,	Carlow County.
O'Keeffe, F. A.,	Limerick, City.
Pinkerton, John,	Galway City.
Power, P. J.,	Waterford, East.
Reynolds, W. J.,	Tyrone, East.
Roche, John,	Galway, East.
Sexton, Thomas,	Belfast, West.
Sheehan, J. D.,	Kerry, East.
Sheehy, David,	Galway, South.
Stack, John,	Kerry, North.
Sullivan, Donal,	Westmeath, South.
Tanner, C. K.,	Cork, Mid.
Tuite, James,	Westmeath, North.
Webb, Alfred,	Waterford, West.

IN AMERICA.

Dillon, John,	Mayo, East.
*Gill, T. P.,	Louth, South.
O'Brien, William,	Cork, North-East.

* Mr Gill afterwards took up a "neutral" attitude.

Member.	Constituency.
O'Connor, T. P.,	Liverpool Scotland Division.
Sullivan, T. D.,	Dublin, College Green.

The Parnellite Pledge-Breakers (33).

Blane, A.,	Armagh, South.
Byrne, G. M.,	Wicklow, West.
Campbell, Henry,	Fermanagh, South.
Carew, J. L.,	Kildare, North.
Clancy, J. J.,	Dublin Co., North.
Conway, M.,	Leitrim Co., North.
Corbet, W. J.,	Wicklow, East.
Dalton, J. J.,	Donegal, West.
Fitzgerald, J. G.,	Longford, South.
Harrington, E.,	Kerry, West.
Harrison, Henry,	Tipperary, Mid.
Hayden, L. P.,	Leitrim Co., South.
Kenny, J. E.,	Cork Co., South.
Lalor, R.,	Queen's Co., Leix.
Leahy, J.,	Kildare, South.
Leamy, E.,	Sligo, South.
Macdonald, W. A.,	Queen's Co., Ossory.
McKenna, Sir J.,	Monaghan, South.
Maguire, J. R.,	Donegal, North.
Mahony, Pierce,	Meath, North.
Nolan, Colonel,	Galway, North.
Nolan, Joseph,	Louth, North.
O'Brien, P.,	Monaghan, North.
O'Connor, John,	Tipperary, South.
O'Hanlon, T.,	Cavan, East.
O'Kelly, J. J.,	Roscommon, North.
Parnell, C. S.,	Cork City.
Power, R.,	Waterford City.
*Quinn, T.,	Kilkenny City.
Redmond, J. E.,	Wexford, North.
Redmond, W. H. K.,	Fermanagh, North.
Sheil, E.,	Meath, South.

In America.

Harrington, T.,	Dublin City, Harbour.

The decision of the majority should have been accepted by any men claiming to be patriotic. It had become an

* Mr Quinn afterwards joined the majority.

axiom, which men of the majority and minority alike had often dwelt on, that without unity among her people Ireland could not be free. Were Mr Parnell an angel, there could not now be unity under his leadership, supposing even only a fraction, and not the great majority of the people, had rejected it. For his followers in the Irish Party there was less excuse than for himself, for some allowance must be made for his wounded pride in being re-elected leader, and thrust from the position a few days afterwards. Seeing that the majority had actually to leave the room, where Mr Parnell presided, before they could depose him, they were termed by the minority " seceders," and on this wretched quibble the Parnellites declared, and affected to believe, that they had not broken their pledges to sit, vote, and act with the Irish Party.

In addition to this, Mr Parnell had his second line of defence, for, even supposing the party had deposed him, was he not, he asked, the leader of the Irish Race?

The bye election in North Kilkenny gave him an opportunity of testing these pretensions. For several years, while the cause of Ireland had to be served, he had not taken any part in the struggle on Irish soil. Now, that it was himself he was fighting for, he crossed the Channel, and was full of activity. But the gifts of cool judgment and self-restraint had deserted him. The possession of these qualities, more than anything else, had marked him out as leader in a party containing at least a score of abler men than himself, representing a race which had given rulers and statesmen to the proudest lands on earth. But there were Irishmen at this time who paraded their " independence," and yet thought so meanly of themselves and of their country as to declare that this self-disgraced man was the only possible leader. The overwhelming mass of our people, particularly here in Great Britain, soon proved that they were not so lost to self-respect as this. Their cause had often known defeat, but never would they submit to have it associated with infamy.

Once in Ireland it seemed as if the fallen leader had ceased to be the same Parnell that millions of men had known and trusted. He abandoned himself to the wildest extravagances of speech and action. One of his first achievements was the seizure, at the head of a mob, of the office and plant of *United Ireland*.

The *Freeman's Journal* was already under his control, so that the two most powerful popular newspapers in Ireland now advocated his claims to the leadership. On behalf of Mr William O'Brien, the editor of *United Ireland*, then in America, an edition, called *Suppressed United Ireland*, was brought out, and, notwithstanding the violent means adopted by the Parnellites to stop the circulation, it would have gone on had not an injunction been obtained from the Vice-Chancellor to stop its production. The British Government, when Mr Forster was Irish Chief Secretary, could not stop *United Ireland*, but now Mr Parnell, but only when aided by a decree of British law, was able to suppress it.

In work like this he displayed an amount of activity such as he had not exhibited for some years. His tenacity of purpose in the wrong direction even exceeded that shown by Mr Biggar and himself in the old "Obstruction" days, when, with Ireland undoubtedly at their backs, they faced a host of enemies in the House of Commons.

He had put forward Sir John Pope Hennessey as a good candidate for the vacancy which had arisen in the representation of North Kilkenny, as indeed he was; but when his candidate ranged himself on the side of the majority of the Irish Party, Mr Parnell, with shameless inconsistency, actually denounced his own nominee as a "place-hunting renegade," a "mongrel," and an "upstart skinner." In the same strain he spoke of his late friends and supporters—men who had almost gone to the verge of betrayal of their country's cause in their generous endeavour, on account of his past services, to still retain him as their leader. These he stigmatised as "miserable gutter-sparrows," "wretches," "scum," and a "cowardly crew." Those who wished to put the most charitable construction upon his conduct, could only suppose that he had been seized with some extraordinary mental aberration. Casting about for supporters in his desperate fortunes, he now made bids for the help of those who believed in physical force as a means for winning Ireland's rights. So evidently insincere was he in this, that it was only the thoughtless and the reckless who could be caught by his bait. He was more successful in winning help from the Tories and Orangemen—indeed the *Times*, which had previously done its best to ruin him, advised that support should be given to the Parnellites, as, on account of their being the weaker party, that would be the best way to perpetuate the unhappy dissensions created amongst the Irish people—arising out of Mr Parnell's crime and his obstinate determination to retain the leadership at any cost.

Having appealed from the decision of his colleagues to that of the Irish people, he at once got a foretaste of what their judgment would be in the result of the Kilkenny election, when Sir John Pope Hennessey was returned by 2527 votes against 1305 given for his nominee. But he still persisted in thrusting himself upon the country.

The remembrance of what he had done for Ireland, and his once noble character, had caused him to be treated with tenderness by many of his former friends—tenderness which he afterwards only jeered and scoffed at as a sign of weakness. Better for the Irish cause—better for Parnell himself — had he been treated with more firmness from the beginning.

For a few weeks after the Kilkenny election there was a kind of one-sided truce, in which he expected the Nationalists to remain with their hands and tongues tied while he struck at them in all directions. This was during the time when what were known as the Boulogne conferences were going on. Mr William O'Brien had crossed from America to France, and it was supposed that he could influence Mr Parnell to accept the verdict of his colleagues, and to "retire" on certain conditions. The well-meant endeavours of Mr William O'Brien, Mr John Dillon, and others in this direction, failed. There can be no doubt but that these conferences, of which most people became as weary as they had been of the proceedings in Room 15, strengthened Mr Parnell's hands in the unscrupulous course he was pursuing, from the suggestion implied in the negotiations that anything other than his absolute and unconditional retirement from the field of Irish politics would satisfy the requirements of the case.

He had already been deposed by the Irish party, and even if his retirement, and that of his followers—men who had broken their solemn pledges—were a debatable matter, it was one *that only the Irish constituencies were now competent to deal with*. After Kilkenny, there could be little doubt as to what their decision would be. The Irish Party, after the general election, may be trusted to see that the next Home Rule Bill is at least as good as that which Mr Parnell accepted in 1886. But why at this particular time—simply because Mr Parnell had disgraced himself—Mr Gladstone should be asked to give a guarantee of his good faith (which none before had ventured to question) as a condition of the ex-leader's retirement from the scene, was more than most Irishmen could understand. They could not see what there was to negotiate about. The matter, however painful to them, was most simple, and they saw it exactly as the Hierarchy saw it—*Mr Parnell had shown himself unworthy to be any longer their leader*. Yet were they most anxious to treat the wretched man with all tenderness and consideration if he would but let them. Anything they would do but sacrifice Ireland to his mad ambition. All they asked was that he would simply stand out of the way and not further obstruct the march of Irish freedom.

On Thursday, April 21st, 1891, there was another byeelection in North Sligo, and here again Mr Parnell's nominee was defeated. He and his friends did their best to explain away the significance of these expressions of the feelings of the Irish people; declaring that, after all, Kilkenny and Sligo were exceptional constituencies, where they could not have hoped to win. But when a vacancy arose in the representation of Carlow, caused by the death of the veteran Nationalist, the O'Gorman Mahon, the Parnellites declared, with much sounding of trumpets, that their day of triumph had now come, and that Carlow would speak with the true voice of Ireland. Their expectations of winning Carlow were really based on the fact that the Orange and Tory voters were more numerous there than in almost any place outside of Ulster. These amounted to about one thousand, and as the Parnellites could confidently reckon upon them —as they could on every other enemy of Ireland—it was hoped that these, with whatever votes they themselves could muster, would cause the defeat of the Nationalist candidate. On Tuesday, July 7th, Carlow did indeed speak with the voice of Ireland by giving 3755 votes for the Nationalist, Hammond, against 1539 recorded for Parnell's candidate. Fully half of these last were Orange and Tory votes, given by men who felt that the wretched Parnell and his faction were doing their evil work against Ireland far more effectually than they could do it themselves.

But the ex-leader still refused to accept what must now evidently be the verdict of the Irish people against him, and declared his determination to persist in the attitude he had taken up, even if he should be defeated at the general election. This opened the eyes of many who, up till then, had believed in him. Others who had at first generously and rashly committed themselves to his leadership—who had, afterwards, in their hearts, felt that they were wrong, but were ashamed to admit it—now took heart to shake off the slough of the Divorce Court, and to array themselves once more on the side of Ireland.

Meanwhile, what was the attitude of the Irish in Britain throughout the unfortunate crisis? None knew better than Mr Parnell himself the significance of their decision. They were generally in advance of popular opinion in Ireland itself, and, as they had been the first to indicate him as the future leader, they were now the first to proclaim his unworthiness. Their judgment could not but have had enormous weight with Irishmen elsewhere. Mr Parnell, finding the Irish on this side of the Channel so overwhelmingly against him, craftily recommended them to remain neutral, and that they should leave the Irish people at home to deal with the crisis. But he showed an extraordinary contempt for their intelligence in thinking they would submit without a murmur to see their kinsmen in Ireland crow-barred, bludgeoned, and plundered by him and his henchmen. They were not to be so deceived. Mr T. P. O'Connor, addressing a magnificent meeting of his constituents in Liverpool, truly spoke their feelings when he said that the one great danger Ireland had to be saved from was Mr Parnell himself.

It will be remembered that, in 1877, the Annual Convention of the Irish Home Rule Confederation of Great Britain, the recognised Irish political organisation on this side of the Channel, elected Mr Parnell as President, in place of Mr Isaac Butt. This was the first indication of the feeling among Irishmen elsewhere which led to his being chosen as leader of the Irish Parliamentary party. It was, therefore, significant that another Annual Convention of the same organisation—which had now become the Irish National League of Great Britain—formed of delegates from all parts of England, Scotland, and Wales, solemnly pronounced against the leadership of Mr Parnell. This Convention was held at Newcastle-on-Tyne, on Saturday, the 16th of May 1891. Mr Parnell had not been President of the organisation since 1883, but eight out of the eighteen who formed the Executive, or governing body, were followers of his, who, in refusing to bow to the majority of their colleagues or to resign their seats, had broken their pledges to their constituents. Mr Parnell had already been deposed by the Irish Party, and this Convention was demanded by the branches of the League several months before the usual time, for the expulsion of his followers from their positions in the organisation. Knowing that this Convention would show the practical unanimity of the Irish of Great Britain against him, and that his friends on the Executive would be expelled, the ex-leader issued another "manifesto." In this he advised his followers to remain away from the Newcastle Convention, and constituted the pledge-breakers who still remained members of the legitimate Executive, with the addition of a few others, the "Executive" of what he styled the "Irish National League of Great Britain;" with himself as "President."

In another chapter it has been shown how the recognised Irish organisation of Great Britain had been founded by men who were working for Irish freedom before Mr Parnell had been heard of. The fact is that he and those of his creatures he had made into an "Executive" of his so-called "Irish National League of Great Britain" had as much claim to the titles they assumed as a merchant or trader has who fraudulently takes the title or trademark of some old-established firm.

Needless to say that the Irish National League of Great Britain, by its assembled delegates, at the Newcastle Convention, purged itself of the Parnellite element on the Executive—for not one of them had the honesty or grace to resign—and elected genuine Nationalists in their places by a unanimous vote.

The following resolution brought forward by the Liverpool Central branch was carried with enthusiasm:—" That we renew the pledges of loyalty made by us, year by year, for so long a time to the old cause of Irish Freedom. That we declare our solemn conviction that Mr Parnell has proved himself both morally and politically unfit for any further trust or confidence, and that the melancholy story of his fall is a convincing proof of the folly and danger of one-man rule and undemocratic methods. That having confidence in the Irish Parliamentary Party, and their respected Chairman, Mr Justin M'Carthy, we assure them of our encouragement and support. That we promise our hearty co-operation and assistance to the Irish National Federation, which we recognise as the authorised and representative Organisation of the people of Ireland."

In this way did the chosen representatives of the two millions of Irish in Great Britain make their unanimous Profession of Faith, and show that as they supported Mr Parnell so long as he was the embodiment of the feeling of unity which pervaded the whole Irish race, so would they reject him and his followers, now they had become factionists and a danger to the Irish cause, which, in the near future, notwithstanding Parnell's treason, they hoped to assist in bringing to a triumphant issue.

Though the great majority of the Irish people had so unmistakably declared against Parnell's leadership, the wretched man still madly persisted in clinging to it. Sunday after Sunday, with almost superhuman activity, he visited the various parts of Ireland to stir up hatred against those of his late followers who preferred loyalty to Ireland and to their pledges to allegiance to him. Irishmen who had heard with such pain of the illness he had suffered from for several years and who saw that he was but the wreck of what he once had been, could not but ask themselves had he really been so ill as had been represented, and was his appearance deceptive. The wondrous activity which he displayed after his fall would have been trying to a robust man. His struggle against Ireland was as fierce and as hopeless as that of Lucifer and the fallen angels against Heaven. His indomitable will for a time conquered the weakened frame, and gave him strength—the feverish strength of a madman. This, to a man in his condition, could have but one termination. The last of his Sunday meetings was at Creggs, in the County Roscommon, where he indulged in the usual reckless defiance of his opponents. He returned, as he usually did after each of these demonstrations, to England, never again to touch Irish soil as a living man. Reaching Brighton, he died after a few hours' illness on October 6th, 1891.

The ever generous Irish people now desired to remember only all that was good of him, and to bury if possible in his grave the memory of the last wretched year of his life. His funeral on the following Sunday, at Glasnevin, showed how deeply their hearts had been moved.

While he lived his followers declared that they supported him because he was "the only possible leader." Now he was gone, according to their own previous arguments, there was no longer any motive for their perseverance in the work of faction. It was possible to understand the ground taken up by many during his lifetime, that, with all the faults of the last wretched years of his life, it was better for the cause of Ireland to still retain Parnell as leader. They had now no longer this excuse. But they had taken the first false step of preferring allegiance to a leader to their duty towards their country, and, with the weakness of perverse human nature, preferred remaining wrong to admitting they were wrong, the downward path being evidently to them, as it often has been for many others, the easiest.

Unfortunately, but too many honest men in Ireland, as was shown by the considerable minorities at the bye-elections, had been deceived by the misrepresentations of the pledge-breakers, who, fearing the verdict of their constituencies at the general election, were trying to offer some reason for their continued political existence. The constituencies

were the only tribunals that were competent to deal with
the factionist leaders, but Ireland was always willing to
receive back into the National fold the erring ones who
had been deceived, or those who, having been Parnellites
while the late leader lived, saw no reason for the continuance of Parnellism after his death.

But the tenderness shown by the Irish race for the memory
of Parnell on the occasion of his death and funeral led his
pledge-breaking followers to suppose there was a reaction
in favour of Parnellism. Accordingly, these declared their
intention still to carry on the struggle against the great bulk
of their fellow-countrymen, on the grounds of being the
leaders of the only "independent" Irish party. As a matter
of fact, they knew right well there was no real difference
among any section of patriotic Irishmen, working on
constitutional lines, as to what Ireland required and the
methods for obtaining it. But the unrepentant factionist
chiefs must find some excuse for their attitude. They therefore continued the dishonest cry that the leaders of the
party which had been loyal to Ireland—including men who
had faced death or spent the best years of their lives in
British dungeons in striving to win freedom for their country
—had submitted to British "dictation."

They thought that while the people were in a melting
mood it would be a good time to win the seat in Cork
vacated by the death of Mr Parnell. One of the pledge-
breakers, Mr John Redmond, knowing how thoroughly the
overwhelming mass of his constituents were against him, gave
up his seat in Wexford, and came forward as the factionist
candidate for Cork.

Singularly enough, Sir John Pope Hennessey died in the
same week as Parnell, so that the seat which he had carried
nearly twelve months before against the ex-leader's nominee
was again vacant; but here the factionists did not dare to
oppose the Nationalist candidate, who was returned without
a contest.

Once more Ireland, by the voice of Cork, however gently
she might deal with the memory of Parnell, pronounced
condemnation on his factionist followers by the election of
a Nationalist.

But the pledge-breakers still declared their determination to perpetuate disunion. Aided by the Orange and Tory vote—ever their chief reliance—and by deluding a number of honest Irishmen, they managed to carry a seat at Waterford, the one solitary success of their twelve months' disgraceful and disastrous campaign against Ireland.

They made the most of this victory, well knowing the doom of most, if not all, of them at the general election.

Foreshadowing this, and as a noble example to the well-meaning Irishmen who had been deluded, the men of gallant Wexford—the sons of '98—who had never yielded to either British or factionist "dictation," when they came to fill the seat from which Redmond had fled, showed that the tide of Irish nationality still swept on strongly and irresistibly. Faction dared not even show its head in North Wexford, so that the Nationalist candidate was returned unopposed.

Seeing the splendid unanimity of the Irish in Great Britain in favour of Ireland, the pledge-breakers tried to persuade the people at home that these had become demoralised by Liberal influence, and had submitted to "British dictation." Those who had so well assisted every Irish National movement, and had given heroes and martyrs on the scaffold for the cause, even in the present generation, could well afford to treat such ravings with contempt. Largely by their aid the success of the cause for which they had struggled for generations was now assured, if they but still kept an unbroken front. Being practical politicians, they saw that their country could, at all events, be made happy, prosperous, and self-governing by peaceful means, while they were as ready as ever, should the occasion demand it, to fight for Ireland on any field where her freedom could be won.

The Hierarchy of Ireland, the most glorious relic of nationality we possess—with an authority handed down in an unbroken line from the days of St Patrick—as the guardians of the purity of life which alone has saved our race from extinction, had denounced the crime of the late leader. For this they were assailed by some of the Parnellites with a malignity worthy of the worshippers of William of Orange. The overwhelming mass of the Irish race, not blinded for the moment by the fury of faction, felt, with the bishops and clergy, that if there was to be a new birth of Irish freedom, it could not be from the slime of the Divorce Court. That was a form of "British dictation" no pure-minded Irishman would submit to. Such a thought was revolting, and never were felt more strongly than now the words of Thomas Francis Meagher, after he had braved death for Ireland, that our cause—as pure and holy as any on earth —should be "Baptised in the Holy Wells." Alike were the lofty thoughts, in which all true Irishmen still join, of our glorious Protestant patriot poet, Thomas Davis, when he sang of the hope that filled his soul—

> It whispered, too, that freedom's ark
> And service high and holy,
> Would be profan'd by feelings dark,
> And passions vain or lowly;
> For freedom comes from God's right hand,
> And needs a godly train;
> And righteous men must make our land
> A NATION ONCE AGAIN.

BOOK XIII.

THE IRISH IN BRITAIN TO-DAY.

CHAPTER XL.

THE CENSUS OF 1881 AND OF 1891.

IT is difficult to form anything like an accurate estimate of the number of the Irish race at present in Great Britain.

We can give an approximation to this, but, after all, the only really reliable figures are the Census returns of the number of Irish-born. The following are the figures for all the counties and principal towns, according to the Census of 1881:—

DISTRIBUTION IN ENGLAND AND WALES OF ENUMERATED IRISH-BORN.

*Counties—Lancashire, 212,350; Middlesex Intra. Met., 56,273; Surrey, Intra. Met., 16,879; Kent, Intra. Met., 7626; Yorkshire, 56,878; Durham, 36,764; Cheshire, 23,615; Cumberland, 14,093; Stafford, 13,100; Northumberland, 12,489; Glamorgan, 11,958; Hampshire, 11,441; Warwick, 9628; Kent, Ex. Met., 8272; Devon, 6256; Gloucester, 5330; Derby, 5219; Monmouthshire, 5218; Middlesex, Ex. Met., 5045; Essex, 4958; Surrey, Ex. Met., 4821; Sussex, 3574; Somerset, 2271; Worcester, 2243; Nottingham, 2225; Lincoln, 1921; Shropshire, 1860; Leicester, 1856; Cornwall, 1693; Berkshire, 1471; Dorset, 1431; Flint, 1394; Northampton, 1073; Norfolk, 1022; Pembroke, 991; Denbigh, 971; Suffolk, 968; Herts, 793; Wilts, 775; Carnarvon, 621; Hereford, 583; Oxford, 562;

* The totals for the counties included those for all the boroughs contained in them.

Cambridge, 510; Bucks, 501; Beds, 494; Brecknock, 444; Anglesey, 426; Westmoreland, 371; Carmarthen, 362; Montgomery, 199; Huntingdon, 153; Merioneth, 136; Cardigan, 103; Rutland, 85; Radnor, 47. Total, 562,342.

Principal Boroughs—London, 80,700; Liverpool, 70,972; Manchester, 25,588; Salford, 12,990; Leeds, 9560; Bradford, 7870; Birkenhead, 7423; Birmingham, 7086; Newcastle-upon-Tyne, 5511; Sheffield, 5005; St Helens, 4893; Bolton, 4611; Oldham, 4443; Sunderland, 4443; Preston, 4274; Cardiff, 4274; Blackburn, 4217; Middlesborough, 3712; Stockport, 3375; Bristol, 3205; Gateshead, 3149; Portsmouth, 3037; Halifax, 2587; Rochdale, 2530; Kingston-upon-Hull, 2474; Bury, 2193; Burnley, 2137; West Ham, 2024; South Shields, 2024; Swansea, 1800; Wolverhampton, 1687; Nottingham, 1518; Huddersfield, 1462; Plymouth, 1406; Derby, 1293; Walsall, 1237; Brighton, 1125; Croydon, 1019; Leicester, 956; Southampton, 767; Bath, 475; Northampton, 450; West Bromwich, 394; Aston Manor, 394; Norwich, 337.

DISTRIBUTION IN SCOTLAND OF IRISH-BORN.

*Counties—Lanark, 115,085; Renfrew, 30,444; Edinburgh, 14,767; Ayr, 14,070; Forfar, 12,405; Dumbarton, 8618; Stirling, 4453; Linlithgow, 3365; Wigtown, 2350; Perth, 2126; Fife, 1475; Haddington, 1425; Argyll, 1249; Aberdeen, 1012; Dumfries, 1001; Kirkcudbright, 856; Roxburgh, 827; Bute, 635; Selkirk, 585; Berwick, 358; Inverness, 357; Peebles, 272; Clackmannan, 257; Ross and Cromarty, 142; Elgin, 141; Banff, 140; Kincardine, 104; Caithness, 67; Orkney, 49; Kinross, 29; Nairn, 23; Shetland, 22. Total, 218,659.

Principal Burghs—Glasgow, 62,555; Dundee, 11,443; Greenock, 10,328; Edinburgh, 7875; Govan, 6958; Partick, 5013; Paisley, 4994; Port-Glasgow, 3272; Dumbarton, 2575; Maryhill, 2309; Leith, 2000; Rutherglen, 1799; Motherwell, 1641; Kinning Park, 1533; Airdrie, 1359; Wishaw, 1342; Ayr, 1277; Kilmarnock, 1146; Hamilton, 1072; Perth, 850; Stirling, 779; Aberdeen, 715; Dum-

* The totals for the counties included those for all the boroughs contained in them.

fries, 636; Falkirk, 548; Hawick, 359; Galashiels, 342; Arbroath, 273; Dunfermline, 304; Forfar, 57; Inverness, 153; Kirkcaldy, 171; Montrose, 179; Peterhead, 37.

TOTAL, Great Britain, . . . 781,001.

These figures show where the Irish were most numerous in 1881, and, by comparison with previous statistics, what changes had taken place in their location since the great immigration into this country which followed the Famine.

In a previous chapter a comparison was made between the Irish-born population in 1841 and 1851, showing that during that time they had nearly doubled. It will be interesting to note the changes which took place between 1851 and 1881. Each succeeding Census showed an increase up to 1861. After that the stream from Ireland slackened. The Census of 1871 showed a reduction, and that of 1881 a still further diminution, so that in the latter year, when they numbered 781,001, they were not much more numerous than in 1851, when they were 733,866. The great rush was during and for some time after the Famine years. After that, the fountain head of Irish life becoming itself drained, the immigrants did not more than make up for the number of deaths among the Irish settlers here. Emigration from Great Britain to America and Australia must also be taken into consideration. The rate of diminution since 1861 is likely to continue with each succeeding decade.

The Census enumerators for 1881, speaking of the decrease in the Irish population at home, said—" If this decline be taken into account it will be found that the Irish in England and Wales, when measured by their proportion to the Irish in their own country, have increased at each successive Census. In 1841 there were 36 Irish in this country to 1000 in Ireland itself; in 1851 there were 80; in 1861 there were 105; in 1871 there were 107; and, finally, in 1881, the proportion had risen to 111 here to a thousand in Ireland."

They then speak of the distribution of the Irish-born throughout England and Wales—" The distribution of the

Irish over the country was most unequal. In the purely agricultural counties their numbers were insignificant, while in the great manufacturing and mining counties they formed a not inconsiderable fraction of the population. Thus in Lancashire they formed 6·1 per cent. ; in Cumberland 5·6 per cent. ; in Durham 4·2 per cent. ; and in Cheshire 3·7 per cent. of the population, the proportion being also over 2 per cent. in Middlesex, Monmouthshire, Northumberland, and Glamorganshire. The proportion they bore to the general population was lowest in the counties of Cardigan, Radnor, Norfolk, Huntingdon, Merioneth, Suffolk, Cambridge, Buckingham, Carmarthen, and Wilts, and in no one of which is it as high as 0·3 per cent.

" Passing from counties to towns, we find that in Liverpool the Irish form 12·8 ; in Birkenhead, 8·8 ; in St Helens, 8·5 ; in Manchester, 7·5 ; and in Salford, 7·4 per cent. of the population, these Lancashire and Cheshire towns being those in which the Irish element was strongest. Then followed in order Middlesboro, Stockport, Cardiff, Gateshead, Preston, Bolton, Bradford, and Oldham, exhausting the list of great towns in which the Irish formed as much as 4 per cent. of the inhabitants.

" Of the aggregate inhabitants of London and of the forty-six great towns, each having a population exceeding 50,000 persons, 3·3 per cent. were natives of Ireland, while the proportion was only 1·5 per cent. in the rest of England and Wales.

" Instead of considering, as we have hitherto done, the proportion borne by the natives of Ireland to the population of the several counties and towns, we may examine their local distribution in another way. Of each 1000 natives of Ireland who were enumerated in this country 378 were enumerated in Lancashire, 176 in London, or the adjoining counties of Middlesex, Surrey, and Kent, 101 in Yorkshire, 65 in Durham, 42 in Cheshire, and over 20 in Cumberland, Staffordshire, Northumberland, Glamorganshire, and Hampshire respectively. With the exception of Hampshire, all these are mining or industrial centres, and the apparent exception presented by Hampshire is explicable by the comparatively large number of soldiers quartered in that county. Passing to the great towns, of 1000 Irish enumerated in England and Wales, 147 were enumerated in London or the adjoining town of West Ham, 139 in Liverpool or Birkenhead, 69 in Manchester or Salford, 17 in Leeds, 14 in Bradford, and 13 in Birmingham. In no other of the great towns was the proportion so high as 10 per 1000."

Turning to Scotland the Census enumerators make the following analysis—" Those of Irish nationality are most numerous in Wigtown, with 6·112 per cent.; in Ayr, with 6·465 per cent.; in Linlithgow, with 7·647 per cent.; in Dumbarton, with 11·023 per cent.; in Lanark, with 12·214 per cent.; and in Renfrew, with 13·494 per cent. They are least numerous in Shetland, with 0·074 per cent., and in the other northern counties.

" The Irish-born, whose average in the whole burghs is 8·634 per cent., bulk most largely in Partick, with 18·289 per cent.; in Dumbarton, with 18·678 per cent.; and in Port Glasgow (Parliamentary), with 30·096 per cent.; being smallest in Forfar, with 0·445 per cent.; in Peterhead, with 0·337 per cent.; and in Dysart, with 0·304 per cent."

The provinces of Ireland are well represented in the various parts of Great Britain. Ulstermen are most numerous in Scotland and the North of England, as might be expected from their contiguity to the northern province of Ireland, while you find the Irish of London and South Wales are mostly from Munster, owing to the convenience of access. The natives of Connaught are probably most numerous in the Midlands. This arises from the fact that most of the harvest men came from the West of Ireland, and that many of these who have not returned have settled down in the Midland counties, nearest to where they had previously been employed at field work. As formerly most of the harvestmen entered England through Liverpool, and from time to time a portion would remain in this country, a good many natives of Connaught are to be found in Lancashire. The Leinstermen are probably more numerous in Lancashire than elsewhere. Indeed the four provinces are well represented in that county, though it is probable there is a preponderance of Connaughtmen. Though as a rule you find that convenience of access accounts for the distribution in Great Britain of the natives of the various parts of Ireland, this is not always the case. It sometimes happens that you come across a colony from some particular spot on the "old sod " because the original settlers came from there, and these brought over, or were followed by, relations, friends, and neighbours from their "own place," while they, in their turn, brought others.

The Census of 1891 showed that the drain on Ireland's life-blood still continued, for the population had decreased from 5,174,836 in 1881 to 4,706,162 in 1891, a loss of nearly 10 per cent. This makes the Home Rule question one of life or death for our nationality, and there cannot be a doubt but that when Lord Salisbury prescribed "twenty years of resolute government" as the cure for Ireland's ills, he had in his mind the thought that if the present state of things continued long enough, there would be so few left in the country that the Irish question would settle itself. During the last ten years about three quarters of a million of persons of Irish birth have emigrated to countries outside of Europe. A number of these would be from various parts of Great Britain. This, with the falling off in the number of those crossing the Channel to settle here, will account for the considerable diminution of Irish-born in England, Scotland, and Wales which the Census Commissioners' returns, when the statistics under this head have been completed, will probably show. It will, no doubt, then be seen, as the information in the following chapter indicates, that our people are more widely diffused throughout the country than ever before. While the Irish-born will no doubt be found to have diminished, there is undoubtedly a large increase, counting those born in this country, of those of purely Irish blood, besides those of partially Irish extraction.

Let us now follow the Irish exiles and their descendants in detail into the various parts of England, Scotland, and Wales, where they have made their homes.

CHAPTER XLI.

THE IRISH IN THE VARIOUS DISTRICTS OF GREAT BRITAIN.

LONDON.

IN dealing with the Irish as we now find them on this side of the Channel, one naturally commences with London, not only on account of the many memories connecting it with the history of Ireland, but also because it contains the greatest number of our race to be found in any one place.

From time to time, in the preceding chapters, we have passed in review the various occasions on which Irishmen have been either voluntary or involuntary residents of London.

It is with the London of to-day we are now dealing. If you want to find out quickly where the London Irish are settled, and the part of Ireland they chiefly hail from, you have only to go to one of the numerous Catholic churches on a Sunday morning. Listen to the banns of marriage being published, and you at once recognise from the names that "rebel Cork" and other Munster counties must have sent a large contingent to the modern Babylon. The announcements also prove to you that the Irish race must be increasing and multiplying in the huge city; not sitting down, as the children of Israel did of old, to weep by the waters of the Assyrian Babylon, but standing up like men, and, with stout hearts and limbs and keen brains, fighting successfully the battle of life.

Many Irishmen have distinguished themselves in London, as elsewhere, during the present century, but it is the great mass of them in the metropolis that shall now claim our special attention. That very interesting book, "London Labour and the London Poor," by Henry Mayhew, gives us glimpses of the precarious modes of living of our poorer fellow-countrymen and women forty years ago.

It is chiefly with the street traders that he deals. At that time, which immediately followed the great Famine, the Irish must have been coming into the metropolis in large numbers. He says—"The parts of London that are most thickly populated with Irish lie about Brook Street, Ratcliff Cross, down both sides of the Commercial Road, and in Rosemary Lane, though nearly all the coster districts have their Irish settlements—Cromer Street, Saffron Hill, and King Street, Drury Lane, for instance, being thickly peopled with the Irish." While Mayhew does not shut his eyes to their weaknesses, he pays a well-deserved tribute to their virtues. Speaking of the Irish female street traders, he says—"But the women present two characteristics which distinguish them from the London costermongers generally—they are chaste, and, unlike the 'coster-girls,' very seldom form any connection without the sanction of the marriage ceremony. They are, moreover, attentive to religious observances." Although those of this class are now chiefly London-born, and what are termed "Irish Cockneys," Mayhew's description is equally true of them to-day.

Probably, as these pages may have already shown, the oldest Irish colony in London formed part of the district lying south of Holborn and Oxford Street, and stretching westward from Lincoln's-Inn-Fields to Regent Street. As in similar portions of the large provincial towns, this district has been much opened out by new streets, so that, as described by Cardinal Manning, in connection with the congregations of the Catholic churches and chapels in this part of London, our people are by no means so numerous now as they once were. They are, in fact, spreading all over the metropolis, and, as a rule, getting into far more satisfactory locations than formerly. They are, however, still numerous enough to exercise considerable political influence in the Holborn Parliamentary division and other adjacent constituencies. This influence does not end merely with the exercise of their own votes. The Irishman is almost invariably patriotic, and generally ahead in political intelligence of his English neighbours of the same class. Besides this, the branches of the Irish National League, which are now to be found in every quarter of London, have exercised a healthy educational influence. As a consequence, the Irishman, either native or London-born—for one is often quite as good as the other—living in such localities as the streets adjoining Drury Lane, Seven Dials, and other parts of the ancient parish of St Giles in the Field, and the surrounding district, is generally able to bring up to the poll on the day of an election a number of his English friends to vote for a supporter of Ireland's demands. Indeed, whether he be a coster, a porter in Covent Garden or some other of the wholesale markets—where the smartest and strongest of the men are Irish or Irish Cockneys—a "docker" at the East end, a gas stoker, a bricklayers' labourer, shoemaker, tailor, or artisan of some other kind, or indeed in the highest walk of life, this is true of the Irishman all over the metropolis.

Then, again, the canvasser for one of our League branches, or one of the Irish church collectors—those veritable pillars of the Catholic Church—can nearly always, by his ready tact and mother wit—they sometimes call it "blarney"—get an apathetic friend to sign a claim to be put on the register of voters, where the English Liberal agent, however zealous, signally fails, because he is so often taken for a School Board visitor, a broker's man, or some other equally obnoxious individual.

At the eastern end of Holborn division, in and about Saffron Hill, there is a considerable Irish population. This is an Italian quarter, too, such as you find about Gerard Street, Liverpool, or Bordesley Street, Birmingham; St Peter's, Hatton Garden, being generally called the Italian church. Though the Italians, like the Irish, are mostly Catholics, there are few intermarriages between them here.

It is an admitted fact that you find a greater amount of political intelligence among tailors than any other class of artisans. The nature of their occupation in some measure explains this. It is not a noisy craft, like the smith's or carpenter's, and, without neglecting their work, a number of them in the one room can readily carry on political and other discussions. It is quite a usual thing in London and elsewhere for the men in a workshop to employ one of their number to read a newspaper, while the rest listen to and digest for future discussion the news of the day and other matters. The Irish are undoubtedly the cream of the craft. In fact, the Irish tailor, being gifted with the imaginative powers of his race, is often a real artist. In some of the best and most fashionable shops in London you will find the Irish cutter at the top of the tree, and, to his credit be it said, he is generally a sterling patriot. He is often a missionary, too, for more than one branch of the League owes its origin to some Irish cutter from London who has got an engagement in a provincial town.

The Irish are numerous in Clerkenwell, where, until recently, when the jail was pulled down, you could see by the new brickwork in the wall where the gap was made by the terrible explosion of 1867. In St Luke's parish, East Finsbury, you also find them in considerable numbers. In these two districts they are mostly of the class to be found in the Holborn division of Finsbury, already referred to. South Hackney, Bethnal Green, and Haggerston are noted centres of the boot and shoemaking trade, which gives employment to a portion of the Irish population in these districts. In Marylebone, North Kensington, Chelsea, Fulham, and Westminster, there are districts where the Irish and their descendants are largely in evidence. As in other parts of London, while there is a satisfactory proportion who have "got on," the bulk of these are in the ranks of labour. It is satisfactory to know that many Irish labourers in connection with the building trades have been able to bring up their sons as masons, carpenters, or bricklayers. Among the artisan class you find many who have received a fair education at the schools in connection with the various Catholic churches—men who have never, perhaps, seen Ireland, but who are among the staunchest upholders of the national cause, as well as being the keenest and most intelligent politicians to be found in the metropolis.

On the south side of the Thames you find small colonies of our people in Camberwell, Peckham, and other centres. In fact they are everywhere—even in places where you never dream of finding them, as any priest will tell you who has ever opened a new mission in London. From the names of the children attending the schools, whose parents are, or ought to be, Catholics, you would not take half of them to be of Irish descent. This, together with the number of genuine or partially altered Irish names borne by many who disclaim both our creed and nationality, shows how, during many generations, thousands of the

Irish have been gradually merged into the general population. An eminent Irish dignitary of the Church in London is of opinion that this contact and intermixing with the English population has produced an undoubted moral deterioration—even among those of purely Irish descent—during the past twenty years. The loss to creed and country must have been still greater when there were so many proselytising influences at work, and fewer priests, churches, and schools than now.

The life of a Catholic priest in London is sufficiently laborious at the present time, but it must have been more so some forty or fifty years ago. Father Lockhart, in a lecture delivered by him, "Thirty years amongst the Irish in London," while paying a tribute to their generosity, describes the viscissitudes he experienced in opening a mission at Kingsland. The first assistance he received was, he says, from an Irish builder named Kelly, who came to him and said he had a good house in which he could say Mass, and that he would give him board and lodging for nothing. With the Irishman's aid he acquired the use of a large paper store, one floor of which he converted into a school and used another for a church. This, he said, was what had been going on through all parts of London and throughout the world wherever the Irish race had gone. His present church, Father Lockhart said, was a real old church, built in the thirteenth century. It had been the chapel of the Bishop of Ely, and when it was for sale some years ago, he sent a well-known Protestant auctioneer to buy it, and he got it, to his surprise, for a very small sum.

Perhaps the densest mass of Irish is to be found among the river-side population stretching for miles eastward of London Bridge, on both sides of the Thames. On the north side you meet them in large numbers in Whitechapel, Wapping, Shadwell, Limehouse, Poplar, Millwall, Barking Road, and Silvertown, their chief employment being in connection with shipping. At the latter place there are also ironworks and chemical works such as you find at Widnes, Flint, Oldbury, and other places, where considerable numbers of Irishmen are employed. On the south side of the Thames the Irish population is largest in Southwark,

Bermondsey, Rotherhithe, and Deptford, and mostly employed at the docks and the river-side. In and about Bermondsey you find a number of them connected with the various branches of the leather trade, for which the district is noted, both as employers and work people.

In a previous chapter it will be found that they were so employed in these districts along the banks of the Thames far back into the last century. So they have been ever since. Considering the constant influx from Ireland during the last and present centuries, and allowing for the natural increase of a prolific race, it must be quite evident that the *known* Catholic population—which is generally supposed to give an approximation to the number of Irish—falls far short of what the Irish and those of Irish descent probably number to-day. Through their having been for so many generations employed at the loading and unloading of vessels in the London docks and by the river-side, a large proportion of them have come to be stevedores, as what may be considered the skilled workmen among the "dockers" are called. A considerable amount of skill is required in the stowing of a vessel. Many a good ship has been lost on account of the shifting of the cargo and other causes arising out of unscientific stowing.

As might be expected many of our river-side population find employment as firemen in the sea-going steamers, or "before the mast" as sailors.

It is computed that nearly half of the "dockers" who took part in the great strike of 1889 were Irish or the sons of Irishmen. Formerly, as in Liverpool, they had the field almost to themselves, but of late years the ordinary English agricultural labourers who come to London make for the docks as the readiest way of getting employment, so that now there are more English than Irish among the casual and unskilled dockers. It was this element that might have caused the defeat of the strike. John Burns, the most prominent advocate and champion of the strikers, said— " The fathers and grandfathers of dockers had been dockers before them," and in speaking of the causes that helped to win, he said—" When the stevedores consented to throw in their lot with the dock labourers, they proved really the backbone of the strike." In speaking of the ancestry of the dockers he might have gone even further back than their grandfathers or even their great-grandfathers, if he had ever read the account of the fight between the Irish coal-heavers and sailors at Shadwell in 1768. It is not extraordinary, then, to find that the Irish having been for so long a period engaged in the river-side work of London, probably 75 per cent. of the stevedores, the skilled hands among the dock labourers, are Irish or of Irish extraction. In standing by their fellow-workmen who were less able to help themselves, it cannot, therefore, but be said that Irishmen are rendering good service in return for the aid our cause is now receiving from the British democracy. Indeed the Irish may be said also to be the backbone of other popular movements in London. Go to Hyde Park on the day of some great democratic demonstration, and you cannot but see this. Not only do you find them in the ranks of the purely Catholic and Irish societies, with their bands, banners, and patriotic emblems, but in connection with other political and temperance organisations—if one may judge from the handsome banners, on which you often see depicted such subjects as "Sarsfield," "The Irish Parliament House," and "O'Connell"; with quotations from Tom Moore and harps and shamrocks *galore*.

It can never be forgotten, by men of all creeds, politics, and nationalities, that the one man who, more than all others, helped to bring the gigantic dock strike to a happy termination was Cardinal Manning. Other princes of the Church—like the Wolseys and the Richelieus—may for a time have made a more splendid figure in history, but, in the end, they must have confessed to themselves that the cause of religion and humanity could never be served by state intrigues; such as those carried on in our own days, in the supposed interest of religion, by creatures of the English government and bitter enemies of Ireland, like Norfolk and Errington. Cardinal Manning was no believer in statecraft and diplomacy as the means of spreading and strengthening the Faith, if we may judge from the following passage in a letter he wrote to the great Irish-American ecclesiastic, Cardinal Gibbons—"Surely the episcopate of the whole world is the most powerful and direct instrument in the hands of the Holy See for getting correct local knowledge and enforcing its decisions. Who can know the temper of America, England, and Ireland, as they who have a finger upon the pulse of the people? Hitherto the world has been governed by dynasties ; *henceforth the Holy See will have to deal with the people*, and it has bishops in daily and personal contact with the people."

Cardinal Manning so identified himself with the aspirations—political as well as religious—of the Irish, that any sketch of them in London would be incomplete without giving to him that magnificently prominent position which he occupied among them. Here is what he said of Ireland and her cause in a letter to an American friend—" The time is come when Ireland shall be handed over to itself. Its people have attained their majority. Mr Parnell has indeed done what no other man has attempted to do. He has filled the place he found vacant. He has known the needs and interpreted the desire of the Irish people. Therefore he leads. But the transfer of self-government is not to Mr Parnell, nor the Parnellites, but to Ireland and the Irish people. . . . The centuries which have ripened England and Scotland with flowers and fruit have swept over Ireland in withering desolation. We are beginning in the nineteenth century to undo the miseries of the seventeenth and eighteenth. But let us not excuse ourselves by alleging the faults of national character. If our Irish brethren have faults they are for the most part what England has made them."

Justin M'Carthy thus speaks of Cardinal Manning and the work he did in London—" For this is the foremost man in the Catholic Church in England. This is the Cardinal Grandison of D'Israeli's 'Lothair,' Cardinal Manning, Catholic Archbishop of Westminster, successor in the office to the late Cardinal Wiseman, an Englishman of Englishmen, with no drop of Irish blood in his veins, he is more Hibernian than the Hibernians themselves in his sympathies with Ireland. A man of social position, of old family, of the highest education, and most refined instincts, he would leave the Catholic noblemen at any time to go down to his Irish teetotallers at the East End of London, for he firmly believes that the salvation of England has yet to be accomplished through the influence of that religious devotion which is at the bottom of the Irish nature."

Mr B. F. C. Costelloe, a Catholic and Irish member of the London County Council, an able barrister, and himself a good type of a class of men who are steadily becoming more numerous among the Irish in Britain, thus speaks of the noble part the great Cardinal took in the "Dockers' Strike" of 1889—"At a time when the Archbishops and Bishops of the establishment were either taking holiday, or taking fright, the octogenarian Cardinal offered his services, and became the very centre and leading spirit of the famous Committee of Conciliation. It was an open secret that his was the one name upon that Committee which commanded the full confidence of both parties. The dockmen, even when the fight was at its hottest, welcomed his arbitration; and their only difficulty was the necessity of finding a few other men of sufficient standing to act with him, and of sufficient wisdom and sympathy not to spoil his work. No one, except those who were on the spot, has any idea of the immense personal labour which the great negotiation involved, or of the wearing anxieties and incessant difficulty of detail which had to be dealt with from hour to hour. Never, perhaps, has a difficult problem been solved with more universal approval. It is worth remembering—as even the least religious of the strike leaders confessed at the time—that the result would never have been possible, if it had not been that half of the men on strike were Catholics themselves, and were not only open to appeals founded in a true conception of Christianity, but inspired with a personal devotion for the saintly character of their ecclesiastical chief."

Just as the Irish river-side population appreciated the character of this truly great prince of the Church—as prince he was in the noblest sense of the word—so did he appreciate them. No one knew better than he what the Church owes to their self-sacrifice. His predecessor, Cardinal Wiseman, in 1856, at the opening of a Catholic Church in East London, described how it had been erected by the penny contributions of dock labourers, bargemen, bricklayers, hodmen, and other toilers. So could Cardinal Manning tell of similar work done all over London, in connection with well nigh a hundred Catholic churches, and with numerous schools and religious houses—all centres of future light and hope for the generations yet to come, and all substantial testimonies that, as of old, the Irish, even in their poverty, are still the missionary nation of Europe.

The living made by the docker, even with the advantages now secured by their Union, is but a precarious one. It is also attended by danger to life and limb. A man may fall into the hold of a vessel, or be disabled in some other way, and if he has made no provision for such an emergency his comrades readily and cheerfully come to his assistance. A collection will be made for him, or they get up what is called a "Friendly Lead" for his benefit. This used to be a very popular institution among the London Irish for the relief of compatriots in misfortune, and there were men among them famous for so conducting them as to produce the most substantial results for the special object of benevolence, combined with the greatest amount of recreation for those who rallied to his or her assistance. The "Friendly Lead," like some other similar institutions, is rapidly becoming a thing of the past, for, being held in licensed premises, where something has to be spent for "the good of the house," it is, of course, discountenanced by the League of the Cross, founded by Cardinal Manning, which is doing such great temperance work in London.

It is a mistake, frequently made, both in London and elsewhere, to suppose that the bulk of our fellow-countrymen live in what have been termed the "Irish quarters." However it may have been formerly, it is not so now. Those who are compelled by circumstances to live in undesirable surroundings do not, perhaps, constitute one-tenth of the whole. As in other large towns these quarters are gradually disappearing. You find that our people are now spreading all over London, and in much healthier localities than formerly. Although not so numerous among the substantial "middle-class" traders as one would wish to find them, they are making fair progress, and it is no uncommon thing to find substantial shopkeepers and wholesale traders who have been costers or are the sons of costers; while in every calling and profession you find Irishmen in most responsible positions. In London, as elsewhere throughout Great Britain, you meet with a numerous body who prove that "with a fair field and no favour" Irishmen are bound to come to the front. These are the Civil Service and Customs Officials. Formerly but few Irishmen could get employment as officials of this kind. In the old days of patronage it was practically "no Irish need apply." Since the competitive examination system has been in operation, the native gifts of Irishmen have proved them to be second to none. As a consequence, you now find in the ranks of the Civil Service and in the Customs a greater proportion of them, perhaps, than of the other nationalities of the empire. As a rule, there are no truer Irishmen, and, being men of education, they are often able to render valuable assistance to the cause. In this connection it must not be forgotten that there are a great number of Irishmen in the Government Ordnance Survey, and among the ablest in the various departments.

Irish doctors are numerous in London, and recognised even by those who have no love for their nationality, as among the most skilful in their noble profession.

Of the devoted body of Irish priests, who can speak in sufficient praise? A dignitary of the Church in London has said that had they the same materials to work upon as the clergy at home in Ireland, and were their difficulties not so much greater, such is their zeal and self-sacrifice that our people here would be all saints. But the noble work of the clergy is taken so much as a matter of course that it is apt to be forgotten.

To sum up the Irish in London, in the higher social grades, they are far better represented in the various professions than in trade, so that besides Government employes, doctors, and clergymen, there are a large number of men of our nationality who are eminent as lawyers, painters, sculptors, actors, musicians, and in every department of literature.

KENT, MIDDLESEX, ESSEX, AND SURREY.

It will have been noted how, as early as the middle of last century, the Irish labourers came each year for the hop-picking in Kent, often lodging as they came and went in Whitechapel, St Giles, and similar neighbourhoods. Some of these, with their native Irish adaptability, would pick up employment in London, and remain. Probably most of those who now go "a-hopping" each year are from London itself, and consist very largely of the ordinary vagrant class among the English population; for during the season the tramps' lodging-houses in London are completely deserted, the "Bohemian" inmates having betaken themselves *en masse* to the pleasant fields of Kent, where, particularly on the Saturday nights, they make Maidstone and the other centres of the hop district rather too lively for the steady-going natives. Large numbers of Irish from all the poorer neighbourhoods go to the hop-picking, and it is no uncommon thing for the houses or rooms to be shut up, and for whole families to go off together. In the season of 1891 as many as eight hundred, chiefly Irish, went from Poplar alone, and it is the same among our poorer fellow-countrymen in other parts of London. Indeed, the season is eagerly looked forward to by them, as besides earning their keep for the time and something over, the annual "hopping" is regarded as a pleasant and healthy month's holiday. "Hopping cases" are constantly turning up in the London Revision Courts. The Tory canvasser, in seeking for "objections," finds the tenement of Jerry Sullivan or Timothy Mahony shut up during the "qualifying period," and in due time each gets a notice of objection to his vote as having "removed." But these devices seldom succeed, as the chances are that the ubiquitous church-collector, or energetic canvasser from the League branch of the district is present in Court to explain that Sullivan or Mahony has only been on his annual holiday, or, better still, the Irishman objected to turns up himself and claims and gets his expenses from the enemy.

Henry Mayhew, in contrasting the English and Irish costers, speaks of the attention of the latter to their religious observances. The same holds good in later years with regard to the Irish hop-pickers, as may be seen from a number of *St George's Magazine*, which speaks of the arrangements being made to send a priest to pitch his tent amongst them during the season.

As a rule, the hop-picking has not left behind it any settled Irish population in the rural parts of Kent. Our fellow-countrymen are, however, increasing in the semi-rural districts around London—situated in Kent, Essex, Surrey, and Middlesex. Many of these come straight from Ireland, a proportion of them returning each year at the end of the season, but a large number must also make their way here from other parts of England, where we find the Irish population diminishing. The fact is that, even yet, a great number of our people are migratory, and having once torn themselves away from the "old sod," will not stay in idleness and poverty in one place if work is to be found elsewhere.

For miles around London the most profitable form of agriculture is market gardening, seeing that a daily supply of fruit and vegetables has to be kept up for the five millions of people who live in the metropolis. This gives employment to an enormous number of hands—far greater than ordinary farming would—and this is what brings the Irish in such numbers to the district, where their intelligence and adaptability are much appreciated. Westward from London, along both banks of the Thames, you find them, men and women, boys and girls, at this employment, in and about Chiswick, Brentford, Isleworth, Mortlake, Barnes, and Kingston. They are numerous, too, in the Dartford division of Kent, where they find employment around Crayford, St Mary's Cray, Swanscombe, and Dartford. Many of those working at the market gardening will tell you they can do better at it than if they or their sons were mechanics, for whereas the latter will, as a rule, only look for a job at their own trade, the Irish labourers will turn their hands to anything. As a consequence you find them employed as gas-stokers—an occupation which Irishmen follow in many places—in the cement works at Northfleet, in the arms factories, and in many other ways. The surest sign that they are settling down and becoming a political power in these Parliamentary divisions around London is the fact that in the Dartford division of Kent there are some four or five hundred Irish voters, in the Kingston division of Surrey about two hundred, and so on with the rest in the four counties into which London more or less extends.

THE SOUTHERN AND SOUTH-WESTERN COUNTIES—THE IRISH IN THE ARMY AND NAVY.

Leaving behind us Kent and Surrey, and turning to the other southern counties of England, and to the south-western counties, we find the greatest body of Irish in any one place in Bristol, which, as we have seen, has many memories connecting it with our country. A considerable number have attained fair positions, but as the city—though still far ahead of its rivals in population, wealth, and importance—has not kept pace in its development with the other rising ports on the Bristol Channel, and as the Irish gravitate to where the most employment is to be had, it is probable that they have diminished in Bristol.

There is a small Irish mining colony at Camborne, in Cornwall, the existence of which was chiefly made known to the world by the savage attack made on them and their church by some of the native population in 1882.

The two southern counties having the largest Irish-born population are Hampshire and Devonshire. The Census Commissioners account for the comparatively large Irish population of Hampshire, including Portsmouth and Southampton, by the number of soldiers quartered there. The same, no doubt, applies to Devonshire.

This will be a suitable place to speak of our fellow-countrymen in the naval and military service of Great Britain.

For about two centuries the Irish have been numerous in the armies of Britain, and, probably, for nearly as long a period in the navy also. Several of the infantry and cavalry regiments raised for King James the Second in Ireland were, after he had been driven from the throne, incorporated into the British army. During the wars of the last century it was no uncommon thing to find Irish troops engaged on both sides. The Fifth, or Royal Irish Regiment of Dragoons, raised in or about the year 1688, served under the Duke of Marlborough during the whole of his wars. They fought in 1706 at the battle of Ramillies, where, says Grose in his "Military Antiquities of the British Army," they gathered fresh laurels. But these were not for Ireland. Yet was her heart uplifted when she heard of the valour of her sons in the opposing ranks, and of the trophies they carried off from the Sassenagh. Who does not remember the soul-stirring ballad of our national poet, Thomas Davis, in which he sings the deeds of the gallant exiles serving in the Irish regiment of Lord Clare, who, from the very gloom of defeat, snatched the only ray of glory that shone on the arms of their allies on "Ramillies' bloody field"?

Grose also tells us that this same Fifth Royal Irish Regiment, which won such laurels for Britain, was disbanded on account of a plot among the recruits to assist the Irish insurgents in 1798.

Our countrymen must have been numerous about this time not only in the British army, but in the navy, if we are to believe Froude, who says that "half the sailors and petty officers in the service were Catholics." He was probably right, for the Irish fisheries, the nurseries of the hardiest seamen, were then flourishing. His statements must, however, be received with caution; for, like Macaulay, he is a notorious romancer, and strains his facts to fit his theories. As there would be no picture at all if he painted everything Irish black, he condescends to commend the courage of Irishmen, though he disparages them in the same breath. "The Irish are," he says, "the spendthrift sister of the Aryan race. . . . Brave to rashness, yet so infirm of purpose, that unless they are led by others, their bravery is useless to them." He shuts his eyes to the fact that Irishmen have led the armies of the most powerful of the nations of the earth—France, Austria, Spain, and America. Moreover, though we take no pride in the fact, some of the most distinguished generals who have commanded the armies of England have been, and are, Irishmen.

Happily, in glancing at the career and position of our countrymen in the land and sea forces of Britain, we have more reliable historians than Froude or Macaulay. General Sir William Butler, himself an Irishman, in his biography of his distinguished fellow-countryman, Sir Charles Napier, gives a vivid and graphic account of the various engagements of the Peninsular War. From this we learn that Sir John Moore's gallant little army were almost all Irishmen, and that the 50th

Regiment, which Napier commanded, was called the West Kent, but that its soldiers were almost to a man Irish. Of the whole British army at this time it has been estimated that from half to two-thirds were Irish.

Many a patriotic Irish heart has beaten under the uniform of the British soldier, and if there was one thing more than another that hastened Catholic emancipation in 1829, it was that many of the troops sent into Ireland to overawe the people cheered for O'Connell as soon as they landed.

The great Famine drove large numbers to enlist in the British army. It will be remembered how, in 1854, at the time of the Crimean War, Frederick Lucas succeeded in gaining a number of concessions for the Catholic soldiers and sailors. In the days of the penal laws it was only when England was engaged in a deadly grapple with foes abroad that any one of these was relaxed. So it was at this time that the Catholics engaged in the Crimea were allowed greater facilities for the practice of their religion.

There is no doubt but that Catholics are not as numerous in this country as might be expected, on account of the many proselytising influences which have been at work for so long a period. Among these were so-called benevolent public institutions, such as the Duke of York's School and the Royal Hibernian Military School in the neighbourhood of Dublin. As late as 1881 "an old Hibernian boy" wrote regarding the latter institution to the *Universe*:—" From its high-sounding title the general public would be led to believe it was opened for the reception of the children of Irish soldiers generally, but such is far from being the case. When I first remember it no Catholic children would be allowed to practise their religion in any way, all having to attend the Protestant church. Later on they became more tolerant, allowing the children to attend mass in the neighbouring village of Chapelizod, and eventually building a small church within the grounds." The writer further stated that the proportion of Catholics then was 170 out of 400, which was most extraordinary, seeing that the bulk of Irish soldiers were, and are, Catholics. In addition to this, he speaks of other temptations to proselytism. In the regimental schools, both at home and in India, a similar system has prevailed. Seeing that all boys are supposed to leave at the age of fourteen, and join the army if capable, one is not so much surprised to find, in almost any garrison town, soldiers or their descendants bearing grand old Irish historic names, but who disclaim both the creed and nationality of their fathers. Against this it must be said, however, that in some of these same military stations, such as Shrewsbury, Brecon, Colchester, Carnarvon, Maidstone, and Norwich, you find among the barrack officials, as well as drill instructors, Irishmen who are sincere lovers of their country. Some of the most capable adjutants in the militia and volunteer regiments are Irishmen. In fact, you find they appear to take more naturally to soldiering as a profession than do most other nationalities. One would expect to find an overwhelming proportion of them in the rank and file as compared with the commissioned officers. This is not so; Irishmen are to be found in about the same proportion in every grade of the army.

Within the last twenty years there has been a great diminution in their number in the British army, but this has not been so great in the number who enlisted as Catholics. Among the non-commissioned officers and men there were in :—

1868—55,583 Irish, and 51,889 Catholics.
1878—39,121 ,, ,, 41,437 ,,
1888—31,335 ,, ,, 39,446 ,,

The numbers given as Irish mean Irish-born. The decrease in the population of Ireland would account for some portion of the diminution, but only for a comparatively small proportion. During these twenty years the population of Ireland had decreased by 10 per cent. During the same period the soldiers entered as Irish had diminished by 43 per cent., and the Catholics by 24 per cent. This probably shows two things—that the class from which England recruited her armies is disappearing, and that Irishmen are losing their taste for wearing the British uniform.

The reason why those entered as Catholics have not diminished so rapidly as the Irish is on account of the number of enlistments of Catholics of Irish extraction, but born in England, Scotland, or Wales, and classed under the heads of these several nationalities.

In the navy it is the same, and probably to a greater degree. The Irish fishing population, formerly a great recruiting ground for the navy, has diminished in even a faster ratio than the agricultural population. Besides this, since the training ships have been withdrawn from the Irish coasts, fewer Irish-born lads enter the navy. On this side of the Channel, however, a very large proportion of Irishmen and their descendants make their living by the industries connected with shipping. Consequently great numbers of men and lads of Irish parentage along the Thames, Mersey, Clyde, Tyne, and elsewhere, go to sea, either " before the mast," or as firemen in the Mercantile Marine, and a proportion of these drift into the Royal Navy.

WALES.

The position we hold in South Wales and Monmouthshire has already been dealt with in these pages in connection with the Tredegar riots. The friendlier relations that now exist between the two nationalities have been shown in a variety of ways. When Irish members of Parliament or other public men have visited, they have met with a cordial reception from the Welsh population. The visit of Michael Davitt to the Rhondda Valley is still remembered with pleasure. There are many proofs of the kindlier feeling mainly due to the initiative of Mr Gladstone. One illustration will be sufficient. An article in the Welsh national magazine, *The Red Dragon*, on "Thomas Davis," excited deep interest among cultured Welshmen, who were the more drawn towards our Protestant national poet on account of his being himself half a Welshman by descent. About this time a gentleman, connected with the Irish National League, was announced to visit a branch of it in a town among the Monmouthshire hills, not far from the scene of the 1882 riots. He was asked by prominent Welshmen of the place to address a larger assembly than he had expected to meet, and to speak on the life and poetry of Thomas Davis. As the subject was a congenial one, he consented, more especially as it gave him an opportunity he had not expected of putting the case of Ireland before an audience of Welshmen as well as of Irishmen. The Baptist minister gave the use of his school for the lecture, and announced it in his chapel. He, himself, with most of his congregation, and the leading people of the town, attended, and the room was filled with an enthusiastic audience, who highly appreciated the noble national sentiments of Davis's poems and the lessons of his life.

While of late years the Welsh and Irish have been united in a common political cause, they have, but too often, in the mining districts, been united in a common sorrow. In the terrible colliery explosions, which have carried death and desolation into these hills and valleys, among the Welsh names on the death roll you invariably find others here and there of unmistakable Irish origin; while among the first to rush to the pit mouth at the appalling sound, which is only too familiar, you never miss the heroic Irish doctor, if there be one in the neighbourhood, as there generally is, with his ready skill and tenderness for the unhappy victims. The success of Irish doctors everywhere, which has been often noted, is largely due to the fact that in addition to being, as a rule, the most skilful in their profession, they possess the sympathetic Celtic nature which is so welcome in affliction.

Outside of Monmouthshire and Glamorganshire there are but few Irish in South Wales. After these two counties they are most numerous in Pembrokeshire, no doubt on account of the passenger traffic coming from Ireland through Milford. Besides those coming by this route from the Munster counties, some come from Wexford.

The Irish are much less numerous in North than in South Wales. There are more in Flintshire than elsewhere. They are chiefly engaged in the mining industries about Bagilt and Flint, as well as at the chemical works in the latter town. There are a few Irish in Mold, who chiefly work at the quarries and coalpits; and also at Holywell—famous for the miraculous well of St Winefride, to which pilgrims from all parts resort. It is a favourite spot for the annual excursions of the various Catholic and Irish Societies of Lancashire and

Cheshire. Mostyn, on the coast of Flintshire, will be remembered as the place where the troops from Ireland landed to fight for King Charles. It is said that in Flintshire and Cheshire there are, to this day, memories of what they term the "Irish invasion." In the Protestant church here there is a monument or tablet erected to the memory of the men of the 23rd Welsh Fusileers, who fell at the Alma, and on the roll of the "gallant Welshmen" so honoured are some unmistakable Irish names. As a rule it is only when Pat commits some delinquency that his nationality is prominently brought forward. In Denbighshire the Irish are chiefly in Wrexham. Carnarvonshire, being on the direct route from Ireland, through Holyhead (where there are some Irish residents), was evidently one of the places where our people first settled down, for in Bangor there is what was probably one of the first Catholic chapels erected in Wales during this century. As in many other districts, the making of a line of railway left a small Irish population behind, and you find them along the track of the Chester and Holyhead railway. The Irish at Bangor are pretty well employed at the slate quarries, and in the various occupations of the place, some being in fairly good positions. There is also a small Catholic population, chiefly Irish, at Carnarvon. They are less numerous than formerly in these places, for, as we have noticed before, in many small agricultural towns in England and Wales, owing to the want of great permanent industries, it is difficult to get employment for the young people at which they can make their living in after life, so that these, as they grow up, generally get away to the larger towns.

The district is full of memories of the days when Wales was in communion with Rome, but, though in the cathedral of Bangor and other buildings there are relics of the ages of Faith, there are but few native Catholics. Though there are about sixty Catholic churches and chapels in Wales— one county only, Radnor, being without one — these are centres not so much of Welsh as of Irish Catholicity. A Breton priest once came to Swansea, and preached in Welsh in one of the Catholic churches. He addressed the congregation as though they were of Welsh nationality, and of a kindred race to himself. There is no doubt a connection of that kind both in blood and in the similarity of their languages. But though a great number could understand the Welsh tongue in which the priest spoke, they were mostly the descendants of Irish parents. Indeed, with the exception of some Breton sailors who were in port at the time, most of those present were Irish.

So far the efforts to convert the Welsh to Catholicity have not met with much success. A few years since a religious house was opened on St Tudwal's island, off the coast of Carnarvon, from which it was hoped in time missionaries might go forth, like the disciples of St Columba from Iona, for the conversion of the Welsh. The pious work did not meet with success, and the place was abandoned. The Welsh lost the Faith in the days of persecution, through the priests being driven out or martyred. They are still an eminently religious people, and would make fervent Catholics. There are but few converts made among them, and these are generally through inter-marriages. It is a question if the Church has not lost more than she has gained from this cause.

MIDLAND AND EASTERN COUNTIES—
CHIEFLY AGRICULTURAL.

The West Midland English counties, Cheshire, Shropshire, Hereford, and Monmouth, form, with North and South Wales, the two Catholic dioceses of Shrewsbury, and of Newport and Menevia.

Cheshire, among English counties, has the fifth largest Irish population. We are most numerous in the larger towns. Birkenhead comes first with an Irish population almost as great as Leeds or Bradford, and greater than Birmingham. They are in a fairly good position. The great bulk, as in Liverpool, on the opposite bank of the Mersey, are at employments connected with shipping. In Stockport, Stalybridge, and Hyde, within a few miles of Manchester, they are well employed at the cotton factories, and much better off than the bulk in Liverpool or Birkenhead, where it is hard to get work for the younger people.

You also find them in a fair position in the ancient city of Chester, which has many memories connected with Ireland. Following the course of the Dee from Chester to where it opens out into an estuary several miles wide, you find, on the right bank, the old-world fishing village of Parkgate, which, until very recent years, modern improvements seemed to have entirely forgotten. Yet this was formerly the principal Irish packet station. It was from Parkgate that William of Orange with his forces embarked to encounter the troops of his royal father-in-law. At Crewe the Irish are chiefly artizans and labourers at the works of the London and North-Western Railway Company. Macclesfield is famous for its silk manufacture. Among those at this trade are some whose fathers or grandfathers came from Ireland after the depression in manufactures which followed the Union. The staple manufacture was introduced here about 1745, and, it is said, by silk, poplin, and tabinet weavers from Dublin. Besides the Irish by birth and descent, there is a considerable proportion of the population of partially Irish extraction, including some in good positions. Our countrymen are tolerably numerous in Runcorn, Congleton, Middlewich, Nantwich, and other towns. To Cheshire, as to other counties more exclusively agricultural, come each year a number of Irish labourers, but not to such an extent as formerly. In past years a few remained behind, finding employment with the farmers in the neighbourhood of the smaller towns and villages. In these quaint old places you usually come across the picturesque-looking, gabled, framed-work houses characteristic of the district. Occasionally you will find one of these used as a lodging-house, with, not unfrequently, over the door, the name of some Connaught harvestman who may have settled here many years ago. They carry with them the faith of St Patrick, and every place has its own history of the struggles made to practise the observances of religion. For instance, in Nantwich, a venerable little town on the Weaver, they will show you where Mass was first said in an old salt-works, the entrance to which was up a ladder, and which building was used until 1855, when the present school-chapel was built.

In Shropshire there are, according to the Census returns,

1880 Irish-born. If those of Irish extraction were added to this the figures would probably be five or six thousand. The greatest number in any one place is at Shrewsbury, the county town, where there is a Catholic (chiefly Irish) congregation numbering about eight hundred. These seem a small portion of 26,478, the whole population of the town, yet it is more than one would expect in a place so far out of the ordinary track of the Irish in England. Shrewsbury itself, with its embattled towers, its ancient abbey and churches, and its time-worn walls, is full of Celtic memories—of associations which call to mind the stout Cymric race, whose descendants in our generation have so nobly rallied to the call of Gladstone. For this is the Pengwerne of the Ancient Britons, built, as one may see, in a position of great natural strength, in a loop of the Severn. Against it, in successive waves of invasion, have beaten the hostile squadrons of the Romans, Saxons, Danes, and Normans; and though pushed back from it into their mountain fortresses, the Welsh, time and again, made gallant efforts to recapture it. The ubiquitous Irish are in it now. The bulk of them live by the most precarious means, and, as a rule, are congregated in the least inviting portion of the place. There are Irish, too, in Wellington, Newport, Oswestry, and others of the Shropshire towns, chiefly employed as labourers on the farms in the districts adjacent, as hawkers, and in other ways. In some of these places fully half of the Irish are intermixed with the English population.

You find a sprinkling of Irish in the old cathedral towns of Hereford and Worcester, some having attained to good positions. The more or less floating populations of them formerly in these places have for the most part disappeared.

Let us now deal more particularly with the agricultural labourers who come and go each year. A Parliamentary return was published in 1882, from which it appeared that in the previous year there were 21,322 Irish migratory labourers. Of these 1444 went from one part of Ireland to another, 17,153 came to England, and 2725 to Scotland. The number coming now is very small in comparison with former years. They come to all the English agricultural districts, but chiefly to the midland and eastern counties.

One of these is Cambridgeshire. The *Freeman's Journal* sent a special commissioner to report on the clearances on the Pollock property in the west of Ireland. To show that the land itself was not able to pay the extortionate rents demanded, he said—" It is important to remember that even the rents that had been paid up to this point were not paid out of the land. In nearly every instance the male members of the family went to England to work. For thirty years and upwards the men on this Creggs portion of the estate have gone to Cambridgeshire, and, as a proof of the poverty of these people I may mention that the English farmers in the Fen country have, over and over again, sent across the money to pay the passage of the harvestmen—and after landing it was quite a custom to give them the half year's rent to send home—the loan to be repaid in labour. The Post Office authorities are able to confirm this fact."

The Fen country spoken of is in Lincolnshire, where there are places almost as well known, and spoken of as familiarly by the firesides of Mayo, as if they were in Ireland itself. Up to 1885 the number coming into Lincolnshire had been gradually decreasing, but after that there set in a slight increase, according to the observation of a patriotic Irish priest of the district. He noticed in 1885 a newspaper paragraph stating that eight hundred harvestmen had left the North Wall, Dublin, for England. He met the same company on their arrival in Boston, one of the Lincolnshire towns called after St Botolph (Botolphstown), possessing a noble old church, some centuries old, roofed with Irish oak. It was singular, the good priest said, to see the celerity with which they distributed themselves to their various destinations among the fens and wolds. This is owing to the fact that each man knows where to go, and is expected. The same men, as a rule, come year after year to the same farmers, and many of the fathers of the present race of harvestmen came over year after year to the fathers of their present employers. They encounter much hardship and sometimes real persecution, although not so much as formerly. Frequently the priests of these Lincolnshire Missions have to go many miles into remote districts to say Mass on Sundays for the harvestmen, it being no uncommon thing to have a congregation of five hundred or more hearing Mass in a barn lent for the occasion. In many cases the farmers compete with each other who shall have the priest for this purpose. The reverend gentleman before referred to is one who believes that if these labourers can be made good Irishmen there is a better hope of keeping them good Catholics. He, therefore, used to get a dozen copies of one or more of the national newspapers for each Sunday and leave them for as many farm houses, and he was always delighted to hear how intelligently the men discussed the contents on the following Sunday. The self-denial some of these poor fellows exhibit in hoarding up their earnings to send home to their families is heroic. The settled Irish population is by no means so great in the Lincolnshire towns as formerly. During the harvesting and potato-digging many slept in the barns, which enabled them to save their lodging money. In the towns there were lodging-houses which were often kept by Irishmen, and mostly used by their fellow-countrymen passing through, as well as by those working in the immediate district within a convenient radius. One street in Boston, North Street, was formerly nearly all lodging-houses of the kind named. The Irish are now nearly all gone. Our people are tolerably numerous in the city of Lincoln, and there are small colonies at Louth and Grantham. In Gainsboro town the Irish are but a handful, but are more numerous in the villages of Crowle, Eastoft, and Luddington, in the same Parliamentary division. It is in remote places like these that you come across relics of the great Famine in the persons of Irishmen, chiefly agricultural labourers, who have been here forty years or more. Of course, as might be expected, in some cases this long absence has sadly deteriorated the character of the people, but in the main the Lincolnshire Irish, in the second and third generation, many of them, are as sound at heart as if they had just left Ireland. In fact they have been treading in the footsteps of the Irish monks who, more than a thousand years ago, traversed these very spots to convert the East Anglians. The Venerable Bede tells how the Irish St Fursey built a monastery in East Anglia ; the parallel case is that of the few Irish working-men of Grimsby, who clubbed together their hard-earned money to bring from Hull, the nearest place where a Catholic church already existed, a priest to administer the sacraments to them and their families. The good Irishmen of Grimsby can show you to-day the room in which, not so very long ago, Mass was celebrated. The next step was the erection of a small iron chapel, which in its turn has given place to the handsome church of St Mary at Holme Hill. By far the largest body of the Irish of Lincolnshire are to be found in Grimsby. Some are employed at the deep sea fisheries, for which the place is famous. It is said that a number of the Catholic fisher-boys have been known to lose their Faith. It need scarcely be said that those lost to creed are generally lost to nationality also.

Many instances can be given in this and the neighbouring counties of the sacrifices made by men in humble circumstances, to obtain for themselves the ministrations of religion. The Irish drovers attending the cattle markets in various places are also frequently generous contributors. The Catholic Chapel at Huntingdon was built, and has been sustained by, the Irish drovers attending St Ives market, and they have been equally generous in other places.

The Midlands—Manufacturing and Mining.

Under this head it is only right that the first place should be given to the great city of Birmingham, the capital of the Midlands.

A sketch of the history of the Irish there, and of their struggles for creed and country, has already been given. This will be a favourable opportunity for reviewing their position now as compared with what it was, as described by A. M. Sullivan, when an unknown young man on the staff of the *Nation*, in May 1856.

A great change has taken place.

The Irish-born had diminished from 9341 in 1851, to 7086 in 1881, and, so long as there is no Irish famine to keep up the supply, are likely to still further diminish, owing to the gradual dying out of the original immigrants.

There has been an increase, no doubt, in those of Irish extraction; though this is not so great as might be expected, owing to so many having gone to other parts of England and to America. The hod-carrier, spoken of by Mr Sullivan, and still later by Father Sherlock, is not altogether extinct. His sons will be found among the artizans of Birmingham, and making fair progress in various other occupations. His daughters still find employment in the manufacture of the multifarious articles fashioned from brass, iron, and other materials, for which Birmingham is world-famed. There are few places where the Irish are more intermixed and intermarried into the general population than in Birmingham. London is the nearest approach to it. This is in striking contrast to Liverpool, Manchester, and other north-country towns, where they are more homogeneous, and but rarely marry outside their own creed and nationality. As a consequence, as Father Sherlock can tell you, there is not among our people in Birmingham, and the Midlands generally, that warmth of feeling he found here forty, or even twenty years ago; though no one can doubt but that, if the occasion demanded it, they would rally to the defence of their homes and their churches and convents as heroically as they did in 1867. Be that as it may, Father Sherlock is as dearly beloved by the present generation as he ever was by the exiles to whom, in his younger days, he ministered in their cherished native tongue; while he still regards them as a father would his children.

This intermixture of Celt and Saxon is, in the Midlands, somewhat perplexing in political matters. Take up a Register of Voters in Liverpool, and any person with a fair knowledge of Irish names could tick off with tolerable certainty nine-tenths of them. In Birmingham, he will frequently find himself deceived, for it is no uncommon thing to come across people bearing such names as Butler, Riley, Crowley, Larkin, Burke, Gorman, &c., who are neither Irish nor Catholics. Some years since they were not so ready to admit it, but if you enquire closely now, as a keen politician only can, you will find there is an Irishman in the pedigree—either father, grandfather, or great-grandfather; and even further back than that. In fact, the Irish have

been steadily coming to Birmingham for over a hundred
years. Though they have to a great extent been gradually
merging into the general population, so that in some cases
there is little trace of them left but the old Irish name, or
some Anglicised form of it, they are not all lost to creed or
country. Take the Register of Voters of one of the seven
Parliamentary divisions of the town, and let a stranger go
through it and pick out the Irish names. He will at once
conclude there is some exaggeration in the estimates he has
heard of the Catholic and Irish population. But let him
take it to one of the priests or zealous school teachers, and
it will be found that the number of available votes is much
larger than would appear. To begin with, there are the
numerous families of Smiths, Whites, Browns, and other
names of that class, who may be of any nationality, and of
whom a proportion will be found to be Irish—the Christian
names often being a good means of distinguishing them.
Then there are many more of purely Irish blood, not distinguishable by their names. Lastly, you have the English
names, brought in by an English father or grandfather,
married to a thorough-going Irishwoman, who has transmitted to her descendants the faith of St Patrick, and sometimes made them "more Irish than the Irish themselves"—
at all events they can be depended upon to go with their
Irish kindred in a Parliamentary or School Board election.

As in London, Liverpool, and elsewhere, there has been
a great change within the last few years in the location of
the Irish of Birmingham. This has been caused by railway
extension and street improvements in the centre of the town.
A large Irish population was displaced by the making of
Corporation Street and the extension of New Street station.
As a consequence they are now more dispersed than formerly. This, on the whole, has been an improvement, as
regards their personal comfort, though it may have somewhat lessened their political power in some wards.

As Birmingham is justly regarded as the capital of the
Midlands, let us, while dealing with the locality, take a
glance at our position in the surrounding district. Here the
most important town of what is termed the " Black Country "
is Wolverhampton. The revival of religion seems to have

commenced here considerably earlier than in Birmingham. Cardinal Manning, who takes a special delight in tracing the history of the Church in the various parts of England from the penal days until our own times, made some researches here. In a visit he paid to Wolverhampton, to be present at the reopening of St Peter's and St Paul's Church, North Street, he in his sermon gave some very interesting reminiscences of the building. It had been, he said, one of the oldest Catholic places of worship in the neighbourhood, Wolverhampton having been in former times the centre of Catholicity for a very considerable district. They were not aware of the exact date of its erection, but as early as 1725 a chapel existed within the building known as "Gifford House." In 1745 the chapel was enlarged, and in 1826 the building was increased, he said, to its present size. The cardinal on the same occasion uncovered a fine mural brass, placed nearly over the tomb of Dr Milner. In doing so he gave some interesting details of the life of the great controversialist, who was Bishop of Castabala, and Vicar Apostolic of the midland district of England, and resided in North Street from the time of his consecration in 1803 until he died in 1826. The Irish here, about thirty years ago, were described by the Rev. Father Hall, of St Patrick's, as, with few exceptions, earning their living by manual labour, some working in the coal pits, some in the foundries, and others as bricklayers' labourers.

There is undoubtedly a great decrease in the Irish population of the district. In Wolverhampton the Irish-born, who were 3491 in 1851, were but 1687 in 1881. After thirty years the survivors out of a given number of people would not be very much greater than this, but the new comers ought to count for a considerable number. The diminution in some of the other towns of the district has been considerably greater than in Wolverhampton, particularly in Bilston and Darlaston, not simply in the Irish-born, among whom you but seldom now hear their native tongue, but also in their descendants.

Perhaps the most graphic description we have of the "Black Country" is from the pen of A. M. Sullivan, who visited the district in 1856. This was but a few years after the rush of our people into England to escape from the Famine. Most of those, therefore, he found at this time were Irish-born. Speaking of them in parts of Darlaston, Oldbury, and Wednesbury, he says—"The Gaelic tongue is now more often heard than the language in which Thor and Woden were praised and glorified." At this time they had become numerous in the district, and their employment was of the most rude, laborious, and unhealthy kind. In fact, he says—"It is lives that are bought and sold in the furnaces and forges of South Staffordshire." He describes the district around Wednesbury, with its "mounds of fire and sheets of flame, with a forest of stacks belching out smoke." Here there was at the time a population of 15,000, of whom he estimated that probably one-fourth were Irish. In describing the part of the town inhabited by the Irish, he says—"In very many of the houses not one of the women could speak English, and I doubt that in a single house the Irish was not the prevalent language." It will be remembered how Father Sherlock was sent to minister to the Irish of Bilston, one of these Black Country towns, because he could hear their confessions in their native tongue.

Mr Sullivan describes the terrible ordeal our people passed through in these early days of their appearance in South Staffordshire, and how the English miners "rose up against them and tried to expel them by fire and sword. Many were," he says, "killed, many were murdered in the works at night of whom no word was ever heard or trace ever found." His informant said—"If we went into a public-house to drink, and that an Englishman came in, we were struck dumb; if he asked for our pipe and didn't get it, he'd pull it out of our mouth. We dare say nothing, for there was neither law nor justice for an Irishman. Many changed their names. We got reckless, too, and used to drink and fight and riot, and would have gone wild and savage outright if it wasn't the mercy of God sent us a priest."

Visiting West Bromwich and Oldbury, he says he "found the Irish employed at laborious tasks that required great physical strength more than skill, such as charging and cleaning out the blast furnaces, and removing the slag.

Having," he continued, "seen the Irish in their homes, I was anxious to see them at their work. Threading my way through smouldering heaps of ironstone, undergoing the process of roasting, and coal being converted into coke, I reached a gateway, in which were lying in all directions piles of pig iron, and masses of metal of every shape and size. A constant roar, as of a hurricane through the shrouds of a frigate, only louder by a hundred times, filled the air to the utter absorption at times of the hundred other noises that assailed the tympanum. On entering the precincts, my profane curiosity changed into awe and wonder. I found myself about to witness a marvellous event—one of King Vulcan's revels! That great, ponderous vat, eighty feet high, belted and ribbed with iron bands as closely as the network of a balloon—that mighty cauldron was about to be tapped; iron was about to run like wine! See how the imps of the iron god prepare for the flow of the liquid fire; through smoke and dust and darkness they flit about naked, their limbs and muscles strong as the metal girders that brace and bind the roof above them. All seems to be ordered by gesture; no voices may be heard here save those raised in the grand chorus which ever and anon swells into thunder on the ear, now sinking, now rising, now allowing the ringing sound of the cold metal, or the heavy blow of the weighty sledges to be for a moment distinguished amidst the thorough bass of the awful roar that stunned the visitor on entering. This proceeds from the powerful steam-bellows —the caged Boreas—that blows the furnace. At every gust the very ground seems to quake and tremble. It takes a little time to acquire confidence and composure in such a scene as this. And now a bustle is observed in the group standing near the surface: a canal has been cut leading to a pit dug in the ground. One of the firemen strikes, with his iron pole, at the base of the furnace wall, a few strokes, and a glare bursts on the faces of the group, and a fiery fluid rushes through the canal, and deposits in the pit. This, however, is not the stream—this is not the libation that is to flow for the Fire King. In a little while the deposit cools, and we discover that it is only the scum or dross—called "slag," that is being drawn off from the metal in the furnace. When it has flowed for ten or twelve minutes a movement is perceptible among the firemen, indicating that something of importance is about to take place. One or two of them run along by the canal that leads to the "furrows," throw themselves on their knees, pat with their hands and smoothen the sides, or dust out the bottom of it most carefully, which done, they take their stand at its head, close to the huge vat, and now—now—shower the blows of their weapons at its base; again and again, when—a shout of horror and dismay bursts from your lips, as you see a fountain of liquid fire dash out almost in their faces; as it sweeps along the canal it fills the whole space, to a distance of twenty yards, with a scorching glow, white, sparkling, and dazzling, quite painful to the sight, and yet these wondrous beings, calm and undismayed, walk by it, play with it, all but handle it and feel it. One can scarcely credit that it is metal he sees there flowing in a stream with ripples and waves, and even spray rising on its surface; a glance at the spot to which it is flowing and we perceive that the furrows are nearly all filled with the molten iron thus cast into "pigs," the canal which fed them being technically called the "sow." When the metal has all run out the opening through which it flowed is once more securely blocked up with fireproof material, and the furnace again charged. I ascended to the platform from whence this operation is performed, and watched half a dozen brave Connaughtmen at the task. The furnace is a circular tower about eighty feet high and thirty feet diameter at the base, tapering to about fifteen or twenty feet at the top; within some ten feet or so of which are large openings through which the charge is shot. The "charge" consists of fixed proportions of coal, coke, limestone, and ironstone: the latter having already been subjected to the process of "roasting." The mass is fired and —in a hot blast furnace—burns twelve hours before tapping, by which time the molten metal has settled at the bottom. In cold blast furnaces twice the time is needed; in the former the air which is blown into it passed through red-hot pipes and entered the furnace at a heat sufficient to melt lead by one puff of its fiery breath.

"Rain was pouring heavily as I held converse with these men on the platform, yet they wore but little clothing, and from this little, saturated and dripping, the heat of the furnaces was driving a dense cloud of steam. In the snows and sleets of December, mid biting frosts and drenching rains, they are in this way exposed to the sudden and extreme changes of temperature—they are at the same moment being drenched and scorched, broiled and frozen; the strongest constitution sinks under subjection to this fearful trial, and the average duration of life, consequently, here is appallingly brief. Accidents, too, are numerous and of constant occurrence."

Speaking of the sympathy of Father Revell with his Irish flock at Wednesbury, and the want of such he found in other priests, Mr Sullivan says—"It is not always that the claims of a common faith ensure for our people from an English born clergyman that forbearance for their peculiarities, that merging of the national antipathy in the religious accord which alone can reconcile him to a congregation of Celts."

Since Mr Sullivan visited the Black Country, and so lovingly traced the footsteps of his poor fellow-countrymen, there has been a great change in the industries he studied so closely.

At Oldbury, one of the places he visited, there has been even more tragic waste of Irish flesh and blood than anything he saw. Those employed at the copper works there or elsewhere may commence the work fine, stalwart, young men, full of life, of powerful bone, and with sinews like iron —but they only last a few years. They have good wages, but no wages could repay their suffering. After a time their teeth become destroyed, they have bleeding at the nose, and other symptoms of arsenical poisoning. In comparatively a few years they become prematurely aged and mere wrecks of humanity. When unable to do the work required they are not discharged, but set at jobs in the yard and kept in employment while they live, which is not very long. It is circumstances like this and those described by Mr Sullivan that, no doubt, account for what one sees with sorrowful eyes in some places in this country—the Irish apparently melting away like a snow wreath.

It will be found that whatever diminution there has been in the Irish population in some places in the district has chiefly arisen from the fact that, when a slackness of trade arises, the Irish are generally the first to feel the pinch, and go elsewhere in search of employment. From this cause you will find them more evenly diffused throughout Great Britain than they ever were before; with less of that gravitation towards certain large centres and the formation of Irish colonies than there used to be. You lose sight of a man from Wednesbury, or Tipton, or Bilston, and you will perhaps pick him up at Dowlais, Middlesboro', or Wigan, and *vice versa.* They go further afield if they can, and the young Irishman, by birth or descent, who can save a few pounds, prefers to make his way to America, so that many of those who have left the British iron-working districts can now be found at Cleveland and other such places in the United States.

The Irish and their descendants are still, as they were in Mr Sullivan's time, chiefly engaged in the more laborious occupations, not only as being best fitted for them by their superior physique, but also from necessity. Of course a fair proportion are making their way in other pursuits, but the bulk have not yet found their way into the ranks of skilled labour. You still find them in the works where ships' cables and other chains and heavy tackle of every kind are made, and in the blast furnaces. By day the Black Country looks cheerless and blighted, but it has a sort of grandeur at night, when the flames leap up through the throats of the furnace chimneys and cast a lurid glare on the blasted landscape around. Inside the works the effect is equally weird and striking, and it might easily have been from one of these Black Country interiors that Samuel Ferguson drew his picture when he wrote the "Forging of the Anchor."

When from slackness of trade a furnace fire goes out it may be the cause of a certain number of Irish leaving the district to seek work elsewhere. At home in Ireland they cling with desperate tenacity to their bit of land, but here they have nothing to cling to. It is the wretchedly poor English who can be best compared to the Irish peasant at home with his single industry—the land. It was among these, rather than among the Irish, who "would not stay to starve," as they would tell you, that the most appalling distress prevailed during the period of depression this country passed through a few years ago. And yet they clung to their miserable lot, just as they used to do in Ireland, as if it were a privilege to be allowed to live. The most wretched place in the Black Country during the time of distress was Cradley Heath, one of the centres where dog, and harness, and other small chains, and also horse shoes are made. The introduction of machinery has lessened the demand for most kinds of nails made by hand. Not far from the Black Country, which is chiefly in Staffordshire, and over the Worcestershire border, in the part nearest to Cradley Heath, the production of hand made nails is an industry extensively carried on in and around Halesowen and Bromsgrove. Here, unlike the adjoining part of Staffordshire, the face of Nature has not suffered from the hand of man. Indeed, there are spots among the Lickey and Hagley Hills that would recall some of the most charming scenes in Wicklow.

In the main street of Bromsgrove the framed-work and gabled houses, with their low ceilings and heavy beams, have that old-world look you so often find in the rural districts of Warwick, Worcester, and Stafford; while, both here and at Halesowen, the cottages—some detached, others built in rows—have a neat appearance. Close to each of these is the miniature forge, where the whole family—father, mother, and children—are literally "busy as nailors." Listening to the hammers ringing briskly on the anvils one feels a wish that such music could be heard among our Irish hills and vales—but the picture is only fair to the outside view. During the worst period of depression among the Cradley Heath nail and chain makers in 1886, much public attention was directed to their position. If you entered one of these little forges and spoke to "the free-born Englishman" there, you would find that in many cases the lot of the African slave was preferable to his. A young woman, the wife or daughter it might be of one of these British nail-makers, whose arms, lean and sinewy, like a man's, showed that the hammer and not the needle was the instrument she plied for her daily bread, had to make 1 cwt. of chain (composed of 3600 links) for four shillings, and to accomplish this it took about a week of ordinary working days. A man at the same description of work earned about seven shillings, and a boy about four or five shillings. But the worm turns at last, and some three thousand of these poor creatures went out on strike for a higher rate of pay. In a short time they were starving. A touching incident occurred at one of the meetings of the strikers. Some of the women had their infants with them, and during one of the speeches a baby cried so incessantly that its mother was asked to take it out. The poor woman, anxious to remain, pleaded—" Maister, her's hungry. Her wouldn't cry if her weren't clemmed, but I've only had one crust in three days, and my milk is goin' away." There was dead silence in the meeting and strong men around wept like children. Facts like these show, and year by year it has been becoming more evident, that there is an " English question " arising, which can only be successfully dealt with by getting the " Irish question " out of the way ; and statesmanlike and really patriotic Englishmen are beginning to see this.

The Irish in Worcestershire are chiefly in Dudley—which being almost surrounded by Staffordshire, may be classed among the Black Country towns—the city of Worcester, and Kidderminster. In Dudley they are fewer in number than formerly, a large number having left during the depression in the iron trade. Most of the Irish labouring population have gone from Worcester. There used to be a colony in Dolday, in that city, but you find few there now. They have mostly gone to the larger towns, where they have a better chance of getting employment for the younger generation, or to America. This, as may be noticed in connection with other places, applies to all the smaller towns in the agricultural districts. The Irish who remain are mostly in a tolerably good position, and engaged in various occupations. The staple trade of Kidderminster is carpet making. Some of our younger people are now employed at it, but on the whole there are but few Irish in the manufactories of the town. They are mostly agricultural and other labourers, with a few mechanics and shopkeepers. Many years ago, when the Irish woollen industry was failing, a considerable number of wool-combers came over and settled in Kidderminster. There are few traces of them now. You find occasional descendants of these men, but most of them drifted into the Yorkshire towns, and, indeed, in Leeds and Bradford you still come across some of the old men or their children, who have, as a rule, good employment. Another centre in Worcestershire where our country people are to be found is Oldbury, near Birmingham. As at Widnes, Flint, Silvertown, and elsewhere, they are chiefly employed at the chemical works. The iron works also employ a considerable number.

Crossing back into South Staffordshire, we find them about Cannock Chase, working at the coal pits, many of them varying this in the slack time in the summer by field work. In Walsall, just on the borders of the Black Country, the Irish, once very numerous, are diminishing. They get to America if they can, and also to the larger towns, and, as in Birmingham, some of those who remain get lost sight of in a generation or two through intermarriages. That there must be a serious diminution in Walsall, not merely among the Irish-born, which might naturally be expected, but among those of Irish extraction, is evident from the fact that there are now only about half the Catholic baptisms that there were some thirty years ago. Our people are mostly employed at the iron works, and as labourers of various kinds. Some few are engaged in the staple trade of the place—saddlery, and the manufacture of bridles, bits, shoemakers' awls, tacks for boots, and such like articles. About Lichfield, Tamworth, and Rugeley, most of the Irish are agricultural labourers. There is a small settled population, but most only come for the season each year from Ireland, and return with the little hoards they have accumulated. At Burton a number of Irishmen are employed at the breweries. At Leek we have an interesting example of the blighting effect of the Union upon Irish industries. The staple trade is silk spinning and weaving, handlooms being employed for the production of the wider breadths of silk. The Irish are not numerous but are as sterling a body as you will find anywhere. Most of them are silk workers who have never seen Ireland, and some are the sons or grandsons of Irish artizans in the same trade, who were forced through want of employment to leave their country. One family of Irish descent have come well to the front in Leek. They have a large and flourishing silk factory, and are among the most respected inhabitants of the place. A number of our fellow-countrymen in Stafford and Stone are engaged in the staple industries of these places—boot and shoe making. It cannot but be noticed that shoemaking and tailoring are the only trades in which, up to the last few years, you found any considerable number of Irish artizans in this country. Perhaps the most compact and numerous body of Irish, not merely in Staffordshire, but in the whole of the Midlands, are to be found in the cluster of North Staffordshire towns and villages known as "The Potteries," from the chief industry of the district. The principal places are Newcastle, Hanley, Stoke, Longton, Burslem, and Tunstall. They lie so closely together as almost to form one town. Our people here marry more among themselves and are more homogeneous than elsewhere in the Midlands; in fact they are more like you find them in the Lancashire towns, resembling them also in their zeal for the national cause. They do not put the young people to trades as often as they might. There are many girls of Irish parentage among the cleverest at the various branches of pottery production, but, too often, instead of the boys being put to this or some other trade, they are sent to work at the coal pits, probably because they can, while still young, earn more in this way than at anything else. You find it the same in many other places. This, with the difficulty which exists in some places of getting trades to put the young people to, is why the Irish so largely swell the ranks of unskilled labour in Great Britain.

Outside of Birmingham the only considerable Irish population to be found in Warwickshire is in Coventry. This ancient city, with its peculiarly tall and tapering spires, and its striking and picturesque streets, is full of historic memories, dating back to a thousand years ago. As is well known, it was famous for its ribbon weaving, but this industry—

though it is still carried on, and there are Irishmen working at it—is now much decayed. Its watch-making industry has also much declined, chiefly through foreign competition. But Coventry, more fortunate than most other towns of its class, has during the last few years developed a new industry which has more than compensated for all the trade it has lost—the manufacture of bicycles and tricycles, and in this, too, Irishmen are to be found engaged. The influx of mechanics into Coventry in connection with this pursuit has a tendency to improve the political atmosphere, for there is no doubt that in the good old times of corruption and bribery the old ribbon weavers of the city had grown to look on their vote as a marketable commodity.

Like most ancient cities, Coventry is full of old charitable foundations, dating back to Catholic times. These have been not only diverted from their original pious objects, but actually turned into sources of corruption. Take, as an example, the Bablake Hospital and School, which was left by a wealthy Coventry draper an endowment of £49, 11s. 7d. a year. Of course all these ancient endowments have enormously increased in value, so it is not surprising to find that the value in this particular case has risen to £1100 per annum. No doubt relief is still given, but it is by no means always to the most deserving, and the education intended for the children of the poor is generally bestowed on those of a class well able to take care of themselves. Then there is a provision made for a " priest to say masses for the souls of the founder, his father, grandfather, and all Christian souls." This was, of course, carried out in the time when Coventry (which literally means " Convent town ") was filled with the churches and religious houses of the Benedictines, Franciscans, Carthusians, and other orders of the church. Sacrilegious hands have been laid upon these holy places, and it is unnecessary to add that from the endowment provided by the pious old draper of Coventry no masses are now said for his soul. However, the "black friars" are back again in the old city, and, sustained by the generous offerings of the ever-faithful Irish people and the English converts they are making day by day, he is still remembered in their prayers. Nevertheless, in simple justice, the community of English Benedictines, who have their noble church (dedicated to St Osburg) and priory, with schools attached, in Hill Street, a few hundred yards off, are surely the rightful heirs and administrators of this fund. At the opening of this fine edifice in 1845, which, if not so spacious, vies in beauty with those two noble fanes (the one dedicated to the Holy Trinity and the other to St Michael) which, standing side by side, are to-day the chief glory of Coventry, High Mass was sung by the famous Dr (afterwards Cardinal) Wiseman, a man of true Celtic blood and genius. This church replaced an older one built on the same site as far back as 1807. The Irish colony here is of old establishment, judging from the names of the freemen's roll, and what one hears of their fathers before them. That some Irish were here a century ago is evident from the fact that there still stands in Little Park Street a building with a cross carved on the wall, which at the end of the last century was known as the " Mass House."

The Irish vote, which numbers about 200, has generally been able to determine the result of the Parliamentary elections. In 1880 they supported the Liberals, whose candidate was returned. In 1885, in accordance with the mandate from their leaders, their votes secured the election of a Conservative. At the General Election of 1886, when Mr Gladstone was defeated, chiefly by Liberal abstentions, the Irish vote failed to secure the return of his candidate, but, at the bye-election of 1887, Coventry, by its aid, became another wave in the "flowing tide " of the " Grand Old Man."

The Irish in Derbyshire are tolerably numerous, a large proportion finding employment as pitmen or coal workers all along the eastern portion of the county from the Yorkshire border to Leicestershire. In and around Eckington, Whittington, Staveley, Chesterfield (which has a large Irish population), Clay Cross, and Ilkeston, you find them numerous, though, in some places, considerably less so than formerly. The Midland Railway works being in Derby, are a considerable source of settled employment to the population, among whom the Irish are tolerably numerous, and fairly to the front in the trade of the place. Besides the places mentioned, the only other considerable body of our people are in the High Peak division of Derbyshire, where you find them in tolerably comfortable circumstances—chiefly in Glossop and Hadfield, which, like the adjoining places in Lancashire and Cheshire, are cotton manufacturing towns.

The bulk of the Irish of Nottinghamshire are in Nottingham town, which gives its name to the Catholic diocese. The bishop, Dr Bagshawe, is a firm friend of our cause. Our countrymen, who are tolerably numerous, are engaged in a variety of occupations, including the staple manufacture of the place, which is lace making. Outside Nottingham itself they mostly work at the collieries, and are to be found chiefly in or about Bulwell, Hucknall, Long Eaton, Eastwood, Mansfield, Newark, Retford, and Worksop. In some of these Catholic Missions our poor working people are deserving of all praise for the way they tax themselves to keep their little chapels and schools going. The priests also have hard times of it in trying to serve isolated congregations, often many miles distant from each other.

The town of Leicester has the chief Irish population of the county of the same name. The staple industry is boot and shoe making, a branch of trade in which Irishmen are tolerably numerous in most places. Outside Leicester you find an Irish population in the colliery village of Whitwick, which is not far from the famous Abbey of Mount St Bernard. There are also small congregations of them at Loughboro and Hinckley.

Northampton, like Leicester, is famous for its boot and shoe manufactories, and here, too, the Irish are engaged in this as well as other occupations; a satisfactory proportion of them filling good positions. They are not so numerous here as formerly.

LANCASHIRE.

Although we have now dealt with the Irish in about three-fourths of the area of England and the whole of Wales, we have still left untouched about two-thirds of their number—being those located in the counties north of the Mersey and Humber. Of these, Lancashire contains more than one-third of the Irish in England, having, according to the Census of 1881, 212,350 Irish-born. This means a population of purely Irish blood of about half a million.

Perhaps the largest proportion to be found in any one place is in Bootle, where the Catholic population is about 51 per cent. of the whole. There is much the same proportion in Widnes.

Let us now glance in detail at their condition in the various parts of Lancashire, beginning with the northern portion, where they are the least numerous.

In most parts of Great Britain you can form an estimate of the Irish population by the number of Catholics, and *vice versa*. In some districts of Lancashire this does not apply, as there are in certain places a considerable number of native English Catholics.

In North Lancashire, comprising the Parliamentary divisions of Lonsdale, Blackpool, Lancaster, and Chorley, there are, outside of Preston and Barrow, nearly 30,000 Catholics, of whom, probably, one-third are Irish. These are principally in the towns. Barrow-in-Furness is one of those rising places which always attract our people. In it there are about 5000 Catholics, chiefly Irish, of whom over 500 are voters. They are generally employed in connection with the iron-works and ship-building. You find them also at Ulverston and Dalton. Preston (Priest town) is the chief centre of English Catholicity, the various congregations numbering over 30,000. About a third of these are Irish. The cotton factories employ a great number of them. In Chorley it is the same, some also being agricultural labourers. About Standish they are mostly colliers.

North-east Lancashire is more Irish than North Lancashire. In it are the following Parliamentary divisions:— Darwen, Clitheroe, Accrington, and Rossendale. The Catholic population, including the boroughs of Blackburn and Burnley, is over 40,000, chiefly Irish, and employed in the cotton factories and other industries. In Rossendale division is the town of Haslingden, the scene of Michael Davitt's early life, already referred to in connection with the Fenian movement.

Coming to South-east Lancashire, you find the Irish

population increasing in density. There are over 150,000 Catholics, the great bulk being Irish. In the rural parts they are mostly employed at the collieries, and in the towns at the cotton factories and multifarious other occupations. At Horwich, in the West Houghton Parliamentary division, there has been a rapid increase, owing to the establishing of the works of the Lancashire and Yorkshire Railway there. The chief manufacturing towns are Manchester and Salford; Bolton, which has a numerous, and, on the whole, thriving Irish population; Oldham, which may almost be said to be a continuation of Manchester; Rochdale, Bury, and Ashton, —memorable for the No-Popery riots.

Taking Manchester and Salford to be one town—which they practically are—they come after London, Liverpool, and Glasgow in extent of Irish population. The Census shows the Irish-born in 1881 to have been 38,578. But as the enumeration of the various congregations gives a Catholic population of about 90,000, we may reckon that fully 80,000 of these are Irish either by birth or extraction.

As these pages have shown, this has always been an active Irish centre, not to speak of the memories that have burned into the Irish heart in connection with the "Manchester Martyrdom" of 1867.

The chief employment is in connection with the cotton factories, and here it may be said of almost all the cotton or woollen manufacturing towns of Lancashire and Yorkshire, that, there being employment for young and old, the position of our people is, as a rule, much better than in places like Liverpool, and some of the seaports and other towns, where it is hard to get employment for the young. A fair number are in trade, although it is quite true, as the Bishop of Salford has said, that one has only to look at the names over the shops, to see how few in proportion to their numbers are those of Catholics—which, practically, means Irish. As Dr Vaughan says, we are well represented in the humbler walks of life, and fairly among the professional classes, but among the middle classes—the traders who possess the solid wealth of the country—we make but a poor figure. The noble churches and schools, built chiefly by the pence of the poor, are a credit to the Irish of Manchester, who are steadily improving in their social and political status, and, owing to better organisation, acquiring positions on the various public bodies. They are pretty well spread all over Manchester and Salford, but are most numerous in the North Parliamentary Division, particularly in St Michael's Ward.

North-east and South-east Lancashire form the Catholic diocese of Salford. From the Diocesan Almanac of a recent date and other sources we learn that there were at that time a considerable number of Catholic public officials, including two Deputy Lieutenants of the County, one County and eight Borough Magistrates, ten Town Councillors, seven Members of Local Boards, eight Members of Boards of Guardians, and fifteen Members of School Boards. Of these, one Magistrate, five Town Councillors, two Members of Local Boards, two Members of Boards of Guardians, and nine Members of School Boards were Irishmen.

South-west Lancashire contains, according to a recent Church census of the diocese of Liverpool, about a quarter of a million of Catholics, fully nine-tenths of these being Irish by birth or blood. The English Catholics, as a rule, are descended from ancestors who kept the Faith through all the horrors of the penal days. In two villages—Little Crosby and Ince Blundell—the whole of the people are Catholics. These are on the estates of two branches of the Blundell family, who have been settled here since the time of the Norman Conquest, and have held on, through every vicissitude, to the faith of their fathers.

Bootle is a Parliamentary division of South-west Lancashire, having a large number of Irish in the town itself. They have not the political influence their numbers would give if they were a more settled population. Bootle has developed enormously since such a large proportion of the trade of Liverpool has moved northward here. This has brought with it a large Irish population, mostly employed in connection with the shipping. In the same degree there has been a corresponding diminution in the Irish population of certain parts of Liverpool.

In Widnes Parliamentary division the Irish are most numerous in Widnes town. They are chiefly employed in connection with the chemical works, for which the place is famous. The most noted of these was founded by the Muspratts, a family of Irish extraction. At Garston our people chiefly work at the docks, or as agricultural and other labourers. They are, of course, more numerous in the towns of South-west Lancashire than in the rural parts. Outside of Wigan, St Helens, Leigh, Tyldesley, and other towns there are a considerable number of Irishmen employed at the collieries. In Warrington they have fairly good employment in the cotton factories, and at Wigan also, where, in addition, they work at the blast furnaces. At St Helens you find them engaged at the chemical and glass works, and at various other occupations. In all the Lancashire towns there are a fair share of Irish artisans, though not so many as one would like to see, with a sprinkling of shopkeepers and professional men.

The diocese of Liverpool consists of North and Southwest Lancashire and the Isle of Man. A recent almanac gave the Catholic officials as follows:—one Deputy Lieutenant of the County, seventeen County Magistrates, five County Councillors, thirty-three Town Councillors, twenty-nine Members of Local Boards, forty-eight Poor-Law Guardians, and twenty-eight Members of School Boards. Of these the following are Irishmen:—one County Magistrate, three Borough Magistrates, sixteen Town Councillors, six Members of Local Boards, ten Poor-Law Guardians, and seventeen Members of School Boards. The Irish officials do not, it will be seen, number one-third of the whole of the Catholics. This is not wonderful. The English have for generations—for centuries, indeed, it may be said—been accumulating wealth, while the Irish have, for the most part, been flung naked on these shores to sink or swim. On the whole, therefore, these figures are not altogether unsatisfactory.

Let us, before leaving Lancashire, turn once more to Liverpool, which contains, next to London, the largest population of Irish in any town in Great Britain. They are not scattered about in handfuls, as you find them in the metropolis, but massed together in great numbers. Among them the late A. M. Sullivan used to say he felt as if he were "not out of Ireland at all, but on a piece cut from the old sod itself." Of the Irishmen holding positions in the diocese the following are in the borough of Liverpool itself:—two Magistrates, nine Town Councillors, four Poor-Law Guardians, and four Members of the School Board. Liverpool is the only place in Great Britain able to return a Nationalist to Parliament for one of its seats against all comers. As this is the only constituency in Great Britain in our hands, Mr T. P. O'Connor may be said to represent not merely Scotland Division, nor Liverpool, but the whole of the Irish of England, Scotland, and Wales. Liverpool has furnished no less than eight members of the Irish Parliamentary Party since its formation. It is not without some justification that some consider it the Irish capital of England.

The Irish-born within the old Parliamentary boundary, according to the 1881 Census, were 70,972. At a very moderate estimate, the Irish by birth and descent must number 150,000. The Census is, of course, the only sure ground, but the Catholic Church statistics for the dioceses of Liverpool and Salford may be considered as fairly accurate as regards those known to be Catholics. The Bishop of Liverpool, however, some years ago, informed the present writer that he considered the figures given of the Catholic Church congregations as being under the mark. This can be readily understood. In all large towns there are thousands of people of whom literally nothing is known, and no priest, however laborious and painstaking, can say he has reached all who are or who "ought to be" Catholics in his district. An effort has been made to ascertain the number of Catholics by assuming the baptisms to represent the births, and multiplying these by a certain figure, varying according to circumstances. Every priest, particularly in the large towns, will tell you that this is but an approximation, as there are many, particularly where there are mixed marriages, who do not get their children baptised. Here, then, is missionary work, to bring back all these stray sheep to the fold, whether Catholic or national.

Reference has already been made to the undesirable districts in which many of our people live in some of the larger towns. In Liverpool, in the quarters inhabited almost exclusively by our poorer people, the mortality has been in some years more than twice as great as in other parts where people in better circumstances live. The attempts at improvements, by opening up the insanitary neighbourhoods in Liverpool and other places, have been much impeded by the slowness with which the operations have been carried out. Blocks of houses have been cleared away, and the sites left vacant for years. As a consequence, the people who have been dispossessed, being obliged to be near their employment, have gone into the dwellings that remained, thus making the overcrowding greater than before, and what was intended for a remedy worse, for a time, than the evil.

There has been, however, a vast change for the better in the surroundings of our people, and, indeed, in every other way, so that there is no town in the country in which we have made greater progress than in Liverpool. Irishmen are gradually emerging from the ranks of unskilled labour and becoming more numerous among the artisans, shopkeepers, merchants, and professional classes. Among these latter they have most distinctly made their mark. Among other Irish lawyers of the highest reputation, Sir Charles Russell may be said to have graduated on this circuit. The Irish doctors of Liverpool are also numerous, and the first in their profession.

Notwithstanding this success, however, there is probably also more wretchedness among our people here than anywhere else in the country. But take them at their worst—take the jail statistics that cannot possibly give the whole truth, and take the lying statements of the no-popery orators—and there cannot be a doubt but that the overwhelming mass of the Irish of Liverpool will compare favourably with the people of any town. Intemperance, and the violence begotten of it, which caused Irish names to figure so often in the police courts, are confined to one wretched class; but even amongst them, these are generally their worst offences. You seldom hear of Irishmen in connection with more serious crimes.

It is often a source of wonder why Liverpool, with such a large Irish population, remains, on the whole, so persistently Tory. Reference has already been made to the Irish-Orange element in Liverpool. This, in point of numbers, would

have been insignificant in itself, but that at its head were a
number of bigoted, virulent, and eloquent Irish parsons,
chief amongst whom was Dr M'Neill, a native of the County
Antrim. These raised the no-popery cry on every occasion,
and encouraged their ignorant followers—men of the Belfast
Sandy Row type—to infuse their own venom into their
fellow-workmen. As a consequence you find more of the
bigoted, ignorant, anti-Irish, no-popery type of Toryism in
Liverpool than probably in any other place in Great Britain.
In fact, owing to the contagion brought in by the Irish-
Orangemen, many have had such a spirit developed in them
that whatever party the Irish supported, they would range
themselves on the opposite side.

From time to time we have had in the previous chapters
glimpses of the religious, social, and political life of the Irish
in Liverpool, since they first began to make their homes
here. We have seen them in the penal days of the last
century, and their struggles in the race of life in the first
half of the present century, and how they came like the
rush of a mighty torrent in the terrible famine years. Then
the newcomer considered himself fortunate if he met some
relative or friend, or someone from his own part of the
country, to hold out to him that helping hand which was
seldom withheld; for "over here in England" the characteristic has not been lost that, however poor, they are always
ready to befriend what seems to them a still poorer neighbour. Those who have lived here for some time are glad to
see someone "from their own place," and, amidst the squalor
of an English city, the imaginative Irish Celt—as he listens to
the gossip about the changes, the marriages, and the deaths
that have taken place since he left "home"—for a brief
moment lives once more on the "old sod." Visions of the
little cabin where dwelt those "near and dear" to him, of
the mountain chapel where he worshipped, of a bright-eyed
Irish girl beloved in the golden days of youth, and a thousand
other associations of the past, come flooding back upon his
memory, as he listens to the story of Dan, or Pat, or Bridget,
who "has just come over." It so happens that, from the
very goodness of the Irish heart, the newcomers are frequently drawn into the same miserable mode of life as the

friends who have come before them to England have fallen into. Irish intellect and Irish courage have, in thousands of cases, brought our people to their proper place in the social scale, but it only too often happens that adverse circumstances drive the great bulk of them to the hardest, the most precarious, and the worst paid employments in the English labour market. The Irish of Liverpool frequently show a remarkable aptitude for dealing, which goes to show that, under the fostering care of a native government, ours would develop into a great commercial people. It is often noted that where an Irishman is steady and has got a good wife—for that is more than half the battle—he is frequently able to save enough from his earnings to open a marine store —a business our people seem partial to throughout the country—a coal yard, or a small shop. By degrees he gets on, for, as a rule, our people are more quick-witted in bargaining than even the Jews—the difference being that Moses sticks to all he gets, while Pat's often too generous nature frequently lets go easily what he has won so hardly. There are, however, hard-headed Irishmen too—men who know how to keep what they have earned. So by degrees they get into the higher circles of the commercial world, and of these there are to be seen, among the merchant princes on 'Change, men who either themselves or whose fathers before them commenced life in Liverpool as corn or cotton porters, or even in some humbler or more precarious occupation.

Fifty years ago there were but five Catholic churches in Liverpool. At the time the jail statistics before referred to were published they had increased to over twenty, so that all could not have been so black in Liverpool as it would then appear. Besides the churches, numerous schools and charitable institutions had been built. The erection of these structures, the money for which was chiefly subscribed by Irishmen, proved that there was a considerable amount of wealth among them. At a very moderate calculation, counting the value of the land, and the cost of the structures —many of which from an architectural point of view are really splendid edifices—it is not far off the mark to say that the Catholic churches, schools, and institutions of

Liverpool represent in money value about a quarter of a million pounds sterling. The same, of course, applies to other parts of Great Britain. As an indication of an improvement in the social position of our people, it may be mentioned that where formerly there was not an Irish priest in the town, or, if one, only for a short time, if the names of the clergy be referred to—including that of the bishop, Dr O'Reilly, who is an Irishman—it is evident that about onehalf are either Irish-born or the sons of Irishmen. We may, therefore, not unreasonably draw the conclusion with regard to the latter, at all events, that their fathers had been able to acquire sufficient means to educate them for the Church. It is a remarkable fact that a great number of the Protestant clergy of Liverpool are Irish also. It is regrettable that, as a rule, these have not made it their mission to preach charity and good will amongst men.

YORKSHIRE.

Among the 56,878 Irish-born of Yorkshire—although there may not be so many who have come into prominent notice as in London, Liverpool, and other places—there has been, on the whole, more substantial social progress than in any other part of Great Britain. Though they may have furnished no members to the Irish Parliamentary Party, there is no place where Irish public opinion has been more intelligently directed than in Yorkshire. Our people are as a rule more prosperous than in most places, as in the manufacturing towns there is generally good employment for young and old. There are not, therefore, the same temptations in the way of the young as in places like Liverpool, where, from an early age, many are driven to earn their living by street trading and in the most precarious callings, which but too often unfit them for lives of steady industry.

As a consequence of the more favourable condition of our people in Yorkshire they are better able to help the cause financially. Fortunately they are not only able but willing, so that, with the exception, perhaps, of South Wales, there is no place where, in proportion to the Irish population, more substantial aid is given to the Irish national organisation than in Yorkshire. As might be expected, too, they are well organised.

In Leeds, Bradford, Halifax, Huddersfield, Wakefield, Keighley, Skipton, Dewsbury, and a number of other towns, the Irish are largely employed in the woollen manufacture—the staple trade of Yorkshire. For several generations, and long before the Irish Famine drove our people here in such vast numbers, they have been so engaged; in many cases in consequence of so many Irish skilled workmen having had to come here for employment on the decline of the woollen trade which followed the Union. Reference has already been made to this in connection with the Irish wool-combers, who first settled in Kidderminster and afterwards made their way to the woollen manufacturing towns of Yorkshire. Many Irishmen, through sheer force of ability and integrity, have attained prominent positions. We have seen, in this history, the numerous disadvantages our people have had to contend against, merely in struggling for the right to live. As a consequence they have often been kept down in the social scale; but speak to any fair-minded manager in a Yorkshire woollen mill, and he will tell you that the Irish, with equal opportunities, are more than able to hold their own against any others: for they have brains and adaptability. Besides the skilled workmen who came to Yorkshire in the first half of the present century, there are those who came, perhaps, as harvestmen or drovers, and who, finding employment, settled here. Their children, as a matter of course, fell into the industries of the district. They could the more readily do this because in the routine work of a large mill it is but comparatively few who can be called highly skilled workmen. The great bulk are but as cogs in a big wheel, or parts of a huge piece of machinery. This is the tendency of the times, and in every branch of trade you see the most minute subdivision of labour. This makes it all the easier for a man with brains and opportunities to rise, and a fair proportion of our people do so.

One of the Yorkshire towns is as noted for its hardware as most of the rest are for their woollens. For many

centuries the cutlery of Sheffield has been famous. In 1859
there was a presentation of cutlery to the distinguished Irish
patriot, William Smith O'Brien, by the Irishmen of Sheffield,
when he visited that town. There are but few Irish
engaged in the staple manufacture. Many girls of Irish
extraction are employed at the silver and silver-plating work.
Though as a rule the bulk of our people are labourers at
the iron-works, at iron plate making, and in other departments, a fair proportion of them are mechanics, and there
are a considerable number in good positions as manufacturers and otherwise. The most Irish quarter in Sheffield
is about the centre of the town, in the group of streets
known as "The Crofts." In one of these—Hawley Croft—
they are almost all Irish, and, in themselves, their children,
and their homes, have all the appearance of a thriving,
steady-going population.

Hull has a considerable Irish population, and being a
noted seaport, you meet here a class such as are to be seen
along the Thames at the east end of London, in Liverpool
and Cardiff, where such a large number are employed as
dock labourers. A great many are, however, skilled
artizans, such as fitters, boilermakers, platers, riveters, and
in other occupations connected with iron shipbuilding. In
fact the Irish here put their children to trades wherever
they can, although the temptation to send a strong young
fellow, sixteen or eighteen years old, to work at the docks
and earn from a pound to thirty shillings a week—rather
than as apprentice to a trade and only to earn a few
shillings—is sometimes irresistible.

In the ancient city of York, with its numerous memories,
so interesting to Irishmen and Catholics, though there are a
few of our fellow-countrymen in fairly good positions, the
bulk are agricultural and other labourers.

On the restoration of the English Catholic Hierarchy the
whole of Yorkshire was formed into the diocese of Beverley.
Not long afterwards it became necessary to make this into
two dioceses—Leeds and Middlesboro. It was natural that
Leeds, as the most important town in Yorkshire, should be
chosen as one See when the division had to be made.
Middlesboro was no doubt chosen as the other, not only

from its geographical position but also on account of the Catholic population having become so numerous through the extraordinary development in the iron trade of the district. The bishop, the Right Rev. Dr Lacy, is an Irishman, born in Navan. The Catholics are nearly all Irish, and chiefly employed at the blast furnaces, at the docks, and other industries of the place. We have seen how the Irish are often the first to move whenever there is a depression in trade, so that you find here a good number who formerly lived in the Black Country, at Dowlais, and other seats of the iron-working industry.

Though woollen is the chief trade of Yorkshire other industries flourish. Thus in Keighley it is chiefly the Irish women and girls who work in the mills. A large proportion of the men are at the iron-works, and, in general, the young people are being put to trades of various kinds. In Wakefield, also, the women and the young are employed at the mills, while the chief part of the men work at the collieries and blast furnaces outside the town.

Throughout Yorkshire a considerable number of Irishmen have attained fair positions in trade. The professions are best represented by the able, generally patriotic, and, one is bound to add, ubiquitous Irish doctor.

There are about eighty Catholic churches and chapels in the diocese of Leeds, and over fifty in Middlesboro, with numerous schools, convents, and religious institutions—all well supported. It would be ungenerous, in this connection, not to pay a high tribute to the English Catholics of noble family, who, through the darkest days of persecution, not only afforded shelter to the hunted priest, but the means of obtaining the ministrations of religion to their humbler brethren. There is more than one Catholic place of worship in Yorkshire dating from previous to the "Reformation," and from the seventeenth century—just previous to the expulsion of the last Catholic King, James II.; about a score founded in the last century, with about a dozen erected in the present century—previous to Catholic emancipation. While every justice must be done to the noble native Catholics who kept the lamp of faith alight, it must also be said that the history of the Yorkshire missions, for the last hundred years, is chiefly a record of self sacrifice made by Irishmen, mostly in humble positions; and to them principally is due the present flourishing condition of religion in the county.

NORTHUMBERLAND, DURHAM, CUMBERLAND, AND WESTMORELAND.

A large proportion of the Irish in the four most northern counties of England are engaged in mining pursuits. The Irish-born number, according to the Census of 1881, 63,717. Every national movement, from that of O'Connell to the Irish National League, has found in them the most ardent and generous supporters. They are chiefly from the north of Ireland, including, as might be expected, a small proportion of Orangemen; but a considerable number hail from the province of Connaught.

Newcastle-on-Tyne is the chief Irish centre, and here our countrymen have made satisfactory progress, a fair number having attained to good social and public positions. Several of them who came here as packmen are now among the foremost citizens of the place. Although as elsewhere the Irish are chiefly labourers, a fair proportion are artizans—chiefly in connection with shipbuilding, for which the Tyne is famous. Along its banks, north and south, and on its bosom you see on all sides unmistakable signs of the industry and enterprise which have created the prosperity of the district. All along the river-side you find our people engaged at the shipbuilding, iron-works, chemical works, and other industries.

Throughout Durham they are mostly engaged at the coal pits, the cinder ovens where the coal is converted into coke, and the iron-works. In many places they live in small one-storied cottages built by their employers, just as in similar districts in Wales and Scotland. Many of them were victims of evictions at home in Ireland. A recent strike at New Silksworth showed them that this was a process not entirely unknown on this side of the Channel. The colliery owner was the Marquis of Londonderry, and on his behalf the work people with whom he had the dispute were evicted from their dwellings. It was singular that, when the first cottage was broken into and the furniture ejected, the first article brought out was a picture of Robert Emmet, and the second a picture of St Patrick. When added to this the "man of the house" was named Dunleavy, there cannot be much doubt as to his faith and nationality.

The most important Irish centre in the county of Durham is Sunderland. Our people have increased in numbers and prosperity with the progress of the town. The young people are generally put to trades, chiefly, as along the Tyneside, in connection with iron shipbuilding, so that you now find a considerable number of Irishmen and boys in the fitting and engine shops, besides those employed as platers and riveters. A large number of labourers are employed in the shipbuilding, of whom many are Irishmen. You also find them at the blast furnaces, collieries, and quarries in and about the town. Darlington, Durham city, the Hartlepools, and Stockton have considerable Irish populations.

This part of what was once the Saxon kingdom of Northumbria has deeply interesting memories for Irishmen, for it was the chief scene of the labours of the disciples of St Columbkille, who taught the savage Saxons the Christian religion and the arts of civilisation. In August 1887 the Catholics of the diocese of Hexham and Newcastle made a pilgrimage to the island of Lindisfarne, in commemoration of the twelfth centenary of St Cuthbert, the Irish patron saint of the diocese. Most of the distance from the mainland was traversed barefooted through the shallow water by the pilgrims, who must have felt the powerful significance of the text of the preacher—"Take thy shoes from off thy feet for the place wherein thou standest is holy ground."

The Irish must have been coming into Cumberland for at least two centuries. The mission of St Begh, in Whitehaven, dates from 1706. St Begh, or Bega, Virgin and Abbess, was an Irish princess, who spent a portion of her life in the district as a recluse, her name (St Bees) being still associated with the topography of the county. She founded a religious house at Hartlepool, and her name is still venerated throughout the north of England.

In addition to St Cuthbert and St Begh the following,

among other Irish saints, are associated with the diocese of Hexham and Newcastle—St Aidan, Monk of Iona, first Bishop of Lindisfarne; St Finan, second Bishop of Lindisfarne; St Colman, third Bishop of Lindisfarne; and St Tuda, fourth Bishop of Lindisfarne. St Kentigern preached in Cumberland, and there is a tradition which connects the name of St Patrick, when a boy, with Banaven (now Whitehaven). The footsteps of Irish missionaries can be traced in the district by the churches they founded, among these being two near Cockermouth which were dedicated to St Bridget.

In our own days, since the Catholic Hierarchy was re-established, the see of Hexham and Newcastle has been filled by men of the same race as St Cuthbert, the patron of the diocese. Dr Chadwick, the second bishop, was a native of Drogheda, and Dr O'Callaghan, the fourth bishop, was born in London of Irish parentage.

Besides St Begh's, there are over a dozen other missions now existing founded previous to the present century.

Our countrymen used to come over in the small trading vessels from the north of Ireland. As in Ayrshire and Wigtownshire, in Scotland, there is no doubt but that many of the descendants of those who came in the last and the early part of the present century, particularly those who were farm labourers, scattered about the agricultural districts, lost the Faith through want of churches and priests. For the same reason, and being so much out of communion with their fellow-countrymen, these also became denationalised. Throughout Cumberland the Catholic churches are not too numerous yet—being less than a score—for such a population; the Irish-born numbering 14,093. The work of the clergy is no doubt well supplemented in the schools, and by the branches of the Irish National League, so that, in one way or another, the cause of creed and country is pretty well kept to the front.

The bulk of the Irish in Cumberland are employed at the coal pits, in the iron ore mines, at the cinder ovens, and the blast furnaces. Though the most are from the north of Ireland there are men in the iron mines who came from the lead and copper mines of Wicklow. Although the great bulk of the Ulstermen who cross into Cumberland are Catholics and staunch nationalists, a number of Orangemen have come over too. Some of these were formerly engaged at the shipbuilding yards at Whitehaven but of late years there has been but little employment for them. Some also work at the pits and iron-works. Formerly these wretched creatures used to deny their nationality, and were greatly despised for this by the Cumberland men—even by those who were of a bigoted anti-Irish type themselves. Of late years, since Mr Gladstone took up the Home Rule question, they have begun to proclaim themselves Irishmen, not from any patriotic motive, but that they might stab their country in the back by declaring that, though they were Irishmen, they did not want Home Rule. This has earned for them from Englishmen even greater contempt than before, as men who are so degraded as to be willing to live in slavery themselves, providing they can still keep their feet on the necks of the "Papishes." The Irish are most numerous in Whitehaven and Carlisle, where many are in fairly good positions. They are also found in considerable numbers in Maryport, Workington, and other towns. The largest number of Irish voters to be found in any constituency here is in the Egremont (west) division of Cumberland. The chief centre of Irish population in this division is Cleator Moor, where nearly half the people are of our nationality. This was the reason why, in 1884, the Orangemen gathered from all parts, resolved in bravado to make this village the scene of their annual carnival. They came armed with deadly weapons, and, by all manner of insulting party emblems, tunes, and cries, did their best to provoke a riot. In the scene of turmoil which they created the Orangemen fired some shots. One of those killed an inoffensive young man who was pursuing his ordinary avocation as a postman. As it happened he was Irish and a Catholic, the Orange Moloch was satiated, though it might just as well have been one of their own sympathisers that they killed in their blind fury.

There is no part of Great Britain where our countrymen are better organised than in Cumberland. It is no exaggeration to say that every Irish nationalist elector is known and can be relied upon to give his vote for his country in the ballot box, or do a man's part in any field wherever the battle of Irish freedom has to be fought out.

SCOTLAND.

Our fellow countrymen are considerably more numerous in Scotland, in proportion to the general population, than in England and Wales. The 1881 Census gives the Irish-born in Scotland as 218,659. This, out of a general population of 3,735,570, gives a proportion of 1 in 17 of Irish-born. In England and Wales the proportion is but 1 in 46.

As may be imagined from the convenience of access, they are mostly from Ulster, although in Edinburgh, Perth, and other places a great number are from the western province of Ireland.

More than half the Irish of Scotland are in Lanarkshire. As in South Wales, Durham, and the "Black Country," a large proportion of these are employed at the collieries and blast furnaces. The principal coal and iron-working centres are Airdrie, Coatbridge, Carluke, Carfin, and Kilsyth. As a rule our people are much better off in the smaller towns of Scotland than in Glasgow, Edinburgh, Greenock, Paisley, or Dundee. In some of the mining villages you see the one-storied, compact-looking stone cottages, generally built by the employers, which are, as a rule, far more comfortable dwelling places than where the people are forced to live in the closes and wynds of the larger cities and towns. In these cottages there is certainly often much room for improvements, but in some places, as at Carluke, they are neat-looking little dwellings, and made all the more cheerful by the small gardens in front and behind. Indeed, the whole surroundings are in marked contrast to the squalor in some parts of the large towns. In Carfin, where nearly half the people are Irish, you find the same satisfactory state of things. They have no wealthy people among them; with their good priest they form a primitive community, and are proud of their handsome little chapel and schools, and all the more so that they built them without external aid.

In the ancient town of Lanark you meet with many warm-hearted Irish exiles, who are foremost in the fight for nationality. Even if he were inclined to forget it, every scene around, and all the memories of the district are calculated to rouse the spirit of freedom in the breast of the Irish as well as of the Scottish Celt. For these old streets once resounded with the battle cries of Wallace and of Bruce, and away to the south can be seen the hill of Tinto, from which the beacon fires summoned the sturdy men of Lanark to battle against the Saxon invader.

In some of the Lanarkshire towns, particularly Airdrie and Coatbridge, it will be noticed that a number of our people are in tolerably good positions as shopkeepers and traders of various kinds. A feature in many Scottish towns —large or small—is the number of Irish publicans and pawnbrokers.

Although the province of Ulster generally sends sterling Nationalists to Lanarkshire, it also sends a certain proportion of those wretched creatures called Orangemen. These last have not succeeded to any great extent in inoculating the native population with their own bigotry, and, as a rule, the Scotch despise them as the only people on earth who have no nationality. In some of the Lanarkshire villages you find as flourishing branches of the Irish National organisation as any in the country. Coatbridge, for instance, in one year, furnished more money to the national treasury than almost any of the great cities. In Lanarkshire, and, indeed, in other parts of Scotland, there are a considerable number of Irishmen filling public positions, who have in many cases risen from the humblest beginnings. Besides the places already named, there are Irish communities in a number of other towns and villages of this great county, in most of which you find a fair proportion in good social positions—some being members of representative bodies. These include Govan and Partick, which are suburbs of Glasgow; Maryhill, Rutherglen, Motherwell, Hamilton, Bailieston, Blantyre, and Larkhall, where their avocations and position are similar to those in the places more minutely referred to.

The city of Glasgow has a deep interest for us, not only on

account of its vast Irish population, but from the memories connecting it with our country. For the ground on which it stands was once hallowed by the footsteps of the glorious Irish saints—Columba and Kentigern. Their countrymen are to-day so numerous in the modern city that it is the third largest Irish centre in Great Britain—only ranking after London and Liverpool.

Although, as in other great cities, there is much to lament in the condition of the Irish in Glasgow, you nowhere find a more sterling and sturdy patriotism. They are gradually rising in the social scale, they are generous supporters of religion, and, every year—as their discipline improves— they are becoming more politically powerful. With the spread of education, and the growing facilities for the practice of their religion, they are gradually rising from the ranks of unskilled labour, and out of the numerous precarious callings in which, some years ago, you frequently found them. They are now to be met with in tolerably large numbers in every rank, trade, and profession. There is just one weakness it is well to point out. In some cases Irishmen who have amassed wealth, after giving their sons a good education, do not put them to useful occupations; or it may be that the son is not satisfied to build upon the foundation laid by the father, as the Scotch generally do. He aims, perhaps, at something he considers more "gentlemanly," and not unfrequently makes a failure for life.

As in other cities, a good many of the insanitary neighbourhoods in Glasgow have been improved, or swept away, and where the bulk of our people were once to be found almost exclusively in such neighbourhoods as the Salt Market, they are now spreading themselves all over the city, and in much better surroundings than formerly. In observing their social condition in the cities and towns of Scotland, and the places in which they live, one is favourably impressed by the appearance of the lofty and substantial looking stone buildings. But internally—not to speak of what you find in the habitations in the more insanitary "wynds" and "closes" —they are, as a rule, in point of substantial comfort and health much below the four-roomed cottages in the smaller English towns.

Passing through the streets of a strange town, some people have a weakness for looking at the names over the shops. It is true that in Scotland, as in England, you do not find as many Irish names as you would like to see, but, on the other hand, you see the absurdity of the parrot cry of "Anglo-Saxonism," or "John Bullism," as Cardinal Newman used to call it. According to some writers and speakers, what they style the Anglo-Saxons—there are really no such people—must be a heaven-born race to whom the rest of humanity must bow. But here in Glasgow—and throughout Scotland—what are the names you see on the places of business or in the local directories? Nine out of ten are of purely Celtic origin. There can be no doubt but that the Irish Celt—now that his religious disabilities have been removed, and that his political enfranchisement is also close at hand—will, before long, find himself as well to the front in the social scale as his Scottish brother. In one of the principal sites in Glasgow is a monument which, in itself, is an exemplification of the genius of the two branches of the Celtic race—the noble statue of the distinguished Scottish soldier, Lord Clyde, by the no less distinguished Irish sculptor, John Henry Foley.

Glasgow Irishmen, although they have on many occasions given splendid assistance to the Irish cause, are by no means the political power they might be, and as they certainly will be under the better discipline that now prevails. For such a population there ought to be considerably more Irish voters. The Census figures of Irish-born are given elsewhere. The Catholic Church statistics, perhaps, help us to form a more accurate idea of the Irish Nationalist strength. The Catholic Directory gives the estimated Catholic population of the diocese of Glasgow at 220,000. Of these, about 120,000 would be in Glasgow. A considerable number of these are Scottish Catholics—chiefly Highlanders—and these would have to be taken off in reckoning the available Irish Nationalist strength. It is extremely probable, for the same reasons that prevail in London, Liverpool, and elsewhere, that the Church statistics of *known* Catholics are an under-estimate, and that with zealous exertions in gathering all the stray sheep into the religious and national fold there would be a great accession to our available strength. It is an undoubted fact that our voting power, in proportion to population, is very much greater in the smaller places—where everybody knows everybody else—than in the larger towns, to which whatever there is of wretchedness among us gravitates.

Leaving Lanarkshire, let us now follow our people along the right bank of the Clyde into Dumbartonshire. At Clydebank we see an illustration of their migratory habits in following industries as they leave or spring up in certain places, causing a diminution in one district and an increase in another. This has been the case here, where there has been a rapid increase, caused by the development of ship building and chemical works, and the building of a large sewing machine factory. Close to, and lying inland from Clydebank, you come to Duntocher, a really thriving Irish colony—a model community, in fact. The good priest, who is like a ruler—or, perhaps, one should say father— among his people, will tell you that this is "Ireland," with all its domestic virtues, with infinitely more domestic comfort, and none of its wretchedness. Here, as in most of the smaller towns north of the Tweed, you see there is solid progress being made, and an absence of the squalor you so frequently meet with in the larger towns of Scotland, and of England too, it may be added. In this district you find a fair number of Irishmen, and the sons of Irishmen, engaged in trade, and well to the front in various avocations, besides holding public representative positions. Passing on to Dumbarton, you find them employed at ship building, as artizans and labourers, and in the various industries of the place; a fair proportion being in business. Northward from here, and not far from the romantic Loch Lomond, you meet with them at Renton and Alexandria. Here the chief industries are dyeing and calico printing. Both are unhealthy occupations. For this work a large number of girls are brought from Donegal and the West of Ireland, as being stronger than those reared on the spot. At Kirkintilloch and Croy our people are mostly pitmen. There is in Dumbartonshire a large and well-organised Irish vote, which can always be relied upon in the fight for fatherland.

Renfrewshire, on the left bank of the Clyde, has, after Lanarkshire, the largest Irish population among the counties of Scotland. About half of these are in the important towns of Greenock and Paisley. Greenock, being a considerable seaport, near the mouth of the Clyde, is, naturally, the first place many touch on coming into Scotland. They will tell you here that the Irish and Highlanders almost have the place to themselves. It has been remarked in connection with the Highland labourers that they seem to feel themselves more akin to the Irish harvestmen, who come each year, than to their lowland fellow-countrymen. They can readily understand each other in their native tongues, as there is a great similarity between the Gaelic and the language spoken by the peasantry from Donegal. The Greenock Irish are mostly from that county. Some people profess to be able to tell what part of Ireland a man hails from by his accent. There is a tolerably well-marked North of Ireland accent, and there is a characteristic Scottish accent, but here the two are so blended, with so many intermediate shades, that none but a specialist in such matters could undertake to say, in Greenock, from his tongue, if a man were Irish or Scotch.

The Irish work at the docks, as mechanics and labourers in the shipyards, and at the sugar refineries. As might be expected, you find among them a proportion of Orangemen. It is estimated that there are 17,000 Catholics in Greenock. Most of these are Irish by birth or parentage, and, as in Glasgow and elsewhere, the Scottish Catholics are about equal in number to the Irish Orangemen. A considerable number are in trade. Here, as in other parts of Scotland, Irishmen appear to take specially to two trades—those of the pawnbroker and the publican. A few years ago it was estimated that one-fourth of the latter class in Greenock were our fellow-countrymen. As a rule, there are no more patriotic Irishmen than these, but one would like to see them equally numerous in the trades that minister to the comfort rather than to the weakness of mankind. In Greenock there is the usual proportion of poverty among our people, but this has not been the only cause why, until recently, they had not that political power their numbers would warrant. Since the various extensions of the franchise, their voting-strength ought to have increased twentyfold. One illustration will show the immensely increased political power now in our hands. Our people in Greenock have always been eminently patriotic, and able to detect the difference between the true metal and the base. In 1849, an address was presented to Charles Gavin Duffy, one of the Young Ireland chiefs, by the Irish electors, who, with the very limited franchise then existing, numbered but sixty. A few years since they had increased to six hundred, and yet this was not half what it might be made, and what it has since really become, through organisation and discipline—thanks chiefly to the clergy and the Irish National League.

After Greenock, the most important Irish centre in Renfrewshire is the flourishing manufacturing town of Paisley. At Johnstone, where they find employment at the flax mills; at Busby, at the calico printing; at Linwood, at the cotton and paper mills, and at the coal-pits, you find thriving Irish colonies.

Though the Irish are more diffused throughout Scotland than formerly, nearly three-fourths of them are still to be found along the banks of the Clyde, in the three counties we have just passed in review—Lanark, Renfrew, and Dumbarton.

Much of Ayrshire is like the coal and iron districts of South Wales. In many parts you see nothing but barren hills—only fit for sheep grazing—but what Nature has denied on the surface she has more than repaid in the mineral wealth beneath. As might be expected, you find a considerable number of Irish engaged in the industries of the district. The colliers are but poorly paid, yet they are most generous in their support of religion and education.

It is singular that in some places in Ayrshire there are fewer Irish now than formerly, when they used to cross over regularly in the fishing boats from the opposite coasts of Antrim and Down. Thus, in Girvan, it is said, there was a larger Catholic congregation at the beginning of the present century than at the present time. This is, no doubt, accounted for by the migration to other centres in search of employment.

An exemplification of what causes our people to be so largely migratory is found here. The chemical works at Ayr were removed to Kilmarnock, which caused a considerable displacement of Irish in the one place and a corresponding increase in the other. It will be noticed that they seem to follow certain industries, of which this chemical working is one. There has been a considerable diminution of their number throughout Ayrshire during the last thirty years.

The greatest decrease in any of the Scottish counties has been in Wigtownshire, which has now less than a third of the Irish-born it had in 1851.

There has been a falling off in Dumfriesshire also. The bulk of the Irish are in the town of Dumfries, and chiefly in the suburb of Maxwelltown. Dumfries has many mementos of the struggle for Scottish freedom and of the genius of the Scottish branch of the Celtic race. The Irish would be a less impressionable people than they are if they could be unmoved by such associations. Here is still the monastery of the Grey Friars, where Bruce slew the Red Comyn, and here, too, Robert Burns lived for some years, and died. His countrymen have erected in Dumfries a statue to his memory, as the national poet of Scotland, a song-writer who reached the hearts of the people as few poets had ever done before, a thorough Celt, and, in his own person, a refutation of the superstition of "Anglo-Saxonism." The Irish community in all its grades in Dumfries is a satisfactory one, for here you find, with the usual number of labourers of various kinds, a fair proportion of artisans, besides traders and professional men, who have risen from the humblest beginnings.

Attention has already been called to the number of Irishmen in certain lines of business in Scotland. To this must be added another class who are numerous not only in most of the towns north of the Tweed, but also in England and Wales. These are often engaged in so many branches of trade that perhaps the only title which would fairly embrace them would be that of "general dealers." These, or their fathers, or it may have been their grandfathers, have generally started at the lowest rung of the social ladder. An

Irish harvestman or labourer out of employment finds himself in one of the small English or Scottish towns, and he tries his luck at dealing—a few pence, or shillings at the outside, often constituting his capital. He becomes a collector of rags, old ropes, bones, old metal, rabbit and hare skins, and other apparently waste materials, for which trade has its uses. Sometimes he gives ready money for his purchases, sometimes he adopts the barter system, and gives, in exchange, crockery, or other articles useful in a household; and, in this way, realises a double profit. By dint of pinching and screwing he is able to leave the hawking to others, and to set up what is termed a "marine store," where, instead of trudging about in search of trade, the trade comes to him. Along with this, in consequence of the barter system, many of these marine store dealers develop large businesses in china and crockery ware, hardware of every kind, fur, wool, and every conceivable article of trade and commerce. Somewhat akin to this class of traders are those who carry on what was formerly a flourishing trade as old clothes dealers. In London and many towns, there were and are still, though to a less extent, whole streets devoted to this business, such as Fontenoy Street, Liverpool. Cheap clothing has considerably lessened the profits, but there is still good business done in the better kind of cast-off clothing by the proprietors of the "wardrobe shops," over which you not unfrequently see an Irish name.

There are few places in Great Britain where, on the whole, our people are in a more satisfactory position than in the towns on the banks of the Tweed, which are famous for the manufacture of the woollen goods which take their name from the border river of England and Scotland. These are Hawick, Galashiels, Selkirk, Peebles, and a few smaller places. The Irish-born are dying out, but they are leaving behind them a generation who are a credit to their creed and to the land of their fathers. There is employment in the factories for young and old, and many have come well to the front. You find Irishmen among the cleverest in designing the patterns which go so far in making a saleable article, and others well skilled in the various departments of the local trade. More than one Irishman born and reared in this district has got an engagement in one of the rising woollen factories in Ireland. Indeed, they will tell you here, as well as in the Yorkshire towns, that for the technical education wanted for the revival of native industry, Ireland need not look beyond her own children in England and Scotland, should she require them, for the most capable teachers.

Unlike most other parts of Scotland, there are in the ancient city of Edinburgh a considerable proportion of people from the province of Connaught. At the time of the no-popery riots in 1779, which heralded and, to some extent, inspired the Gordon riots in London, there was already an Irish colony gathering here. Since then they have been gradually coming, but here, as elsewhere, the famine was what brought about the great increase in the Irish population. As in many other towns, there was, and, though not to the same extent, is, an "Irish quarter," the district principally inhabited by our people being in the older part of the city, in the neighbourhood of Cowgate and High Street. With the spread of education and the more tolerant spirit which now prevails, it is easier to get an Irish youth apprenticed to a trade than formerly. A fair proportion have made good progress in Edinburgh in various trades and industries. In Leith the Irish are mostly dock labourers, as in other seaports. There are various places in Edinburghshire where you find Irish populations like those you meet with in Lanarkshire.

Crossing the Forth we come to Kirkcaldy, where there are a number of our people. The most striking feature of the place to a traveller, either passing casually on the railway or entering the town, is the immense pile of solid stone buildings, devoted to the manufacture of floorcloth and such like material, owned by the firm of John Barry, Ostlere, & Co. Anyone who has the pleasure of the acquaintance of the guiding spirit of this gigantic factory can tell you that John Barry is one of the most capable and enterprising Irishmen that our times have produced. His success is a proof that in the race of life, with anything like a fair chance, Irishmen need fear no competitors. It need scarcely be said that the founder of the Home Rule Confederation of Great Britain is a sterling patriot.

Still going northward, you reach "Bonnie Dundee," with its "West Port," famous in song, where, to-day, the Irish are so numerous. They are not the first of their race who came here, for the town and district are memorable in connection with the dashing campaign of Montrose, in which Alaster M'Donnell and his hardy followers from the glens of Antrim bore so brave a part; while the gallantry of the Irish troops later still, under Lord Viscount Dundee, can never be forgotten. About one-fifth of the population of Dundee at the present time are Irish or of Irish extraction.· They are extensively employed in connection with the manufacture of jute, now so largely used for sailcloth, sacking, and other coarse fabrics, for which Dundee, Arbroath, and others of the neighbouring towns are famous. They are also employed at the iron shipbuilding on the Tay. The Irish of Dundee are fairly representative of the various parts of Ireland, and many of them occupy good positions in the trade of the town. They are genuinely patriotic, and though in the past there has been much room for improvement in their political organisation, the branches of the League are bringing the people more into line every day, and showing them the necessity for possessing votes with which to fight the battle of Ireland.

Not far from Dundee is the famous city of Perth, which in days gone by also witnessed the prowess of Irishmen. The Irish here are chiefly from the province of Connaught, and though they are all over the place, you find them most in evidence in and about Meal Vennel and Queen Street. The older generation are mostly, as one may imagine, labourers, but the rising youth are now being put to various trades, so that in times to come there will be an improvement in their position. There are a fair number of successful Irish traders in Perth.

There are several other places where you meet our people in greater or lesser numbers in Scotland, but the principal districts have now been dealt with, and these will enable the reader to form an idea of the rest. It will be noticed that the overwhelming mass of them are to be found in the great industrial centres.

There is one Catholic diocese in Scotland—Argyle and

the Isles—which has a supreme interest for Irishmen. Here it was, as our opening chapters show, that, many centuries ago, the colony from Ireland which laid the foundation of the Scottish nation and monarchy made their first settlement. After a time the glorious St Columba and his disciples, having made their home in Iona, went forth on their great mission for the conversion of the Picts and Saxons, founding numerous centres of religion and enlightenment, and gaining such fame for the parent house that for ages it shone a beacon light for all Christendom.

Hence Iona is to us the most sacred spot in all Britain. Our days have witnessed a memorable pilgrimage to this holy island. On the 13th of June 1888, a number of the bishops, clergy, and laity from all parts of Scotland, with some from Ireland and England, landed at Iona to honour the memory of the grandest of the saints of our country. It is true that the vessel which conveyed them thither was one that would have filled the mariners of primitive times with wonder could they have seen it. But, after all, the pilgrims who came in the steamship of modern civilisation were filled with the same spirit as those who, with St Columbkille, traversed those stormy northern seas in their rude hide-covered coracles to make their abode in this lonely island. As the pilgrims formed into procession on the beach and moved onward, headed by the emblem of man's redemption, which was borne aloft by a cowled figure that might well have been one of the old Culdees, the hymns of the Church were chanted here for the first time since the "Reformation," while the islanders, sad to say, no longer professing the faith of Columbkille, looked on and listened in wonder.

What is called Iona Cathedral and the numerous ruins on the island have often been described. The main buildings date from about the twelfth century. Some of the other ruins are considerably older. The fury of the fanatical "Reformers" destroyed the grand old crosses which were once the glory of Iona, with the exception of two, which in form are the same as those at Monasterboice and other places in Ireland, and which, in recognition of the race that erected them, are known the world over as Celtic crosses.

Mass was said in the roofless ruin. The solemn Gregorian music, sung by the black monks of St Benedict, in their habits and cowls, mingled as it was with the hoarse screams of the wild sea birds, must have been just such a simple chaunt as Columba's followers raised when the saint celebrated the sacrifice of the Mass in their first rude timber or wicker-work oratory. In some of the Western islands which he visited, to preach Christ crucified, the people have kept the faith he taught their ancestors to this day. The stormy weather which preceded the day of the pilgrimage prevented a number of these Catholic islanders from coming in their fishing boats to take part in it. Of the two sermons that day, one was by Angus McDonald, Bishop of Argyle and the Isles, preached in Gaelic—the still living tongue used by St Columbkille himself, centuries before the English language came into existence. The theme was the life, labours, virtues, and miracles of the great Irish saint. The simple story, told after an interval of thirteen centuries, on the very spot sanctified by his footsteps, and where his fiery eloquence had so often resounded, was something to remember for a lifetime. Surely the spirit that once animated the majestic form of St Columbkille must have been present in that solemn hour. Surely as the multitude—exiles, most of them, like himself, from Erin—knelt at his shrine, he, who had struggled so nobly for the freedom of the young Scottish nation, must, at that moment, have interceded with God to end the centuries of sorrow that have passed over the land he loved with all the passionate ardour of his race.

CHAPTER XLII.

DISTINGUISHED IRISHMEN OF THE NINETEENTH CENTURY.

IN dealing with the condition of the Irish of Great Britain to-day, attention has been chiefly given to those in the humbler ranks of life, to which, for obvious reasons sufficiently set forth in this book, most of them belong. For these same reasons Irishmen are not as well represented in the trade and commerce of this country as one would like to see them.

But in those positions where the more intellectual faculties come into play it will be found that their progress in this century has been marvellous. So numerous have those Irishmen who have so distinguished themselves been, that a record of their struggles and triumphs could not be given, to do them justice, within the compass of this book. We shall, therefore, have to be satisfied to take as representative men, in their various arts and professions, those whose lives, as recorded here, have blended into the general history of the Irish in Britain during the present century.

Although they may not in all cases have held the same religious or political faith as the majority of us, our meed of admiration cannot be withheld from the thousands of Irishmen who have, during that period, won renown on every field—whether of peace or war, art or literature. They have made their mark as statesmen at home, as well as having been the most capable rulers of the great colonies and dependencies of the empire; while, notwithstanding the sneers of Macaulay and Froude at their want of capacity as leaders, they are still Irishmen who command the armies of Britain, and who have carried her flag into the most distant and perilous seas.

Although we have amongst the present Irish political leaders, men distinguished in their various professions, those whose actions have been recorded must only be taken as representatives of a host of others. Justin M'Carthy, the present leader of the Irish Parliamentary party, though he holds such a prominent position in English literature, is not the only novelist and historian the Irish in Britain have produced. His son, Justin Huntly M'Carthy, is not the only Irish dramatist of the century, though his is the only name which has come into this history. T. P. O'Connor and others of our political leaders are but a handful among the host of brilliant Irishmen whose pens have adorned the newspaper and other literature of our times. T. D. Sullivan, the veteran poet-laureate of our race, whom we can now surely claim as one of the Irish in Britain—he is so often amongst us—is but the example which has fired the emulation of a host of rising poets who are determined to prove that Ireland is still the " Land of Song." Sir

Charles Russell, pre-eminent as he stands to-day, is but one of a numerous band of able Irish lawyers and orators, while in music, painting, and sculpture we have had, and still have, many famous Irishmen. In the annals of the stage our countrymen occupy the most prominent positions, and among men of science and philosophers they are well represented.

It would take many pages of this book to give merely the names of those who have distinguished themselves in these various fields, while to give even a few lines of passing notice to each would fill a large volume. Even these constitute but a fraction of the capable Irishmen rising up amongst us, whose names are bound to be famous in days to come, and who now vie with their fellow-countrymen in the humbler ranks of life in their endeavours to uplift the Irish name.

CHAPTER XLIII.

A FEW PARTING WORDS.

SHOULD the foregoing pages appear somewhat fragmentary it will not be extraordinary. They embody the experiences of nearly half a century, and have been jotted down at various times, and amid changing scenes, in brief periods of leisure extending over the last seven years.

During that time the writer, a humble missionary of Irish nationality, has often found himself, in his journeyings through England, Scotland, and Wales, treading in the footsteps and inspired by the example of the saints of our land, whose labours have been described in the opening chapters. With such inspirations, it is not strange if this does not pretend to be a cold-blooded, "impartial" history. It only claims to be true, though the writer does indeed confess to a strong partiality for his own kith and kin. It has been to him a labour of love, in many parts of Great Britain, to gather into the national fold, wherever he has found them, however remote, or few, or scattered, the warm-hearted exiles of

> "—— That brave old Irish race,
> That fire or sword could not efface,
> That lives and thrives—and grows apace,
>   However its foes assail it;
> That, point by point, and day by day,
> Wins back its rights, and works its way,
> And bursts its bonds. Hurrah! Hurrah!
>   With a hundred cheers we'll hail it!"

In these pages, while the faults of our people—chiefly the inheritance of ages of slavery—have not been ignored, their capacity for self-government and their reputation for virtue, valour, learning, and genius, have been upheld. Ground down and persecuted as they have been, the wonder is that an Irish race exists at all to-day. Only their purity of life could have given them the extraordinary vitality which has enabled them to survive every vicissitude. It may seem that too much prominence has been given to the religious history and condition of the Irish in Britain. While all honour has been paid to nationalists not of the faith of the majority of our people, and to fair-minded Britons who have espoused our cause, with us creed and country have been so closely blended that this would be but half a history of our race if due prominence were not given to the struggles for the practice and advancement of our religion. At the risk, then, of being deemed a most partial historian, the writer has now to say for himself that, besides being an Irishman who loves his country beyond all others, he is a Catholic who believes in the faith he professes.

In this spirit these pages have been written. From them it will be seen that the golden age of the Irish in Ireland—the centuries following their conversion by St Patrick—was also their golden age here. It would seem that, with Columba, Adamnan, Aidan, Cuthbert, and the other holy men of that age, the line of the canonized Irish saints of Britain ended. Let us take one rapid parting glance at the after fate and fortunes of the Irish in Britain since then, as already described in detail.

Their history at home, during the last seven centuries, is, for the most part, a saddening story. The same must be said of their history here. Since Ireland's night of sorrow began, the records of our race at home and here have been often interwoven. It is so at the present moment, when every pulsation of the national heart at home meets with a warm and ready response throughout Britain.

First we have the evil-omened visit of the traitorous Diarmid M'Murrough, and his sojourn in the ancient city of Bristol, and among the banditti of the Welsh marches.

Then we read how, as time went on, men of the best blood of our race were held captives in the Tower of London. We find them, too, as combatants, generally on the patriot side, in the stubborn battles which resulted in Scottish independence. Next we hear of them in the train of some Anglo-Irish noble—a Fitzgerald, it might be, or a Butler—fighting in the "Wars of the Roses," or embarking for foreign fields under the banners of the Anglo-Norman kings; while, all through, they were not unrepresented at Oxford and other abodes of learning, which were afterwards diverted from the uses for which pious souls in the Ages of Faith had endowed them.

Then came England's change of faith, and the bitter persecution of our countrymen here, for as early as the days of Elizabeth small Irish colonies were gradually forming in such places as London, Bristol, and Liverpool. During those dark days, Oliver Plunkett, Archbishop of Armagh, and other Irishmen won the crown of martyrdom, while, still later, the horrors of the Penal Laws were intensified for the Irish "Papists" in Britain by the cowardly and brutal attacks of British mobs. In fact, for about two hundred years, as these pages have shown, our history would appear to be one long series of struggles for the mere right of existence.

But, like the children of Israel in bondage, we have, despite persecution and innumerable proselytizing influences, increased and multiplied, and become a mighty power, that statesmen must reckon with; permeating, in numerous ways, the religious, social, and political life of Britain.

APPENDIX.

THE CENSUS OF 1891.

WHEN the first edition of "The Irish in Britain" appeared, the figures in the Census of 1891, showing the birth-places of the people, had not been published. The following are the returns since issued of the Irish-born in the various counties and burghs in Great Britain. It will be interesting to compare them with previous returns given in this book.

DISTRIBUTION IN ENGLAND AND WALES OF ENUMERATED IRISH-BORN.

Counties.—Lancashire, 164,489; Middlesex, Surrey, and Kent, Intra. Met., 66,465;* Yorkshire, 43,098; Durham, 27,663; Cheshire, 20,006; Hampshire, 11,848; Glamorgan, 11,256; Northumberland, 10,414; Cumberland, 9698; Stafford, 9,212; Kent, Ex. Met., 8155;† Essex, 7224; Warwick, 7084; Devon, 6537; Middlesex, Ex. Met., 5834;† Surrey, 5291;† Gloucester, 4409; Derby, 4234; Sussex, 3963; Monmouth, 3807; Somerset, 2236; Nottingham, 1994; Worcester, 1797; Leicester, 1697; Cornwall, 1626; Lincoln, 1454; Berks, 1422; Shropshire, 1284; Dorset, 1240; Norfolk, 1152; Northampton, 1095; Suffolk, 934; Flint, 912; Herts, 841; Denbigh, 819; Pembroke, 784; Wilts, 758; Bedford, 663; Carnarvon, 630; Westmoreland, 625; Oxford, 584; Hereford, 531; Bucks, 496; Cambridge, 438; Anglesey, 409; Carmarthen, 343; Brecon, 308; Huntingdon, 140; Montgomery, 130; Cardigan, 98; Merioneth, 85; Rutland, 71; Radnor, 32. Total, 458,315.

* Population of Registration County of London.
† The totals of the figures marked thus represent the Irish-born population of these three counties outside of the Registration County of London.

APPENDIX.

Principal Boroughs, &c.—London (Registration County of), 66,465; Liverpool, 47,243; Manchester, 23,005; Salford, 9265; Leeds, 7166; Birkenhead, 6145; Bradford, 5352; Birmingham, 5043; Newcastle-on-Tyne, 4898; St Helens, 4487; Barrow, 4249; Cardiff, 4114; Portsmouth, 3844; Sheffield, 3779; Oldham, 3539; Wigan, 3476; Bolton, 3401; Preston, 3348; Middlesboro, 3150; Blackburn, 3122; West Ham, 2822; Gateshead, 2572; Sunderland, 2554; Bristol, 2511; Stockport, 2424; Merthyr, 2405; Warrington, 2254; Burnley, 2115; Hull, 2053; Devonport, 1878; Halifax, 1877; Bury, 1699; Rochdale, 1660; Newport, 1624; Swansea, 1614; South Shields, 1480; Plymouth, 1469; York, 1374; Nottingham, 1332; Huddersfield, 1131; Wolverhampton, 1108; Derby, 1055; Croydon, 1050; Brighton, 1032; Leicester, 974; Walsall, 889; Hanley, 754; Southampton, 662; Bath, 614; Hastings, 553; Norwich, 490; Northampton, 419; Reading, 400; Aston Manor, 373; Coventry, 346; Ipswich, 274; West Bromwich, 262; Grimsby, 242.

DISTRIBUTION IN SCOTLAND OF IRISH-BORN.

Counties.—Lanark, 107,863; Renfrew, 24,668; Edinburgh, 12,912; Ayr, 11,074; Dumbarton, 9845; Forfar, 8525; Stirling, 4001; Linlithgow, 3646; Perth, 1745; Fife, 1732; Wigtown, 1453; Argyle, 1073; Haddington, 897; Aberdeen, 890; Dumfries, 746; Kirkcudbright, 577; Roxburgh, 552; Bute, 490; Clackmannan, 424; Selkirk, 366; Inverness, 291; Peebles, 212; Berwick, 199; Banff, 135; Elgin, 120; Ross and Cromarty, 114; Kincardine, 80; Orkney, 46; Kinross, 39; Caithness, 33; Sutherland, 27; Nairn, 20; Shetland, 12. Total, 194,807.

Principal Burghs, &c.—Glasgow, 59,822; Dundee, 7918; Greenock, 7860; Edinburgh, 6950; Govan, 5814; Partick, 5140; Coatbridge, 4693; Paisley, 4639; Port-Glasgow, 3354; Dumbarton, 2574; Motherwell, 2331; Rutherglen, 1786; Kinning Park, 1623; Leith, 1557; Hamilton, 1525; Wishaw, 1477; Pollokshaws, 1373; Clydebank, 1234; Airdrie, 1076; Kilmarnock, 1000; Ayr, 915; Falkirk, 673; Aberdeen, 624; Perth, 584;

Stirling, 554; Dumfries, 434; Dunfermline, 263; Hawick, 261; Galashiels, 252; Alloa, 247; Arbroath, 191; Kirkcaldy, 187; Inverness, 120; Montrose, 75; Dysart, 47; Peterhead, 35; Forfar, 31.

NOTE.—The totals for the counties include those for all the boroughs, &c., contained in them.

TOTAL, Great Britain, . . . 653,122.

www.ingramcontent.com/pod-product-compliance
Lightning Source LLC
Chambersburg PA
CBHW051855300426
44117CB00006B/409